Passion and Power

Butch-fem couple, New Orleans, 1956.

Critical Perspectives on the Past
A series edited by Susan Porter Benson, Stephen Brier, and Roy Rosenzweig

A *Radical History Review* book

Passion and Power

Sexuality in History

Edited by Kathy Peiss

and Christina Simmons

with Robert A. Padgug

Temple University Press
Philadelphia

Temple University Press, Philadelphia 19122
Copyright © 1989 by MARHO: The Radical Historians Organization. All rights reserved
Published 1989
Printed in the United States of America

The paper used in this publication meets the minimum
requirements of American National Standard for Information
Sciences—Permanence of Paper for Printed Library Materials,
ANSI Z39.48-1984

Library of Congress
Library of Congress Cataloging-in-Publication Data
Passion and power : sexuality in history / edited by Kathy Peiss and
Christina Simmons with Robert A. Padgug.
p. cm. — (Critical perspectives on the past)
Bibliography: p.
Includes index.
ISBN 0-87722-596-6 (alk. paper)
1. Sex customs—United States—History. I. Peiss, Kathy.
II. Simmons, Christina. III. Padgug, Robert A. IV. Series.
HQ18.U5P37 1989
306.7'0973—dc19   88-21670
                                                                  CIP

The frontispiece photograph was provided courtesy of the
Lesbian Herstory Educational Foundation and Joan Nestle.

Contents

up b 1989.10.6

Sexuality and
Historical Meaning

1

Passion and Power: An Introduction

Kathy Peiss
Christina Simmons

In 1979 the *Radical History Review* published a pathbreaking issue entitled "Sexuality in History." At that time American historians were only beginning to explore the notion that sexuality was not an unchanging biological reality or a universal, natural force, but was, rather, a product of political, social, economic, and cultural processes. Sexuality, that is, had a history. Moreover, the *RHR* authors claimed, sexuality had historical *significance*, in itself and in relationship to other parts of human experience, such as gender, race, class, and power. The challenge to reinsert sexuality into history, issued so directly in the late seventies, has subsequently provoked a flourishing scholarship. This volume encompasses some of those early forays into the history of sexuality originally published in *Radical History Review*, as well as more recent explorations that push historical inquiry in exciting new directions.

Why, at this historical moment, has it become possible to speak of a "history of sexuality"? To speak of "sexuality" at all presupposes that sexuality is itself a separate subject, detachable from other areas of life. Yet this very concept of sexuality was itself formed historically. As Robert Padgug notes in "Sexual Matters," his introduction to the original *RHR* issue, conceiving of sexuality as an entity apart from the rest of human experience coincides with emerging capitalism's division of life into public (political and economic) and private (sexual and familial) spheres. Freud intellectualized this division when he described individual psychology as a result of the dynamic evolution within the family of a biologically based sex drive. He helped to shape the widespread popular sense in the twentieth century that sexuality dominated or even determined individual personality and action. Alfred Kinsey's influential study of sexual "outlets" in the 1940s argued that the sexual urge was pervasive, important, and expressed itself in many forms, although ultimately he understood it as a biological force. By the mid-twentieth century sexuality was considered an important independent variable in human development. The idea of what sexuality *was*, however, remained for the most part static and ahistorical, until political challenges from feminism and gay liberation in the 1960s and 1970s opened up that issue to inquiry.[1]

Although feminism has a tradition of radicals, utopians, and bohemians who attacked dominant marital relations and sexual practices even in the nineteenth century, it was not until the 1960s that feminists foregrounded sexual politics—heterosexual relationships, lesbianism, the family, parenting, and housework—as the central problem of women's liberation. Feminists began to question essentialism, the assumption that existing social and sexual arrangements between women and men were natural, normative, and inevitable. The attack took a variety of forms: Shulamith Firestone, for example, explored the underside of romantic love as an ideology oppressive to women; lesbian–feminist Adrienne Rich described heterosexuality as a compulsory institution. Feminists found that the essentialist discourse of sexuality masked relations of power, indeed, comprised a tool for the perpetuation of male supremacy by asserting its inevitability. Historicizing gender and sexuality was a crucial means of opposing this conceptualization.[2]

Similarly, the gay liberation movement called into question the concept of heterosexual normalcy when it rejected the label of deviance. The gay civil rights movement had begun in the 1950s to assert a positive social identity for homosexual men and women. But the radical gay liberationists after 1969 challenged the very boundaries of sexual identities, moving toward the vision of a freer, more open-ended human sexuality. Gay historians contributed to this project by arguing that the homosexual role and gay consciousness were historical developments. Older essentialist categories of sexual behavior and identity have been exploded.[3]

The essays in this volume, taken together, explore the way that sexuality has increasingly become a core element of modern social identity, constitutive of being, consciousness, and action. The logic of this historical development (a framework most fully articulated by Michel Foucault) is a dialectical one, in which efforts to control the organization and meaning of sexuality both delimit and open up the possibilities of sexual expression. The authors examine sexuality as a field of contention in itself *and* as part of other struggles along the fault lines of gender, class, and race. Out of such struggles came new assertions of political power and cultural authority by dominant groups seeking to classify and control sexuality. Many of these essays examine the emergent institutions, ideologies, and tools deployed for the regulation of sexuality in the last 150 years, particularly the medical, social-scientific, and psychological modes of analysis and intervention, and the growth of state power in channeling sexual energies to preserve existing social order. But as other essays point out, these struggles also produced resistance by subordinate and stigmatized groups, new explorations of alternative sexualities, and positive assertions of sexual identities at odds with the norm of marital heterosexuality.

How can we best understand this historical process? To begin with, economic, demographic and social changes occurring with the rise of a capitalist order altered the relationship between sexuality, reproduction, and the family. As an economy based on agricultural and artisan labor became transformed into a commercial and industrial one, new family forms within the bourgeoisie emerged in response. In this changed economy, middle-class parents were less able to provide children with land through inheritance or specific skills through apprenticeships, but could offer them education and "character" as resources. Nor was the labor power of children so useful in the new economy; parents' greater investment of time, money, and attention in their offspring produced a logic for limiting fertility. For the middle class in the nineteenth century, an emergent ideology, spread through advice literature and sermons, asserted the notion of the passionless lady and the Christian gentleman as constructions associated with postponing and limiting children in the interests of the new family order. Although men were encouraged to adopt sexual self-restraint in conjunction with their roles as responsible breadwinners and men of character, women were most affected by the new ideology. Enjoined to internalize self-control, they assumed the character of asexual beings whose most important duty was motherhood. This ideological position shored up the traditional notion of sex being only for reproduction, but the larger change, the precipitous decline in the white birth rate, diminishing by half from the late eighteenth to the early twentieth century, laid the material basis for a weakening of the "natural" linkage between reproduction and sexuality.[4]

Changing relations of power between women and men were clearly implicated in these developments in the sexual economy that shaped modern sexual identity. Attacks on female control over sexuality and reproduction have long served to maintain male dominance. The American Medical Association, for example, attacked women's common law right to abortion in the mid–nineteenth century, a period when abortion rates were rising and efforts to use contraceptive measures increased. Abortion made sexuality and reproduction more separable, allowing women some degree of control over reproduction and the potential, in the long run, for sexual autonomy. The greater visibility of abortion made it even more threatening, however, and the AMA, representative of male elite groups, mounted an effort to limit the threat of women's increased power by asserting the necessity and inevitability of women's reproductive role.[5]

The centrality of gender relations to the social construction of sexuality is a theme running through most of the articles in this volume.

Social relations of class and race have also been articulated through sexual categories, which in turn have been a ground of cultural conflict and political struggle. For the white middle class and elite, the projection of promiscuity and deviant sexuality onto working-class and black Americans reinforced the boundaries of respectability in the dominant culture, particularly those regulating women's behavior. The distinction between "good" and "bad" women has historically been coded in class and racial terms. Middle–class white women's "purity"—the elevation of chastity, motherhood, and spiritual values—was contrasted to working-class and African-American women, who were depicted as loose, rowdy, carnal, and debased. The sexualization of subordinate groups has been a mechanism legitimizing intervention in working-class and black social life by bourgeois reformers and by an increasingly powerful state apparatus.

In the nineteenth century, for example, the criminalization of prostitution and the creation of red light districts in urban centers transformed many working-class women, who engaged in sexual commerce as they did other income-earning activities, into social outcasts. Moreover, the middle–class association of prostitution and promiscuity generally with the working class shaped public policies that limited working women's legal, economic, and sexual self-determination, particularly their ability to conduct a life independent from the protection and control of fathers or husbands.[6] As Marybeth Hamilton Arnold shows in her study of sexual assault in working–class New York from 1790 to 1820, eighteenth-century misogynistic views of women as carnal and depraved were embedded in the criminal justice system when it adjudicated rape cases involving working–class women. While women and men asserted different conceptions of rape in the trials, the courts' rulings reflected patriarchal assumptions. Decisions were concerned primarily with upholding men's property rights in women; women's bodily self–determination, far from being affirmed, aroused fear, hostility, and stigmatization.

In the antebellum South, the accusation of sexual promiscuity was essential to the view promulgated by slaveholders that blacks were incapable of family relations and were dangerous to civilized society if uncontrolled. Black women were defined as temptresses, but this ideology mystified the reality of white men's sexual privilege. Their access to black women became an integral tool of white supremacy and patriarchy, enforcing and symbolizing their institutional and coercive power over black women, black men, and white women. After the Civil War black men were labeled as potential aggressors threatening white womanhood and "race purity." The specter of black men raping white women was used in justification for the lynching, torture, and harassment of blacks, in what was an accepted if unofficial state policy intended to control black political, economic, and social assertion.[7]

The emergence of new languages for expressing ideas about sexuality was another crucial element shaping the construction of modern sexual identity. Beginning in the late nineteenth century, a vast medical literature on masturbation, child and adolescent sexuality, female reproductive diseases, homosexuality, and abortion created a new framework for understanding sexuality, through the classification of sexuality into categories of normality and deviance. This marked a signal shift from an earlier religious framework that had cast sexuality in marriage in moral terms as God-given, sacred, and natural, and specific sexual *acts* outside marital relations, such as sodomy and masturbation, as sinful. In a theological sense, any human being could be a transgressor, but the commission of such sins did not mark one with a specific sexual identity. The medical classification of sexual normality and deviance, in contrast, described not only sexual acts but character traits, as Jeffrey Weeks explains in his essay on homosexual identity, "Movements of Affirmation."[8]

However, the sexual discourses that accompanied the development of medicine, science, and the state did not in and of themselves create our modern sense of sexual identity, but were in large part responses to changes already taking place. Like the campaign against abortion, the aggressive use of medicine against women in the nineteenth century—radical gynecological surgery, enforced rest cures, and the designation of women as "hysterical" and "neurasthenic"—were efforts to restrict the expanding range of women's social and sexual choices in the late nineteenth century. Similarly, the elaboration of categories of sexual inversion and homosexuality were efforts by physicians, sexologists, and others to put a name on sexual and social behavior of women and men that departed from the prescribed norms of marital heterosexuality and family relations. As George Chauncey argues in "From Sexual Inversion to Homosexuality: The Changing Medical Conceptualization of Female 'Deviance,'" doctors did not invent the homosexual or lesbian.[9]

What had occurred? Social and economic changes accompanying the expansion of capitalism, particularly the growth of wage labor and urbanization, created new opportunities for some women and men to live outside the marital and familial social order. New sexual and social relations were possible in urban spaces that permitted anonymity and experimentation among populations of single men. As early as the 1870s, a gay male culture, located in bars, clubs, halls, and certain neighborhoods, emerged in many U.S. metropolitan areas, like New York's Greenwich Village. As Jeffrey Weeks indicates in his discussion of parallel developments in Britain, distinctive patterns of dress, self-presentation, and social interaction helped to shape homosexual identity.[10]

Women also experienced the increased possibilities of an independent life that allowed new forms of sexual expression to emerge. Although occupational segregation and pay inequity made marriage a necessity for most women, the historical expansion of women's economic and educational opportunities gave some women enough income to avoid dependency on husbands or fathers. Wage-earning, education, political activism, and even leisure and consumption contributed to a new sense of self among women that underlay and shaped the possibility of asserting an alternative sexual identity.[11]

In the Victorian period, close, sensuous, and passionate female friendships had coexisted with marriage, but by the late 1800s, this world of women could flourish independent of men. For middle-class women, social settlement houses, women's colleges, salons, and female residences permitted the elaboration of female-centered and lesbian relationships. Working-class women, especially those who lived outside families in furnished rooms and apartments, also developed lesbian relationships. A lesbian bar culture can be traced to the early twentieth century; by the 1940s and 1950s, Elizabeth Kennedy and Madeline Davis contend, it was central to the development of lesbian identity. Arguing against the notion of lesbian identity as an internal or biological essence, they show instead how the social roles of butch and fem structured the bar community. Interestingly, a number of the women they interviewed explained their lesbianism in terms of the essentialist medical model that has been described by George Chauncey. This suggests that mid–twentieth-century lesbians appropriated physicians' labels and used them in their own ways to describe their relationships and form a self-conscious identity.

Heterosexual women also experienced the expansion of possibilities for nonmarital relationships. The bohemians of Greenwich Village, who experimented with trial marriages, cohabitation, and other living arrangements, were only the most visible participants in the development of alternative sexual and social arrangements between women and men. A sense of the freedom, playfulness, and experimentation of these relationships may be seen in Judith Schwarz's evocative photo essay on the Heterodoxy Club, a club of lesbian and heterosexual women that accepted, even celebrated, the independent sexual choices of its members.

But women without Heterodoxy's self-consciousness about a new sexual order were also involved in reshaping sexual definitions and practices. Working-class women, Kathy Peiss argues in her essay, found in new forms of commercial leisure the social spaces for sexual experimentation: dancing sensually and provocatively, picking up men, engaging in premarital sex, defining their sexual behavior according to a more flexible standard of morality than their middle-class counterparts. Such activity among working women had existed earlier, but now it became more public and visible, offering an alternative model of behavior that could be appropriated by other women.

The challenge to traditional marital sexuality also took overtly political forms. The feminist birth control movement of the 1910s marked a new willingness of large numbers of women to demand the uncoupling of reproduction and sexuality as a requisite to their liberation. Newly willing to use mechanical means of contraception instead of sexual restraint or abortion, they asserted the existence and legitimacy of nonprocreative female sexuality. However, the feminist (and socialist) direction of the birth control movement was undercut by eugenicists seeking to regulate the sexuality and limit the fertility of black and poor women.[12] Nevertheless, as Jessie Rodrique shows in her essay on birth control and the black community, extensive grassroots support for contraception existed among African–Americans, who sought to direct the birth control movement in ways that would enhance racial progress and economic independence.

In the twentieth century new cultural authorities have arisen to reformulate and regulate dominant sexual arrangements. If the emergence of the medical model was crucial in the nineteenth century, since the early 1900s psychologists, sociologists, social workers, family counselors, and the like have played an increasingly important role in constructing sexual ideology and practices. As Christina Simmons shows in her article, "Modern Sexuality and the Myth of Victorian Repression," social scientists and commentators in the 1910s and 1920s responded to feminist demands by articulating a concept of companionate marriage that emphasized sexual comradeship, accepted divorce and birth control, and allowed some equality for women within marriage. However, Simmons argues, sex educators and social scientists drew new boundaries around acceptable forms of female sexuality, limiting women to marital heterosexuality and making men the arbiters of sexual relations.

This ideological repositioning of gender and sexual roles became more rigid from the twenties into the fifties. By the mid–twentieth century, psychiatric and functionalist modes of analysis dominated thinking about sexuality, prescribing standards of normality and deviance. Disseminated by new agents of mass communication, these views attained a powerful hold. Estelle Freedman's essay on the response to the "sexual psychopath," for example, demonstrates the role of psychiatry, the media, and politicians in targeting a new sexual outcast— the aggressive, violent, heterosexual male. In making men the new subject of sexual discourse, she argues, these groups used fears of extreme male violence to sanction the control of nonviolent forms of sexual deviance and redefine the boundaries of sexual normality.

In the twentieth century the state has become increasingly willing to intervene in matters of sexuality, health, and public order, deploying scientific and social-scientific methods of intervention. But the seemingly objective standards employed by the new experts have masked continued efforts to judge, control, and punish the sexual behavior of outcast groups. As Elizabeth Fee's study of public policy and venereal disease from 1920 to 1950 demonstrates, a biomedical approach to syphilis, which viewed it as just another infection by a microorganism, contended with a moralistic perspective, which perceived disease as a consequence of sin. Whites held the black community largely responsible for syphilis, accusing it of unrestrained and immoral sexual behavior. The parallels between this historical example and the contemporary struggle over the interpretation of AIDS are striking.[13]

Much of the public attention to sexuality has been in the form of "sex panics." Heightened fears of perceived sexual pathologies—the lesbian threat of the 1920s, the sexual psychopath of the 1930s, the "homosexual menace" of the 1950s—have recurred throughout the century and continue unabated, as the contemporary hysteria over child molestation and AIDS as the "gay plague" indicates. Such panics represent efforts to interpret and control changes in sexual behavior, but they also speak metaphorically to the dangers nonconformity of any sort presents to the social order. John D'Emilio, for example, explores the attack on homosexuality in the 1950s in terms of Cold War politics, with its fears about family breakdown and social disorder through the "infection" of the body politic by such outcasts as homosexuals and Communists.

The twentieth-century obsession with sex cuts another way, however, as the marketplace colonizes the terrain of sexual pleasure. The growth of mass consumer and entertainment industries has relied upon the commercial exploitation of sexual images and transactions. The depiction of women as objects of sexual desire permeates advertising, movies, television, and other media, and is a core element in the contemporary construction of gender. Women's work reinforces this understanding. Waitresses, models, personal secretaries, and other service workers perform jobs that often involve overt or disguised forms of "sex appeal," and until recently, sexual harassment of women workers has been an unquestioned privilege of male employers.[14]

The expansion of pornography and the sex industry for men is an outgrowth of these larger developments in capitalist and patriarchal relations. In the mid-fifties *Playboy* used female sexual images to legitimize new kinds of personal consumption for men, unrelated to the breadwinner role. Male endorsement of the sexual revolution of the 1960s fostered efforts to end censorship of movies, literature, and other forms of cultural production. And after 1970 the male backlash against feminism fueled the continued expansion of the sex industry.[15]

The commercialization of sex has taken other forms when the market consists of women, as can be seen in the mass marketing of romance novels. While this genre emerged in the eighteenth century, its modern form revolves around a more sexualized dynamic of attraction and courtship between women and men. Ann Snitow provocatively raises the question of whether such romances constitute pornography for millions of women readers. She argues that their semi-pornographic content provides ideological support for traditional women's roles while attempting to reduce some of the tensions that stem from those very roles.[16]

Since the late 1970s women's demands for freedom from male domination, as well as the assertiveness of gay men and lesbians in public life, have been checked by the growth of a right-wing political reaction. The attackers have framed their argument in terms of conservative Christian theology, protesting the breakdown of patriarchal family life and values. In this arena of highly polarized debate, intense struggles have revolved particularly around abortion, pornography, and AIDS.

The emergence of female sexuality from the bonds of reproduction has been challenged by the Right-to-Life movement, since the Supreme Court upheld abortion rights in the 1973 decision *Roe v. Wade.* For opponents, abortion represents women's wrongful denial of a God-given obligation to bear children and their "selfish" assertion of pleasure-seeking sexual activity outside marriage. Following the reasoning of the Court, supporters have generally argued that a constitutional right to privacy forms the basis for abortion rights. It has been more difficult, however, to justify abortion rights on the basis of women's right to an active and self-determined sexual life. Despite the impact of feminism, women's claim to sexual autonomy is not yet well established.[17]

Right-wing opposition to the sexual revolution has intersected with the feminist analysis of male sexual violence to exacerbate an important tension within the women's movement. Feminist critiques of rape, sexual harassment, and women battering gave rise in the late 1970s to an attack on pornography as both reflection and stimulant of male domination and violence. Daphne Read's article analyzes how feminists interpreted pornography as the essence of misogyny, a construction that resonated powerfully with many women, but played into conservative goals of silencing sexual expression. By sustaining traditional fears of an active and diverse sexuality, she argues, anti-pornography work also clashed with other feminist demands for sexual freedom and experimentation.[18]

In the 1980s the crisis of AIDS has been another instance of the confrontation between forces of regulation and control and forces opening up sexual possibilities. Robert Padgug, in his article "Gay Villain, Gay Hero," juxtaposes two ways of understanding AIDS that have been shaped by historical constructions of homosexuality. On the one hand, conservative moralists interpret AIDS as an apocalyptic judgment on a corrupt and unnatural sexuality. On the other hand, the gay community's creative response to this crisis has reaffirmed the positive self-definition and collective consciousness originating in the gay liberation movement.[19]

It is our intention that these articles provide a historical context and conceptual framework for understanding the ongoing political struggles over sexual meanings. It is our belief that understanding the history of sexuality is empowering. Through history we can see the mutability of sexual definitions and practices, the evolution of sexual possibilities. We are struck by the weight of political and cultural authority, its entrenched and oppressive power. We are also moved by the heroic persistence of people choosing and defending their own sexual lives. We hope this and other work in the history of sexuality will help make possible more humane and creative ways of understanding and engaging with the momentous changes now taking place.

■ Notes

1. See also Jeffrey Weeks' discussion in *Sexuality* (London: 1986). On the twentieth century sexual authorities, see Paul Robinson, *The Modernization of Sex* (New York: 1976); Nancy Chodorow, *The Reproduction of Mothering: Psychoanalysis and the Sociology of Gender* (Berkeley: 1978), 141–58; Alfred Kinsey et al., *Sexual Behavior in the Human Male* (Philadelphia: 1948) and *Sexual Behavior in the Human Female* (New York: 1953).

2. Linda Gordon, *Woman's Body, Woman's Right: A Social History of Birth Control in America* (New York: 1976); Hester Eisenstein, *Contemporary Feminist Thought* (Boston: 1983); Alix Kates Shulman, "Sex and Power: The Sexual Bases of Radical Feminism," *Signs* 5 (1980): 590–604; Shulamith Firestone, *The Dialectic of Sex* (New York: 1970); Adrienne Rich, "Compulsory Heterosexuality and Lesbian Existence," *Signs* 5 (1980): 631–60.

3. John D'Emilio, *Sexual Politics, Sexual Communities: The Making of a Homosexual Minority in the United States, 1940–1970* (Chicago: 1983); Jeffrey Escoffier, "Sexual Revolution and the Politics of Gay Identity," *Socialist Review* no. 82/83 (1985): 119–53.

4. Nancy Folbre, "Of Patriarchy Born: The Political Economy of Fertility Decisions," *Feminist Studies* 9 (Summer 1983): 261–84; Mary Ryan, *Cradle of the Middle Class: The Family in Oneida County, New York, 1790–1865* (Cambridge: 1981); Nancy Cott, "Passionlessness: An Interpretation of Victorian Sexual Ideology," in *A Heritage of Her Own*, ed. Nancy Cott and Elizabeth Pleck (New York: 1979); Charles Rosenberg, "Sexuality, Class and Role in 19th-Century America," *American Quarterly* 25 (1973): 131–53; Rosalind Petchesky, *Abortion and Woman's Choice: The State, Sexuality and Reproductive Freedom* (New York: 1984).

5. James Mohr, *Abortion in America: The Origin and Evolution of National Policy, 1800–1900* (New York: 1978); Gordon, *Woman's Body, Woman's Right*; Carroll Smith-Rosenberg, "The Abortion Movement and the AMA, 1850–1880," in *Disorderly Conduct: Visions of Gender in Victorian America* (New York: 1985); James Reed, *From Private Vice to Public Virtue: The Birth Control Movement and American Society Since 1830* (New York: 1978).

6. Judith R. Walkowitz, *Prostitution and Victorian Society* (Cambridge: 1980); Ruth Rosen, *The Lost Sisterhood: Prostitution in America, 1900–1918* (Baltimore: 1982); Christine Stansell, *City of Women: Sex and Class in New York, 1789–1860* (New York: 1986); Barbara Meil Hobson, *Uneasy Virtue: The Politics of Prostitution and the American Reform Tradition* (New York: 1987); Elizabeth Pleck, "Feminist Responses to 'Crimes Against Women,' 1868–1896," *Signs* 8 (1983): 451–70. See also Howard I. Kushner, "Nineteenth Century Sexuality in the 'Sexual Revolution' of the Progressive Era," *Canadian Review of American Studies* 9 (1978): 34–49.

7. Deborah Gray White, *Ar'n't I a Woman: American Female Slavery in the Plan-

tation South (New York: 1985); Bettina Aptheker, *Woman's Legacy: Essays on Race, Sex and Class in American History* (Amherst: 1982); Jacqueline Dowd Hall, " 'The Mind That Burns in Each Body': Women, Rape and Racial Violence," and Barbara Omolade, "Hearts of Darkness," both in *Powers of Desire: The Politics of Sexuality,* ed. Ann Snitow *et al.* (New York: 1983), 328–49, 350–87.

8. See also Michel Foucault, *The History of Sexuality,* vol. I, *An Introduction* (New York: 1978).

9. On women, see Barbara Ehrenreich and Deirdre English, *For Her Own Good: 150 Years of the Experts' Advice to Women* (Garden City, N.Y.: 1978); John S. Haller and Robin M. Haller, *The Physician and Sexuality in Victorian America* (New York: 1974). On homosexual identity, see also Jeffrey Weeks, *Sex, Politics and Society: The Regulation of Sexuality Since 1800* (New York: 1981).

10. John D'Emilio, "Capitalism and Gay Identity," in *Powers of Desire,* ed. Snitow *et al.,* 100–13.

11. Carroll Smith-Rosenberg, "Female World of Love and Ritual" and "The New Woman as Androgyne," in *Disorderly Conduct;* Kathy Peiss, *Cheap Amusements: Working Women and Leisure in Turn-of-the-Century New York* (Philadelphia: 1986); Joanne Meyerowitz, *Women Adrift: Independent Wage Earners in Chicago, 1880–1930* (Chicago: 1988); Peter Filene, *Him/Her/Self: Sex Roles in Modern America,* 2nd ed. (Baltimore: 1986); Judith Schwarz, *The Radical Feminists of Heterodoxy,* rev. ed. (Norwich, Vt.: 1986); Mari Jo Buhle, *Women and American Socialism* (Urbana, Ill.: 1981), 246–87.

12. Gordon, *Woman's Body, Woman's Right.*

13. See also Allan M. Brandt, *No Magic Bullet: A Social History of Venereal Disease in the United States Since 1880* (New York: 1985).

14. On female sexuality and representation, see, for example, Rosemary Betterton, ed., *Looking On: Images of Femininity in the Visual Arts and Media* (London: 1987). On sexuality and women's work, see Catherine MacKinnon, *Sexual Harassment of Working Women: A Case of Sex Discrimination* (New Haven: 1979).

15. Barbara Ehrenreich, *The Hearts of Men: American Dreams and the Flight from Commitment* (Garden City, N.Y.: 1983).

16. For a provocative alternative interpretation, see Janice Radway, *Reading the Romance: Women, Patriarchy and Popular Literature* (Chapel Hill: 1984).

17. Petchesky, *Abortion and Woman's Choice;* see also Zillah R. Eisenstein, *Feminism and Sexual Equality: Crisis in Liberal America* (New York: 1984).

18. The anti-pornography analysis has been articulated in Laura Lederer, ed., *Take Back the Night: Women on Pornography* (New York: 1980). Two anthologies that in various ways challenge this perspective are Snitow *et al.,* eds., *Powers of Desire,* and Carol Vance, ed., *Pleasure and Danger: Exploring Female Sexuality* (Boston: 1984). See also B. Ruby Rich, "Feminism and Sexuality in the 1980's," *Feminist Studies* 12 (1986): 525–61.

19. See also Cindy Patton, *Sex and Germs: The Politics of AIDS* (Boston: 1985); and Dennis Altman, *AIDS in the Mind of America* (Garden City, N.Y.: 1986).

2

Sexual Matters: On Conceptualizing Sexuality in History

Robert A. Padgug

Sexuality—the subject matter seems so obvious that it hardly appears to need comment. An immense and ever-increasing number of "discourses" has been devoted to its exploration and control during the last few centuries, and their very production has, as Foucault points out,[1] been a major characteristic of bourgeois society. Yet, ironically, as soon as we attempt to apply the concept to history, apparently insurmountable problems confront us.

To take a relatively simple example, relevant to one aspect of sexuality only, what are we to make of the ancient Greek historian Alexis' curious description of Polykrates, sixth-century B.C. ruler of Samos?[2] In the course of his account of the luxurious habits of Polykrates, Alexis stresses his numerous imports of foreign goods, and adds: "Because of all this there is good reason to marvel at the fact that the tyrant is not mentioned as having sent for women or boys from anywhere, despite his passion for liaisons with males. . . ." Now, that Polykrates did not "send for women" would seem to us to be a direct corollary of "his passion for liaisons with males." But to Alexis—and we know that his attitude was shared by all of Greek antiquity[3]—sexual passion in any form implied sexual passion in all forms. Sexual categories which seem so obvious to us, those which divide humanity into "heterosexuals" and "homosexuals," seem unknown to the ancient Greeks.

A problem thus emerges at the start: the categories which most historians normally use to analyze sexual matters do not seem adequate when we deal with Greek antiquity. We might, of course, simply dismiss the

Reprinted from *Radical History Review* 20 (Spring/Summer 1979): 3–23.

Greeks as "peculiar"—a procedure as common as it is unenlightening—but we would confront similar problems with respect to most other societies. Or, we might recognize the difference between Greek sexuality and our own, but not admit that it creates a problem in conceptualization. Freud, for example, writes:

> The most striking distinction between the erotic life of antiquity and our own no doubt lies in the fact that the ancients laid the stress upon the instinct itself, whereas we emphasize its object. The ancients glorified the instinct and were prepared on its account to honor even an inferior object; while we despise the instinctual activity in itself, and find excuses for it only in the merit of the object.[4]

Having made this perceptive comment, he lets the subject drop: so striking a contrast is, for him, a curiosity, rather than the starting point for serious critique of the very categories of sexuality.

Most investigators into sexuality in history have in fact treated their subject as so many variations on a single theme, whose contents were already broadly known. This is not only true of those who openly treat the history of sexuality as a species of entertainment, but even of those whose purpose is more serious and whose work is considered more significant from a historical point of view. One example, chosen from the much-admired *The Other Victorians* of Steven Marcus,[5] is typical. Marcus describes a very Victorian flagellation scene which appears in the anonymous *My Secret Life*. After describing its contents, he states categorically:

> But the representation in *My Secret Life* does something which the pornography cannot. It demonstrates how truly and literally childish such behavior is; it shows us, as nothing else that I know does, the pathos of perversity, how deeply sad, how cheerless a condemnation it really is. It is more than a condemnation; it is —or was—an imprisonment for life. For if it is bad enough that we are all imprisoned within our own sexuality, how much sadder must it be to be still further confined within this foreshortened, abridged and parodically grotesque version of it.

Marcus already *knows* the content and meaning of sexuality, Victorian or otherwise. It was not *My Secret Life* which gave him his knowledge, but rather his predetermined and prejudged "knowledge" which allowed him to use *My Secret Life* to create a catalog of examples of a generalized and universal sexuality, a sexuality which was not the result but the organizing principle of his study. Given this pre-knowledge, sexuality in history could hardly become a problem—it was simply a given.

Not surprisingly, for Marcus as well as for many other "sex researchers"— from Freudians to positivists—the sexuality which is "given," which is sexuality *tout court*, is what they perceive to be the sexuality of their own century, culture, and class, whether it bears a fundamentally "popular" stamp or comes decked out in full scientific garb.

In any approach that takes as predetermined and universal the categories of sexuality, real history disappears. Sexual practice becomes a more
or less sophisticated selection of curiosities, whose meaning and validity
can be gauged by that truth—or rather truths, since there are many com-
petitors—which we, in our enlightened age, have discovered. This procedure is reminiscent of the political economy of the period before, and
all too often after, Marx, but it is not a purely bourgeois failing. Many of
the chief sinners are Marxists.

A surprising lack of a properly historical approach to the subject of
sexuality has allowed a fundamentally bourgeois view of sexuality and its
subdivisions to deform twentieth-century Marxism. Marx and Engels
themselves tended to neglect the subject and even Engels' *Origin of the
Family, Private Property and the State* by no means succeeded in making
it a concern central to historical materialism. The Marxism of the Second
International, trapped to so great a degree within a narrow economism,
mainly dismissed sexuality as merely superstructural. Most later Marxist
thought and practice, with a few notable exceptions—Alexandra Kollon-
tai, Wilhelm Reich, the Frankfurt School—has in one way or another accepted this judgment.

In recent years questions concerning the nature of sexuality have been
re-placed on the Marxist agenda by the force of events and movements.
The women's movement and, to an increasing degree, the gay movement,
have made it clear that a politics without sexuality is doomed to failure or
deformation; the strong offensive of the American right wing which combines class and sexual politics can only re-enforce this view.[6] The feminist insistence that "the personal *is* political," itself a product of ongoing
struggle, represents an immense step forward in the understanding of
social reality, one which must be absorbed as a living part of Marxist
attitudes toward sexuality. The important comprehension that sexuality,
class, and politics cannot easily be disengaged from one another must
serve as the basis of a materialist view of sexuality in historical perspective as well.

■ **Sexuality as Ideology**   The contemporary view of sexuality which
underlies most historical work in this field is the major stumbling block
preventing further progress into the nature of sexuality in history. A brief
account of it can be provided here, largely in the light of feminist work,
which has begun to discredit so much of it. What follows is a composite
picture, not meant to apply as a whole or in detail to specific movements
and theories. But the general assumptions which inform this view appear
at the center of the dominant ideologies of sexuality in twentieth-century

capitalist societies, and it is against these assumptions that alternative theories and practices must be gauged and opposed.

In spite of the elaborate discourses and analyses devoted to it, and the continual stress on its centrality to human reality, this modern concept of sexuality remains difficult to define. Dictionaries and encyclopedias refer simply to the division of most species into males and females for purposes of reproduction; beyond that, specifically human sexuality is only described, never defined. What the ideologists of sexuality describe, in fact, are only the supposed spheres of its operation: gender; reproduction, the family, and socialization; love and intercourse. To be sure, each of these spheres is thought by them to have its own essence and forms ("*the* family," for example), but together they are taken to define the arena in which sexuality operates.

Within this arena, sexuality as a general, overarching category is used to define and delimit a large part of the world in which we exist. The almost perfect congruence between those spheres of existence which are said to be sexual and what is viewed as the "private sphere" of life is striking. As Carroll Smith-Rosenberg, working partly within this view of sexuality, puts it, "The most significant and intriguing historical questions relate to the events, the causal patterns, the psychodynamics of private places: the household, the family, the bed, the nursery, and kinship systems."[7] Indeed, a general definition of the most widely accepted notion of sexuality in the later twentieth century might easily be "that which pertains to the private, to the individual," as opposed to the allegedly "public" spheres of work, production, and politics.

This broad understanding of sexuality as "the private" involves other significant dualities, which, while not simple translations of the general division into private and public spheres, do present obvious analogies to it in the minds of those who accept it. Briefly, the sexual sphere is seen as the realm of psychology, while the public sphere is seen as the realm of politics and economics; Marx and Freud are often taken as symbolic of this division. The sexual sphere is considered the realm of consumption, the public sphere that of production; the former is sometimes viewed as the site of use value and the latter as that of exchange value. Sexuality is the realm of "nature," of the individual, and of biology; the public sphere is the realm of culture, society, and history. Finally, sexuality tends to be identified most closely with the female and the homosexual, while the public sphere is conceived of as male and heterosexual.

The intertwined dualities are not absolute, for those who believe in them are certain that although sexuality properly belongs to an identifiable private sphere, it slips over, legitimately or, more usually, illegitimately, into other spheres as well, spheres which otherwise would be definitely desexualized. Sexuality appears at one and the same time as narrow and limited and as universal and ubiquitous. Its role is both overestimated as the very core of being and underestimated as a merely private reality.

Both views refer sexuality to the individual, whom it is used to define. As Richard Sennett suggests, "Sexuality we imagine to define a large territory of who we are and what we feel. . . . Whatever we experience must in some way touch on our sexuality, but sexuality *is*. We uncover it, we discover it, we come to terms with it, but we do not master it."[8] Or, as Foucault rather more succinctly states, "In the space of a few centuries, a certain inclination has led us to direct the question of what we are to sex."[9] This is, after all, why we write about it, talk about it, worry about it so continuously.

Under the impulse of these assumptions, individuals are encouraged to see themselves in terms of their sexuality. This is most easily seen in such examples of "popular wisdom" as that one must love people for their inner, that is, sexual, selves, and not for "mere incidentals," like class, work, and wealth, and in the apparently widespread belief that the "real me" emerges only in private life, in the supposedly sexual spheres of intercourse and family, that is, outside of class, work, and public life. Sexuality is thereby detached from socioeconomic and class realities, which appear, in contrast, as external and imposed.

The location of sexuality as the innermost reality of the individual defines it, in Sennett's phrase, as an "expressive state," rather than an "expressive act."[10] For those who accept the foregoing assumptions, it appears as a *thing*, a fixed essence, which we possess as part of our very being; it simply *is*. And because sexuality is itself seen as a thing, it can be identified, for certain purposes at least, as inherent in particular objects, such as the sex organs, which are then seen as, in some sense, sexuality itself.

But modern sexual ideologues do not simply argue that sexuality is a *single* essence; they proclaim, rather, that it is a *group* of essences. For although they tell us that sexuality as a general category is universally shared by all of humanity, they insist that subcategories appear within it. There are thus said to be sexual essences appropriate to "the male," "the female," "the child," "the homosexual," "the heterosexual" (and indeed to "the foot fetishist," "the child molester," and on and on). In this view, identifiable and analytically discrete groups emerge, each bearing an appropriate sexual essence, capable of being analyzed as a "case history," and given a normative value. Krafft-Ebing's *Psychopathia Sexualis* of 1886 may still stand as the *logical* high point of this type of analysis, but the underlying attitude seems to permeate most of contemporary thought on the subject.

In sum, the most commonly held twentieth-century assumptions about sexuality imply that it is a separate category of existence (like "the economy," or "the state," other supposedly independent spheres of reality), almost identical with the sphere of private life. Such a view necessitates the location of sexuality within the individual as a fixed essence, leading to a classic division of individual and society and to a variety of psychological determinisms, and, often enough, to a full-blown biological determinism as well. These in turn involve the enshrinement of contemporary sexual categories as universal, static, and permanent, suitable for the analysis of all human beings and all societies. Finally, the consequences of this view are to restrict class struggle to nonsexual realms, since that which is private, sexual, and static is not a proper arena for public social action and change.

■ **Biology and Society**   The inadequacies of this dominant ideology require us to look at sexuality from a very different perspective, a perspective which can serve both as an implicit critique of the contemporary view as well as the starting point for a specifically Marxist conceptualization.

If we compare human sexuality with that of other species, we are immediately struck by its richness, its vast scope, and the degree to which its potentialities can seemingly be built upon endlessly, implicating the entire human world. Animal sexuality, by contrast, appears limited, constricted, and predefined in a narrow physical sphere.

This is not to deny that human sexuality, like animal sexuality, is deeply involved with physical reproduction and with intercourse and its pleasures. Biological sexuality is the necessary precondition for human sexuality. But biological sexuality is only a precondition, a set of potentialities, which is never unmediated by human reality, and which becomes transformed in qualitatively new ways in human society. The rich and ever-varying nature of such concepts and institutions as marriage, kinship, "love," "eroticism" in a variety of physical senses and as a component of fantasy and religious, social, and even economic reality, and the general human ability to extend the range of sexuality far beyond the physical body, all bear witness to this transformation.

Even this bare catalog of examples demonstrates that sexuality is closely involved in *social* reality. Marshall Sahlins makes the point clearly, when he argues that sexual reproduction and intercourse must not be

> considered *a priori* as a biological fact, characterized as an urge of human nature independent of the relations between social persons . . . [and] acting *upon* society from without (or below). [Uniquely among human beings] the process of "conception" is always a double entendre, since no satisfaction can occur without the act and the partners as socially defined and contemplated, that is, according to a symbolic code of persons, practices and proprieties.[11]

Such an approach does not seek to eliminate biology from human life, but to absorb it into a unity with social reality. Biology as a set of potentialities and insuperable necessities[12] provides the material of social interpretations and extensions; it does not *cause* human behavior, but conditions and limits it. Biology is not a narrow set of absolute imperatives. That it is malleable and broad is as obvious for animals, whose nature is altered with changing environment, as for human beings.[13] The uniqueness of human beings lies in their ability to create the environment which alters their own—and indeed other animals'—biological nature.

Human biology and culture are both necessary for the creation of human society. It is as important to avoid a rigid separation of "Nature" and "Culture" as it is to avoid reducing one to the other, or simply uniting them as an undifferentiated reality. Human beings are doubly determined by a permanent (but not immutable) natural base and by a permanent social mediation and transformation of it. An attempt to eliminate the biological aspect is misleading because it denies that social behavior takes place within nature and by extension of natural processes. Marx's insistence that "human beings make their own history but they do not make it just as they please" applies as well to biological as to inherited social realities.[14] An attempt—as in such disparate movements as Reichian analysis or the currently fashionable "sociobiology"—to absorb culture into biology is equally misleading, because, as Sahlins puts it, "Biology, while it is an absolutely necessary condition for culture, is equally and absolutely insufficient; it is completely unable to specify the cultural properties of human behavior or their variations from one human group to another."[15]

It is clear that, within certain limits, human beings have no fixed, inherited nature. We *become* human only in human society. Lucien Malson may overstate his case when he writes, "The idea that man has no nature is now beyond dispute. He has or rather is a history,"[16] but he is correct to focus on history and change in the creation of human culture and personality. Social reality cannot simply be "peeled off" to reveal "natural man" lurking beneath.[17]

This is true of sexuality in all its forms, from what seem to be the most purely "natural" acts of intercourse[18] or gender differentiation and hierarchy to the most elaborated forms of fantasy or kinship relations. Contrary to a common belief that sexuality is simply "natural" behavior, "nothing is more essentially transmitted by a social process of learning than sexual behavior," as Mary Douglas notes.[19]

Even an act which is apparently so purely physical, individual, and biological as masturbation illustrates this point. Doubtless we stroke our genitals because the act is pleasurable and the pleasure is physiologically rooted, but from that to masturbation, with its large element of fantasy, is a social leap, mediated by a vast set of definitions, meanings, connotations, learned behavior, shared and learned fantasies.

Sexual reality is variable, and it is so in several senses. It changes within individuals, within genders, and within societies, just as it differs from gender to gender, from class to class, and from society to society. Even the very meaning and content of sexual arousal vary according to these categories.[20] Above all, there is continuous *development and transformation* of its realities. What Marx suggests for hunger is equally true of the social forms of sexuality: "Hunger is hunger, but the hunger gratified by cooked meat eaten with a knife and fork is a different hunger from that which bolts down raw meat with the aid of hand, nail and tooth."[21]

There do exist certain sexual forms which, at least at a high level of generality, are common to all human societies: love, intercourse, kinship, can be understood universally on a very general level. But that both "saint and sinner" have erotic impulses, as George Bataille rightly claims,[22] or that Greece, Medieval Europe, and modern capitalist societies share general sexual forms, do not make the contents and meaning of these impulses and forms identical or undifferentiated. They must be carefully distinguished and separately understood, since their inner structures and social meanings and articulations are very different. The content and meaning of the eroticism of Christian mysticism is by no means reducible to that of Henry Miller, nor is the asceticism of the monk identical to that of the Irish peasants who delay their marriages to a relatively late age.[23]

The forms, content, and context of sexuality always differ. There is no abstract and universal category of "the erotic" or "the sexual" applicable without change to all societies. Any view which suggests otherwise is hopelessly mired in one or another form of biologism, and biologism is easily put forth as the basis of normative attitudes toward sexuality, which, if deviated from, may be seen as rendering the deviant behavior "unhealthy" and "abnormal." Such views are as unenlightening when dealing with Christian celibacy as when discussing Greek homosexual behavior.

■ **Sexuality as Praxis (I)**   When we look more directly at the social world itself, it becomes apparent that the general distinguishing mark of human sexuality, as of all social reality, is the unique role played in its construction by language, consciousness, symbolism, and labor, which, taken together—as they must be—are *praxis*, the production and reproduction of material life. Through *praxis* human beings produce an ever-changing human world within nature and give order and meaning to it, just as they come to know and give meaning to, and, to a degree, change, the realities of their own bodies, their physiology.[24] The content of sexuality is ultimately provided by human social relations, human productive activities, and human consciousness. The *history* of sexuality is therefore the history of a subject whose meaning and contents are in a continual process of change. It is the history of social relations.

For sexuality, although part of material reality, is not itself an object or thing. It is rather a group of social relations, of human interactions. Marx writes in the *Grundrisse* that "Society does not consist of individuals, but expresses the sum of interrelations, the relations within which these individuals stand."[25] This seems to put the emphasis precisely where it should be: individuals do exist as the constituent elements of society, but society is not the simple multiplication of isolated individuals. It is constituted only by the relationships between those individuals. On the other hand, society does not stand outside of and beyond the individuals who exist within it, but is the expression of their complex activity. The emphasis is on activity and relationships, which individuals ultimately create and through which, in turn, they are themselves created and modified. Particular individuals are both subjects and objects within the process, although in class societies the subjective aspect tends to be lost to sight and the processes tend to become reified as objective conditions working from outside.

Sexuality is relational.[26] It consists of activity and interactions—active social relations—and not simply "acts," as if sexuality were the enumeration and typology of an individual's orgasms (as it sometimes appears to be conceived of in, for example, the work of Kinsey and others), a position which puts the emphasis back within the individual alone. "It" does not do anything, combine with anything, appear anywhere; only people acting within specific relationships create what we call sexuality. This is a significant aspect of what Marx means when he claims, in the famous Sixth Thesis on Feuerbach, that "the essence of man is no abstraction inherent in each single individual. In its reality it is the ensemble of the social relations."[27] Social relations, like the biological inheritance, at once create, condition, and limit the possibilities of individual activity and personality.

Praxis is fully meaningful only at the level of sociohistorical reality. The particular interrelations and activities which exist at any moment in a specific society create sexual and other categories which, ultimately, determine the broad range of modes of behavior available to individuals who are born within that society. In turn, the social categories and interrelations are themselves altered over time by the activities and changing relationships of individuals. Sexual categories do not make manifest essences implicit within individuals, but are the expression of the active relationships of the members of entire groups and collectivities.

We can understand this most clearly by examining particular categories. We speak, for example, of homosexuals and heterosexuals as distinct categories of people, each with its sexual essence and personal behavioral characteristics. That these are not "natural" categories is evident. Freud, especially in the *Three Essays on the Theory of Sexuality*, and other psychologists have demonstrated that the boundaries between the two groups in our own society are fluid and difficult to define. And, as a result of everyday experience as well as the material collected in surveys like the Kinsey reports, we know that the categories of heterosexuality and homosexuality are by no means coextensive with the activities and personalities of heterosexuals and homosexuals. Individuals belonging to either group are capable of performing and, on more or less numerous occasions, do perform acts, and have behavioral characteristics and display social relationships thought specific to the other group.

The categories in fact take what are no more than a group of more or less closely related acts ("homosexual"/"heterosexual" behavior) and convert them into case studies of people ("homosexuals"/ "heterosexuals"). This conversion of acts into roles/personalities, and ultimately into entire subcultures, cannot be said to have been accomplished before at least the seventeenth century, and, as a firm belief and more or less close approximation of reality, the late nineteenth century.[28] What we call "homosexuality" (in the sense of the distinguishing traits of "homosexuals"), for example, was not considered a unified set of acts, much less a set of qualities defining particular persons, in pre-capitalist societies. Jeffrey Weeks, in discussing the act of Henry VIII of 1533 which first brought sodomy within the purview of statute law, argues that

> the central point was that the law was directed against a series of sexual acts, not a particular type of person. There was no concept of the homosexual in law, and homosexuality was regarded not as a particular attribute of a certain type of person but as a potential in all sinful creatures.[29]

The Greeks of the classical period would have agreed with the general principle, if not with the moral attitude. Homosexuality and heterosexuality for them were indeed groups of not necessarily very closely related acts, each of which could be performed by any person, depending upon his or her gender, status, or class.[30] "Homosexuals" and "heterosexuals" in the modern sense did not exist in their world, and to speak, as is common, of the Greeks as "bisexual" is illegitimate as well, since that merely adds a new, intermediate category, whereas it was precisely the categories themselves which had no meaning in antiquity.

Heterosexuals and homosexuals are involved in social "roles" and attitudes which pertain to a particular society, modern capitalism. These roles do have something in common with very different roles known in other societies—modern homosexuality and ancient pederasty, for example, share at least one feature: that the participants were of the same sex and that sexual intercourse is often involved—but the significant features are those that are not shared, including the entire range of symbolic, social, economic, and political meanings and functions each group of roles possesses.

"Homosexual" and "heterosexual" *behavior* may be universal; homosexual and heterosexual *identity and consciousness* are modern realities. These identities are not inherent in the individual. In order to be gay, for example, more than individual inclinations (however we might conceive of those) or homosexual activity is required; entire ranges of social attitudes and the construction of particular cultures, subcultures, and social relations are first necessary. To "commit" a homosexual act is one thing; to *be* a homosexual is something entirely different.

By the same token, of course, these are changeable and changing roles. The emergence of a gay movement (like that of the women's movement) has meant major alterations in homosexual and heterosexual realities and self-perceptions. Indeed it is abundantly clear that there has always existed in the modern world a dialectical interplay between those social categories and activities which ascribe to certain people a homosexual identity and the activities of those who are so categorized. The result is the complex constitution of "the homosexual" as a social being within bourgeois society. The same is, of course, true of "the heterosexual," although the processes and details vary.[31]

The example of homosexuality/heterosexuality is particularly striking, since it involves a categorization which appears limited to modern societies. But even categories with an apparently more general application demonstrate the same social construction.

For example, as feminists have made abundantly clear, while every society does divide its members into "men" and "women," what is meant by these divisions and the roles played by those defined by these terms varies significantly from society to society and even within each society by class, estate, or social position. The same is true of kinship relations. All societies have some conception of kinship and use it for a variety of purposes, but the conceptions differ widely and the institutions based on them are not necessarily directly comparable. Above all, the modern nuclear family, with its particular social and economic roles, does not appear to exist in other societies, which have no institution truly analogous to our own, either in conception, membership, or in articulation with other institutions and activities. Even within any single society, family/kinship patterns, perceptions, and activity vary considerably by class and gender.[32]

The point is clear: the members of each society create all of the sexual categories and roles within which they act and define themselves. The categories and the significance of the activity involved will vary as widely as do the societies within whose general social relations they occur, and categories appropriate to each society must be discovered by historians.

Not only must the categories of any single society or period not be hypostatized as universal, but even the categories which are appropriate to each society must be treated with care. Ultimately, they are only parameters within which sexual activity occurs or, indeed, against which it may be brought to bear. They tend to be normative—and ideological—in nature, that is, they are presented as the categories within which members of particular societies *ought* to act. The realities of any society only approximate the normative categories, as our homosexual/heterosexual example most clearly showed. It is both as norms, which determine the status of all sexual activity, and as approximations to actual social reality that they must be defined and explored.

■ **Sexuality as Praxis (II)**   Within this broad approach, the relationship between sexual activity and its categories and those that are nonsexual, especially those that are economic in nature, becomes of great importance.

Too many Marxists have tried to solve this problem by placing it within a simplified version of the "base/superstructure" model of society, in which the base is considered simply as "the economy," narrowly defined, while sexuality is relegated to the superstructure; that is, sexuality is seen as a "reflex" of an economic base.[33] Aside from the problems inherent in the base/superstructure model itself,[34] this approach not only reproduces the classic bourgeois division of society into private and public spheres, enshrining capitalist ideology as universal reality, but loses the basic insights inherent in viewing sexuality as social relations and activity.

Recently, many theorists, mainly working within a feminist perspective, began to develop a more sophisticated point of view, aiming, as Gayle Rubin put it in an important article,[35] "to introduce a distinction between 'economic' system and 'sexual' system, and to indicate that sexual systems have a certain autonomy and cannot always be explained in terms of economic forces." This view, which represented a great advance, nonetheless still partially accepted the contemporary distinction between a sphere of work and a sphere of sexuality.

The latest developments of socialist-feminist theory and practice have brought us still further, by demonstrating clearly that both sexuality in all its aspects and work/production are equally involved in the production and reproduction of *all* aspects of social reality, and cannot easily be separated out from one another.[36] Above all, elements of class and sexuality do not contradict one another or exist on different planes, but produce and reproduce each other's realities in complex ways, and both often take the form of activity carried out by the same persons working within the same institutions.

This means, among other things, that what we consider "sexuality" was, in the pre-bourgeois world, a group of acts and institutions not necessarily linked to one another, or, if they were linked, combined in ways very different from our own. Intercourse, kinship, the family, and gender did not form anything like a "field" of sexuality. Rather, each group of sexual acts was connected directly or indirectly—that is, formed a part of—institutions and thought patterns which we tend to view as political, economic, or social in nature, and the connections cut across our idea of sexuality as a thing, detachable from other things, and as a separate sphere of private existence.

The Greeks, for example, would not have known how, and would not have sought, to detach "sexuality" from the household (*oikos*), with its economic, political, and religious functions; from the state (especially as the reproduction of citizenship); from religion (as fertility cults or ancestor worship, for example); or from class and estate (as the determiner of the propriety of sexual acts, and the like).[37] This is even more true of so-called primitive societies, where sexuality (mediated through kinship, the dominant form of social relations) seems to permeate all aspects of life uniformly.

It was only with the development of capitalist societies that "sexuality" and "the economy" became separable from other spheres of society and could be counterposed to one another as realities of different sorts.[38] To be sure, the reality of that separation is, in the fullest sense of the word, ideological; that is, the spheres do have a certain reality as autonomous areas of activity and consciousness, but the links between them are innumerable, and both remain significant in the production and reproduction of social reality in the fullest sense. The actual connections between sexuality and the economy must be studied in greater detail, as must the specific relations between class, gender, family, and intercourse,[39] if the Marxist and sexual liberation movements are to work in a cooperative and fruitful, rather than antagonistic and harmful, manner.

A second major problem-area stands in the way of a fuller understanding of sexuality as *praxis*. The approach to sexuality we have outlined does overcome the apparently insurmountable opposition between society and the individual which marks the ideological views with which we began our discussion. But it overcomes it at a general level, leaving many specific problems unsolved. The most important of these is the large and thorny problem of the determination of the specific ways in which specific individuals react to existing sexual categories and act within or against them. To deal with this vast subject fully, Marxists need to develop a psychology—or a set of psychologies—compatible with their social and economic analyses.[40]

Much the most common approach among western Marxists in the last fifty years toward creating a Marxist psychology has been an attempt, in one manner or another, to combine Marx and Freud. Whether in the sophisticated and dialectical versions of the Frankfurt School, Herbert Marcuse, or Wilhelm Reich, or in what Richard Lichtman has called "the popular view that Freud analyzed the individual while Marx uncovered the structure of social reality,"[41] these attempts arose out of the felt need for a more fully developed Marxist psychology in light of the failure of socialist revolutions in the west.

None of these attempts has, ultimately, been a success, and their failure seems to lie in real contradictions between Marxist and Freudian theory. Both present theories of the relationship between individual and society, theories which contradict each other at fundamental levels.

Freud does accept the importance of social relations for individual psychology. For him, sexuality has its roots in physiology, especially in the anatomical differences between the sexes, but these distinctions are not in themselves constitutive of our sexuality. Sexuality is indeed a process of development in which the unconscious takes account of biology as well as of society (mediated through the family) to produce an individual's sexuality.[42]

The problems begin here. Society, for Freud, is the medium in which the individual psyche grows and operates, but it is also in fundamental ways antipathetical to the individual, forcing him or her to repress instinctual desires. Freud's theory preserves the bourgeois division between society and the individual, and ultimately gives primacy to inborn drives within an essentially ahistorical individual over social reality. In a revealing passage, Freud argues:

> Human civilization rests upon two pillars, of which one is the control of natural forces and the other the restriction of our instincts. The ruler's throne rests upon fettered slaves. Among the instinctual components which are thus brought into service, the sexual instincts, in the narrow sense of the word, are conspicuous for their strength and savagery. Woe if they should be set loose! The throne would be overturned and the ruler trampled under foot.[43]

In spite of the fact that Freud does not view instincts as purely biological in nature,[44] he certainly sees sexuality as an internal, biologically based force, a thing inherent in the individual. This is a view which makes it difficult to use Freud alongside Marx in the elucidation of the nature of sexuality. This is not to say that we need necessarily discard all of Freud. The general theory of the unconscious remains a powerful one. Zillah Eisenstein pointed in a useful direction when she wrote, "Whether there can be a meaningful synthesis of Marx and Freud depends on whether it is possible to understand how the unconscious is reproduced and maintained by the relations of the society."[45] But it is uncertain whether the Freudian theory of the unconscious can be stripped of so much of its specific content and remain useful for Marxist purposes. The work of Lacan, which attempts to "de-biologize" the Freudian unconscious by focusing on the role of language, and that of Deleuze and Guattari, in their *Anti-Oedipus*, which attempts to provide it with a more fully sociohistorical content, are significant beginnings in this process.[46]

At the present time, however, Marxism still awaits a psychology fully adequate to its needs, although some recent developments are promising, such as the publication in English of the important non-Freudian work of the early Soviet psychologist L. S. Vygotsky.[47] But if psychology is to play a significant role in Marxist thought, as a science whose object is one of the dialectical poles of the individual/society unity, then it must have a finer grasp of the nature of that object. At this point, we can only agree with Lucien Seve that the object of psychology has not yet been adequately explored.[48]

■ **Conclusion**   The historical study of sexuality has an important role to play in contemporary struggles. Through a better understanding of how capitalist societies developed, and are continuing to develop, the modern ideology of sexuality—including the struggles which have occurred around it, both between and within classes—we will better understand the specific role it plays in legitimating contemporary society and in defusing class struggle, as well as its contradictory potentialities for undermining the capitalist system. We can also begin to develop specific socialist strategies for political activity which combines economic and sexual struggle in fruitful ways. And, finally, we will be in a better position to examine the possible outlines of sexuality in a socialist society, with the useful comprehension that the sexuality of the future cannot be a simple unveiling of something which capitalism "repressed" or distorted, but must be an essentially new creation within the total configuration of the developing social relations of a future society.

■ **Notes**

Acknowledgments: The author would like to thank Betsy Blackmar, Edwin Burrows, Victoria de Grazia, Elizabeth Fee, Joseph Interrante, Michael Merrill, David Varas, and Michael Wallace for their invaluable comments on earlier drafts.

1. Michel Foucault, *The History of Sexuality*, vol. I, *An Introduction* (New York: 1978), pt. 1.

2. As reported in Athenaeus, *Deipnosophistae* 12.450 d-f (= F. Jacoby, *Fragmente der Griech. Historiker* no. 539, fragment no. 2).

3. Cf. for other examples, Lucian, "The Ship" (Loeb Classical Library edition of Lucian, vol. VI, 481), or the "Love Stories," attributed to Plutarch (*Moralia* 771E-775E), which provide pairs of similar love tales, each consisting of one involving heterosexual love and one involving homosexual love.

4. Sigmund Freud, *Three Essays on the Theory of Sexuality* (New York: 1964), 38; the footnote was added in the 1910 edition.

5. Steven Marcus, *The Other Victorians*, 2nd ed. (New York: 1974), 124ff.; the passage quoted is from 127.

6. Cf. Linda Gordon and Allen Hunter, "Sex, Family and the New Right," *Radical America* 11, no. 6/12, no. 1 (Nov. 1977–Feb. 1978): 9–26.

7. Carroll Smith–Rosenberg, "The New Woman and the New History," *Feminist Studies* 3 (1976): 185.

8. Richard Sennett, *The Fall of Public Man* (New York: 1977), 7.

9. Foucault, *History of Sexuality*, vol. I, 78.

10. Sennett, *Fall of Public Man*, 7.

11. *New York Review of Books*, 23 Nov. 1978, 51.

12. On biology as a realm of the necessary, cf. S. Timpanaro, *On Materialism* (London: 1978).

13. Cf. Helen H. Lambert, "Biology and Equality," *Signs* 4 (1978): 97–117, esp. 104.

14. These points are strongly insisted upon by Timpanaro, *On Materialism*. See also Raymond Williams, "Problems of Materialism," *New Left Review* no. 109 (1978): 3–18.

15. M. Sahlins, *The Use and Abuse of Biology* (Ann Arbor: 1976), xi.

16. L. Malson, *Wolf Children* (New York: 1972), 9.

17. Cf. *ibid.*, 10.

18. Cf. *ibid.*, 48.

19. Mary Douglas, *Natural Symbols* (New York: 1973), 93.

20. Cf. W. H. Davenport, "Sex in Cross-Cultural Perspectives," in *Human Sexuality in Four Perspectives*, ed. F. Beach (Baltimore: 1977), ch. 5.

21. Karl Marx, *Grundrisse*, ed. Nicolaus (London: 1973), 92.

22. George Bataille, *Death and Sensuality* (New York: 1962).

23. Cf. the important analysis of this and similar points in Denis de Rougement, *Love in the Western World* (New York: 1956), 159 ff.

24. Cf. Adolfo Sanchez Vazquez, *The Philosophy of Praxis* (London: 1977).

25. Marx, *Grundrisse*, 265.

26. Cf. the work of the so-called symbolic interactionalists, best exemplified by Kenneth Plummer, *Sexual Stigma* (London: 1975). Their work, although not Marxist and too focused on individuals *per se*, does represent a major step forward in our understanding of sexuality as interpersonal.

27. K. Marx, F. Engels, *Collected Works*, vol. 5 (New York: 1976), 4.

28. Mary McIntosh, "The Homosexual Role," *Social Problems* 16 (1968): 182–91, the pioneer work in this field, suggests the seventeenth century for the emergence of the first homosexual subculture. Randolph Trumbach, "London's Sodomites: Homosexual Behavior and Western Culture in the Eighteenth Century," *Journal of Social History* 11 (1977/78): 1–33, argues for the eighteenth century. Jeffrey Weeks, in two important works, "Sins and Disease," *History Workshop* 1 (1976): 211–19, and *Coming Out* (London: 1977), argues, correctly, I believe, that the full emergence of homosexual role and subculture occurs only in the second half of the nineteenth century. Cf. the articles by Weeks and Hansen in volume 20 of *Radical History Review* (Spring/Summer 1979). All these works deal with England, but there is little reason to suspect that the general phenomenon, at least, varies very considerably in other bourgeois countries.

29. Weeks, *Coming Out*, 12.

30. The best work available on Greek homosexual behavior is K. J. Dover, *Greek Homosexuality* (London: 1978), which contains further bibliography.

31. Cf. Foucault, *History of Sexuality*, I, pts. 4–5, as well as Guy Hocquenghem, *Homosexual Desire* (London: 1978).

32. On the conceptualization of family, kinship, and household, see the important collective work by Rayna Rapp, Ellen Ross, and Renate Bridenthal, "Examining Family History," *Feminist Studies* 5 (1979): 174–200, as well as Rayna Rapp, "Family and Class in Contemporary America," *Science and Society* 42 (1978): 278–300. Cf. Mark Poster, *Critical Theory of the Family* (New York: 1978), and the critique of it by Ellen Ross, "Rethinking the Family," *Radical History Review* 20 (Spring/Summer 1979): 76–84.

33. This appears to be true even of such relatively unorthodox thinkers as Louis Althusser (*Lenin and Philosophy* [New York: 1971], 127–86); E. Balibar (*Reading Capital* [New York: 1970], pt. III); P. Hindess and B. Hirst (*Pre-Capitalist Modes of Production* [London: 1975], esp. ch. 1); and Claude Meillassoux, (*Femmes Greniers et Capitaux* [Paris: 1975], pt. I).

34. Cf. Raymond Williams, *Marxism and Literature* (New York: 1977), esp. pt. II.

35. "The Traffic in Women," in *Towards an Anthropology of Women*, ed. R. Reiter (New York: 1975), 157–210, at 167. For other views similar to those of Rubin, on this point at least, cf. R. Bridenthal, "The Dialectics of Production and Reproduction in History," *Radical America* 10, no. 2 (1976): 3–11; Nancy Chodorow, "Mothering, Male Dominance and Capitalism," in *Capitalist Patriarchy and the Case for Socialist Feminism*, ed. Z. Eisenstein (New York: 1979), 83–106; and Juliet Mitchell, *Woman's Estate* (London: 1975).

36. Among recent works which come to this conclusion, and whose bibliographies and notes are useful for further study, see Joan Kelly, "The Doubled Vision of Feminist Theory," *Feminist Studies* 5 (1979): 216–27; Lise Vogel, "Questions on the Woman Question," *Monthly Review* (June 1979): 39–60; Renate Bridenthal, "Family and Reproduction," the third part of a joint essay cited in note 32, above; Eli Zaretsky, *Capitalism and Personal Life* (New York: 1976), 24ff.; and Ann Forman, *Femininity as Alienation* (London: 1977).

37. On the Greek *oikos* and related institutions, see W. K. Lacey, *The Family in Classical Greece* (London: 1968).

38. Cf. Foucault, *History of Sexuality*, vol. I, and Zaretsky, *Capitalism and Personal Life*, for attempts to conceptualize the emergence of these categories. On the non-emergence of a separate sphere of the economy in non-capitalist societies, cf. Georg Lukacs, *History and Class Consciousness* (London: 1968), 55–59, 223–255; and Samir Amin, "In Praise of Socialism," in *Imperialism and Unequal Development* (New York: 1977), 73–85.

39. For works which begin this process, cf. those cited in notes 35 and 36 above, plus the articles collected in Z. Eisenstein, *Capitalist Patriarchy*.

40. For a full discussion of this need and what it involves, see Lucien Seve, *Marxisme et théorie de personnalité*, 3rd ed. (Paris: 1972). Seve is best on the social conditioning of individual psychology and weakest on individual psychic processes themselves.

41. "Marx and Freud," pt. 1, *Socialist Review* no. 30 (1976): 3–56, at 5. This article, along with its two successors in *Socialist Review* no. 33 (1977): 59–84, and no. 36 (1977): 37–78, form a good introduction to the study of the relationship between Marx and Freud, arguing for their incompatibility.

42. An important recent attempt to demonstrate the social underpinnings of

Freud's thought is Juliet Mitchell, *Psychoanalysis and Feminism* (New York: 1974). Eli Zaretsky, "Male Supremacy and the Unconscious," *Socialist Review* no. 21/22 (1975): 7–55, demonstrates several defects in Freud's understanding of socio-historical reality, but suggests that they are remediable.

43. Sigmund Freud, "The Resistance to Psycho-Analysis," *The Standard Edition of the Complete Psychological Works of Sigmund Freud*, trans. James Strachey *et al.* (London: 1961), vol. 19, 218.

44. Cf. Freud, "Instincts and their Vicissitudes," *Standard Edition* (London, 1957), vol. 14, 105–40.

45. Eisenstein, *Capitalist Patriarchy*, 3.

46. G. Deleuze and F. Guattari, *Anti-Oedipus* (New York: 1977). Cf. also the work of Herbert Marcuse, especially *Eros and Civilization* (Boston: 1955), and Norman O. Brown, *Life Against Death* (Middletown, Conn.: 1959).

47. L. S. Vygotsky, *Mind in Society* (Cambridge, Mass.: 1977); cf. Stephen Toulmin's essay on Vygotsky, "The Mozart of Psychology," *New York Review of Books*, 28 Sept. 1978, 51–57.

48. Seve, *Marxisme et théorie de la personnalité*, pt. 1.

II

The Emergence
of Modern Sexuality,
1790 to 1930

3

"The Life of a Citizen in the Hands of a Woman": Sexual Assault in New York City, 1790 to 1820

Marybeth Hamilton Arnold

The man who dares forcibly to violate female honor, who dares to insult a sex whom it is his duty to defend, deserves the greatest punishment the vengeance of man can inflict.

When New York City attorney Robert Troup made this statement in 1793, while defending aristocrat Henry Bedlow on charges of raping sewing girl Lanah Sawyer, he chose his words carefully.[1] The Bedlow case, because of the nature of those involved—"Harry" Bedlow, a notorious libertine and his alleged victim, the daughter of a sea captain well-known in the laboring community—had become a local *cause célèbre*, and Troup faced a large, hostile courtroom audience in his effort to persuade the jury of his client's innocence.

To win his case, Troup could not afford to dismiss the seriousness of the crime with which Bedlow was charged—nor, most likely, would it have occurred to him to do so. In Troup's eyes and, he would have anticipated, in those of his audience, rape was indeed a horrid crime, an abomination exciting (in the words of Troup's colleague Brockholst Livingston) a "universal abhorrence."[2]

But, as Troup's words indicate, that abhorrence did not rest on the factual nature of the crime, its legal definition as "the carnal knowledge of a woman, forcibly and against her will."[3] Troup stressed the violation not of a woman's will, but of her honor; rape thus was hateful as a perversion of each man's duty to protect chaste and helpless females. In com-

A different version of this article appears in William Pencak and Conrad Edick Wright, eds., *New York and the Rise of American Capitalism: 1780–1870* (New-York Historical Society, 1988).

35

mitting his crime, the rapist exploited a woman's guileless trust, thereby robbing her of the purity which "was dearer to her than life."[4] Such an act, Troup's forceful rhetoric implied, constituted an attack against the bases of social order, and an outrage against every man's deeply felt sense of the way things ought to be.

Troup's pronouncement points to a larger truth: rape in early national America was hardly a dispassionately defined, readily recognizable "fact." A formal definition of rape, as a forced and nonconsensual sexual attack, had been operative in America since the colonial period, the legacy of English common law; but a gulf existed between that legal understanding and rape's practical definition. The latter, in contrast, was shaped—and changed—by social conditions, political structures, and, above all, ideologies of sex and gender.

That rape has been perceived and defined in ideologically slanted ways is not, of course, a point applicable to the early nineteenth century alone. Over the past two decades, feminist activists and scholars have contrasted the high incidence of rape in our own time with the crime's treatment in the American judicial system: only a fraction of rapes reported, few of those actually prosecuted, and a low rate of convictions, with many accused rapists acquitted on the basis of the woman's "irregular" sexual past. From these investigations and from public "speakouts" in which women have voiced their own experiences of sexual assault has emerged a potent feminist analysis of the social function of rape as a means of male domination—used, as both physical fact and psychological menace, to limit women's movements, mandate their sexual modesty and reinforce their dependence on men. To Susan Brownmiller, one of the movement's most articulate voices, the fear of rape has cemented patriarchy itself, serving, "from prehistoric times to the present," as "a conscious process of intimidation by which *all men* keep *all women* in a state of fear."[5]

Brownmiller and other anti-rape activists have performed an invaluable service by encouraging women to view rape not as a private shame but as a social and political affront. But their stance on sexual violence has troubling overtones. Susan Brownmiller's grim vision of universal male dominance, unchanged since "prehistory," casts women in a role of ceaseless passivity and neglects the rich history of resistance to oppression (a history that varies with differences in women's class, race, and social and political context) that feminist historians have revealed. Even more troubling, however, is the tone of much anti-rape crusading. At times, the enemy seems to be not institutionalized sexism, but sexuality itself: an unchanging, aggressive male sexuality of which women have been eternally the victims. A feminist politics that sees sex throughout history as simply a force for women's exploitation is a dangerously simplistic politics. By ignoring women's interest in sexual expression, it runs the risk of cooptation by conservative forces whose repressive agenda must ultimately stunt feminist aims.[6]

In this essay I have departed from the ahistorical and antisexual stance of much scholarship on sexual violence by looking closely at rape within a specific historical context—in the working-class districts of post-revolutionary New York City. There, in a milieu structured by political turmoil, poverty, and a volatile conception of sexual relations, rape took shape as a battle between neighbors; in the tenements and on the streets, working-class women and men fought out conflicting understandings of sex, courtship, and female autonomy. By looking at the words of these laboring women and the men they prosecuted for rape, I examine their differing expectations of sex and perceptions of sexual violence and the fate of those expectations and perceptions before the young republican state. Like Brownmiller, I am concerned with how the threat of rape curtailed poor women's movements, limited their freedom, and mandated their submission. Unlike Brownmiller, however, I have tried to see these women as historical agents as well as victims and to understand how their expectations of sex, their stake in sex, shaped their understanding of sexual assault.

■   Between 1790 and 1820 at least forty-eight women came before the New York County Court of General Sessions to bring charges of rape or attempted rape (or, as the court itself termed it, assault and battery with intent to ravish). The remaining records are sketchy: a formal indictment, handed down by the Grand Jury, containing a few details about the identity of the defendant and the location of the crime; often, a transcript of the woman's original complaint to the police court; occasionally, statements from others immediately involved—her parents, her neighbors, her doctor, and, in eleven of forty-eight cases, her alleged assailant; and, finally, in thirty-four instances, a notation of the case's final outcome.

Fragmentary as they are, these records, along with the transcripts of the more sensational trials, provide a revealing glimpse of sexual violence in early national New York. Rape, at least as it came before the judicial system, was overwhelmingly a crime of the poor.[7] In all of the thirty-seven indictments providing enough information about the victim to give some idea of her situation in life, the women involved lived in modest circumstances at best. They included the wives of shopkeepers, day laborers, and craftsmen; single women, working as domestic servants and seamstresses; and children as young as six years of age, the daughters of cartmen, masons, and small shopkeepers, who occasionally worked as domestic servants themselves. They were, with three exceptions, white. Their assailants included three men listed as "gentlemen," but by far the majority came from roughly the same station in life as the women. Overwhelmingly white (in all but five cases), they worked as artisans, laborers, and small shopkeepers and lived like the women they assaulted, in the ramshackle tenements and small wooden shacks of the central and outer wards.

Those districts were increasingly distinct and isolated in the early nineteenth century as they became home to the growing numbers of the city's poor, a population that increased dramatically between 1790 and 1820. Those years saw rapid growth in the city's economy, but also brought recurrent depressions, brief but severe, that caused New York's unemployment to skyrocket. With fewer jobs and limited resources for charity, the struggle to get by grew more competitive, burdensome, and demanding, especially as thousands of penniless migrants and immigrants ventured to the city in search of work and then could not afford to go elsewhere.[8] By 1817 close to 1,800 people were housed in the city's Almshouse (nearly triple the Almshouse population in the 1790s), and fully 15,000, or one-seventh of New York's total population, required some sort of municipal assistance to survive. Still more scraped by from hand to mouth as day laborers, hucksters, seamstresses, rag pickers, and, when necessary, petty thieves and prostitutes.[9]

The presence of poverty was nothing new to the city, but its attendant circumstances during this thirty-year period often were. The slow but unmistakable growth of capitalist social relations in the city's workshops meant that many laborers found themselves sliding into poverty in new ways.[10] Once there, they and their families lived in subtly but significantly changing surroundings, as hostilities between rich and poor took concrete physical form with the growing segregation of New York City's neighborhoods by class. By 1820 the laborers, artisans, and small shopkeepers who made up New York's working classes were settling in the newer and cheaper sections of town, the central and outer wards, at a distance from the more well-to-do residents of the older, better established first and second wards. These laborers crowded two or more families into subdivided dwellings, the poorer among them crammed into "mean, small and low" wooden houses perched on landfills over disease-breeding swamps in Roosevelt, James, Bancker, Oliver, Catherine, and Rutgers Streets and in the notorious Five Points slum.[11]

To study rape in early national New York is to study those households and their surrounding streets: in all but two of the thirty-two cases in which the fact can be determined, working-class women were assaulted by fellow neighborhood dwellers, often their co-residents in crowded tenements. Thus assailants, from these women's perspective, were the most everyday of men, individuals whose attire and demeanor marked them as neighborhood dwellers and whose faces must often have been familiar even when their names were not: laborers whom women brushed past in the street, lodgers with whom they shared a breakfast table, fellow residents of subdivided houses who frequented the same hallways. In turn, the crimes themselves took place on this familiar terrain, in the households and on the neighboring streets these men and women shared. Women were attacked, in other words, not on extraordinary excursions into the city's unfamiliar nether reaches, but in the most mundane of settings, in the same locations where they lived and worked, as they carried on their daily lives.

These neighborhoods and the ramshackle houses within them were crowded, convivial places where bantering with housemates, neighbors, and casual passersby served as a constant source of diversion.[12] Sexual assaults seem often to have been rooted in that gregarious framework. In their opening moments they were instances of the easy familiarity of household and street life, as the men's language in the court records—friendly, relaxed, and jovial—occasionally attests. Charles Carpenter, for example, accosting seventeen-year-old domestic servant Ellen Carsen in the nursery of her employer's home in 1818, approached her with the words, "I want to stay with you all night," a casually seductive statement, not a bluntly violent one, despite the fact that he subsequently chased her down a staircase into an alley, propped her leg on a barrel, and pushed himself inside her.[13] Similarly, George Bowman approached his housemate Margaret Heyser in 1798 not with threats but with an appeal to desire—her husband, he argued (before forcing himself upon her after she refused his advances), was "good for nothing," and she would do better to sleep with him.[14] And shopkeeper Patterson Lolly in 1815 strolled into the entryway of housemate Mary Ann Marsh, placed an arm companionably around her waist, and remarked, "Let us go and try whether the bed is well corded" before dragging her into her room, throwing her onto the bed, and pulling up her skirts.[15]

Yet the casual familiarity of neighborhood life does not in itself explain what is most striking about these encounters—the juxtaposition of the men's tone of calm, assured jocularity with their rough, brutal conduct. To judge by their actions, they viewed violent pursuit as entirely compatible with amiable seduction. In a jovial, friendly manner, they made advances and asked the woman's consent, but were not particularly concerned to obtain it before getting things under way, perhaps in the belief that every sexual encounter required a bit of a struggle to overcome most women's veneer of reluctance. And veneer, to these men's way of thinking, was surely all it was. As their air of assurance indicates, they assumed the women involved to be, at heart, as willing as they.

In that assumption they would not have been alone in early national New York. Whatever these men's individual histories, they could have bolstered their supposition of female acquiescence with the harsh and

overt misogyny that pervaded the wider culture of New York City, reso-
nating through the etiquette manuals of the well-to-do, the songs and
jokes of the popular classes, and the "commonsense" pronouncements
of attorneys in trials for sexual assault.

This misogyny had its roots in the suspicions of female sexual in-
satiability that had persisted for centuries in western culture. Protestant-
ism, by elevating wives to the status of "helpmeets," had tempered those
suspicions somewhat, but with the decline of religious fervor in the eighteenth century, those suspicions grew more intense and more fully elaborated. Women—"the sex," as popular terminology labeled them—were
reputed to have strong and imperious sexual desires that they were unable, or unwilling, to control. From women's sexual voracity sprang a
slew of "feminine" vices: greed, vanity, deceit, and manipulativeness, all
foibles of weak, emotionally unstable beings who were incapable of
rationality.[16]

This conception of feminine nature was applied, to a degree, to all
women, regardless of class. Even aristocratic ladies, to judge by the British proscriptive literature devoured by New York's anglophilic upper
crust, were regarded as manipulative and artful, plying their schemes in
the "guerilla war of wits" that was eighteenth-century courtship.[17] Yet
the social status of aristocratic women protected them from the more
malicious characterizations of feminine vice to which poorer women
were subject. The women of New York's laboring class, as Christine Stansell has noted, were made the repositories of all the most venal qualities
the city's upper-class women had shed in their ascent to ladyhood—
their insatiable passions and grasping, greedy brand of treachery. In the
rowdy male preserves of saloons and bawdy houses (terrain frequented
by both gentlemen and laborers), jokes, songs, and tales depicted poor
women as greedy whores and lusty, manipulative molls, creatures whose
violent passions led them readily to vengefulness and deceit.[18] In such a
cynical milieu, some men could easily dismiss any woman's rejection of
their advances and see force as a legitimate weapon in, and indeed inseparable from, sexual conquest.

Such a perception was articulated explicitly by Richard Harison, one of
a number of attorneys defending Henry Bedlow in his trial for the rape of
Lanah Sawyer. Without denying that sexual intercourse had taken place
between the pair, intercourse against which Sawyer had most likely put up
a struggle, Harison justified his client's actions:

> Some degree of force possibly might have been used by the Prisoner at
> the Bar; but it was a force only to save the delicacy and feelings of the
> Prosecutrix. Any woman who is not an abandoned Prostitute will appear
> to be averse to what she inwardly desires; a virtuous girl on the point of
> yielding will not appear to give a willing consent, though her manner
> sufficiently evinces her wishes.[19]

To Harison (and, he must have assumed, to the male jurors to whom he spoke), roughness seemed a normal and acceptable component of Bedlow's pursuit. If Lanah Sawyer had struggled, moreover, that resistance could only have been feigned: Sawyer, in Harison's eyes, like all lower-class women, had strong sexual urges that would manifest themselves at the beckoning of any male admirer, particularly one as wealthy and well-connected as Bedlow. Another counsel for the defense, Brockholst Livingston, stated the matter more bluntly: Sawyer, though characterized by neighbors and family as a quiet, modest young woman, was simply "innocent for want of opportunity." She "had the art to carry a fair outside, while all was foul within."[20]

This notion of laboring women's "foul" interior could only be reinforced by their far from pristine surroundings—the crowded tenements and overflowing streets of the city's evolving laboring-class neighborhoods. In those areas even the most intimate aspects of human life necessarily took on a public character. Constrained by the fast-rising rents of the growing city, laboring families jammed themselves into a few rooms, often stretching whatever extra space remained to accommodate one or more boarders. In such densely packed households, nothing could remain private, especially given their thin wooden walls, whose cracks and knotholes hid little of what went on from the eyes and ears of fellow residents, neighbors, and curious passersby.[21]

The city streets, particularly such bustling thoroughfares as Broadway and the Bowery, could offer escape from those prying eyes. Precisely because of the relative anonymity they provided the adventurous, however, those avenues brimmed with sexual tension and excitement. From early in the morning until late at night, even the more obscure neighborhood byways overflowed with crowds—crowds composed of women as well as men, for both material necessity and desire for pleasure dictated that the women and girls of New York's laboring class would spend much of their lives out of doors. Married women, though forced by domestic duties to stick close to home, still ventured outside their walls to fetch water from street pumps, beat rugs, journey to neighboring markets, and, when weather allowed, wash clothes. Their daughters, even the very young, took up residence in neighboring homes as domestic servants, where many of their chores would carry them outdoors, or simply roamed the streets to supplement the family's scanty income—scavenging for odds and ends, peddling, and taking on paying chores where they could find them.[22]

On the streets they encountered a wealth of sexual possibilities. There women could banter and flirt with men they met while fetching water from street pumps or vegetables from corner markets. There they negotiated their way around crowds of "bloods," young men from merchant and laboring families who lounged on city sidewalks and, affecting the contemptuous stance of the aristocratic libertine, tossed provocative remarks at any single woman who passed. And there they had the chance to "walk out"—to pair off with the men of their choice for strolls amidst the evening crowds. On such excursions, far from the watchful eyes of parents and neighbors, young women could trade sexual favors ranging from companionship to intercourse for an evening of urban excitement or, if they chose, cash. The latter option was by no means unusual—in a city where prostitution was not yet a statutory offense, such casual encounters could provide young women with a quick income, enabling them to obtain small luxuries otherwise out of their reach, and for that reason were sometimes sought by girls as young as eleven or twelve.[23]

The gregarious lives of New York's laboring women within this sexually public milieu seem to have provided some men with, in effect, a sense of entitlement to women's bodies. That sense can be glimpsed in the preceding cases; it appears with more jarring clarity, however, in the court documents concerned with assaults against female children.

Fully one-third of the forty-eight cases of sexual assault brought before the Court of General Sessions in the early national period involved girls under the age of fourteen. To be sure, one should not assume that the widespread suspicions of laboring women's sexuality were applied to six-year-old serving girls in the same manner as to their mothers or older sisters. Sexual assaults of young children were indeed treated by the courts as particularly heinous crimes—indictment papers took care to specify attacks on "infants" (apparently defined as ten years or younger until 1813, when the age of consent was raised to fourteen).[24] Yet the fact remains that, in a milieu like that of the laboring poor, where children early shouldered the responsibilities and to some degree the freedoms of adulthood, a wide latitude for uncertainty existed as to when a female child had made the fateful transition to womanhood. As Brockholst Livingston argued in his defense of Richard Croucher on charges of raping thirteen-year-old Margaret Miller in 1800:

> [If] anything of an improper nature passed between them, I am inclined
> to believe that it has been with her consent. The passions may be as
> warm in a girl of her age as in one of more advanced years, and with very
> little enticement she may have consented to become his mistress. . . . [It]
> is said her youth renders it impossible she should have been a lewd girl.
> Who is acquainted with the dissolute morals of our city, and does not
> know that females are to be found living in a state of open prostitution at
> the early ages of 12 and 13 years?[25]

The young daughters of the city's laborers of necessity led active, peripatetic existences in a milieu where sex was a clearly visible element of community life. As Livingston's remarks indicate, their very sociability lay all such girls open to contempt for supposed "lewdness." In some cases, as the court records attest, it lay them open as well to advances from men who viewed them, like their older sisters, as available targets for pursuit.

In 1813 Kent Cotton, a black oyster vendor working at the corner of James and Chatham Streets, was accused of attempting to rape Susan Johnson, the seven-year-old sister of twelve-year-old Sally Johnson, who lived with Cotton and worked at his stand. Late one afternoon, according to the girls' father, Cotton sent Sally off on an errand, leaving Susan alone with him. Once Sally had left, Cotton lifted Susan onto a nearby bench, laid atop her, and entered her, causing the girl great bodily injury.

Cotton's response to the charges leveled against him is illuminating. As the police recorded his defense:

> About sunset while Sally was gone some wheres and he and Susan were alone in the oyster stand, he went to playing with Susan and with his fingers operated upon her private parts—which is all he did. She made no objections to anything he did to her. . . . There was no blood about Susan nor did she make any noise or outcry.

Clearly, claiming that "operating upon" her genitals with his fingers was "all he did" was not a convincing defense in light of the injuries Susan sustained—her father said that she appeared "almost torn asunder"—and Cotton was found guilty of the assault.[26] But the point here is that Kent Cotton could consider his statement to be a valid defense of his conduct. In Cotton's view Susan's silence accorded him full license to her seven-year-old body; if she made no objection to his actions, it could only mean that she desired and welcomed them. As a female she had to brim with sexual passions that waited to be stirred, and he had as much right as any man to partake of them.

Kent Cotton's is not the only case reflecting such a sentiment. It can be sensed in shopkeeper John Conlon's contemptuous dismissal of thirteen-year-old Maria Forshee, his domestic servant, as a "whore" after she informed neighbors, her mother, and Conlon's wife of his attempt to rape her in 1818.[27] It appears more openly in carpenter John Dolphin's unabashed outrage when in 1819 he was pulled from atop the body of six-year-old Madelina Bentley in the shop at the rear of the lot he shared with her family in Corlear's Hook: "in a great rage he cursed and swore at [Madelina's] mother and brother] and said the child should lie with him."[28]

Finally, this sense that even the youngest girls were fair game for male advances is apparent in the case of Morris Matthews, accused of attempting to rape ten-year-old Caroline Earle in 1816. If the examples detailed thus far can be dismissed as the responses of "deviants" or people willing to say anything to save their skins—as not, in other words, reflective of any wider cultural ambivalences about girlhood, womanhood, and sex—the Matthews case cannot, for the crucial evidence there comes not from the accused or his attorney, but from the principal witness on behalf of the injured girl.

Thomas Leslie was a lodger at 55 Maiden Lane, a boarding house oper- ated by John Anderson. On the night of December 31, a visitor, Morris Matthews, arrived at Anderson's establishment and, after some conversa- tion, retired to his room for the night, a room where he was to share a bed with lodger Leslie. The pair had lain in bed for about twenty minutes, Leslie testified, when Matthews arose and left the room. Leslie sat up and listened, trying to ascertain what Matthews was doing, but heard noth- ing, and lay down again. A few minutes later, however, he heard a noise "which he could not account for some thing like a person being stifled." With that, he left his bed immediately and headed in the direction of the noise—the children's bedroom, occupied by Anderson's niece, Caroline Earle. Reaching the door, Leslie heard Caroline cry out as if hurt. He entered the room "and by the light of the moon which shone directly on the bed Caroline slept in he saw Morris Matthews in the bed and upon the body of Caroline who appeared . . . to be asleep." In the moonlight, Leslie testified, he could clearly see Matthews "meddling" with the young girl.

At this point in his testimony, it seems, one can easily predict Leslie's next action—he doubtless seized Matthews and pulled him off of the girl. But, in fact, Leslie did nothing of the kind.

> [He] stood for some time within about four feet of Morris . . . at first doubting whether he had better to seize the said Morris or to go and alarm Mr. Anderson. Finally [he] concluded that he would go and tell Mr. Anderson, and then went back to his own bedroom and put on his clothes and then went and informed Mr. Anderson.[29]

Clearly, Leslie was in no hurry about any of this. Though objecting to Matthews' conduct, he did not do so, it seems obvious, out of outrage at Matthews' violation of Caroline Earle's bodily integrity and will. Instead, his chief concern was to inform Caroline's uncle of Matthews' actions, indicating that he viewed John Anderson as the injured party in the af- fair, and that he was angered that a man staying under Anderson's roof had presumed to take possession of his niece without his knowledge. In other words it was not Matthews' right to the girl, but his flaunting of another man's authority, that Leslie disputed.

It is impossible to know with certainty what went through Thomas Leslie's mind as he stood "for some time" watching Morris Matthews and Caroline Earle by the light of the moon. But the possibility seems strong that he hesitated to seize Matthews because he believed Caroline a will- ing participant in the act. He had, of course, heard her scream in pain, but when he entered the room she was silent. Perhaps he believed her resistance had been conquered or that it had been feigned to begin with.

She was a female, after all, with all the qualities attendant on that fact, despite her youth.

Laboring-class women of all ages in early national New York faced a daunting task: to scrape together a subsistence for themselves and their families within a culture whose prevailing myths identified poor women's machinations with lewdness and insatiable, grasping passion. Yet to conclude from the above that these women lived lives of unalloyed fear and victimization would be to do them an injustice. However charged with potential harassment and violence their lives may have been, many women comported themselves throughout with strength and assertiveness. Economic necessity, the demands of household chores, and the simple desire for pleasure made the streets indispensable to poor women, and they walked them at all hours. When harassed, many did not scoot meekly past, but retorted sharply and stridently. In physical battles with assailants, some were well able to hold their own, among them Mary Ann Marsh, who fought off her assailant, shopkeeper and housemate Patterson Lolly, and Margaret Heyser, who did the same with assailant George Bowman.[30]

Yet these instances of physical strength and assertiveness, though important, only go part of the way in describing how the women of New York City's laboring poor negotiated their everyday lives. To maintain their hold on subsistence in a turbulent economy, women needed toughness and a combative spirit, and it should come as no surprise that the assault records provide glimpses of precisely that. Yet they carry suggestions of something more. In prosecuting for rape, these women asserted that from their perspective the boundaries of permissible sexual advance had been crossed. Their testimony allows us to piece together where, for some, those boundaries lay—at what point, in other words, the act became intolerable and in what elements in particular its odiousness resided. Through their words—what the women leave unmentioned as well as what they stress—we gain a hint of the way in which, in their everyday encounters, New York's laboring women sought to manipulate the sexual tensions that surrounded them and to use those tensions to their own advantage when they could.

In 1818 Mary Brett, an eleven-year-old domestic servant, swore out a complaint on charges of attempted rape against her employer, grocer Dennis Hosey. Brett's description of the attack vividly demonstrates one young girl's attempt to maneuver as best she could within a sexually charged situation. Early in the morning of July 28, after his wife had left to sell vegetables in the market, Dennis Hosey had offered Mary Brett some milk punch made with alcohol. She drank it, and then at his direction lay down on his bed in a back room off the grocery store. She had been resting quietly for a few minutes, lying on her side at the foot of the bed with her back toward its head, when Hosey came into the room and—assuming, she supposed, that she was asleep—tried to lift her skirts.

Brett reacted not with panic but with a great deal of control. In an understated but effective act of resistance, she wrapped her skirts tightly around her feet while stiffening her body so Hosey could not flip her onto her back. He managed, after a long struggle, to raise her skirts as high as her knees but was unable to turn her over. Failing that, he unbuttoned his pants and lay down on the bed behind her. As Brett told the police court, "He then laid behind her and attempted to enter her body . . . from behind but she shooed it away with her hand. He kept saying only let me have a little taste and she told him she would not while he was laying with her in that situation."

Their struggles ceased abruptly when a customer entered the store. Hosey left the room, and Brett went into the kitchen to fix breakfast. When she called her employer in to eat, she found him sitting with her father, who had arrived for a visit. The three sat down together for the meal, and no mention was made of the struggle that had just taken place. Once her father had left, Hosey again offered some milk punch and, after some persuasion, Brett drank it—"but," she said in her statement, "it was not strong." During the rest of the day she resisted all of Hosey's pleas to return to his bed.

Dennis Hosey's assault, however, was not without side effects. During their early morning struggle, he had apparently penetrated Brett with his finger, and as the day wore on the pain began to take its toll. By nightfall, Brett had collapsed, violently ill, in her room. Thinking some fresh air might help her, Hosey carried her outside and placed her in a chair in the yard. Within a few minutes neighbors had gathered around the visibly sick young girl, speculating about what had happened to her; one woman asked Brett directly and, "in agony or fits," she told her. Neighborhood furor soon reached such proportions that Hosey himself went to Mary Brett's mother to tell her of the incident, "saying to her he was determined to tell her the first story as he knew she would hear about it."[31]

Mary Brett's description of her struggle with Dennis Hosey, while certainly a story of exploitation, is as well an account of careful, strategic maneuvering, of a sexually charged encounter that both players sought to manipulate to their own advantage. Brett, for her part, obtained a brief rest from her household chores, as well as two glasses of milk punch. (Given the centrality of alcohol to the lives of laborers in this period, it is highly unlikely that even an eleven-year-old would not have known the effects it could have on her or suspected Hosey's motive in offering it. Indeed, the fact that she could have put up such a struggle after taking a full drink, and that she had a basis by which to judge that the second drink was "not strong," suggests that she was familiar with alcohol's effects herself.) In return she had to cope with Hosey's advances, which she did quite skillfully, her response temperate enough to forestall his anger yet effective enough to prevent him from fully gratifying his desires.

They engaged throughout the day in a genuine battle, one in which power was more heavily weighted on Hosey's side. Yet Brett also retained some leverage. As her own account attests, it was Hosey who did the pleading; Brett herself managed to wield a tone of authority and indeed seems to have taken his actions very much in stride. (While one could interpret her failure to tell her father of the assault as resulting from terror of her employer's wrath, this seems unlikely given the assertiveness with which she had refused his advances only a short time before.)

What seemed crucial to Mary Brett in her complaint was not the sexual nature of Hosey's assault but the fact that she grew sick as a result. Nor, indeed, was Mary Brett's the only complaint to emphasize the physical damage incurred far more than the sexual violation itself. In several cases the woman's testimony centered on the violence she had suffered: that since the attack she had been confined to bed, requiring a doctor's care; that her back had been injured to the extent that she had trouble moving; that her face had been scarred so severely she hesitated to go out in public.[32]

The testimony of some, in addition, laid particular emphasis on whether their assailants reached orgasm—or, as they themselves phrased it, whether the men "left them wet." Indeed, that fact, not penetration alone, seems to have determined in all of these cases whether the crime would be judged rape or attempted rape.

Here, however, one must beware of inferring too much. The Court of General Sessions indictment papers provide not the women's voices directly but their stories as they were recorded in the police court. The officials taking their complaints may have asked these women specific questions about the extent of their injuries in order to comply with court requirements.[33]

Yet, though much more research remains to be done, it makes sense to consider the possibility that in stressing injury and ejaculation in their police court statements women were expressing their own primary grievances. These women and girls were scraping by at the very margins of existence. A physical injury or a pregnancy sustained in a sexual assault could incapacitate them for work and destroy the precarious sustenance they had managed to eke out. As Bridget Waters, an unmarried domestic servant with a child, made clear, such a circumstance formed her key complaint in charging her employer, Matthias Hays, with rape in 1803: "Since the affair before stated has happened she has not been able to do any work on account of the bruises she then received."[34] Yet this strong emphasis on physical injury, at times to the exclusion of all else, suggests that some women of the laboring class were willing to allow noninjurious sexual acts to proceed to a relatively advanced degree before seeking legal redress for a criminal violation.

If this was in fact true, we need not read it automatically as yet another grim example of victimization. While belief in poor women's inherent lewdness opened them up to exploitation by some men, it could also be turned to their advantage. As "the sex" they had a valuable bargaining tool for material and social gain in a world where they had almost no other such device to claim. Stated most simply, they had something men wanted, and that gave them at least a small amount of leverage in making their way through a hostile environment.[35]

That sexual nature, moreover, gave these women common ground with others of their sex, who often became sources of advice, comfort, and even retribution in cases of assault. Nearly all of the women in these cases who sought outside help after an attack turned to another woman, whether a relative, an employer's wife, or a neighbor. Such help could be invaluable, as in both Mary Brett's and Maria Forshee's cases, in which neighboring women seem to have banded together in condemnation of the offending man, to the point that Dennis Hosey, at least, felt obliged to protect himself from further scorn by informing Mary Brett's mother of his actions himself.[36]

Yet such banding together had its limits. Women did turn to other women for advice, aid, and support in cases of sexual assault, as, one would suspect, in sexual matters more generally. But though such loyalties between women perhaps tempered the informal justice dispensed in neighborhoods, they could have little effect on the formal verdicts handed down in the courts.

This should not, however, imply that men could rape poor women with impunity, or that laboring women who prosecuted could never obtain convictions. Guilty verdicts were handed down in at least eighteen of the cases in the Court of General Sessions records. Those convicted of rape were subject to execution until 1796 and to life imprisonment thereafter; those convicted of assault with intent to ravish were subject to one to fourteen years' imprisonment for the first offense and life imprisonment for the second.[37]

But only a particular sort of rape case was capable of bringing a guilty verdict. The more closely the circumstances of the crime resembled a scenario of male villainy and female helplessness, the greater the likelihood that the case would result in a conviction. Of the eleven cases ending in convictions that provide sufficient information for such an assessment, fully nine contained complaints by women that strongly stressed their helplessness and dependence on men—either the women were rescued by valiant males, or they brought their husbands or fathers to court to testify to the validity of their charges. A woman who fought off her assailant alone or pressed charges with no man to stand up for her stood a slim chance of gaining a conviction.[38]

Such a depiction of sexual assault—as the diabolical exploitation of a defenseless woman—was not simply a legal convention. It pervaded the culture of early national New York, figuring centrally in the Richardsonian novels of rape and seduction that became the era's best sellers and in the melodramas of feminine victimization beginning to make their way onto the New York City stage.[39] Such a depiction prevailed for a reason—it meshed with the tenets of a severely patriarchal culture, a culture that scorned women as lewd and irrational and demanded their subordination to husbands and fathers in return for protection and support. In that culture sexual assault could be conceived of only in specific terms—as an exploitation of women's presumed dependence on men. If a woman had herself violated patriarchal norms by straying out of her dependent position—if she had fought off her attacker, asserted her rights alone in court, or behaved in too self-reliant a manner more generally—the term "rape" no longer applied, no matter how forceful the attack visited upon her.

In one sense this was probably nothing new. Little detailed evidence exists for rape trials in pre-revolutionary New York City, but it is probable that, in previous decades as in later, the cultural suspicions of feminine lewdness that seem to have intensified with the waning of Calvinism encouraged jurists to define rape in ways that mandated women's dependence and subordination. Yet in one important respect, a rape victim's position *had* worsened in early national New York. The political climate of the post-revolutionary era in many ways intensified jurists' insistence upon poor women's dependence. The ascendance of republican politics had provided all men with a new and powerful measure of their shared dignity and self-worth—their status as "citizens," an identity that by definition could be assumed by men alone. In the early years of the nineteenth century, some educated women were able to turn republican precepts to their own advantage—to argue for an expansion of women's rights based on their duty to rear responsible republican citizens—but no such sophisticated argument was available to the women of the city's poor. In contrast they bore the brunt of long-standing cultural suspicions that republicanism had newly deepened and legitimated, by implicitly stigmatizing "unprotected" poor women as dangers to social stability.

No case illustrates this more clearly than that of Lanah Sawyer, who accused Henry Bedlow of rape in September 1793. One evening near the end of August, Sawyer, a seventeen-year-old sewing girl who lived with her parents in Gold Street in the fourth ward, was taking a stroll on Broadway and was harassed by a group of Frenchmen. A chivalrous gentleman came to her rescue, silencing the offenders and steering her safely out of their reach. As he escorted her home, he told her his name was "Lawyer Smith," but he was in reality Henry Bedlow, the son of a prominent New York City family and, as would be made clear in the trial, a notorious rake.

Bedlow met Sawyer again the following Sunday and, after some persuasion, extracted a promise to walk with him on the Battery on Wednesday. He greeted her in front of her home Wednesday evening and assured her that they would be accompanied by another couple, including a young woman whom Sawyer knew, but when they reached that young woman's house she was not in. At Bedlow's suggestion the pair continued on to the Battery and, after strolling there for some time, walked back along Broadway to Ann Street. There, according to Sawyer, Bedlow grabbed hold of her, covered her mouth, and dragged her to a brothel run by a Mrs. Cary. (According to Bedlow, Sawyer came with him peaceably.) Once Mrs. Cary had placed them in a room, Bedlow several times asked Sawyer to consent to his sleeping with her; after she repeatedly refused, Sawyer asserted, he took her by force.[40]

In the subsequent trial the prosecution portrayed the case as a perfect instance of villainous ravishment. Bedlow, a scoundrel, had deluded the helpless Lanah Sawyer. Working his way into her affections in the guise of a protector by coming to her rescue on the street, he had taken advantage of her dependence and used the trust she placed in him for his own vile gain. In prosecuting attorney Hoffman's florid words:

> Through the natural simplicity of youth, through inexperience in the wiles of mankind, [Sawyer] . . . placed too great a confidence in the Prisoner at the Bar. . . . [He] made use of her security in his honor to get her more effectually in his power. . . . The Prisoner finding his prey in his power, exulting in the success of his schemes, now seizes the unhappy victim, forcibly tears off her cloaths, and accomplishes his diabolical scheme.[41]

Bedlow's defense team, however, composed of some of the city's most prominent lawyers, interpreted the encounter differently. While accepting the defense's characterization of rape, they emphasized how sharply Lanah Sawyer's behavior departed from its tenets. She had, after all, been walking the streets alone and at night when she and Bedlow first met. Of her own accord she had formed a quick acquaintance with the man, even after being warned against him and informed of "Lawyer Smith" 's true identity by her neighbor Samuel Hone. She had walked with this near-stranger on the Battery with no other man present and had remained out with him even after she had heard the clock strike midnight. Though they employed other evidence as well in their defense—crucially, producing a string of residents from Mrs. Cary's "bad house" to dispute Sawyer's contention that she put up a struggle—Bedlow's attorneys placed at the center of their argument the presentation of Sawyer as an imprudently assertive young woman.[42] As such, she could never convincingly claim rape, a charge that in practice relied upon a woman's injured innocence and victimized dependence.

Under attack by Bedlow's attorneys, the prosecution's portrait of Sawyer as a "discreet, prudent young woman [who] never kept much company" quickly grew unconvincing.[43] Sawyer, like other young women in the gregarious neighborhoods of the working poor, kept a great deal of company and sought diversion on the city streets far from her father's supervision. Such freedom of movement, from the defense's perspective, demonstrated Sawyer's abandonment of both dependence and innocence; indeed, it provided proof, in defense attorney John Cozine's words, of "her desire of gratifying her passions."[44] As Cozine stated in summarizing the defense's argument, "The manner of her acquaintance with the Prisoner, her indiscretion throughout the whole of her behavior to him, affords a strong presumption of her consent."[45] Such reasoning evidently had great force with the jury—it acquitted Bedlow after fifteen minutes' deliberation.

In presenting their case, Bedlow's lawyers relied not simply upon the jury's agreement that female prudence was necessary on the city streets. They relied, more fundamentally, upon the jury's unquestioned acceptance of the female subordination imbedded in the social structure of early national New York. The terms in which they phrased their argument, moreover, make clear how fully that patriarchal tradition had been reinforced within the political climate of post-revolutionary America. The Bedlow case, after all, carried a strong political appeal from the prosecution's standpoint—a crime certain to outrage the honor of any plain, proud laborer, in which a vicious aristocratic libertine violated the honor of a young girl of common but honest background.[46] To counteract that image's force, Bedlow's lawyers changed the terms of the presentation in a critical way. Bedlow in their portrayal was not a corrupt aristocrat but, as they stressed repeatedly, a "fellow citizen." He had his faults, of course, but he was a citizen nonetheless: a self-reliant, property-holding, civic-minded male whose independence was being jeopardized by a devious, passionate, poor (and consequently grasping and manipulative) girl. Defense attorney Thompson drove this point home in his opening address, warning the jury that rape "is an offense . . . so easily charged by the woman . . . putting the life of a citizen in the hands of a woman, to be disposed of almost at her will and pleasure."[47]

The Bedlow–Sawyer case was thus transformed into a dispute between a citizen and an outsider—potent rhetoric in a post-revolutionary climate in which the glories of citizenship had been so recently hard-won. Defining social dignity and political worthiness on the basis of rationality, material self-reliance, and independence from the will of others, the ideal of citizenship bound together men of all classes, bringing aristocrats like Bedlow down to the common level and providing poorer laborers with a new means to self-respect. Yet the concept of citizenship by definition excluded women—indeed, by implication, it reviled them. As Linda Kerber has noted, revolutionary republican politics, in which the concept of citizenship was grounded, implicitly equated female passion, trickery, and extravagance with the corruption ever threatening civic virtue.[48] Thus, although eighteenth-century misogyny had already dictated women's dependence, republicanism provided that status with a powerful political justification. In their lewdness and venality, women had to be corralled, held fast by the "protective" bonds of the family; unleashed, they formed a potent threat to the young republic's stability.

■   Republicanism did not legitimize rape in early national New York. Yet it did make heavier the burdens under which poor women labored. Struggling to scrape together a subsistence within the volatile quarters of the working poor, they survived through toughness, aggression, and adeptness at sexual maneuvering. Sex, from their perspective, was simply another arena for struggle: a charged and dangerous terrain requiring cunning and vigilance, but to which they did bring some resources of their own. Sexual assault undoubtedly enraged them, but not, as the courts would have had it, as an insult to a cherished sexual purity. For many poor women rape was most onerous as a violent, debilitating attack on their mobility and their capacity to fend for themselves.

To survive, and to enrich their lives with any degree of pleasure, poor women had to enmesh themselves in the gregarious, sexually charged life of their neighborhoods and streets. Yet precisely that expansive behavior gave at least some laboring men a sense of entitlement to these women's bodies. Imbued with their culture's suspicions of feminine lust and cunning, they interpreted poor women's sociability and freedom of movement as open invitations to sexual advances. Whether women refused, protested, or tried to fight them off was unimportant: all sex, from their perspective, consisted of struggle and conquest. Viewing sex as an inherently volatile adventure, they drew no real distinction between persuasive seduction and violent assault.

Such men were a minority in the laboring community, but their "deviance" most likely rested more in the degree of their violence (and in the fact that they were unlucky enough to be prosecuted for it) than in the nature of their actions. As Christine Stansell has shown, courtship and marriage were contentious, combative enterprises within the early national working class. Not all men, of course, turned violent, any more than all became rapists. The point, however, is that within the culture of which these men were a part, it was possible to view aggression and hostility as simply normal, unremarkable consequences of sexual relations. Their bawdy, vehemently masculine plebian culture glorified male sexual adventuring and stigmatized women as lewd, scheming whores. Under that culture's sway some men saw sexual relations as rough-and-tumble battles of bodies and of wits, encounters demanding that they prey upon women before being preyed upon themselves. Such a construction of sex could blur the line between "persuasion" and force: all working-class women could potentially be seen as fair game for sexual pursuit.

In adopting such a vision, moreover, a laboring man stood a good chance of being supported by New York's judicial system. Rape, as we have seen, was harshly condemned by the courts, but only when presentable as a villainous example of libertinism, a brutal violation of feminine helplessness and dependence. That appearance of helplessness was critical to the success of a woman's complaint, yet it was an appearance that many poor women found exceedingly difficult to give. Assertive, gregarious, often sexually tough, they faced in the immediate postwar years a political climate that feared and reviled female sexuality as a potent threat to the state. Before New York's judicial system, concerned above all to guard the republican city from danger, the more assertive and contentious women of the laboring class lost all claim to protection from attack.

■ Notes

Acknowledgments: I owe special thanks to John Carson, Daniel Ernst, Christine Stansell, Rachel Weil, and Sean Wilentz for their advice and encouragement.

1. William Wyche, *Report of the Trial of Henry Bedlow for Committing a Rape on Lanah Sawyer* (New York: 1793), 35.

2. *Ibid.,* 32.

3. William Blackstone, *Commentaries on the Laws of England,* American ed. (Philadelphia: 1771), vol. IV, 210.

4. Wyche, *Report of the Trial of Henry Bedlow,* 58.

5. Susan Brownmiller, *Against Our Will: Men, Women and Rape* (New York: 1975), 15.

6. For a recent, dramatic example of such an argument, see Andrea Dworkin, *Intercourse* (New York: 1987). An insightful discussion of the repressive implications of some feminist work on sexual violence can be found in Ellen Carol DuBois and Linda Gordon, "Seeking Ecstasy on the Battlefield: Danger and Pleasure in Nineteenth Century Feminist Sexual Thought," in *Pleasure and Danger: Exploring Female Sexuality,* ed. Carole S. Vance (Boston: 1984), 31–49.

7. I can only speculate on why this was the case and how court statistics compared to the "true" distribution of rape in early national New York City. Perhaps poor women were simply the group most likely to register a complaint—some historians have suggested that, until the mid–nineteenth century, the poor habitually made vigorous use of the courts as the most effective, accessible forum for redressing their grievances. See, for example, Allen Steinberg, "The Criminal Courts and the Transformation of Criminal Justice in Philadelphia, 1815–1874" (Ph.D. dissertation, Columbia University, 1983). I also suspect, however, that the overwhelming predominance of poor women bringing complaints did reflect the actual distribution of the crime. As I hope to demonstrate here, poor women's freedom of movement and the cultural suspicions of their lewdness and greed made them easy prey for attack.

8. Sidney I. Pomerantz, *New York, An American City, 1783–1803: A Study of Urban Life* (1938; rpt. Port Washington, N.Y.: 1965), 203–216.

9. Sean Wilentz, *Chants Democratic: New York City and the Rise of the American Working Class, 1788–1850* (New York: 1984), 26–27.

10. *Ibid.,* 23–60.

11. Betsy Blackmar, "Re-walking the 'Walking City': Housing and Property Relations in New York City, 1780–1840," *Radical History Review* 21 (1979): 131–48; Pomerantz, *New York, An American City,* 230.

12. For a detailed discussion of these neighborhoods and the life within them, see Christine Stansell, *City of Women: Sex and Class in New York, 1789–1860* (New York: 1986), 41–62.

13. *The People v. Charles Carpenter* (filed 9 December 1818), New York County Court of General Sessions Indictment Papers, Municipal Archives, New York City.

14. *The People v. George Bowman* (filed 24 July 1798), New York County Court of General Sessions Indictment Papers, Municipal Archives, New York City.

15. *The People v. Patterson Lolly* (filed 6 October 1815), New York County Court of General Sessions Indictment Papers, Municipal Archives, New York City.

16. Stansell, *City of Women,* 20–25.

17. *Ibid.* See also Janet James, *Changing Ideas About Women in the United States, 1776–1825* (New York: 1981), ch. 1.

18. Christine Stansell examines these popular sources in detail in *City of Women,* 28–29.

19. Wyche, *Report of the Trial of Henry Bedlow,* 45.

20. *Ibid.,* 22.

21. Many a rape case would have gone uncorroborated had it not been for neighbors' habits of scrutinizing the sexual goings-on around them—their readiness to peer through windows, listen at doorways, and speculate at length about the rakish inclinations of neighboring men. See, for example, *The People v. George Bowman* (filed 4 July 1798), *The People v. Grant Cottle* (filed 1 February, 1 March, and 11 August 1800), *The People v. David Crawford* (filed 16 May 1810), *The People v. Garret Fitzgerald* (filed 12 February 1815), *The People v. Morris Matthews* (filed 31 December 1816), and *The People v. Dennis Hosey* (filed 28 July 1818), all in New York County Court of General Sessions Indictment Papers, Municipal Archives, New York City; see also the above-cited transcripts of the Bedlow, Croucher, and Wakely trials, all of which rely heavily on the observations of scrupulously watchful neighbors. For a more general discussion of the neighborhoods of New York City's poor, see Stansell, *City of Women,* 41–62. For discussion of the effect of material conditions on sexual experience in other locales, see Nancy Cott, "Eighteenth Century Family and Social Life Revealed in Massachusetts Divorce Records," in *A Heritage of Her Own: Toward a New Social History of American Women,* ed. Nancy F. Cott and Elizabeth H. Pleck (New York: 1979), 107–35; and G. R. Quaife, *Wanton Wenches and Wayward Wives: Peasants and Illicit Sex in Early 17th Century England* (London: 1979).

22. Christine Stansell, "Women, Children, and the Uses of the Streets: Class and Gender Conflict in New York City, 1850–1860," *Feminist Studies* 8 (Summer 1982): 309–35.

23. *Ibid.,* 317; Stansell, *City of Women,* 180–92.

24. I could not, however, find confirmation of this in New York's legal code. My

statement is based simply on a change in the wording of the indictments themselves, which in 1813 ceased specifying "an infant under the age of ten years" and noted instead "an infant under the age of fourteen years."

25. *Report of the Trial of Richard D. Croucher, on an Indictment for a Rape on Margaret Miller, on Tuesday, the 8th day of July, 1800* (New York: 1800), 15, 18.

26. *The People v. Kent Cotton* (filed 13 April 1813), New York County Court of General Sessions Indictment Papers, Municipal Archives, New York City.

27. *The People v. John Conlon* (filed 4 March 1818), New York County Court of General Sessions Indictment Papers, Municipal Archives, New York City.

28. *The People v. John Dolphin* (filed 10 June 1819), New York County Court of General Sessions Indictment Papers, Municipal Archives, New York City.

29. *The People v. Morris Matthews* (filed 12 February 1817), New York County Court of General Sessions Indictment Papers, Municipal Archives, New York City.

30. *The People v. Patterson Lolly* (1815); *The People v. George Bowman* (1798).

31. *The People v. Dennis Hosey* (filed 5 August 1818), New York County Court of General Sessions Indictment Papers, Municipal Archives, New York City.

32. See, for example, *The People v. William Van Tassell* (filed 8 February 1800); *The People v. Anthony A Yellow Boy* (filed 7 August 1811); *The People v. Samuel Summers* (filed 8 January 1812); *The People v. Kent Cotton* (1813); all in New York County Court of General Sessions Indictment Papers, Municipal Archives, New York City.

33. Whether American courts required ejaculation as well as penetration in order to bring a rape charge remains unclear. The British jurists most often cited in New York trials, Matthew Hale and Edward Hyde East, argued against a requirement of emission, stating instead that penetration alone could constitute rape. Some British courts, however, did require proof of emission until 1828, when the requirement was abolished by law. See Edward Hyde East, *A Treatise on the Pleas of the Crown,* American ed. (Philadelphia: 1806), vol. I, 436–37; and Joseph Chitty, *Practical Treatise on Medical Jurisprudence,* American ed. (Philadelphia: 1836), 381–82. I am grateful to Anna Clark, in her as yet untitled, unpublished monograph on rape in eighteenth- and nineteenth-century England (Rutgers University, 1985), for these references.

34. *The People v. Matthias Hays* (filed 17 December 1803), New York County Court of General Sessions Indictment Papers, Municipal Archives, New York City.

35. The possibility that poor women could turn sexual tensions to their own advantage, not simply be exploited by them, is explored as well by Kathy Peiss in "'Charity Girls' and City Pleasures: Historical Notes on Working-Class Sexuality, 1880–1920," in this volume.

36. *The People v. Dennis Hosey* (1818); *The People v. John Conlon* (1818).

37. *Collection of Penal Laws and Laws Concerning the State Prison* (New York: 1799), 3–5.

38. Anna Clark reaches a similar conclusion for nineteenth-century Britain in "'Shameful Occurrences': Controversies over Sexual Assault in Early Nineteenth Century England," paper delivered at the Fifth Annual Graduate History Conference, Rutgers University, 1983.

39. James, *Changing Ideas About Women,* 52; David Grimsted, *Melodrama Unveiled: American Theater and Culture, 1800–1850* (Chicago: 1968), ch. 1.

40. Wyche, *Report of the Trial of Henry Bedlow,* 3–14.

41. *Ibid.,* 51–55.

42. *Ibid.,* 9–45.

43. *Ibid.,* 18.

44. *Ibid.,* 40.

45. *Ibid.,* 41.

46. Anna Clark explores the political implications of this scenario in Britain in "Seduction: Myth, Melodrama, and the Politics of Class and Gender," Women's History Seminar Paper, Rutgers University, 1983.

47. Wyche, *Report of the Trial of Henry Bedlow,* 9.

48. Linda Kerber, *Women of the Republic: Intellect and Ideology in Revolutionary America* (Chapel Hill: 1980).

4

"Charity Girls" and City Pleasures: Historical Notes on Working-Class Sexuality, 1880–1920

Kathy Peiss

Uncovering the history of working-class sexuality has been a particularly intractable task for recent scholars. Diaries, letters, and memoirs, while a rich source for studies of bourgeois sexuality, offer few glimpses into working-class intimate life. We have had to turn to middle-class commentary and observations of working people, but these accounts often seem hopelessly moralistic and biased. The difficulty with such sources is not simply a question of tone or selectivity, but involves the very categories of analysis they employ. Reformers, social workers, and journalists viewed working-class women's sexuality through middle-class lenses, invoking sexual standards that set "respectability" against "promiscuity." When applied to unmarried women, these categories were constructed foremost around the biological fact of premarital virginity, and secondarily by such cultural indicators as manners, language, dress, and public interaction. Chastity was the measure of young women's respectability, and those who engaged in premarital intercourse, or, more importantly, dressed and acted as though they had, were classed as promiscuous women or prostitutes. Thus labor investigations of the late nineteenth century not only surveyed women's wages and working conditions, but delved into the issue of their sexual virtue, hoping to resolve scientifically the question of working women's respectability.[1]

Nevertheless, some middle-class observers in city missions and settlements recognized that their standards did not always reflect those of working-class youth. As one University Settlement worker argued, "Many of the liberties which are taken by tenement boys and girls with one another, and which seem quite improper to the 'up-towner,' are, in fact, practically harmless."[2] Working women's public behavior often seemed to fall between the traditional middle-class poles: they were not truly promiscuous in their actions, but neither were they models of decorum. A boarding-house matron, for example, puzzled over the behavior of Mary, a "good girl": "The other night she flirted with a man across the street," she explained. "It is true she dropped him when he offered to take her into a saloon. But she does go to picture shows and dance halls with 'pick up' men and boys."[3] Similarly, a city missionary noted that tenement dwellers followed different rules of etiquette, with the observation: "Young women sometimes allow young men to address them and caress them in a manner which would offend well-bred people, and yet those girls would indignantly resent any liberties which they consider dishonoring."[4] These examples suggest that we must reach beyond the dichotomized analysis of many middle-class observers and draw out the cultural categories created and acted on by working women themselves. How was sexuality "handled" culturally? What manners, etiquette, and sexual style met with general approval? What constituted sexual respectability? Does the polarized framework of the middle class reflect the realities of working-class culture?

Embedded within the reports and surveys lie small pieces of information that illuminate the social and cultural construction of sexuality among a number of working-class women. My discussion focuses on one set of young, white working women in New York City in the years 1880 to 1920. Most of these women were single wage earners who toiled in the city's factories, shops, and department stores, while devoting their evenings to the lively entertainment of the streets, public dance halls, and other popular amusements. Born or educated in the United States, many adopted a cultural style meant to distance themselves from their immigrant roots and familial traditions. Such women dressed in the latest finery, negotiated city life with ease, and sought intrigue and adventure with male companions. For this group of working women, sexuality became a central dimension of their emergent culture, a dimension that is revealed in their daily life of work and leisure.[5]

■   These New York working women frequented amusements in which familiarity and intermingling among strangers, not decorum, defined normal public behavior between the sexes. At movies and cheap theaters, crowds mingled during intermission, shared picnic lunches, and commented volubly on performances. Strangers at Coney Island's amusement parks often involved each other in practical jokes and humorous escapades, while dance halls permitted close interaction between unfamiliar men and women. At one respectable Turnverein ball, for example, a vice investigator described closely the chaotic activity in the barroom between dances:

> Most of the younger couples were hugging and kissing, there was a general mingling of men and women at the different tables, almost everyone seemed to know one another and spoke to each other across the tables and joined couples at different tables, they were all singing and carrying on, they kept running around the room and acted like a mob of lunatics let lo[o]se.[6]

As this observer suggests, an important aspect of social familiarity was the ease of sexual expression in language and behavior. Dances were advertised, for example, through the distribution of "pluggers," small printed cards announcing the particulars of the ball, along with snatches of popular songs or verse; the lyrics and pictures, noted one offended reformer, were often "so suggestive that they are absolutely indecent."[7]

The heightened sexual awareness permeating many popular amusements may also be seen in working-class dancing styles. While waltzes and two-steps were common, working women's repertoire included "pivoting" and "tough dances." While pivoting was a wild, spinning dance that promoted a charged atmosphere of physical excitement, tough dances ranged from a slow shimmy, or shaking of the hips and shoulders, to boisterous animal imitations. Such tough dances as the grizzly bear, Charlie Chaplin wiggle, and the dip emphasized bodily contact and the suggestion of sexual intercourse. As one dance investigator commented, "What particularly distinguishes this dance is the motion of the pelvic portions of the body."[8] In contrast, middle-class pleasuregoers accepted the animal dances only after the blatant sexuality had been tamed into refined movement. While cabaret owners enforced strict rules to discourage contact between strangers, managers of working-class dance halls usually winked at spieling, tough dancing, and unrestrained behavior.[9]

Other forms of recreation frequented by working-class youth incorporated a free and easy sexuality into their attractions. Many social clubs and amusement societies permitted flirting, touching, and kissing games at their meetings. One East Side youth reported that "they have kissing all through pleasure time, and use slang language, while in some they don't behave nice between [sic] young ladies."[10] Music halls and cheap vaudeville regularly worked sexual themes and suggestive humor into comedy routines and songs. At a Yiddish music hall popular with both men and women, one reformer found that "the songs are suggestive of everything but what is proper, the choruses are full of double meanings, and the jokes have broad and unmistakable hints of things indecent."[11] Similarly,

Coney Island's Steeplechase amusement park, favored by working-class excursionists, carefully marketed sexual titillation and romance in attractions that threw patrons into each other, sent skirts flying, and evoked instant intimacy among strangers.[12]

In attending dance halls, social club entertainments, and amusement resorts, young women took part in a cultural milieu that expressed and affirmed heterosocial interactions. As reformer Belle Israels observed, "No amusement is complete in which 'he' is not a factor."[13] A common custom involved "picking up" unknown men or women in amusement resorts or on the streets, an accepted means of gaining companionship for an evening's entertainment. Indeed, some amusement societies existed for this very purpose. One vice investigator, in his search for "loose" women, was advised by a waiter to "go first on a Sunday night to 'Hans'l & Gret'l Amusement Society' at the Lyceum 86th Str & III Ave, there the girls come and men pick them up."[14] The waiter carefully stressed that these were respectable working women, not prostitutes. Nor was the pickup purely a male prerogative. "With the men they 'pick up,' " writer Hutchins Hapgood observed of East Side shop girls, "they will go to the theater, to late suppers, will be as jolly as they like."[15]

The heterosocial orientation of these amusements made popularity a goal to be pursued through dancing ability, willingness to drink, and eye-catching finery. Women who would not drink at balls and social entertainments were often ostracized by men, while cocktails and ingenious mixtures replaced the five-cent beer and helped to make drinking an acceptable female activity. Many women used clothing as a means of drawing attention to themselves, wearing high-heeled shoes, fancy dresses, costume jewelry, elaborate pompadours, and cosmetics. As one working women sharply explained, "If you want to get any notion took of you, you gotta have some style about you."[16] The clothing that such women wore no longer served as an emblem of respectability. "The way women dress today they all look like prostitutes," reported one rueful waiter to a dance hall investigator, "and the waiter can some times get in bad by going over and trying to put some one next to them, they may be respectable women and would jump on the waiter."[17]

Underlying the relaxed sexual style and heterosocial interaction was the custom of "treating." Men often treated their female companions to drinks and refreshments, theater tickets, and other incidentals. Women might pay a dance hall's entrance fee or carfare out to an amusement park, but they relied on men's treats to see them through the evening's entertainment. Such treats were highly prized by young working women; as Belle Israels remarked, the announcement that "he treated" was "the acme of achievement in retailing experiences with the other sex."[18]

Treating was not a one-way proposition, however, but entailed an exchange relationship. Financially unable to reciprocate in kind, women offered sexual favors of varying degrees, ranging from flirtatious companionship to sexual intercourse, in exchange for men's treats. "Pleasures don't cost girls so much as they do young men," asserted one saleswoman. "If they are agreeable they are invited out a good deal, and they are not allowed to pay anything." Reformer Lillian Betts concurred, observing that the working woman held herself responsible for failing to wangle men's invitations and believed that "it is not only her misfortune, but her fault; she should be more attractive."[19] Gaining men's treats placed a high premium on allure and personality, and sometimes involved aggressive and frank "overtures to men whom they desire to attract," often with implicit sexual proposals. One investigator, commenting on women's dependency on men in their leisure time, aptly observed that "those who are unattractive, and those who have puritanic notions, fare but ill in the matter of enjoyments. On the other hand those who do become popular have to compromise with the best conventional usage."[20]

■   Many of the sexual patterns acceptable in the world of leisure activity were mirrored in the workplace. Sexual harassment by employers, foremen, and fellow workers was a widespread practice in this period, and its form often paralleled the relationship of treating, particularly in service and sales jobs. Department store managers, for example, advised employees to round out their meager salaries by finding a "gentleman friend" to purchase clothing and pleasures. An angry saleswoman testified, for example, that "one of the employers has told me, on a $6.50 wage, he don't care where I get my clothes from as long as I have them, to be dressed to suit him."[21] Waitresses knew that accepting the advances of male customers often brought good tips, and some used their opportunities to enter an active social life with men. "Most of the girls quite frankly admit making 'dates' with strange men," one investigator found. "These 'dates' are made with no thought on the part of the girl beyond getting the good time which she cannot afford herself."[22]

In factories where men and women worked together, the sexual style that we have seen on the dance floor was often reproduced on the shop floor. Many factories lacked privacy in dressing facilities, and workers tolerated a degree of familiarity and roughhousing between men and women. One cigar maker observed that his workplace socialized the young into sexual behavior unrestrained by parental and community control. Another decried the tendency of young boys "of thirteen or fourteen casting an eye upon a 'mash.'" Even worse, he testified, were the

many men who are respected—when I say respected and respectable, I mean who walk the streets and are respected as working men, and who would not under any circumstances offer the slightest insult or disrespectful remark or glance to a female in the streets, but who, in the shops, will whoop and give expressions to "cat calls" and a peculiar noise made with their lips, which is supposed to be an endearing salutation.[23]

In sexually segregated workplaces, sexual knowledge was probably transmitted among working women. A YWCA report in 1913 luridly asserted that "no girl is more 'knowing' than the wage-earner, for the 'older hands' initiate her early through the unwholesome story or innuendo."[24] Evidence from factories, department stores, laundries, and restaurants substantiates the sexual consciousness of female workers. Women brought to the workplace tales of their evening adventures and gossip about dates and eligible men, recounting to their co-workers the triumphs of the latest ball or outing. Women's socialization into a new shop might involve a ritualistic exchange about "gentlemen friends." In one laundry, for example, an investigator repeatedly heard this conversation:

"Say, you got a feller?"
"Sure. Ain't you got one?"
"Sure."[25]

Through the use of slang and "vulgar" language, heterosexual romance was expressed in a sexually explicit context. Among waitresses, for example, frank discussion of lovers and husbands during breaks was an integral part of the work day. One investigator found that "there was never any open violation of the proprieties but always the suggestive talk and behavior." Laundries, too, witnessed "a great deal of swearing among the women." A 1914 study of department store clerks found a similar style and content in everyday conversation:

While it is true that the general attitude toward men and sex relations was normal, all the investigators admitted a freedom of speech frequently verging upon the vulgar, but since there was very little evidence of any actual immorality, this can probably be likened to the same spirit which prompts the telling of risqué stories in other circles.[26]

In their workplaces and leisure activities, many working women discovered a milieu that tolerated, and at times encouraged, physical and verbal familiarity between men and women, and stressed the exchange of sexual favors for social and economic advantages. Such women probably received conflicting messages about the virtues of virginity, and necessarily mediated the parental, religious, and educational injunctions concerning chastity, and the "lessons" of urban life and labor. The choice made by some women to engage in a relaxed sexual style needs to be understood in terms of the larger relations of class and gender that structured their sexual culture.

Most single working-class women were wage earners for a few years before marriage, contributing to the household income or supporting themselves. Sexual segmentation of the labor market placed women in semi-skilled, seasonal employment with high rates of turnover. Few women earned a "living wage," estimated to be $9.00 or $10.00 a week in 1910, and the wage differential between men and women was vast. Those who lived alone in furnished rooms or boarding houses consumed their earnings in rent, meals, and clothing. Many self-supporting women were forced to sacrifice an essential item in their weekly budgets, particularly food, in order to pay for amusements. Under such circumstances, treating became a viable option. "If my boy friend didn't take me out," asked one working woman, "how could I ever go out?"[27] While many women accepted treats from "steadies," others had no qualms about receiving them from acquaintances or men they picked up at amusement places. As one investigator concluded, "The acceptance on the part of the girl of almost any invitation needs little explanation when one realizes that she often goes pleasureless unless she does accept 'free treats.' "[28] Financial resources were little better for the vast majority of women living with families and relatives. Most of them contributed all of their earnings to the family, receiving only small amounts of spending money, usually 25¢ to 50¢ a week, in return. This sum covered the costs of simple entertainments, but could not purchase higher priced amusements.[29]

Moreover, the social and physical space of the tenement home and boarding house contributed to freer social and sexual practices. Working women living alone ran the gauntlet between landladies' suspicious stares and the knowing glances of male boarders. One furnished-room dweller attested to the pressure placed on young, single women: "Time and again when a male lodger meets a girl on the landing, his salutation usually ends with something like this: 'Won't you step into my place and have a glass of beer with me?' "[30]

The tenement home, too, presented a problem to parents who wished to maintain control over their daughters' sexuality. Typical tenement apartments offered limited opportunities for family activities or chaperoned socializing. Courtship proved difficult in homes where families and boarders crowded into a few small rooms, and the "parlor" served as kitchen, dining room, and bedroom. Instead, many working-class daughters socialized on street corners, rendezvoused in cafes, and courted on trolley cars. As one settlement worker observed, "Boys and girls and young men and women of respectable families are almost obliged to carry on many of their friendships, and perhaps their love-making, on tenement stoops or on street corners."[31] Another reformer found that girls whose parents forebade men's visits to the home managed to escape into the streets and dance halls to meet them. Such young women demanded greater independence in the realm of "personal life" in exchange for their financial contribution to the family. For some, this new freedom spilled over into their sexual practices.[32]

■   The extent of the sexual culture described here is particularly difficult to establish, since the evidence is too meager to permit conclusions about specific groups of working women, their beliefs about sexuality, and their behavior. Scattered evidence does suggest a range of possible responses, the parameters within which most women would choose to act and define their behavior as socially acceptable. Within this range, there existed a subculture of working women who fully bought into the system of treating and sexual exchange, by trading sexual favors of varying degrees for gifts, treats, and a good time. These women were known in underworld slang as "charity girls," a term that differentiated them from prostitutes because they did not accept money in their sexual encounters with men. As vice reformer George Kneeland found, they "offer themselves to strangers, not for money, but for presents, attention, and pleasure, and most important, a yielding to sex desire."[33] Only a thin line divided these women and "occasional prostitutes," women who slipped in and out of prostitution when unemployed or in need of extra income. Such behavior did not result in the stigma of the "fallen woman." Many working women apparently acted like Dottie: "When she needed a pair of shoes she had found it easy to 'earn' them in the way that other girls did." Dottie, the investigator reported, was now known as a respectable married woman.[34]

Such women were frequent patrons of the city's dance halls. Vice investigators note a preponderant number of women at dances who clearly were not prostitutes, but were "game" and "lively"; these charity girls often comprised half or more of the dancers in a hall. One dance hall investigator distinguished them with the observation, "Some of the women . . . are out for the coin, but there is a lot that come in here that are charity."[35] One waiter at La Kuenstler Klause, a restaurant with music and dancing, noted that "girls could be gotten here, but they don't go with men for money, only for good time." The investigator continued in his report, "Most of the girls are working girls, not prostitutes, they smoke cigarettes, drink liquers and dance dis.[orderly] dances, stay out late and stay with any man, that pick them up first."[36] Meeting two women at a bar, another investigator remarked, "They are both supposed to be working girls but go out for a good time and go the limit."[37]

Some women obviously relished the game of extracting treats from men. One vice investigator offered to take a Kitty Graham, who apparently worked both as a department store clerk and occasional prostitute, to the Central Opera House at 3 A.M.; he noted that "she was willing to go if I'd take a taxi; I finally coaxed her to come with me in a street car."[38] Similarly, Frances Donovan observed waitresses "talking about their engagements which they had for the evening or for the night and quite frankly saying what they expected to get from this or that fellow in the line of money, amusement, or clothes."[39] Working women's manipulation of treating is also suggested by this unguarded conversation overheard by a journalist at Coney Island:

"What sort of a time did you have?"
"Great. He blew in $5 on the blow-out."
"You beat me again. My chump only spent $2.50."[40]

These women had clearly accepted the full implications of the system of treating and the sexual culture surrounding it.

While this evidence points to the existence of charity girls—working women defined as respectable, but who engaged in sexual activity—it tells us little about their numbers, social background, working lives, or relationships to family and community. The vice reports indicate that they were generally young women, many of whom lived at home with their families. One man in a dance hall remarked, for example, that "he sometimes takes them to the hotels, but sometimes the girls won't go to [a] hotel to stay for the night, they are afraid of their mothers, so he gets away with it in the hallway."[41] While community sanctions may have prevented such activity within the neighborhood, the growth of large public dance halls, cabarets, and metropolitan amusement resorts provided an anonymous space in which the subculture of treating could flourish.

■   The charity girl's activities form only one response in a wide spectrum of social and sexual behavior. Many young women defined themselves sharply against the freer sexuality of their pleasure-seeking sisters, associating "respectability" firmly with premarital chastity and circumspect behavior. One working woman carefully explained her adherence to propriety: "I never go out in the evenings except to my relatives because if I did, I should lose my reputation and that is all I have left." Similarly, shop girls guarded against sexual advances from co-workers and male customers by spurning the temptations of popular amusements. "I keep myself to myself," said one saleswoman. "I don't make friends in the stores very easily because you can't be sure what any one is like."[42] Settlement workers also noted that women who freely attended "dubious resorts" or bore illegitimate children were often stigmatized by neighbors and workmates. Lillian Betts, for example, cites the case of working women who refused to labor until their employer dismissed a co-worker who had borne a baby out of wedlock. To Betts, however, their adherence to the standard of virginity seemed instrumental, and not a reflection of moral absolutism: "The hardness with which even the suggestion of looseness is treated in any group of working girls is simply an expression of self-preservation."[43]

Other observers noted an ambivalence in the attitudes of young working women toward sexual relations. Social workers reported that the critical stance toward premarital pregnancy was "not always unmixed with a certain degree of admiration for the success with the other sex which the difficulty implies." According to this study, many women increasingly found premarital intercourse acceptable in particular situations: "'A girl can have many friends,' explained one of them, 'but when she gets a "steady," there's only one way to have him and to keep him; I mean to keep him long.'"[44] Such women shared with charity girls the assumption that respectability was not predicated solely on chastity.

Perhaps few women were charity girls or occasional prostitutes, but many more must have been conscious of the need to negotiate sexual encounters in the workplace or in their leisure time. Women would have had to weigh their desire for social participation against traditional sanctions regarding sexual behavior, and charity girls offered to some a model for resolving this conflict. This process is exemplified in Clara Laughlin's report of an attractive but "proper" working woman who could not understand why men friends dropped her after a few dates. Finally she receives the worldly advice of a co-worker that social participation involves an exchange relationship: "Don't yeh know there ain't no feller goin' t'spend coin on yeh fer nothin'? Yeh gotta be a good Indian, Kid— we all gotta!"[45]

For others, charity girls represented a yardstick against which they might measure their own ideas of respectability. The nuances of that measurement were expressed, for example, in a dialogue between a vice investigator and the hat girl at Semprini's dance hall. Answering his proposal for a date, the investigator noted, she "said she'd be glad to go out with me but told me there was nothing doing [i.e., sexually]. Said she didn't like to see a man spend money on her and then get disappointed." Commenting on the charity girls that frequented the dance hall, she remarked that "these women get her sick, she can't see why a woman should lay down for a man the first time they take her out. She said it wouldn't be so bad if they went out with the men 3 or 4 times and then went to bed with them but not the first time."[46]

For this hat girl and other young working women, respectability was not defined by the strict measurement of chastity employed by many middle-class observers and reformers. Instead, they adopted a more instrumental and flexible approach to sexual behavior. Premarital sex *could* be labeled respectable in particular social contexts. Thus charity girls distinguished their sexual activity from prostitution, a less acceptable practice, because they did not receive money from men. Other women, who might view charity girls as promiscuous, were untroubled by premarital intimacy with a steady boyfriend.

This fluid definition of sexual respectability was embedded within the social relations of class and gender, as experienced by women in their daily round of work, leisure, and family life. Women's wage labor and the demands of the working-class household offered daughters few resources for entertainment. At the same time, new commercial amusements offered a tempting world of pleasure and companionship beyond parental control. Within this context, some young women sought to exchange sexual goods for access to that world and its seeming independence, choosing not to defer sexual relations until marriage. Their notions of legitimate premarital behavior contrast markedly with the dominant middle-class view, which placed female sexuality within a dichotomous and rigid framework. Whether a hazard at work, fun and adventure at night, or an opportunity to be exploited, sexual expression and intimacy comprised an integral part of these working women's lives.

■ Notes

1. See, for example, Carroll D. Wright, *The Working Girls of Boston* (1889; rpt. New York: 1969).

2. "Influences in Street Life," University Settlement Society *Report* (1900), 30.

3. Marie S. Orenstein, "How the Working Girl of New York Lives," New York State, Factory Investigating Commission, *Fourth Report Transmitted to Legislature*, 15 February 1915, Senate Doc. 43, vol. 4, app. 2 (Albany: 1915), 1697.

4. William T. Elsing, "Life in New York Tenement-Houses as Seen by a City Missionary," *Scribner's* 11 (June 1892): 716.

5. For a more detailed discussion of these women, and further documentation of their social relations and leisure activities, see my Ph.D. dissertation, "Cheap Amusements: Gender Relations and the Use of Leisure Time in New York City, 1880 to 1920," (Brown University, 1982). [Editor's note: see also my book *Cheap Amusements: Working Women and Leisure in Turn-of-the-Century New York* (Philadelphia: 1986).]

6. Investigator's Report, Remey's, 917 Eighth Ave., 11 February 1917, Committee of Fourteen Papers, New York Public Library Manuscript Division, New York.

7. George Kneeland, *Commercialized Prostitution in New York City* (New York: 1913), 68; Louise de Koven Bowen, "Dance Halls," *Survey* 26 (3 July 1911): 384.

8. Committee on Amusements and Vacation Resources of Working Girls, two-page circular, in Box 28, "Parks and Playgrounds Correspondence," Lillian Wald Collection, Rare Book and Manuscripts Library, Columbia University, New York.

9. See, for example, Investigator's Report, Princess Cafe, 1206 Broadway, 1 January 1917; and Excelsior Cafe, 306 Eighth Ave., 21 December 1916, Committee of Fourteen Papers. For an excellent discussion of middle- and upper-class leisure activities, see Lewis A. Erenberg, *Steppin' Out: New York Nightlife and the Transformation of American Culture, 1890–1930* (Westport, Conn.: 1981).

10. "Social Life in the Streets," University Settlement Society *Report* (1899), 32.

11. Paul Klapper, "The Yiddish Music Hall," *University Settlement Studies* 2, no. 4 (1905): 22.

12. For a description of Coney Island amusements, see Edo McCullough, *Good Old Coney Island: A Sentimental Journey into the Past* (New York: 1957), 309–13; and Oliver Pilot and Jo Ransom, *Sodom by the Sea: An Affectionate History of Coney Island* (Garden City, N.J.: 1941).

13. Belle Lindner Israels, "The Way of the Girl," *Survey* 22 (3 July 1909): 486.

14. Investigator's Report, La Kuenstler Klause, 1490 Third Ave., 19 January 1917, Committee of Fourteen Papers.

15. Hutchins Hapgood, *Types from City Streets* (New York: 1910), 131.

16. Clara Laughlin, *The Work-A-Day Girl: A Study of Some Present Conditions* (1913; rpt. New York: 1974), 47, 145. On working women's clothing, see Helen Campbell, *Prisoners of Poverty: Women Wage-Earners, Their Trades and Their Lives* (1887; rpt. Westport, Conn.: 1970), 175; "What It Means to Be a Department Store Girl as Told by the Girl Herself," *Ladies Home Journal* 30 (June 1913): 8; "A Salesgirl's Story," *Independent* 54 (July 1902): 1821. Drinking is discussed in Kneeland, *Commercialized Prostitution*, 70; and Belle Israels, "Diverting a Pastime," *Leslie's Weekly* 113 (27 July 1911): 100.

17. Investigator's Report, Weimann's, 1422 St. Nicholas Ave., 11 February 1917, Committee of Fourteen Papers.

18. Israels, "Way of the Girl," 489; Ruth True, *The Neglected Girl* (New York: 1914), 59.

19. "A Salesgirl's Story," 1821; Lillian Betts, *Leaven in a Great City* (New York: 1902), 251–52.

20. New York State, Factory Investigating Commission, *Fourth Report*, vol. 4, 1585–86; Robert Woods and Albert Kennedy, *Young Working-Girls: A Summary of Evidence from Two Thousand Social Workers* (Boston: 1913), 105.

21. New York State, Factory Investigating Commission, *Fourth Report*, vol. 5, 2809; see also Sue Ainslie Clark and Edith Wyatt, *Making Both Ends Meet: The Income and Outlay of New York Working Girls* (New York: 1911), 28. For an excellent analysis of sexual harassment, see Mary Bularzik, *Sexual Harassment at the Workplace: Historical Notes* (Somerville, Mass.: 1978).

22. Consumers' League of New York, *Behind the Scenes in a Restaurant: A Study of 1017 Women Restaurant Employees* (1916), 24; Frances Donovan, *The Woman Who Waits* (1920; rpt. New York: 1974), 42.

23. New York Bureau of Labor Statistics, *Second Annual Report* (1884), 153, 158; *Third Annual Report* (1885), 150–51.

24. Report of Commission on Social Morality from the Christian Standpoint, Made to the Fourth Biennial Convention of the Young Women's Christian Associations of the U.S.A., 1913, Records File Collection, Archives of the National Board of the YWCA of the United States of America, New York, N.Y.

25. Clark and Wyatt, *Making Both Ends Meet*, 187–88; see also Dorothy Richardson, *The Long Day*, in *Women at Work*, ed. William L. O'Neill (New York: 1972); Amy E. Tanner, "Glimpses at the Mind of a Waitress," *American Journal of Sociology* 13 (July 1907): 52.

26. Committee of Fourteen in New York City, *Annual Report for 1914*, 40; Clark and Wyatt, *Making Both Ends Meet*, 188; Donovan, *The Woman Who Waits*, 26, 80–81.

27. Esther Packard, "Living on Six Dollars a Week," New York State, Factory Investigating Commission, *Fourth Report*, vol. 4, 1677–78. For a discussion of women's wages in New York, see *ibid.*, vol. 1, 35; and vol. 4, 1081, 1509. For an overview of working conditions, see Barbara Wertheimer, *We Were There: The Story of Working Women in America* (New York: 1977), 209–48.

28. Packard, "Living on Six Dollars a Week," 1685.

29. New York State, Factory Investigating Commission, *Fourth Report*, vol. 4, 1512–13, 1581–83; True, *Neglected Girl*, 59.

30. Marie Orenstein, "How the Working Girl of New York Lives," 1702. See also Esther Packard, *A Study of Living Conditions of Self-Supporting Women in New York City* (New York: 1915).

31. "Influences in Street Life," 30; see also Samuel Chotzinoff, *A Lost Paradise* (New York: 1955), 81.

32. On the rejection of parental controls by young women, see Leslie Woodcock Tentler, *Wage-Earning Women: Industrial Work and Family Life in the United States, 1900–1930* (New York: 1979), 110–13. For contemporary accounts, see True, *Neglected Girl*, 54–55, 62–63, 162–63; Lillian Betts, "Tenement House Life and Recreation," *Outlook* (11 February 1899): 365.

33. "Memoranda on Vice Problem: IV. Statement of George J. Kneeland," New York State, Factory Investigating Commission, *Fourth Report*, vol. 1, 403. See also Committee of Fourteen, *Annual Report* (1917), 15, and *Annual Report* (1918), 32; Woods and Kennedy, *Young Working-Girls*, 85.

34. Donovan, *The Woman Who Waits*, 71; on occasional prostitution, see U.S. Senate, *Report on the Condition of Women and Child Wage-Earners in the United States*, U.S. Sen. Doc. 645, 61st Cong., 2nd Sess. (Washington, D.C.: 1911), vol. 15, 83; Laughlin, *The Work-A-Day Girl*, 51–52.

35. Investigator's Report, 2150 Eighth Ave., 12 January 1917, Committee of Fourteen Papers.

36. Investigator's Report, La Kuenstler Klause, 1490 Third Ave., 19 January 1917, Committee of Fourteen Papers.

37. Investigator's Report, Bobby More's, 252 W. 31st Street, 3 February 1917, Committee of Fourteen Papers.

38. Investigator's Report, Remey's, 917 Eighth Ave., 23 December 1916, Committee of Fourteen Papers.

39. Donovan, *The Woman Who Waits*, 55.

40. Edwin Slosson, "The Amusement Business," *Independent* 57 (21 July 1904): 139.

41. Investigator's Report, Clare Hotel and Palm Gardens/McNamara's, 2150 Eighth Ave., 12 January 1917, Committee of Fourteen Papers.

42. Marie Orenstein, "How the Working Girl of New York Lives," 1703; Clark and Wyatt, *Making Both Ends Meet*, 28–29.

43. Betts, *Leaven in a Great City*, 81, 219.

44. Woods and Kennedy, *Young Working-Girls*, 87, 85.

45. Laughlin, *The Work-A-Day Girl*, 50.

46. Investigator's Report, Semprini's, 145 W. 50th Street, 5 October 1918, Committee of Fourteen Papers.

5

Movements of Affirmation: Sexual Meanings and Homosexual Identities

Jeffrey Weeks

It is now widely recognized by sociologists, and even by some historians, that the concept of "the homosexual" is a historical creation, and that a necessary distinction has to be made between homosexual behavior, which the evidence shows is present in most cultures, and homosexual identities, which the same evidence shows to be comparatively rare, and in our own culture of fairly recent origin. But it is still by no means clear what the necessary conditions were for the emergence of the category "homosexual," and the social contours of the correlative homosexual identity are very obscure. This essay will attempt to explore some of the problems in understanding the interrelations of sexual meanings and homosexual identities by: (1) tracing the history of the emergence of "the homosexual" in Britain; (2) discussing some of the explanations given for such a development; (3) exploring the impact of homosexual self-activity, and the issues that need to be clarified in understanding the patterns of the (largely male) homosexual life style; (4) examining briefly the impact of the modern gay movement.

■ **The Emergence of "The Homosexual"**   The historical evidence points to the latter part of the nineteenth century as the crucial period in the conceptualization of homosexuality as the distinguishing characteristic of a particular type of person, the "invert" or "homosexual," and the corresponding development of a new awareness of self among "homosexuals."[1] The word "homosexuality" itself was not invented until

Reprinted from *Radical History Review* 20 (Spring/Summer 1979): 164–179.

1869 and did not enter English usage until the 1880s and 1890s, and then largely as a result of the work of Havelock Ellis. The widespread adoption of these neologisms marks a crucial turning point in attitudes to homosexuality comparable to the adoption of "gay" as a self-description of homosexuals in the 1970s. It indicates not just a changing usage but the emergence of a whole new set of assumptions. In Britain (as in Germany and elsewhere) the reconceptualization coincided with the development of new legal and ideological sanctions, particularly against male homosexuality.

Until 1885 the only law dealing directly with homosexual behavior was that relating to sodomy[2] and legally, at least, little distinction was made between sodomy between man and woman, man and beast, and man and man. This had been a capital crime from the 1530s, when the state incorporated traditional ecclesiastical sanctions into law as part of the assumption of many of the powers of the Medieval church. Prosecutions under this law had fluctuated, partly because of changing rules on evidence (for example, a legal judgment of the late eighteenth century made it necessary to prove emission as well as penetration), partly through other social pressures. There seems, for instance, to have been a higher incidence of prosecutions (and executions) in times of war; penalties were particularly harsh in cases affecting the discipline of the armed services, particularly the navy.[3] In the nineteenth century "sodomite" became the typical epithet of abuse for the sexual deviant.[4] Oscar Wilde at the end of the century responded to the accusation that he was "posing" as a sodomite with his disastrous libel case against the Marquess of Queensberry. The power of the taboo is also illustrated in the sustained attempts of the first generation of sex reformers (Ellis, J. A. Symonds, Edward Carpenter in Britain, Magnus Hirschfeld in Germany) to deny that most "homosexuals" indulged in buggery.

There is, however, a crucial distinction between traditional concepts of sodomy and modern concepts of homosexuality. The former was seen as a potentiality in all sinful nature, unless severely execrated and judicially punished (it is striking, for example, that death penalties for many crimes were abolished in the 1820s, but not for sodomy). Contemporary social sciences have treated homosexuality as the characteristic of a particular type of person, a type whose specific characteristics (such as inability to whistle, penchant for the color green, adoration of mother or father, age of sexual maturation, "promiscuity") are exhaustively detailed in many twentieth-century textbooks. In the present century psychology undertook the task of explaining the etiology of the homosexual "condition."[5] Authors of early articles on homosexuality in the 1880s and 1890s discussed the subject as if they were entering a strange continent (and indeed many of those interested in homosexuality were anthropologists, for example, Westermarck, or in close touch with anthropologists, for example, Havelock Ellis with Malinowski). An eminent doctor, Sir George Savage, described in the *Journal of Mental Science* (Oct. 1884) the homosexual case histories of a young man and woman, and wondered if "this perversion is as rare as it appears," while Havelock Ellis was to claim that he was the first to record any homosexual cases unconnected with prison or asylums. The "sodomite," as Michel Foucault has put it, was an aberration; the "homosexual" is a species, and social science during this century has made various—if by and large unsuccessful—efforts to explore this phenomenon.

These changing concepts do not mean, of course, that those who engaged in a predominantly homosexual life style did not regard themselves as somehow different until the late nineteenth century. There is evidence for the emergence of a distinctive male homosexual subculture in London and one or two other cities from the late seventeenth century, often characterized by transvestism and gender-role inversion.[6] By the mid-nineteenth century, it seems the male homosexual subculture at least had characteristics not dissimilar to the modern, with recognized cruising places and homosexual haunts, ritualized sexual contact, and a distinctive argot and "style." But there is also abundant evidence until late into the nineteenth century of practices which modern standards would regard as highly sexually compromising. Lawrence Stone[7] describes Oxbridge male students sleeping with male students in the eighteenth century with no sexual connotations, while Smith-Rosenberg has described the intimate—and seemingly nonsexualized—relations between women in the nineteenth century.[8] In the latter part of the nineteenth century, however, the controversy about "immorality" in public schools, various sexual scandals, a new legal situation, the beginnings of a "scientific" discussion of homosexuality, and the emergence of the "medical model," provoked awareness of homosexuality as a social concern. The subject, as Edward Carpenter put it at the time, "has great actuality and is pressing upon us from all sides."[9] Within this developing context those with homosexual inclinations began to perceive themselves as "inverts," "homosexuals," "Uranians"—a crucial stage in the prolonged and uneven process whereby homosexuality began to take on a recognizably modern configuration.

The changing legal and ideological situations were crucial markers in this development. The 1861 Offences Against the Person Act removed the death penalty for sodomy (which had not been used since the 1830s), replacing it by sentences of between ten years and life. But in 1885 the famous Labouchere Amendment to the Criminal Law Amendment Act made all male homosexual activities (acts of "gross undecency") punishable by up to two years hard labor. And in 1898, the laws on importuning for "immoral purposes" were tightened and effectively applied to male homosexuals (this was clarified by the Criminal Law Amendment Act of

1912 with respect to England and Wales—Scotland has different provisions). Both acts significantly extended the legal controls on male homosexuality.[10] Though formally less severe than capital punishment for sodomy, the new legal situation probably affected a much wider circle of people. A series of sensational scandals, culminating in the trials of Oscar Wilde, drew a sharp dividing line between permissible forms of behavior, but at the same time the publicity given to these trials contributed to the creation of a male homosexual identity.[11] It must be noted, however, that the new legal situation did not apply to women, and the attempt to extend the 1885 provisions to women in 1921 failed.

The development of a medical model of homosexuality was intimately connected with the legal situation. The most commonly quoted European writers on homosexuality in the mid-nineteenth century were Casper and Tardieu, the leading medico-legal experts of Germany and France respectively. Both, as Arno Karlen has put it, were "chiefly concerned with whether the disgusting breed of perverts could be physically identified for courts, and whether they should be held legally responsible for their acts."[12] The same problem was apparent in Britain.[13] Most of the 1,000 or so works on homosexuality that, according to Magnus Hirschfeld, appeared between 1898 and 1908, were directed, in part at least, at the legal profession. Even J. A. Symond's privately printed pamphlet, *A Problem in Modern Ethics*, was explicitly addressed "especially to Medical psychologists and jurists," while Havelock Ellis' *Sexual Inversion* was condemned for not being published by a medical press and for being too popular in tone. The medicalization of homosexuality—a transition from notions of sin to concepts of sickness or mental illness—was a significant move. Around it the poles of scientific discourse ranged for decades: was homosexuality congenital or acquired; ineradicable or susceptible to cure; to be quietly if unenthusiastically accepted as unavoidable (even the liberal Havelock Ellis felt it necessary to warn his invert reader not to "set himself in violent opposition" to his society) or to be resisted with all the force of one's Christian will. Old notions of the immorality or sinfulness of homosexuality did not die in the nineteenth century; they still survive, unfortunately, in many dark corners. But from the nineteenth century they were inextricably entangled with "scientific" theories that formed the boundaries within which homosexuals had to begin to define themselves.

■ **Explanations**   The emergence of the category "homosexual" was not arbitrary or accidental. On one level the scientific and medical speculation can be seen as a product of the tendency of social sciences to differentiate traditionally execrated and monolithic crimes against nature into discrete deviations and to map their etiologies. On another level, the emergence of the concept of homosexual corresponded to the clarification and articulation of a variety of social categories: the sexual child, the hysterical woman, the congenitally inclined prostitute (or indeed, in the work of Ellis and others, the congenital criminal). Perhaps most significantly, the formation of public concepts of sexual identity was part of the contemporaneous debate over an ideological definition of the role of the housewife and mother. Discussion of homosexual meanings has centered on the development of the bourgeois family. As Plummer has put it, "The family as a social institution does not of itself condemn homosexuality, but through its mere existence it implicitly provides a model that renders the homosexual experience invalid."[14]

The significance of the family in bourgeois ideology has long been recognized.[15] In particular the ideology of domesticity was of central importance in shaping the stereotype of femininity. Perhaps unnecessarily overlooked in this debate has been the ideology of sexuality within the family. An important strand in Puritan thought saw sex-in-marriage as an essential binding act, a holy communion, and this was a factor in the hostility to the double standard of morality, which made gross and self-indulgent what could be spiritual and binding (Elizabeth Blackwell in the *Human Element in Sex* expresses this in the 1880s too). But as the sexual family was increasingly shrouded in privacy, secrecy, and discretion in the nineteenth century,[16] homosexuality, which inevitably transgressed the framework of the family and of sexuality within it, was considered incompatible with it. As the Holy Family became purer, especially with the late nineteenth century attack on the double standard, male homosexuality appeared even less compatible with married love. This was in fact in line with the traditional Puritan abhorrence of homosexuality.[17] It is striking that the social purity campaigners of the 1880s saw both prostitution and male homosexuality as products of undifferentiated male lust,[18] and equally significant, if generally unremarked, that the major enactments affecting male homosexuality from the 1880s (the Labouchere Amendment, the 1898 Vagrancy Act) were primarily concerned with female prostitution. Indeed, as late as the 1950s it was seen as logical to set up a single government committee—the Wolfenden Committee—to study both prostitution and male homosexuality.

There is, then, an obvious if so far inadequately analyzed link between a sharpening definition of homosexuality and the evolution of the family. Most attempts to explain this link have relied on variations of role theory. Male homosexuality has been seen as a threat to the assumptions about male sexuality and perceived as a challenge to the male heterosexual role within capitalism.

In Britain sexual intercourse has been contained within marriage which has been presented as the ultimate form of sexual maturity . . . the heterosexual nuclear family assists a system like capitalism because it produces and socialises the young in certain values . . . the maintenance of the nuclear family with its role-specific behaviour creates an apparent consensus concerning sexual normalcy.

So that,

Any ambiguity such as transvestism, hermaphrodism, transexuality, or homosexuality is moulded into 'normal' appropriate gender behaviour or is relegated to the categories of sick, dangerous, or pathological. The actor is forced to slot into patterns of behaviour appropriate to heterosexual gender roles.[19]

The result is the emergence of a specific male "homosexual role," a specialized, despised, and punished role which "keeps the bulk of society pure in rather the same way that the similar treatment of some kinds of criminals helps keep the rest of society law abiding."[20] Such a role has two effects: it helps to provide a clear-cut threshold between permissible and impermissible behavior; and secondly, it helps to segregate those labeled as deviant, and thus contains and limits their behavior patterns. In the same way, a homosexual subculture, which is the correlative of the development of a specialized role, provides access to the socially outlawed need (sex) yet contains the deviant. Male homosexuals can thus be conceptualized as those excluded from the sexual family, and as potential scapegoats whose oppression can keep the family members in line.

Although persuasive, and indeed influential,[21] there are problems in this theory rooted as it is in functionalist sociology. One relates to the whole question of "social control" and the intentionality that it implies.[22] Historical evidence points to the centrality of ideologies of sex and science rather than of policy in the evolution of new attitudes in the late nineteenth century, and if ideology is a lucid relationship rather than a set of imposed ideas, a role theory as described above can easily become static and ahistorical, descriptive rather than theoretical. This model has been helpful in tracing the contours of the male homosexual subculture rather than in linking this development historically to wider social processes. And perhaps it is also significant that there have been few attempts to explain the absence of a comparable lesbian role, for this is more complexly related to the whole problematical area of female sexuality, which in itself poses major historical difficulties.

Secondly, problems arise when we confront the question of the acquisition of sexual meanings. Much as the category "homosexual" is a historical creation, sexual meanings are ascribed and learned in social interaction. But this simple formula presents various problems when trying to grasp change and historical determinacy. A brief description of two different (if sometimes surprisingly overlapping) theories will help clarify this problem.

Symbolic interactionism has been the most potent theoretical tool for recent discussions of homosexuality in Britain[23] and its major significance is that it calls into question, in opposition to traditional drive/repression theories, the very category of "sexuality" itself. Sexuality, in the words of Gagnon and Simon, is subject to "socio-cultural moulding to a degree surpassed by few other forms of human behavior."[24] Hence, what is sexual in one culture, or indeed in one situation, might not be in another. It is, classically, an idealist theoretical perspective: ideas are not treated in terms of their historical roots or practical effect but are seen as forming the background to every social process. Social processes are treated essentially in terms of ideas, and it is through ideas that we construct social reality itself. Its sexual theorists (Gagnon and Simon, Plummer) postulate a potentially infinite series of sexual scripts in which the individual actor creates his or her sexual identity. In the study of homosexuality[25] this method has clearly delineated the ways in which a homosexual identity is constructed in social interaction, thus supporting attempts to delineate a homosexual role, while giving added strength to the notion that homosexuals define their own identities, particularly by subcultural interaction. For historians it can also be of significance, suggesting situations in which identities are assumed or strengthened. A research program to trace the development of the homosexual identity in Britain would include both wider social forces such as urbanization in creating the conditions[26] for the development of distinct subcultures, and the changing role of the state through legislation and its support of family modes antipathetical to homosexual life styles, with an investigation of the labeling effect of major public scandals and trials (such as the Oscar Wilde trial in the 1890s, the *Well of Loneliness* furor in the 1920s). Furthermore, research should focus on the changing role of media in creating and sustaining public images and stereotypes, the development of medical categorizations and the influence of the medical profession, *and* the homosexual response, both in the formation of individual identities and life styles and in subcultural organization.

But symbolic interactionism has so far been unable of itself to theorize the sexual variations it can describe so clearly (why, for instance, some individuals acquire homosexual identities rather than heterosexual); nor has it been able to conceptualize the relations between possible sexual patterns and other social variables, nor explain why there are constant shifts in the location of historical taboos on sexuality (why, for instance, it seems that in the 1970s the taboo on homosexuality in the West is shifting increasingly from adult male relations to lesbianism and pedophilia). Furthermore, if meanings are entirely ascribed on social interaction, it suggests that they can be transformed by an act of individual or collective will, whereas sexuality is in fact experienced as a deeply rooted characteristic. Finally, related to this, symbolic interaction is unable to theorize why, if there are endless possibilities of sensualization, the genitals continue to have a deeply rooted role in sexual imagination and identity. Symbolic interactionism, therefore, stops precisely at the point where theorization is now essential: at the point of historical determination and ideological structuring in the creation of subjectivity.

It is for this reason that we are now witnessing a reassessment, particularly among feminists, of Freud and psychoanalysis with a view to employing it as a tool for developing a theoretical understanding of patriarchy. It is becoming apparent that if the emergence of a distinct homosexual identity is linked to the evolution of the family, then within this it is the role of the male—theorized in terms of the symbolic role of the Phallus and the Law of the Father—that is of central significance. Analysis of patriarchy will allow historians to begin to understand the relationship between gender and sex (for it is in the family that the anatomical differences between the sexes acquire their social significance) and also, to begin to uncover the specific history of female sexuality, within which the social history of lesbianism must ultimately be located. The focal point for most discussion so far has been Juliet Mitchell's *Psychoanalysis and Feminism* which, as was recently put by a sympathetic critic, "opens the way to a re-evaluation of psychoanalysis as a theory which can provide scientific knowledge of the way in which patriarchal ideology is maintained through the production of psychological 'masculinity' and 'femininity.' "[27]

This comment appears, interestingly, in an Australian journal, *Working Papers in Sex, Science and Culture* (now *Working Papers: Studies in the discourses of sex, subjectivity and power*), which developed from a gay liberation paper. Though the question of sexuality has now been strategically linked to the whole problematic of patriarchy, there has been no sustained effort as yet in the English-speaking world—not even in *Working Papers*—to theorize the specific role of homosexuality in a patriarchal society.

The French have proven a little less reticent, which gives particular interest to the recent appearance in English translation of Guy Hocquenghem's *Homosexual Desire* (published in France as *Le desir homosexuel* in 1972). The essay comes out of the Lacanian reinterpretation of Freud, linguistic theory, and the question of ideology, but its specific debt is to the work of Gilles Deleuze and Felix Guattari, *L'Anti Oedipe*, their critique of Freudian (and Lacanian) categories, and their subsequent theory of schizoanalysis. As in our argument, Hocquenghem recognizes the culturally specific function of the concept of "the homosexual" and draws on Michel Foucault's essay on *Madness and Civilization*, suggesting the analogy between the growth in the eighteenth century of the social concept of madness as a specific individual quality and the conceptualization of homosexuality. Hocquenghem argues that the "growing imperialism" of society seeks to attribute a social status to everything, even the unclassified, resulting in a sharpening definition of homosexuality. Foucault's recent work *La volonte de savior* makes this point explicit.

Hocquenghem argues that "homosexual desire," like indeed the heterosexual, is an arbitrary division of the flux of desire, which in itself is polyvocal and undifferentiated so that the notion of exclusive homosexuality is a "fallacy of the imaginary," a misrecognition and ideological misperception. Nevertheless, homosexuality has a vivid social presence, and this is because it expresses an aspect of desire which appears nowhere else. The direct manifestation of homosexual desire opposes the relations of roles and identities necessarily imposed by the Oedipus complex in order to ensure the reproduction of society. Capitalism, in its necessary resort to Oedipalization, manufactures "homosexuals" just as it produces proletarians, and what is manufactured is a psychologically repressive category. Hocquenghem argues that the principal ideological means of thinking about homosexuality are ultimately, though not mechanically, connected with the advance of western capitalism. They amount to a perverse "reterritorialization," a massive effort to regain social control, in a world tending toward disorder and decoding. As a result the establishment of homosexuality as a separate category goes hand in hand with its repression. On the one hand we have the creation of a minority of "homosexuals"; on the other, the transformation in the majority of the repressed homosexual elements of desire into the desire to repress. Hence sublimated homosexuality is the basis of the paranoia about homosexuality which pervades social behavior, which in turn is a guarantee of the survival of Oedipal relations, the victory of the law of the father. Hocquenghem argues that only one organ is allowed in the Oedipal triangle, what Deleuze and Guattari call the "despotic signifier," the Phallus. And as money is the true universal reference point for capitalism, so the Phallus is the reference point for heterosexism. The Phallus determines, whether by absence or presence, the girl's penis envy, the boy's castration anxiety; it draws on libidinal energy in the same way as money draws on labor. And as this comment makes clear, this Oedipalization is itself a product of capitalism and not, as the Lacanian school might argue, a law of culture, or of all patriarchal societies.

Without going into further details, several difficulties emerge. The first relates to the whole question of homosexual paranoia (reminiscent in many ways of the recent discussions of homophobia in Britain and the U.S.[28]). The idea that repression of homosexuality in modern society is a product of suppressed homosexuality comes at times very close to a hydraulic theory of sexuality, which both symbolic interactionism and Lacanian interpretations of Freud have rejected. It is not a sufficient explanation simply to reverse the idea that homosexuality is a paranoia, peddled by the medical profession in the present century, into the idea that hostile attitudes to homosexuality are themselves paranoid. Nor does the theory help explain the real, if limited, liberalization of attitudes that has taken place in some western countries or the range of attitudes in different countries and even in different families.

Secondly, following from this, there is the still unanswered problem of why some individuals become "homosexual" and others do not. The use of the concept of Oedipalization restores some notion of social determination that symbolic interactionism lacks, but by corollary, loses any sense of the relevance of the specific family pressures, the educational and labeling processes, the media images that reinforce the identity.

Finally, there is the still ambiguous relationship of capitalism to patriarchy. If Mitchell can be rightly criticized for creating two separate areas for political struggle, the economic (against capitalism) and the ideological (against patriarchy), then Hocquenghem can be criticized for collapsing them together. And again the weakness of *Homosexual Desire* is that it does not attempt to explain the modalities of lesbianism.[29] Nevertheless, Hocquenghem's work raises important questions. In particular, it points to the relevance of two key points made by Michel Foucault in *La volonte de savoir*. The first is Foucault's rejection of the repression hypothesis. He argues that sexuality is not a given of nature which "power" is trying to "repress" but the name given to a historical apparatus. For the past few centuries rather than a regime of silence and censorship we have seen a massive discursive explosion around sex. The implication is that bourgeois society, far from excluding "sex," has actually incited an explosion of sexualities; and it is an expression of bourgeois power that sex has become a major organizing principle. Bourgeois society, that is, creates sexualities rather than denies them.

Secondly, Foucault rejects a simple relationship between capitalism and sexuality. He argues that there is no single, global strategy bearing on the whole of society, and uniformly on all manifestations of sex. He locates four strategic ensembles at work since the eighteenth century, developing specific apparatuses of power and knowledge in relation to sex: the hysterization of the woman's body; the pedagogization of the sex of the child; socialization of procreative behavior; psychiatrization of perversities. The result is the emergence in the nineteenth century of four privileged objects of knowledge: the hysterical woman, the masturbating child, the malthusian couple, and the perverse adult.[30] Foucault's work is as yet only at the stage of theoretical outline, and its ramifications have still to be fully absorbed in the study of sexuality. There are difficulties in his central concept of "power," and its relationship to orthodox Marxist theorization is problematical. But in attempting to theorize sex in terms of discursive practices Foucault has been able to break with a simple concept of "repression" while maintaining a vista of historical process. His work may therefore be central to any further theorization of homosexuality.

■ **Homosexual Identities**   Foucault has noted that "as soon as there is a power relation, there is a possibility of resistance."[31] The late nineteenth century, as we have noted, was the crucial period in the emergence of a male homosexual identity. Within the boundaries suggested by the wider social changes, there developed gradually and unevenly a consciousness of self among a layer of "homosexuals" who "seized upon the pathologizing discourse of 'perverse implantation' and reversed it into a discourse of defiant self-affirmation."[32] The process can be traced in the life of J. A. Symonds,[33] Edward Carpenter,[34] various "Uranian" poets,[35] and many others.[36] It was a contradictory consciousness: often aggressively sexual, but also defensive and guilt-ridden. Law and its penalties made homosexuals into outsiders, religious residues gave them a high sense of guilt, and medicine and science gave them a deep sense of inferiority and inadequacy. Goldsworthy Lowes Dickinson, a well known liberal humanist and rationalist, believed that he had a "woman's soul in a man's body." But he also believed this to be a "misfortune . . . I am like a man born crippled." Roger Casement enjoyed his homosexual adventures and recorded the size of his pick-ups' sexual organs in his diary, but felt his homosexuality to be a "terrible disease" which ought to be cured.[37] These were, it must be noted, articulate and highly educated members of the intelligentsia. For countless others their homosexuality was conceived of as a disability, a sickness, a personal disaster. The self-consciousness of male homosexuals was deeply fractured by the prevailing norms.

Several other factors need to be noted. We stress, for instance, the male nature of the homosexual self-consciousness. Lesbianism encounters no comparable social pressure. There were indeed individuals who identified themselves as lesbian, and in these we can detect many of the same characteristics as in men.[38] Even Radclyffe Hall's lesbian novel, *The Well of Loneliness*, a determined defense of lesbian love, is pervaded by stereotyping and a final sense of the tragic destiny of the born invert.

But the lesbian sense of self was much less pronounced than the male homosexual, and the subcultural development was exiguous. If the Wilde trials were major labeling events for men, the comparable event for lesbianism, the trial of Hall's novel, had a much less devastating impact, and then a generation later. Even science, so anxious to detail the characteristics of male homosexuals, largely ignored lesbianism. Gagnon and

Simon noted recently that "the scientific literature on the lesbian is exceedingly sparse."[39] These factors indicate that what is needed is not so much a monist explanation for the emergence of a "homosexual identity" as a differential social history of male homosexuality and lesbianism.

The homosexual subculture, in which sexual meanings were defined and sharpened, was then predominantly male, revolving around meeting places, clubs, pubs, etc. Indeed perhaps it was less a single subculture than a series of overlapping subcultures, each part supplying a different need. In its most organized aspect there was often an emphasis on transvestism, a self-mocking effeminacy, an argot, and a predominance of "camp." In its most ubiquitous form (casual sexuality revolving around public lavatories) the overlap between the homosexual subculture and the parent culture was masked.

Secondly, homosexual subculture displayed a notable predominance of upper-middle-class values. Perhaps on one level only middle-class men had a sufficient sense of a "personal life" through which to develop a homosexual identity.[40] Male homosexual writers stressed cross-class liaisons and youth (typically, the representative idealized relationship is between an upper-middle-class man and a working-class youth) in a manner comparable, it may be noted in passing, to certain middle-class heterosexual patterns of the nineteenth century and earlier (see for example the author of *My Secret Life*[41]). The impossibility of same-class liaisons is a constant theme of homosexual literature, demonstrating the strong elements of guilt (class and sexual) that pervade the male identity. But it also illustrates a pattern of what can be called "sexual colonialism," which saw the working-class youth or soldier as a source of "trade," often coinciding uneasily with an idealization of the reconciling effect of cross-class liaisons.

But if the idealization of working-class youth was one major theme, the attitude of these working-class men themselves is less easy to trace. They appear in all the major scandals (for instance, the Wilde trials, the Cleveland Street Scandal) but their self-conceptions are almost impossible to discover. We may hypothesize that the spread of a homosexual consciousness was much less strong among working-class men than middle-class—for obvious family and social factors, even though the law (on, for example, importuning) probably affected more working-class men than middle-class. We can also note the evidence regarding the patterns of male prostitution, as for example in the Brigade of guards, that suggests a reluctance on the part of the "prostitute" to define himself as homosexual.[42]

Among middle-class homosexuals the sense of self occasionally developed into a more political consciousness. There is some evidence for a highly developed sense of homosexual oppression among male homosexuals, such as Edward Carpenter but also in the early twentieth century among a younger generation associated with the writers George Ives and Laurence Housman. These were the focus of a secretive homosexual reform grouping, formed in the late 1890s and active at least until the 1930s. This had all the elements of a defensive coterie, including Masonic rituals and codes, but it was self-consciously a political grouping attempting, by discrete pressure on highly placed people, to change attitudes and the law.[43] There were links with the male culturalist tendencies of homosexual reformers in Germany, but also links with lesbians such as Radclyffe Hall and Una Troubridge. Such evidence suggests continuing effort to articulate an identity in a social climate which was hostile, if not directly persecutory.

Finally, we may note that if it is difficult to map subcultural organizations it is even more difficult to discover the patterns of sexual interaction. There are records of sustained homosexual partnerships but we must also note the predominance of casual promiscuity, a feature for which the male homosexual community has always been excoriated. Many of the best known sites of male homosexual contact, such as public lavatories ("cottages") and Turkish baths which underline casual contact,[44] can be related both to traditional middle-class male attitudes toward casual promiscuity, and to the difficulties of living an openly homosexual life in a hostile milieu, and therefore the necessity for a double life and for "passing." It is difficult to assess the historical and social meaning of this aspect of homosexual life. Hocquenghem sees promiscuity as in itself a positive challenge to heterosexual monogamy, while many contemporary feminists view it as a representative example of male sexual objectification. It is, nevertheless, a deeply rooted part of the male homosexual consciousness, and quite different from lesbian patterns. It illustrates again the important point that "the patterns of overt sexual behavior on the part of homosexual females tend to resemble those of heterosexual females and to differ radically from the sexual patterns of both heterosexual and homosexual males."[45]

■ **The Impact of the Gay Movement**   This leads us finally to a brief assessment of the ways in which this homosexual consciousness has been changed by the impact of the modern gay movement. On the one hand we can see what has happened over the past ten years as the culmination of the long and uneven effort toward self-definition which has been the underlying theme of the emergence of the homosexual identity. Beginning with the hostile labeling, the socially constructed notion of homosexuals as a race apart, it has rejected the stigmas and stressed the positive ("gay is good"). Though starting both in the U.S. and Britain as an explicitly political movement (the name "Gay Liberation Front" was an explicit analogy with national liberation movements) its real impact so far has been as a stimulus to the massive expansion of the male homosexual subculture over the past ten years. Even the personnel of the gay movement (usually male, middle-class) has not been entirely dissimilar to the traditional articulators of a homosexual self-awareness over the past hundred years or so, and certainly most of the gains in terms of subcultural expansion, greater openness, the removal of guilt, have as yet been enjoyed to the fullest only by the metropolitan middle-class gay male. In this way the modern gay movement, though a product of specific social changes, is the climax of a prolonged process of defini-tion and self-definition: its stress on "ethnicity," the search for the roots of "its" history is complicit with the social categorization of homosex-uality which we have traced. We can say that an open and defiant affir-mation of our sexuality is a necessary and essential stage in claiming control of our lives. But of itself it poses no radical challenge, which is why, in the U.S., there now appears to be a complete overlap between the commercial gay scene and the gay movement, to the extent that the an-nual Gay Pride Marches are largely funded by (gay) commercial interests.

On the other hand implicit in the rhetoric, and sometimes the practice, of the gay movement has been not only an attack on the objectifying and oppressive elements of the male subculture but also an identification with women's struggles against patriarchy. Central to this is a challenge to the hegemony of compulsory heterosexuality and the dominance of patriarchal and familial norms. The evolution of sexual meanings and identities that we have traced over the past hundred years or so are by no means complete, but for the first time on a large scale, and openly, homo-sexuals are in a position to attempt to shape their own destinies.

■ **Postscript (1988)**   This essay, first written in 1978, was intended as a state of the art paper, indicating the point which lesbian and gay studies had reached at that particular time. It was also a deliberate chal-lenge to the taken-for-granted essentialism of most previous writing about homosexuality. Ten years later I can see points where my empha-sis might be slightly different. I am certainly aware of a profusion of scholarship that has amplified or attempted to modify certain of my (ten-tative) conclusions. But I have not fundamentally altered my general position; in fact, because I believe it has stood the test of time, I have not revised the article for this re-publication. For developments in my own thinking, the interested reader is referred to my subsequent work.[46]

I would, however, like to make two points, one about the theoretical context of the paper, the second about concurrent and subsequent work. First, the context. This article represented my first attempt to come to terms with the theoretical contribution of Michel Foucault. My first book, *Coming Out: Homosexual Politics in Britain from the Nineteenth Century to the Present*, published in 1977,[47] had been written before I engaged in any serious way with Foucault's work, and certainly before I read the first volume of his *History of Sexuality.*[48] I finished *Coming Out* at the end of 1976, at about the same time *La Volunte de savoir* appeared in Paris.

I was subsequently very captured by Foucault's writings on sexuality.[49] However, my own work was not inspired (as has sometimes been suggested) by Foucault's, but predates any encounter with his thinking on sexuality. More important, the implicit argument of this article, and one I now want to underline more sharply, is that Foucault's work is itself a product of many currents that were forcing a rethinking of the social meaning and historical construction of sexuality. Some are described in this article. Inevitably, the deceptive lucidity of his *History* has been an enormous stimulus (though not always a sensible one) to subsequent work, but that work, it cannot be stated too forcibly, had independent roots and was already ongoing among feminist, lesbian, and gay historians.

This brings me to the second point, concerning concurrent and subsequent work. I wrote *Coming Out* with an acute sense of intellectual isolation. My main intellectual mentors were sociologists (such as Ken Plummer and Mary McIntosh) rather than historians. I did not know until I had almost finished that book that other historians, particularly in the U.S., were engaging on similar themes with closely related intellectual concerns, though not always with concordant conclusions, of course. This paper, which was concerned with stating a position, did not attempt to come to grips with that complementary work of Katz, Trumbach, Smith-Rosenberg, and others which I was only just encountering.[50]

I want to stress that the absence of names such as these is not a comment on their work, rather an index of the relative infancy of the debate on the nature of homosexual history when this article was written. In 1978 there was no sense of a common intellectual endeavor linking historians in a search for an understanding of the complex history of the meanings, categories, and identities around homosexuality. Today that is not true: an "invisible college" of scholars is making major contributions to our understanding of the past, and hence also to our grasp of the elusive present.[51]

Clearly, a full picture of the complexities of sexual meanings and homosexual identities will come to the reader only after exploring this subsequent work. Nevertheless, the lines of argument laid down here are still sufficient to point in the right direction.

■ **Notes**

1. Jeffrey Weeks, *Coming Out: Homosexual Politics in Britain from the Nineteenth Century to the Present* (London: 1977), chs. 1–3.

2. F. Lafitte, "Homosexuality and the Law," *British Journal of Delinquency* 9 (1958–59).

3. See L. Radzinowicz, "The Africane Court Martial," *Journal of Homosexuality* 1 (Fall 1974); "Buggery and the British Navy, 1700–1861," *Journal of Social History* 10 (Fall 1976).

4. *Grappling for Control* (London: 1968).

5. M. McIntosh, "The Homosexual Role," *Social Problems* 16 (1968).

6. *Ibid.*

7. L. Stone, *The Family, Sex and Marriage* (London: 1977), 516.

8. C. Smith-Rosenberg, "The Female World of Love and Ritual," *Signs* 1 (Fall 1975).

9. E. Carpenter, *The Intermediate Sex* (London: 1908), 9.

10. F. B. Smith, "Labouchere's Amendment to the Criminal Law Amendment Act," *Historical Studies* (Melbourne) 17 (1976); Weeks, *Coming Out*, 14–22.

11. H. Ellis, *Studies in the Psychology of Sex*, vol. 2 (New York: 1936), 352.

12. A. Karlen, *Sexuality and Homosexuality* (London: 1971), 185.

13. Weeks, *Coming Out*, 26.

14. K. Plummer, *Sexual Stigma* (London: 1975), 210.

15. R. Gray, "Bourgeois Hegemony in Victorian Britain," in *Class, Hegemony and Party* (1977).

16. M. Foucault, *The History of Sexuality*, vol. I, *An Introduction* (New York: 1979).

17. L. Stone, *The Crisis of the Aristocracy* (London: 1966).

18. Weeks, *Coming Out*, 17.

19. M. Brake, "I May Be A Queer, But At Least I Am A Man," in *Sexual Divisions and Society: Process and Change*, ed. Diana Leonard Barker and Sheila Allen (London: 1976), 178, 176.

20. McIntosh, "The Homosexual Role," 184.

21. Weeks, *Coming Out*, introduction.

22. G. Stedman Jones, "Class Expression versus Social Control," *History Workshop* 4 (1977).

23. Plummer, *Sexual Stigma*.

24. J. H. Gagnon and W. Simon, *Sexual Conduct* (London: 1973), 26.

25. Plummer, *Sexual Stigma*.

26. J. Harvey, "Urbanization and the Gay Life," *Journal of Sex Research* 10 (August 1974).

27. R. Albury, "Two Readings of Freud," *Working Papers in Sex, Science and Culture* 1 (1976): 7.

28. G. Weinberg, *Society and the Healthy Homosexual* (New York: 1972).

29. J. Weeks, Preface to Hocquenghem, *Homosexual Desire* (London: 1978).

30. Foucault, *History of Sexuality*, vol. I; C. Gordon, "Birth of a Subject," *Radical Philosophy* 17 (Summer 1977).

31. M. Foucault, "Power and Sex: An Interview with Michel Foucault," *Telos* (Summer 1977): 160.

32. Gordon, "Birth of a Subject," 25.

33. P. Grosskurth, *John Addington Symonds* (London: 1964).

34. S. Rowbotham, "Edward Carpenter: Prophet of the New Life," in *Socialism and the New Life*, ed. Sheila Rowbotham and Jeffrey Weeks (London: 1977).

35. T. D'Arch Smith, *Love in Earnest* (London; 1970).

36. Weeks, *Coming Out*.

37. *Ibid.,* 31–32.

38. *Ibid.,* chs. 7–9.

39. Gagnon and Simon, *Sexual Conduct,* 176.

40. E. Zaretsky, *Capitalism, the Family, and Personal Life* (London: 1976).

41. S. Marcus, *The Other Victorians* (London: 1967).

42. A. J. Reiss, S. Raven, "Boys Will Be Boys," and "The Social Integration of Queers and Peers," in *The Problem of Homosexuality in Modern Society,* ed. H. M. Ruitenbeck (New York: 1963).

43. Weeks, *Coming Out,* 118–127.

44. X. Mayne, *The Intersexes* (Florence: 1910); H. M. Hyde, *The Other Love* (London: 1972); L. Humphreys, *Tea Room Trade* (New York: 1970).

45. Gagnon and Simon, *Sexual Conduct,* 180.

46. See Jeffrey Weeks, *Sex, Politics and Society: The Regulation of Sexuality Since 1900* (Harlow, England: 1981); *Sexuality and its Discontents: Meanings, Myths and Modern Sexualities* (London: 1985); *Sexuality* (Chichester and London: 1986). See also my contribution, together with those of Mary McIntosh and Kenneth Plummer, in *The Making of the Modern Homosexual,* ed. Kenneth Plummer (London, 1981).

47. Weeks, *Coming Out.*

48. Foucault, *The History of Sexuality,* I.

49. See, for example, my comments in *Sexuality and its Discontents* and *Sexuality,* as cited above.

50. For example, Jonathan Katz, *Gay American History: Lesbians and Gay Men in the USA* (New York: 1976); Randolph Trumbach, "London's Sodomites: Homosexual Behaviour and Western Culture in the 18th Century," *Journal of Social History* (Fall 1977); Smith-Rosenberg, "The Female World of Love and Ritual."

51. See, for example, my report of the lesbian and gay history conference held in Toronto in 1985: "Sex and the State: Their Laws, Our Lives," *History Workshop Journal* 21 (Spring 1986): 206–9.

6

From Sexual Inversion to Homosexuality: The Changing Medical Conceptualization of Female "Deviance"

George Chauncey, Jr.

Historians have recently identified the end of the nineteenth century as a crucial transitional period in the conceptualization and social experience of homosexual relations. Jeffrey Weeks suggests that the "medical model of homosexuality" replaced the religious one during this period, characterizing homosexuality as the condition of certain, identifiable individuals rather than as a form of sinful behavior in which anyone might engage, while Lillian Faderman assigns the medical profession responsibility for the "morbidification" of relationships between women during these years. It was on the basis of the new medical models, they suggest, that individuals came to identify themselves—and distinguish themselves from others—as lesbians and gay men, members of a sexual minority.[1] The last years of the nineteenth century did witness a dramatic increase in medical interest in "deviant" sexual behavior. The first medical article on what was then termed sexual inversion was published in Germany in 1870 and was followed by American studies within the decade; by the mid-1910s, several U.S. journals devoted regular columns to sexology which frequently reported on the study of homosexuality.[2]

But it would be wrong to assume, I think, that doctors created and defined the identities of "inverts" and "homosexuals" at the turn of the century, that people uncritically internalized the new medical models, or even that homosexuality emerged as a precisely defined category in the medical discourse itself in the 1870s. Such assumptions attribute inordinate power to ideology as an autonomous social force; they oversimplify the complex dialectic between social conditions, ideology, and con-

This essay originally appeared in *Salmagundi* no. 58–59 (Fall 1982/Winter 1983).

sciousness which produced gay identities, and they belie the evidence of preexisting subcultures and identities contained in the literature itself. Although the literature is one of the sources most easily accessible to historians, we must guard against attributing to it a more central role in the formation of sexual identities than it actually may have played. It has not yet been adequately documented that medical models and homosexual identities appeared at the same time, even for the members of elite society who have been the subjects of existing studies. But even if we did know this to be the case, it would not necessarily indicate that one caused the other; both may have resulted from more fundamental historical processes. Only extensive and original research in more intimate records such as diaries and correspondence will enable us to measure the influence of the medical discourse on the emergence of gay identities and subcultures. (I use the plural deliberately, for the structure and social experience of sexuality and gender have varied along lines of class, race, and ethnicity.)

Nevertheless, analysis of the medical literature can make an important contribution to our study of the history of sexuality if we consider it a response to and one reflection of changes in the organization and ideology of sexuality that occurred in American culture at the turn of the century. As such, it can provide a key to our understanding of the transformation of the sex/gender system during that period, for the cultural definition of deviance, which it represents, indicates with particular clarity the parameters of the acceptable.[3]

It is highly significant in this light that the turn of the century witnessed the development not only of a new explanation of homosexual behavior but also—and more centrally—of the very concept of homosexual desire as a discrete sexual phenomenon. Sexual inversion, the term used most commonly by doctors in the nineteenth century, did not denote the same conceptual phenomenon as homosexuality. "Sexual inversion" referred to a broad range of cross-gender behavior (in which males behaved like women, and vice-versa), of which homosexual desire was only a logical but indistinct aspect, while "homosexuality" focused on the narrower issue of sexual object choice. The differentiation of homosexual desire from cross-gender behavior at the turn of the century reflects a major reconceptualization of the nature of human sexuality, its relation to gender, and its role in one's social definition.

While the changing focus of medical inquiry into sexual deviance reflected this broad shift in conceptualization, each stage of that inquiry can be analyzed as a response to particular changes in and challenges to the Victorian sex/gender system, such as the women's movement, the growing visibility of urban gay male subcultures, and the changing gender structure of the economy. Medical theories achieved general acceptance and influence because they reflected a much broader cultural uneasiness with and antipathy to these challenges, and because they took ideological forms commonly used to resist social change. Indeed, the early biological explanations offered for sexual deviance were an integral part of that nineteenth-century scientific discourse that sought to validate the existing social order by asserting its biological inevitability. Just as the contemporaneous theory of social Darwinism served to legitimate racism and colonialism by postulating a biologically based racial hierarchy of social development, so the early sexology sought to justify the particular form of women's subordination to men during this period by asserting its biological determination.[4] Subsequent theories emphasized the psychological rather than biological "abnormalities" that resulted in sexual nonconformity, but accepted many of the premises of earlier work. In the process of debate, the literature developed many of the terms and categories that continue to structure our thinking about sexuality and gender.

The following pages, based on a review of approximately eighty-five medical books, articles, and reviews published in the United States between 1880 and 1930, examine the medical literature on inversion and homosexuality as a response to and reflection of changes in the sex/gender system at the turn of the century. After examining the changing focus of medical inquiry during these years, they analyze the assumptions about sexuality revealed by the explanations offered for sexual deviance, and then consider further the reasons for the emergence of medical concern about this subject.

■ **The Changing Focus of Medical Inquiry**   The Victorian assertion of male sexual aggressiveness and denial of female sexual interest established the logical framework for the earliest medical inquiry into sexual nonconformity, and determined the manner in which researchers defined it. The major current in Victorian sexual ideology declared that women were passionless and asexual, the passive objects of male sexual desire. In the 1880s and nineties, as Havelock Ellis noted in 1903, this belief was so deeply rooted a tendency in medical thought that many sexologists considered a woman's expression of sexual desire even in her romantic life to be pathological.[5] Such an assessment of women's sexuality had fundamental implications for the medical conceptualization of lesbian relations. Indeed, in the context of female passionlessness, there was no place for lesbianism as it is currently understood: if women could not even respond with sexual enthusiasm to the advances of men, how could they possibly stimulate sexual excitement between themselves?

In the Victorian system, therefore, a complete inversion (or reversal) of a woman's sexual character was required for her to act as a lesbian; she had literally to become man-like in her sexual desire. That this logic governed early thinking about lesbianism is suggested by the descriptions of lesbians provided by early sexologists. In 1883 in one of the first articles on a "Case of Sexual Perversion," P. M. Wise described the behavior of a woman institutionalized after having been discovered passing as a man: "In passing to the ward, she embraced the female attendant in a lewd manner and came near overpowering her before she received assistance. Her conduct on the ward was characterized by the same lascivious conduct, and she made efforts at various times to have sexual intercourse with her associates."[6] This description, typical of the early literature, emphasizes the sexual aggressiveness of the female "pervert" in terms closely paralleling descriptions of male sexual lust prominent in nineteenth-century thought. At mid-century, for instance, the Female Moral Reform Society thought the "male lecher . . . a creature controlled by base sexual drives which he neither could nor would control," according to Carroll Smith-Rosenberg; woman, "innocent and defenseless, gentle and passive," was just the opposite.[7] This polarization of masculine and feminine sexuality suggests that the perversion described by Wise was not so much in the object of the woman's sexual desire as in the masculine, aggressive form it took: the woman had inverted her whole sexual character.

Sexual inversion, the term used in most of the nineteenth century literature, thus had a much broader meaning than our present term, homosexuality, which denotes solely the sex of the person one sexually desires. Sexual inversion, rather, connoted a complete reversal of one's sex role.

But in Victorian thought, people's sex roles were not limited to their behavioral roles in intimate sexual relations; rather, a woman's sexual passivity served as a paradigm for her complete gender role. In the thinking of many doctors, sexual inversion referred not only to sexual excesses or to nonprocreative sexual activity, as some have argued,[8] but, even more centrally, to aberrations in one's sex-defined social role. As George Beard wrote in the 1880s, when "the sex is perverted, they hate the opposite sex and love their own; men become women and women men, in their tastes, conduct, character, feelings, and behavior."[9] Richard von Krafft-Ebing explained that a person's thought, character, and behavior "correspond with the peculiar sexual instinct [i.e., "the sexual role in which they feel themselves to be"], but not with the sex which the individual represents anatomically and physiologically."[10] Transvestism was therefore seen as characteristic of sexual inversion, and the case histories regularly observed that many inverts revealed their true nature as children by their queer behavior. "She was peculiar in girlhood," observed Wise, "in that she preferred masculine sports and labor; had an aversion to attentions from young men and sought the society of her own sex."[11] P. M. Lichtenstein's list of the "male characteristics" of female sex perverts in a conservative 1921 article included the fact that "they wear strictly tailor-made clothing, low shoes, and they seldom wear corsets. The hair is usually bobbed."[12] Another doctor observed with astonishment that "some of the women inverts can whistle admirably"; and Douglas McMurtrie characterized an invert by her drinking, smoking, and being "very independent in her ways."[13] W. C. Rivers, on the other hand, thought it significant that a male pervert "never smoked and never married; [and] was entirely averse to outdoor games," while two other researchers described as perverted a man who, among other things, was "fond of looking in the mirror . . . [and] talk[ed] in a squeaking, effeminate voice."[14]

Havelock Ellis provided perhaps the most comprehensive description of female sexual inversion. Although on the one hand claiming that transvestism was unrelated to homosexuality, Ellis nonetheless provided numerous examples of lesbian transvestites in his major work, *Sexual Inversion*, and noted that even those lesbians who wore female attire usually showed "some traits of masculine simplicity" in their dress. Furthermore,

> The brusque, energetic movements, the attitude of the arms, the direct speech, the inflexions of the voice, the masculine straightforwardness and sense of honor . . . will all suggest the underlying psychic abnormality to a keen observer. In the habits not only is there frequently a pronounced taste for smoking cigarettes, often found in quite feminine women, but also a decided taste and tolerance for cigars. There is also a dislike and sometimes incapacity for needlework and other domestic occupations, while there is often some capacity for athletics.[15]

These examples suggest not only the paradigmatic nature of woman's sexual role for her social role, but also the polarization of masculine and feminine modes of behavior in Victorian thought. In their discussions of sexual behavior the doctors were unable to conceive of a single person simultaneously embodying both: a woman could not invert any aspect of her gender role without completely inverting that role.

The occasional medical accounts of the heterosexual relations of married inverts emphasize the importance of sexual role inversion rather than homosexual object choice in these discussions. Inverts were occasionally involved in heterosexual relations, doctors noted, if only because of social convention, but they were always attracted to someone whose sex role was opposite their own. Ellis thought that the man attracted to an inverted woman, for instance, must be exceptionally effeminate, and he cited the case of one such man he knew who was "of slight physique, . . . with a thin voice, . . . considerate to others to a feminine degree, . . . and very domesticated in his manner of living—in short, the man who might easily have been attracted to his own sex."[16] William Lee

Howard, writing four years later, in 1900, warned that feminists and sexual perverts alike, both of whom he classed as "degenerates," married only men whom they could "rule, govern and cause to follow [them] in voice and action."[17] J. F. W. Meagher claimed in 1929 that "a homosexual woman often wants to possess the male and not to be possessed by him. . . . With them," he added, "orgasm is often only possible in the superior position."[18] If a female behaved like a man, it seemed, she could only relate to a male who would be her "woman."

By 1900, however, a fundamental shift in conceptualization was under way, as medicine began to specify and narrow the definition of the sexual, and to distinguish and classify sexual deviations in ever more discrete categories, particularly in the case of men. While early investigators had maintained that male sexual inversion involved transvestism, effeminacy, and such unmasculine characteristics as the inability to whistle, as well as sexual desire for men instead of women,[19] Ellis and other writers tried at the turn of the century to redefine male sexual inversion in narrowly sexual terms. Ellis emphatically distinguished it from transvestism and other forms of gender inversion (initially called sexo-aesthetic inversion, and later Eonism), which he claimed were often practiced by heterosexual men. Sexual inversion, he told a meeting of the Chicago Academy of Medicine in 1913, correctly referred "exclusively [to] such a change in a person's sexual impulses, . . . that the impulse is turned towards individuals of the same sex, while all the other impulses and tastes may remain those of the sex to which the person by anatomical configuration belongs."[20] He had already written that a man could invert his sexual object and behavior—becoming the "passive," "feminine" sexual partner to another man—while "remain[ing] masculine in his nonsexual habits."[21]

Sigmund Freud clarified this distinction by introducing the concepts of sexual object and aim in the first of his *Three Essays on the Theory of Sexuality* (1905). Sexual aim, in Freud's view, referred to a person's preferred mode of sexual behavior, such as genital or oral sex, or passive or active roles. Sexual object referred to the object of sexual desire; Freud classified children, animals, and persons of the same sex as "deviations in respect of the sexual object."[22]

The introduction of this distinction between aim and object, which may seem self-evident today, was a highly significant change at a particular moment in the intellectual history of sexuality, and it reflects the changes that occurred in the sex/gender system around the turn of the century. In the late nineteenth century, as we have seen, the fact of active or passive sexual aim—seen as paradigmatic for one's complete gender role—was at least as important as sexual object in the classification of sexuality. Investigators classified a woman as an invert because of her aggressive, "masculine" sexual and social behavior, and the fact that her sexual object was homosexual was only the logical corollary of this inversion; "men," whether biologically male or female, necessarily chose passive women as their sexual objects. By the turn of the century, however, researchers increasingly distinguished passive or aggressive sexual behavior from sexual object, and the latter became the more important element in the medical classification of sexuality.

Although discussions of both male and female sexuality reflect investigators' growing concern about sexual object choice, the change in focus occurred first in the study of men. Ellis, as noted, distinguished men's homosexual object choice from their sexual and social behavior. Freud maintained that although the "secondary and tertiary characteristics" of one sex often appeared in the other, which he attributed to a kind of hermaphroditism, there was no correlation between their appearance and homosexual desire in the case of men. "The most complete mental masculinity," he observed, "can be combined with [male] inversion."[23] For many subsequent theorists, then, a man's sexual object choice, rather than his actual role in intimate sexual relations, was the primary determinant in the classification of his sexuality, and they no longer saw his sexual role as paradigmatic of his social role. Doctors postulated that he could be the passive partner to another man's sexual advances without necessarily being passive and effeminate in his social role, while creating the new category of heterosexual men whose deviance was embodied in their effeminacy. As Michel Foucault has argued, the varieties of perversion thus multiplied, as ever more discrete categories were labeled and distinguished—transvestism from homosexuality, effeminate behavior from taking the "passive" role in intercourse, and so forth.[24]

The growing differentiation of sexual object choice from sexual roles and gender characteristics, and the growing importance of object choice in the classification of sexuality, were reflected, albeit inconsistently, in the increasing frequency with which the term "homosexuality" was used in the place of "sexual inversion" after 1900. While "sexual inversion" referred to an inversion in the full range of gender characteristics, "homosexuality," precisely understood, referred only to the narrower issue of homosexual object choice and did not necessarily imply gender or sexual role inversion. Although during the transition in medical thinking I have described, some doctors, as one would expect, used the terms interchangeably, others distinguished them quite carefully, and in general the terminology of homosexuality achieved currency in the literature at the same time that concern about object choice began to supercede concern about gender inversion.[25]

The change in the focus of sexual inquiry was slower and more complicated in the case of women. As with men, sexual object choice became relatively more important than character inversion, but doctors were less willing—perhaps culturally less able—to distinguish a woman's behavior in sexual relations from other aspects of her gender role. Doctors continued to characterize women who took the aggressive, "masculine" role in sexual relations as masculine in character and social role, even after they had determined that men who were "passive" sexually could engage in the social behavior that was masculine. The long statement by Ellis cited above, for instance, in which he characterized female inverts as masculine, appeared in the third edition of *Sexual Inversion*, which was published two years after his address to the Chicago Academy of Medicine. Freud, like Ellis and the whole of turn-of-the-century sexology, continued to assert that "character inversion" was a regular feature of *female* inversion, although no longer maintaining that this was true of male inversion.[26]

There were, however, changes in medical descriptions of women involved in lesbian relationships between 1880 and 1930 that paralleled the changes in ideas about male sexual deviance. Most of the early accounts of sexual inversion discussed only the invert, leaving her sexual partner anonymous and undefined. In the earliest accounts of this form of sexual deviance, those concerning women who dressed and passed as men, for instance, the women's "wives" received virtually no attention. In the nineteenth century accounts of passing women who married other women collected by Allan Berube and Jonathan Katz, the wives usually play only a minor role, and (when they are considered at all) are not labeled deviant in the same manner as their husbands. Many accounts simply treated them as normal wives, playing their proper feminine roles, as if it did not matter that their "husbands" were biologically female.[27] Further research would be required to substantiate this point, but it seems that many nineteenth-century doctors considered the truly serious offense to be the invert's assumption of the opposite gender role rather than either her or her "wife's" homosexual object choice.

Although later observers considered the role of the wifely partner in increasingly sexual and pathological terms, the nature of her relationship as wife to a female husband remained the fundamental paradigm that governed medical thought. In the Victorian context this might appropriately be termed the "heterosexual paradigm," for it represented conventional wisdom about the proper relation of husband to wife and man to woman. In a culture that polarized the acceptable behavioral and emotional characteristics of men and women, marriage was to represent a union of opposed but complementary characteristics, in which men were dominant and women submissive. This paradigm appears to have been so fundamental to Victorian concepts of marriage that when doctors began to scrutinize homosexual relationships—as well as individuals—around the turn of the century, they were unable to think of them in any other terms. No matter what the anatomical sex of the two partners, they thought, one must play the man and the other the woman; one was an invert, and the other subject to homosexual tendencies.[28]

The "actively inverted woman," wrote Ellis in 1895, was distinguished from her partner by "one fairly essential character: a more or less distinct trace of masculinity." It was she who took the initiative in relations with other women. The second group of women were those "to whom the actively inverted woman is most attracted." Ellis described these women as "plain" in appearance and as almost asexual, with a "genuine, though not precisely sexual, preference for women over men"; they were "always womanly." He did not refer to these women as inverts, but rather as "a class in which homosexuality, while fairly distinct, is only slightly marked."[29] Allan MacLane Hamilton, writing in 1896, observed the same distinction between active and passive lesbians, emphasizing, like most writers, the correlation between inversion in sexual behavior and social role:

> The offender was usually of a masculine type, . . . [holding views which were] erratic, "advanced," and extreme, and she nearly always lacked the ordinary modesty and retirement of her sex. The passive agent was, as a rule, decidedly feminine, with little power of resistance, usually sentimental or unnecessarily prudish. . . . [T]he weak victim can be made the tool of the designing companion.[30]

Hamilton's description, like the one by Ellis, suggested that the passive, feminine woman was almost asexual, simply the recipient (or victim) of active lesbian advances, much as other women might be considered the sexual victims of men. Her prudishness and sentimentality were also hallmarks of the Victorian lady's prescribed sexual consciousness—precisely the reverse of the invert's sexually aggressive, man-like character. As another writer later put it, one could imagine her remaining involved with inverts only until she came "under the influence of a man."

The passive homosexual woman thus occupied an ambiguous position in medical thinking, for although she responded to another woman's advances, her deviation from social norms was qualitatively different from the more easily recognizable perversion of her seducer, the invert. By the end of the nineteenth century, however, the medical profession had begun expressing greater concern about such women. Hamilton himself complained about the lack of attention paid to them in earlier years, citing the difficulties he had once faced in a case involving one, since "at that time her mental perversion was not of a recognized kind."[31] In explaining the difficulty—but urgency—of detecting female homosexuality, Ellis pointed out that "we are accustomed to a much greater familiarity and intimacy between women than between men, and we are less apt to suspect the existence of any abnormal passion."[32]

Doctors increasingly subjected to medical inquiry relations between women that they previously had considered properly asexual, and they sought to identify both active and passive lesbians. Doctors began to discern homosexual elements in such single-sex institutions as "convents, boarding schools, manufacturing establishments, etc.," and the "smashes" common to girls' schools—powerful emotional relationships between students—were studied by doctors in the United States and several European and Latin American countries.[33] The researchers viewed both active and passive lesbians as pathological because of their object choice. Douglas McMurtrie, for instance, who wrote prolifically on lesbianism in the mid-1910s, agreed that in "the relations of Lesbian couples we find that the sexuality of the two individuals is comparative [i.e., 'complementary']." One would be the "more masculine" and "play the male part" both by courting the other and "play[ing] the active role in the sexual relations." But McMurtrie evinced none of the older nineteenth-century sympathy for the woman seduced. He even argued that these roles were reversible; the female who played the masculine role in one relationship might be forced to play the woman to another, even more masculine partner.[34]

The role of the "wife" in lesbian relationships was increasingly sexualized in the medical literature, which saw her no longer as simply victimized by the invert's advances but as fully complicit in homosexual perversion. In later years the heterosexual paradigm itself seemed less satisfactory to doctors. In 1913 Margaret Otis published a study of interracial sexual relationships at a girls' reformatory ("A Perversion Not Commonly Noted"). Although keen to discover who "seemed the man" in the relationships, it was not obvious to her, and she defined the young women's perversion in terms of their homosexuality and interracialism rather than their role inversion.[35] It was only twenty years later, however, that researchers began to reject the heterosexual paradigm. Lura Beam and Robert Latou Dickinson carefully explained that every lesbian in their study who had been asked "whether she or the other person took the male part" answered that it was not she; "the typical reply was that they did not think of it in that way."[36] Beam emphasized that "no transposition to male feeling or manifestation of male sexuality" appeared in the case histories, and that the women alternately assumed various *female* roles such as child, equal, and mother in their relationships.[37] By refuting the paradigm, however, Beam's study highlighted the increasing importance attached to sexual object choice instead of gender characteristics in classifying women's sexual deviance.

■ **The Explanation of the Perverse**   Given the nature and purposes of the medical profession at the turn of the century, it is not surprising that so profound a redefinition of sexual deviance and the role of gender in sexual identity should have occurred. The medical profession's reconsideration of the nature of mental disease and disorder during this period also provided the context for the emergence of quickly changing and often contradictory explanations of inversion and homosexuality. Changes in theories concerning sexual deviance paralleled those concerning mental disease in general; doctors' growing conviction in the late nineteenth century that nervous disorders had a somatic (physical) basis and demonstrated somatic symptoms, for instance, profoundly influenced studies of inversion. Once sexual inversion had been successfully classified as a disease, therefore, its intellectual history was significantly influenced by broader trends in the history of medicine. Within this general context, the emergence of medical theories concerning inversion was related particularly closely to medical theories of women's and men's biological and social roles, physical ailments, and sexual disorders. Inversion theories were thus part of a logical system whose structure reveals the medical profession's and society's basic assumptions about sexuality and gender.

Before the medical profession could explain inversion authoritatively, it had to demonstrate that inversion was symptomatic of a disease and thus a matter properly in the domain of medicine, rather than religion or the law. Numerous doctors in the 1880s and nineties had to argue that "conditions once considered criminal are really pathological, and come within the province of the physician."[38] As G. Frank Lydston wrote in 1889,

> The subject has been until a recent date studied solely from the standpoint of the moralist, and from the indisposition of the scientific physician to study the subject, the unfortunate class of individuals who are characterized by perverted sexuality have been viewed in the light of their moral responsibility rather than as the victims of a physical and incidentally of a mental defect.[39]

But although early medical theorists criticized the religious precept that sexual inversion represented a sinful act of will, for a short while their theories gave willful antisocial behavior a central role in its etiology. The earliest medical model considered inversion to be an acquired disease, which the individual could avoid by refraining from improper activity. This is particularly evident in the role Krafft-Ebing, Beard, and others attributed to masturbation in inversion's etiology in the 1870s and eighties. Krafft-Ebing's concern about the effects of masturbation, for instance, resulted from his conviction that normal, "civilized" sexual relations could occur only in the emotional context of a loving, monogamous, heterosexual relationship, the result of "noble and ideal sentiments."[40] To masturbate was to seek the mere gratification of lust, and put one "at once on a level with the beast" thus "despoil[ing] the unfolded bud of perfume and beauty, and leav[ing] behind only the coarse, animal desire for sexual satisfaction."[41] The results could be ominous: a loss of interest in the other sex, preference for masturbation over "the natural mode of satisfaction," or even homosexual desire.[42] Self-abuse was thus a vice that one properly avoided, and inversion was only one of its worst consequences.[43]

New theories that emphasized inversion's congenital nature and biological basis superceded older concerns about environmental and volitional factors in the 1880s and nineties. This was simply one instance of the growing influence of somatically based theories in the explanation of nervous disease, but the form taken by the somatic explanation of inversion highlights both the polarization of gender roles implicit in the broad definition given sexual inversion and the assertion by late Victorian medicine of the biological determination of the sex/gender system. Medical theory tied men and women's gender characteristics so closely to their respective biological sexes that a somatic explanation had to be found for those people who threatened to contradict the theory by appearing to be one sex while assuming the gender role of the other (the so-called opposite sex).

One of the most influential theories at the turn of the century proposed a radical solution to this dilemma, by asserting that inverts simply were not the sex they first appeared to be, but were hermaphrodites, incorporating biological elements of both sexes. For Herbert Claiborne in 1914, for instance, this provided the only possible explanation not only for lesbianism but also for the "violent and vicious methods" employed by English suffragists and businesswomen, whose acts, he thought, "are certainly not in any sense feminine." The cause of both phenomena, he wrote in an article nominally on hypertrichosis (excessive hair growth) in women, "lies in the possession by the individual of structural cellular elements of the opposite sex."[44] James Kiernan argued that the ancestors of the human race were "bisexual" (i.e., hermaphroditic), but that highly differentiated gender roles had evolved during the course of human civilization. Disease or congenital defects in a particular individual, however, could eliminate the "inhibitions" which prevented people from acting on their atavistic impulses.[45] Ellis incorporated a version of this theory in *Sexual Inversion* when he argued that each person contained male and female "germs" of varying strengths, arranged in a variety of configurations that determined the individual's physical and psychic states.[46] Thus masculine physical attributes could be a sign of psychic masculinity and perversion in women. "Bearded women approach the masculine type," Claiborne observed, and an exceptionally high percentage of them (68 percent in one 1881 survey he cited) were unmarried.[47]

Scientific concern about hermaphroditism has often resulted from challenges to the sex/gender system in Western history,[48] but it took particular form in the scientific discourse of the late nineteenth century. Victorian medical conceptions of woman, for instance, centered on her reproductive role and organs, as Smith-Rosenberg has shown; puberty and menopause were the two great endpoints and crises of womanhood, and menstruation her fundamental identifying characteristic.[49] The early medical case histories of lesbians thus predictably paid enormous attention to their menstrual flow and the size of their sexual organs. Several doctors emphasized that their lesbian patients stopped menstruating at an early age, if they began at all, or had unusually difficult and irregular periods. They also inspected the women's sexual organs, often claiming that inverts had unusually large clitorises, which they said the inverts used in sexual intercourse as a man would his penis.[50] Underlying all such descriptions and inquiries was the assumption that persons who behaved as the female invert did simply could not be women.

As somatically oriented psychological theories began to wane in the early years of this century, however, the theory of psychic hermaphroditism superceded that of the physical. The evidence against somatically based theories of nervous and mental disease became overwhelming in the general scientific literature during this period, and this was the case in studies of inversion as well. For although scrupulous attention was paid to physical organs in the case histories, many investigators did, after all, have to report that there were no physical abnormalities.[51] Some doctors continued to argue, however, that even if the hermaphrodite's anatomical features were of its biological sex, its mind must surely be of the other sex. Karl Ulrichs, the first German writer (and for decades the only openly gay man) to discuss inversion in a public forum, had first characterized male inversion as representing a "woman's spirit in a man's body" in the 1860s. Many of the next generation of gay intellectuals, including Edward Carpenter and Magnus Hirschfeld, adopted a version of this theory at the turn of the century, claiming that they were best characterized as an "intermediate sex" (the loose but popular translation of *sexuelle Zwischenstufe*), hermaphroditically combining psychic qualities of both the male and female.[52]

Krafft-Ebing introduced degeneration theory as a means of explaining inversion in the early editions of his monumental work, *Psychopathia Sexualis*. His explanation quickly gained wide currency in the United States, for in the last years of the nineteenth century degeneration theory had come to dominate explanations of nervous and mental disease in general. The theory drew from those currents in late Victorian thought that postulated an organic relationship between the processes of evolution and civilization. The development of sexual morality and order, according to Krafft-Ebing, laid the "basis upon which social advancement is developed." Lust ran wild in primitive society, which tolerated acts civilized society considered criminal, he argued, while the Victorian sexual order represented at once the pinnacle and the necessary basis of the world's most advanced civilization. Maintaining such a society required that human sexual relations be based on love and monogamy; sexual relations outside of the heterosexual institution of marriage thus represented not only a degeneration to an earlier, lower state of evolution, but threatened civilization itself.[53]

Krafft-Ebing's theory led investigators to consider the relationship of social development to the evolution of sexual morality and resulted in the publication of numerous anthropological studies of "primitive" sexual morality in medical journals. Several studies described the institutionalization of homosexual relations or inversion in Native American and Pacific societies (usually involving transvestism and mirroring the heterosexual paradigm), thus lending support to the argument that primitive cultures could be characterized by their tolerance of such practices.[54] Early gay scholars devoted much of their attention to the refutation of this argument, however, and the work of John Addington Symonds and others on the role of homosexuality in ancient Greek civilization was widely cited to that end. If homosexuality not only was tolerated but flourished in the culture that represented the epitome of Western civilization, they asked, how could it be associated with degeneration? Carpenter argued that inverts had made special contributions to civilization as artists, spiritualists, and warriors in primitive societies.[55] Such arguments doubtless did not persuade many doctors, but they dominated the medical literature by the mid-teens.

Several theories, including that of degeneration, embodied middle-class assumptions about the class nature of sexual morality as well as a concern about the standards of the "civilized West." For the medical profession grew out of the white middle class and reflected its values and concerns in an extremely class-conscious manner; it perceived not only non-Europeans but also America's own lower classes as immoral. Doctors assumed that sexual license and sensuality characterized the poor and working classes, that only the middle and upper classes had "achieved" a sense of sexual propriety.[56] Degeneration theory explained the immorality of the poor—as well as their poverty—by asserting the degeneration of the class as a whole. Some nineteenth-century alienists maintained that sanity and morality alike were socially constructed and a function of class: behavior common to the "immoral" classes, when it appeared in a person from a higher class, could thus be a sign of insanity. Others maintained that the working class suffered from a high incidence of sexual disorders and disease because of its sexual excess.

Each of these tendencies is evident in the medical literature on homosexuality. A number of doctors who described inversion as a disease when it afflicted their middle-class patients considered it to be an immoral, willfully chosen mode of behavior on the part of the poor. This distinction was sometimes expressed as the difference between congenital or disease-induced "perversion" and willful, immoral "perversity"; the person suffering from perversion was to be pitied, while those who were simply perverse, perhaps responding to the pervert's advances, were "worse than the pervert and deserve no sympathy."[57] Furthermore, many doctors accused servants, the representatives of the working class in the middle-class household, of introducing perversion into respectable homes. Highlighting one of the most frightful aspects of the Victorian "servant problem," doctors charged that servants showed children how to masturbate, which resulted in their becoming involved in homosexual activity.

Prostitutes, of whom Hirschfeld, Ellis, and other major sexologists asserted a quarter or more were lesbian, came under particular attack in this context. Female prostitutes chose to respond to the perverse sexual demands of their diseased clients, in and of itself damnable behavior; many doctors maintained that in so doing the prostitutes further perverted their sexuality. In one widely accepted theory, the lesbianism of prostitutes was but one of the sexual perversities resulting from their "satiation" with "normal" sex.[58] For others, however, prostitution necessarily indicated a partial, organic inversion, since the women were without "feminine honor." Ellis argued in this vein that the "prevalence of homosexuality among women in prison [presumably working class women] is connected with the close relationship between feminine criminality and prostitution."[59] To many doctors, prostitutes seem to have embodied the sensuality and sexual immorality of the working class, but doctors did not believe perversity was restricted to them. Female hotel servants and factory workers were also frequently accused of lesbian behavior. In part this seems to have reflected the growing concern about women in single-sex institutions such as boarding schools and convents, but the doctors' descriptions of autoeroticism, mutual masturbation, and other sexual activity among women workers were especially lurid and morbid. Even Ellis deviated from his normal position to characterize lesbianism in factories as "homosexual *vice* . . . common and recognized."[60]

One of Ellis' major purposes was to establish the congenital basis of homosexuality; he considered the theory to have politically progressive implications, since it might remove homosexual behavior from the purview of the law.[61] By 1900 the medical profession had accepted the congenital theory in the explanation not only of inversion but also of a wide range of other supposed mental diseases. Ellis and other sexologists also postulated the importance of heredity in its etiology, but how exactly it might have entered the hereditary chain continued to be disputed. The degenerationists themselves had claimed that, once acquired, sexual perversion was inheritable, each generation suffering an exacerbated form. Doctors such as Beard, who associated inversion with a variety of other mental disorders, frequently noted the incidence of neurasthenia and other nervous disorders in the invert's family history.[62] Later theorists, such as Ellis, were careful to specify the incidence of inversion itself, though often in conjunction with other neuroses.[63] The hermaphroditic theory that Kiernan, Lydston, and others espoused was not wholly incompatible with the congenital theory, and thus continued as an important theoretical tendency even after the demise of other aspects of the degeneration theory.

But the new psychological theories of Freud and his American followers challenged the hegemony of the congenital theory in the early 1900s. In his most radical thought, Freud proposed that exclusive heterosexuality was as problematic as homosexuality, since the suppression of any aspect of the libido required explanation.[64] But although he maintained that many inverts neither desired nor needed treatment, his now familiar theory that the "aberration" of homosexuality resulted from the child's failure to resolve psychosexual relations with one or another parent presupposed a preferred, healthier course of development.[65] Freud's work reintroduced the acquired theory of homosexuality so forcibly that congenital theorists such as Ellis were compelled to devote much of their later work to its refutation.[66]

Nevertheless, Freud's American followers and other non-Freudian psychiatrists continued to mix his radically mental explanation of homosexuality with those that attributed the "disorder" to congenital defects and even to vice. C. P. Oberndorf, for instance, argued in 1919 that only the behavior of "objective," passive lesbians, or "subjective," aggressive gay men, could be explained by psychotraumatic processes. For an aggressive gay man behaved sexually as a man should, he argued, and the "abnormal" fact that he chose to initiate sexual relations with a man instead of a woman was explicable in terms of a traumatic heterosexual experience in childhood and could be cured by psychoanalysis. But Oberndorf believed this theory was inadequate to explain the behavior of the "objective" gay man (i.e., the passive "object" of sexual activity), the man called an invert in the nineteenth-century literature. These men, he argued, represented "biological anomalies of development which are often coupled with unmistakable physical signs."[67] Not only was their sexual object abnormal, but also their sexual aim, and only with the older theories of hermaphroditism and sexual intermediacy could Oberndorf adequately account for so fundamental an inversion of the man's (or obverse woman's) role.

Oberndorf's interweaving of several traditions of conceptualization and explanation in his analysis of homosexuality accurately reflects the intellectual confusion and anachronism of the period under consideration. While increasing numbers of doctors distinguished homosexual desire from sexual (or gender) inversion in the 1910s and twenties, the heterosexual paradigm, which assumed that all sexual pairings were organized between "masculine" and "feminine" partners, continued to structure much medical thought. But while the inconsistencies and fluctuations in explanations offered for inversion and homosexuality resulted in part from confusion about what needed to be explained, they were also a consequence of the more general crisis of medical thought at the turn of the century. Speculation about the etiology of homosexuality was but an aspect of a more general reconsideration of the nature and etiology of nervous disease and closely adhered to the more general pattern.

■ **The Instrumentality of the Perverse**   To note the relationship between theories of inversion and of other supposed mental disorders, however, does not explain why gender deviance and homosexual relations became the subject of medical inquiry when they did, nor does it account for the changing focus of the inquiry. To examine these questions we must assess the broader cultural context in which the medical inquiry emerged. Such analysis can be only tentative and suggestive at this stage in our research, although recent scholarship in women's history has made it possible to understand more deeply the social context of the study of female sexuality than of male. The analysis I suggest here focuses on the reasons for the study of lesbianism, although it also considers inquiry into male inversion and homosexuality. I think three developments in American society during this period were particularly important in this context: the increasing visibility of urban gay male subcultures, the political and economic challenges posed to the Victorian sex/gender system by women in the late nineteenth century, and the related "resexualization" of women in mainstream sexual ideology in the first decades of the twentieth. The professionalization of medicine and its rise to ideological hegemony over religion and, in certain arenas, the state apparatus, were also crucial to the process, but I will only note those developments here.[68]

In the late nineteenth century, increasing numbers of women began to question and challenge the limits placed on their social role, both politically through the suffrage movement and more generally through their movement into the wage-labor force and the efforts of many to achieve economic and social independence. The declining marriage and birth rates of the native-born middle class and the general movement of women into men's sphere alarmed many men. Joe L. Dubbert has argued that a "masculinity crisis" developed in the years 1880–1920 because of the challenge posed to masculine sex-role definitions by both the women's movement and men's perception that women exerted undue influence over key cultural and socializing institutions.[69] The declining autonomy of both working-class men at the factory and middle-class men at the office, due to the introduction of scientific management, the undermining of the crafts, and the rationalization of clerical work, also may have contributed to this crisis.[70] Men who had lost power at the workplace may have needed to reassert power and to redefine their masculinity in their marriages and families. Conservative medical pronouncements played a key role in the ideological reaction to these challenges, and as Smith-Rosenberg and Rosenberg have argued, "would-be scientific arguments were used in the rationalization and legitimization of almost every aspect of Victorian life, with particular vehemence in those areas in which social change implied stress in existing social arrangements.[71]

The sudden growth in the medical literature on sexual inversion, I would argue, was part of the general ideological reaction by the medical profession to women's challenge to the sex/gender system during this period. The designation of their challenge as the *disease* of sexual inversion allowed male doctors both to explain the phenomenon in a non-threatening way and to stigmatize it as deviant behavior which should be avoided by "healthy" women. Thus the observation by A. M. Hamilton in 1896, that "the views of such a person were erratic, 'advanced,' and extreme, and she nearly always lacked the normal modesty and retirement of her sex," was not simply a curious addendum to his description of her homosexuality, as some have assumed, but was central to his concept of women's sexuality and social place, and the nature of the "invert's" disorder.[72]

The implicit concern about challenges to the sex/gender system that pervades these medical accounts was made quite explicit in some, which linked the apparent rise in sexual inversion to the influence of the women's movement. Ellis asserted such a relationship: "Having been taught independence of men and disdain for the old theory which placed women in the moated grange of the home to sigh for a man who never comes, a tendency develops for women to carry this independence still farther and to find love where they find work."[73] Ellis had to qualify his argument by noting that the "unquestionable influences of modern movements cannot *directly* cause sexual inversion" (my emphasis), since otherwise it would contradict his congenital theory, but his point was clear. He quoted without qualification the opinion of "a well informed American correspondent" that one of the "obvious reasons" for the increase in sexual inversion was "the growing independence of the women, their lessening need for marriage." He also reported on the extensive debate within advanced German medical and feminist circles about this relationship.[74] Other doctors attributed the supposed increase in inversion to the repudiation of motherhood by women influenced by feminism. The progeny of the woman who "prefers the laboratory to the nursery," warned Howard in 1900, "are perverts, moral or psychical." By forsaking their proper social role, he claimed, these "emancipated" women produced effeminate sons and masculine daughters.[75]

While some doctors indicated their concern about the women's movement by warning that it could lead to an increase in sexual inversion, others were even more explicit in postulating a literally organic relationship between the two. Kiernan's comments in 1914 on the Claiborne article on hermaphroditism are interesting in this light, for they suggest that such an association was often proposed. "As might be expected," Kiernan wrote, "Claiborne does not finish his paper [nominally on hypertrichosis] without touching upon the influence of defective sexuality in women upon political questions. While, of course, he does not think every suffragist an invert, yet he does believe that the very fact that women in general of today are more and more deeply invading man's sphere is indicative of a certain impelling force within them."[76] Other doctors were less restrained in their appraisal of the organic relationship between the women's movement and inversion. Howard warned in his article of 1900 that

> the female possessed of masculine ideas of independence; the viragint who would sit in the public highways and lift up her pseudo-virile voice, proclaiming her sole right to decide questions of war or religion, or the value of celibacy and the curse of women's impurity, and that disgusting anti-social being, the female sexual pervert, are simply different degrees of the same class—degenerates.[77]

The same historical processes that generated concern about female gender deviance contributed to social apprehension about male inversion. Values under attack are likely to be reasserted with particular vigor, and, as Joe L. Dubbert has argued, many men reacted to the crisis in masculine role definition at the turn of the century by reasserting the traditional values of masculinity. In this context any man who behaved as if he had rejected his masculinity must have generated considerable anxiety on the part of other men, since his behavior implicitly challenged the biological basis attributed to the prescribed male role. Indeed, much of the nineteenth-century literature on male inversion treats these men as veritable traitors to the sex, and the inverts' supposed fear of women was seen as one of their most damning unmasculine traits.

Concern about men who refused to conform to masculine gender norms was exacerbated by the increasing visibility of gay male subcultures, which many observers attributed to urbanization. That doctors were aware of these subcultures and considered them to be a crucial subject of their inquiry is evidenced in some of the earliest articles on male inversion. Lydston observed in 1889 that there was "in every community of any size a colony of male sexual perverts; they are usually known to each other and are likely to congregate together."[78] The phenomenon seemed especially evident in New York; even in the early 1880s, Beard thought that many male inverts lived there, while by 1913 A. A. Brill confidently estimated there were "many thousands of homosexuals in New York City among all classes of society." Three years later, Kiernan noted that gay men were popularly called "fairies" in New York and "brownies" in Philadelphia; he also knew of interracial gay cafes in Chicago.[79] Furthermore, doctors realized that the subjects of their inquiry already identified themselves as part of a sexual underground; two articles reporting the case histories of male inverts in the 1880s noted that "these patients claim to be able to recognize each other."[80] The very existence of such subcultures motivated doctors' interest in male inversion and homosexuality; they considered it their proper domain—and responsibility—to map the emerging sexual underground and classify its inhabitants in ever more discrete categories. They were investigating a subculture rather than creating one.

Despite the ideological attacks on feminist and wage-earning women, their challenge to the Victorian sex/gender system resulted in limited but significant changes. The number of employed women continued to increase; women secured new positions in the professions; and they won two major political campaigns, for suffrage and prohibition. Their economic and political advances led to changes in the cultural conception of middle-class womanhood. The early decades of the century witnessed a "new freedom in manners and morals" for women, and the resexualization of women in mainstream sexual ideology. Although that ideology continued to postulate the greater sexual interest and aggressiveness of men, it increasingly acknowledged women's capacity for sexual interest and initiative.[81] To a limited extent, gender norms changed to recognize the greater complexity of actual gender roles in the society. Particularly notable was the weakening of the holistic character of masculinity and femininity in the ideological system; doctors began to question whether one aspect of one's behavior—sexual passivity or aggressiveness—was paradigmatic for one's entire gender role, although more decisively in the case of men than of women. Thus the increasing differentiation of "perversions" in medical thought may itself have reflected the decline of the older holistic concepts of gender and the increasing complexity of gender roles in American ideology.

But the liberalization of gender norms in the face of women's activism did not alter the fundamental power relations between men and women, and it was in this context that the "homosexual" replaced the "invert" as the subject of medical concern. For if it no longer was considered a deviation from the norm for a woman to initiate sexual relations, then it no longer needed to be considered an inversion of her sexual or social role to do so. But once all women were considered able to experience and act on sexual desire, medical concern shifted logically from the *fact* of women's sexual activity to their *choice* of sexual and social partners. The fact that some women chose other women rather than men as sexual partners thus became the primary fact to be explained and condemned, despite the narrowness of this issue compared to inversion; as we have seen, both the "active" and "passive" partners came under scrutiny. Indeed, the resexualization of women—in one sense a progressive development—was used to tie them to men, as the culture increasingly postulated the importance of women's sexual desire as a basis for their involvement in heterosexual institutions such as marriage, which their employment supposedly rendered less of an economic necessity than before. The new complexity—and restrictiveness—of sex/gender roles was epitomized by the flapper, who was at once both sexually precocious and profoundly heterosexual.

The new celebration of heterosexual bonding and the increasing hostility to homosexual relations between women evident in both the medical literature and the broader culture were central to the general subversion of women's culture and solidarity that Estelle Freedman and other historians have identified as instrumental in the decline of the women's movement after the attainment of suffrage in 1920. The growth of the movement, and the very ability of numerous activists and professional and working-class women to work, had depended in part on the development in the nineteenth century of a women's culture of supportive friendships and networks.[82] The most striking indication of this development is that in the closing years of the century many feminist activists and professional women chose not to marry at all, but to be sustained by their relationships with other women. Heterosexual marriage and motherhood, as constituted in Victorian society—unlike relationships with women—would have left them little chance to pursue their chosen work.

In this context, the increasing denigration of single sex institutions and relations and the new urgency attached to the development of women's relations with men in the 1910s and twenties constituted—to modify a current phrase—a veritable "Heterosexual Counterrevolution." The available evidence suggests that this was a pervasive phenomenon in middle class culture; the newly burgeoning advertising industry did its part, and the marriage manuals of the 1920s and thirties, according to Christina Simmons, emphasized the need for men to develop "companionate marriages" to make marriage more attractive and satisfying to women. The results were also widely evident. Some observers noted that dyadic, heterosexual dating had replaced same-sex group activities as the dominant pattern of youth culture by the 1920s, while autobiographical material from the decade suggests that increasing numbers of professional women chose to marry, often to the detriment of their careers. A full explanation of the decline of the women's movement after 1920 would have to consider many factors, including outright political repression and more subtle processes such as the reconstitution of women as "consumers" upon the rapid expansion of the consumer economy during this period. But the increasing hostility to a women's culture of supportive relationships and networks was also crucial to the movement's decline,[83] and it is in this context that we may best understand the growing medical concern about homosexual desire. Scientific discourse reflected and was but one aspect of a much broader subversion of women's culture and reconstitution of sexual and gender relations in a manner that linked women to men.

■ **Conclusion**   Sexuality is socially structured in a complex relationship with gender, class, and other lines of social demarcation, and a recognition of how profoundly sexual categories and norms can change is essential to the development of a satisfactory conceptual framework for the historical and political analysis of sexuality. Examining the changing focus of sexological inquiry points out how important it is in our study of the history of homosexuality to reconstruct the conceptual frameworks in which homoerotic desire and relations have been understood. As in the late nineteenth century, such conceptual schemas may not even have recognized homoeroticism as a discrete sexual phenomenon.

The medical literature on sexual deviance was not the central force in the transformation of popular attitudes and the social relations of sexuality between 1880 and 1930. But it does provide us with a key to understanding the politics of sexuality during that period. It developed in response to challenges to the Victorian sex/gender system and the emergence of sexual subcultures in the cities, and it changed in a manner that reflected changes in the actual organization of sex/gender roles in the society. The medical profession's increasing concern about homosexual desire, and its differentiation of homosexual object choice from deviant gender behavior, represent both a reorientation of gender norms and a continuing imperative to define and delimit the range of acceptable social relations.

■ **Postscript (1988)**   This is a slightly revised version of an article originally written in 1980 and published in 1982. I still consider the paper's argument sound but would now emphasize the extent to which medical writers continued to be confused, throughout the period under discussion, about the categories and explanations they should employ. A growing number of doctors distinguished homosexuality from gender inversion in the 1910s and twenties, as the paper argues, but inversion continued for decades to be a major medical concern and to be linked to homosexuality; the shift, as I may not have indicated clearly enough, was hardly decisive or unanimous by the 1920s.[84] Indeed, the intellectual history of homosexuality throughout the twentieth century has to some extent been concerned with the working out of the boundaries and relationship between "sexuality" and "gender."

I should also have emphasized the differences in doctors' discussions of male and female inversion, particularly in my analysis of the origins of medical inquiry. Doctors frequently commented on the "colonies" of male inverts they noticed about them, with their own meeting places, argot, and social codes, for instance, but almost never on similar lesbian groupings. The differences in men's and women's public cultures during this period were reflected in the different forms taken by lesbian and gay male social networks.

Finally, I would now argue even more strongly (and have, in another article[85]) that the medical discourse did not "invent" the homosexual; doctors did not create new categories on which people based their identities as homosexual or lesbian. Subsequent research has shown that doctors reproduced the categories and prejudices of their culture. The men doctors called "inverts" in their medical journals were already called "fairies" and "queers" on the streets and in the popular press, and many of them, as several doctors noted in astonishment, resisted doctors' efforts to condemn them as "perverts."[86] As in other new fields of social history, historians of homosexuality first considered the literature of the elite before grappling with the more elusive evidence of the ordinary. It is to that more difficult project that we must now turn.

■ Notes

Acknowledgments: I would like to thank Lisa Biow, John Boswell, Jeanne Boydston, Nancy Cott, Mitchell Katz, Harry Scott, Chris Stansell, Tony Stellato and Jack Winkler for their comments on earlier drafts of this paper. Discussions with Jeanne Boydston were particularly helpful in developing some of the arguments presented in the third section.

1. Jeffrey Weeks, *Coming Out: Homosexual Politics in Britain from the Nineteenth Century to the Present* (London: 1977); Lillian Faderman, "The Morbidification of Love Between Women by 19th-Century Sexologists," *Journal of Homosexuality* 4 (1978): 73–90; Faderman,"Lesbian Magazine Fiction in the Early Twentieth Century," *Journal of Popular Culture* 2 (1978): 700–17. Faderman's major work, *Surpassing the Love of Men* (New York: 1981), unfortunately appeared too late for me to incorporate its findings in this article.

2. Nancy Sahli notes the increasing medical attention to sexual deviance as evidenced by the number of articles cited in the *Surgeon-General's Index Catalog* during these years in her article, "Smashing: Women's Relations Before the Fall," *Chrysalis* 8 (1979): 17–27. James Kiernan, one of the earliest writers on homosexuality, edited a "Sexology" column for the *Urologic and Cutaneous Review* from the early teens at least. It included abstracts of articles appearing in other medical journals and short editorial comments, including three or four a year on homosexuality. *The Psychoanalytic Review*, begun in 1913 by William A. White and Smith Ely Jeliffe, included original articles, translations, and regular abstracts of articles published in major German-language psychoanalytic journals, including many on homosexuality. William J. Robinson established the short-lived *Journal of Sexology and Psychoanalysis* in 1923, to supercede the *American Journal of Urology and Sexology*, published from 1904 to 1922. The first issue of *JSP* carried

an article by Stella Browne, "Studies in Feminine Inversion," 51–58. Thus by the early teens the number of articles or abstracts concerning homosexuality regularly available to the American medical profession had grown enormously.

3. Gayle Rubin introduced the term "sex/gender system" in her article, "The Traffic in Women: Notes on the 'Political Economy' of Sex," in *Toward an Anthropology of Women*, ed. Rayna R. Reiter (New York: 1975), 157–210. Somewhat analogous to "political economy" in scope and purpose, "sex/gender system" is the general term for the many social systems by which sexuality, gender, and procreation are structured.

4. In recent years historians have written extensively on the role of medical arguments in the ideological struggles over gender roles in the late nineteenth century, and in some respects the discussion that follows should be seen as another aspect of the process they have described. See Ann Douglas Wood, "'The Fashionable Diseases': Women's Complaints and their Treatment in Nineteenth-Century America," in *Clio's Consciousness Raised*, ed. Mary S. Hartman and Lois Banner (New York: 1974), 1–22; Carroll Smith-Rosenberg, "The Hysterical Woman: Sex Roles and Role Conflict in Nineteenth Century America," *Social Research* 39 (1972): 654–78; Charles Rosenberg and Carroll Smith-Rosenberg, "The Female Animal: Medical and Biological Views of Women," *Journal of American History* 60 (1973): 332–56.

5. See, e.g., the assertion by H. Fehling that "the appearance of the sexual side in the love of a young girl is pathological" (*Die Bestimmung der Frau*, 1892, 18, quoted in Havelock Ellis, *Studies in the Psychology of Sex*, 2nd ed., rev. (1903, Philadelphia: 1913), 3, 195. Ellis cited similar opinions by other major European sexologists who were influential in the United States, including Krafft-Ebing, Moll, Naecke, and Lombroso (194–96). Carl Degler's study of women's sexuality in the nineteenth century suggests that this ideology had begun to change earlier than historians previously thought ("What Ought to Be and What Was: Women's Sexuality in the Nineteenth Century," *American Historical Review* 79 [1974]: 1467–90), but it relies on sources published only in the last third of the century. My evidence suggests that the assertion of women's sexual subjectivity, which had become common by the 1920s, remained only a minority medical opinion in the closing years of the nineteenth century. For a reinterpretation of the origins and instrumentality of passionlessness, see Nancy F. Cott, "Passionlessness: A Reinterpretation of Victorian Sexual Ideology, 1790–1850," *Signs* 4 (1978): 219–36.

6. P. M. Wise, "Case of Sexual Perversion," *Alienist and Neurologist* 4 (1883): 87–88.

7. Carroll Smith-Rosenberg, "Beauty, the Beast, and the Militant Woman: A Case Study in Sex Role and Social Stress in Jacksonian America," *American Quarterly* 23 (1971): 571.

8. Vern Bullough, "Homosexuality and the Medical Model," *Journal of Homosexuality* 1 (1974): 99–110.

9. George M. Beard, *Sexual Neurasthenia*, ed. A. D. Rockwell (New York: 1884), 106.

10. Richard von Krafft-Ebing, *Psychopathia Sexualis, With Especial Reference to the Antipathic Sexual Instinct*, trans. F. J. Rebman (Brooklyn: 1908), 336.

11. Wise, "Case of Sexual Perversion," 88; P. Leidy and C. K. Mills, "Reports of Cases of Insanity from the Insane Department of the Philadelphia Hospital," *Journal of Nervous and Mental Disease* 13 (1886): 712; Perry M. Lichtenstein, "The

Fairy and the Lady Lover," *Medical Review of Reviews* 27 (1921): 370, 373–74; George F. Shrady, "Perverted Sexual Instinct," *Medical Record* 26 (1884): 70; Ralph Werther, "Studies in Androgynism," *Medical Life* 27 (1920): 243–45.

12. Lichtenstein, "The Fairy and the Lady Lover," 372.

13. "Review of Havelock Ellis' *Sexual Inversion*," *Alienist and Neurologist* 23 (1902): 111; Douglas C. McMurtrie, "Principles of Homosexuality and Sexual Inversion in the Female," *American Journal of Urology* 9 (1913): 147.

14. W. C. Rivers, "A New Male Homosexual Trait (?)," *Alienist and Neurologist* 41 (1920): 22; Leidy and Mills, "Reports of Cases of Insanity," 713.

15. Havelock Ellis, *Sexual Inversion*, 3rd rev. ed., *Studies in the Psychology of Sex*, vol. 2 (Philadelphia: 1915), 250. For other accounts that conceptualize inversion in these broad terms, rather than focusing exclusively on homosexual object choice, see William Lee Howard, "Effeminate Men and Masculine Women," *New York Medical Journal* 71 (1900): 686; Allan MacLane Hamilton, "The Civil Responsibility of Sexual Perverts," *American Journal of Insanity* 52 (1896): 505; Herbert J. Claiborne, "Hypertrichosis in Women: Its Relation to Bisexuality (Hermaphroditism): With Remarks on Bisexuality in Animals, Especially Man," *New York Medical Journal* 99 (1914): 1181; J. Allen Gilbert, "Homosexuality and its Treatment," *Journal of Nervous and Mental Disease* 52 (1920): 297–322; James G. Kiernan, "Sexual Perversion and the Whitechapel Murders," *Medical Standard* 4 (1888): 170–72; Richard von Krafft-Ebing, "Perversions of the Sexual Instinct: Report of Cases," *Alienist and Neurologist* 9 (1888): 556–70, 579–81; Douglas C. McMurtrie, "Manifestations of Sexual Inversion in the Female: Conditions in a Convent School, Evidence of Transvestism, Unconscious Homosexuality, Sexuality of Masculine Women, Masturbation Under Homosexual Influences, Indeterminate Sexuality in Childhood," *Urologic and Cutaneous Review* 18 (1914): 444–46; "Psychology of a Tribadistic Uxoricide: A Lombrosian Case Record," *ibid.* 18 (1914): 480; Shrady, "Perverted Sexual Instinct," 70–71.

16. Havelock Ellis, "Sexual Inversion in Women," *Alienist and Neurologist* 16 (1895): 154.

17. Howard, "Effeminate Men and Masculine Women," 687.

18. J. F. W. Meagher, "Homosexuality: Its Psychobiological and Pathological Significance," *Urologic and Cutaneous Review* 33 (1929): 513.

19. One of the more bizarre—and late—examples of the literature that used this broad definition of male inversion was W. C. Rivers' article, "A New Male Homosexual Trait (?)." The newly discovered trait was cat-loving, and Rivers concluded that "If fondness for cats be entitled to a place among male homosexual traits, the reason will be that it is a woman's taste" (27).

20. Havelock Ellis, "Sexo-Aesthetic Inversion," *Alienist and Neurologist* 34 (1913): 156. In this speech Ellis presented the case of a male homosexual transvestite and cited a case originally reported by Krafft-Ebing of what might now be termed male transsexualism. Magnus Hirschfeld's massive work, *Die Transvestiten*, which appeared in 1910 and made the same distinction between homosexuality and transvestism, obviously influenced Ellis a great deal, as he acknowledges.

21. Havelock Ellis, "Sexual Inversion in Men," *Alienist and Neurologist* 17 (1896): 142.

22. Sigmund Freud, *Three Essays on the Theory of Sexuality*, trans. James Strachey *et al.* (New York: 1962), 1–2.

23. *Ibid.*, 8.

24. Michel Foucault, *The History of Sexuality*, vol. I, *An Introduction*, trans. Robert Hurley (New York: 1978).

25. Two additional points should be made. First, although "inversion" and "homosexuality" were the most common terms used and reflect the changes in the conceptualization of sexuality I have outlined, they were not the only terms used during this period to denote these concepts. Second, inversion has never entirely disappeared as a term or concept. A major study appearing in the mid-sixties, for instance, used the term in its title (J. Marmor, ed., *Sexual Inversion: The Multiple Roots of Homosexuality* [New York: 1965]), while individual researchers, particularly in periods of acute gender role distress such as postwar years, have attempted to revive the concept.

26. Freud, *Three Essays*, 8.

27. A few of the many accounts collected by Allan Bérubé are reported in his article, "Lesbian Masquerade," *Gay Community News* (17 November 1979). See also the numerous accounts reprinted in the chapter on "Passing Women, 1782–1920," in Jonathan Katz, *Gay American History* (New York: 1978), 317–423.

28. Only further research will reveal the actual organization and phenomenology of lesbian and gay male relationships during this period. In the mid-twentieth century, certainly, "butch–fem" relationships were the norm for many couples. For an important reappraisal of lesbian role-playing, see Joan Nestle, "Butch-Fem Relationships: Sexual Courage in the 1950s," *Heresies* 12 (1981): 21–24.

29. Ellis, "Sexual Inversion in Women," 147–48. Ellis used the same wording in the third edition of *Sexual Inversion* (1915), 222.

30. Hamilton, "Civil Responsibility of Sexual Perverts," 505.

31. *Ibid.*, 507.

32. Ellis, "Sexual Inversion in Women," 142.

33. Douglas McMurtrie, "Sexual Inversion Among Women in Spain"; "Principles of Homosexuality and Sexual Inversion in the Female"; Ellis, *Sexual Inversion*, 214–16. Ellis appended an essay on "The School Friendships of Girls" to *Sexual Inversion*, 368–84, which mentions studies in the United States, Italy, England, and Argentina. The U.S. study was by E. G. Lancaster, "The Psychology and Pedagogy of Adolescence," *Pedagogical Seminary* (July 1897). See also Nancy Sahli, "Smashing: Women's Relations Before the Fall," and Lillian Faderman, "Lesbian Magazine Fiction in the Early Twentieth Century." Faderman mentions several popular short stories that unselfconsciously describe intense, emotional relationships between girls and young women at school. For particularly charming examples, see Jeanette Lee, "The Cat and the King," *Ladies Home Journal* (October 1919): 10, 67–68, 71—an unusually late example; and "The Evolution of Evangeline," in Josephine Dodge Daskam, *Smith College Stories* (New York: 1900), 247–78.

34. McMurtrie, "Principles of Homosexuality and Sexual Inversion in the Female," 152. Elsewhere McMurtrie noted that "the authorities on this matter" believed all lesbians took on "active" or "passive" roles ("Manifestations of Sexual Inversion in the Female," 424).

35. Margaret Otis, "A Perversion Not Commonly Noted," *Journal of Abnormal Psychology* 8 (1913): 113–16.

36. Robert Latou Dickinson and Lura Beam, *The Single Woman: A Medical Study in Sex Education* (New York: 1929), 212.

37. *Ibid.*, 214, 203.

38. Shrady, "Perverted Sexual Instinct," 71; R. W. Shufeldt, "Dr. William Lee Howard on 'The Perverts,'" *Pacific Medical Journal* 45 (1902): 143–50; Wise, "Case of Sexual Perversion," 91; William Lee Howard, "Sexual Perversion," *Alienist and Neurologist* 17 (1896): 6.

39. George Frank Lydston, "Sexual Perversion, Satyriasis and Nymphomania," *Medical and Surgical Reporter* 61 (1889): 253.

40. Krafft-Ebing, *Psychopathia Sexualis*, 286.

41. *Ibid.*, 1, 286.

42. The conviction that sexual relations were "healthy" only in the context of a romantic heterosexual relationship persisted. In 1929 Lura Beam noted that the famous gynecologist Robert Latou Dickinson considered "sex expression without avowed emotional interest in other persons" as well as homosexual desire to be "regress[ive]" (*Single Woman*, xiii).

43. Even after theories attributing a causal role to masturbation in the etiology of homosexuality were discarded, many medical observers continued to claim a correlation between the two. Wilhelm Stekel, *Bisexual Love*, trans. J. S. Teslaar (Boston: 1922), 13–15, e.g., while specifically criticizing Krafft-Ebing's reasoning, also asserted a correlation. See also William Lee Howard, "Psychical Hermaphroditism: A Few Notes on Sexual Perversion with Two Clinical Cases of Sexual Inversion," *Alienist and Neurologist* 17 (1897): 111–18; Ellis, *Sexual Inversion*, 276–77.

44. Claiborne, "Hypertrichosis in Women," 1183, 1181.

45. Kiernan, "Sexual Perversion and the Whitechapel Murders," 129; Lydston, "Sexual Perversion, Satyriasis and Nymphomania," 254–55; George Frank Lydston, *The Disease of Society (The Vice and Crime Problem)* (Philadelphia: 1904).

46. Ellis, *Sexual Inversion*, 310–11.

47. Claiborne, "Hypertrichosis in Women," 1178. The survey cited in Claiborne was reported in Max Bartell, "Ueber abnorme Behaarung beim Menschen," *Zeitschrift fuer Ethnologie* 13 (1881). Of 146 women surveyed, 106 were single.

48. Hermaphroditism has long been associated with inversion and been a subject of medical inquiry. In 1836, for instance, a woman discovered passing as a married, male factory worker in Patterson, New Jersey, tried to persuade a court that she was an hermaphrodite. Although "surgical examination prove[d] her statement to be false," the newspaper account of the incident suggests the court might have considered this a reasonable excuse for her behavior (*The National Laborer* [New York], 25 August 1836; thanks to David Roediger for drawing my attention to this document). For discussion of earlier appearances of hermaphroditism as a subject of medical inquiry, see John Boswell, *Christianity, Social Tolerance, and Homosexuality: Gay People in Western Europe from the Beginning of the Christian Era to the Fourteenth Century* (Chicago: 1980), and Michel Foucault, *Herculine Barbin: Being the Recently Discovered Memoirs of a Nineteenth-Century Hermaphrodite*, trans. Richard McDougall (New York: 1980).

49. Carroll Smith-Rosenberg, "Puberty to Menopause: The Cycle of Femininity in Nineteenth-Century America," in *Clio's Consciousness Raised*, ed. Hartman and Banner, 23–37.

50. See, for example, Wise, "Case of Sexual Perversion," 90; Lichtenstein, "The Fairy and the Lady Lover," 372; J. C. Shaw and G. N. Ferris, "Perverted Sexual Instinct," *Journal of Nervous and Mental Disease* 10 (1883): 185–204, which sum-

marizes the cases previously reported in the European literature; and James Kiernan's comment in 1916, when his opinion had changed, that although earlier doctors had usually looked for "an enlarged clitoris as a stigma of perversion," Havelock Ellis had since demonstrated that it was not characteristic of lesbians ("Increase of Sexual Perversion," *Urologic and Cutaneous Review* 20 [1916]: 45).

51. Trignant Burrow, "The Genesis and Meaning of 'Homosexuality' and its Relation to the Problem of Introverted Mental States," *Psychoanalytic Review* 4 (1917): 272–84, and James Kiernan, "Comment on Burrows: The Genesis and Meaning of Homosexuality and its Relation to the Problem of Introverted Mental States," *Urologic and Cutaneous Review* 21 (1917): 467.

52. For a brief statement of Edward Carpenter's views, see his essay, "The Intermediate Sex," in his *Love's Coming-of-Age*, 12th enl. ed. (London: 1923), 130–49. See also Florence Beery, "The Psyche of the Intermediate Sex," *Medico-Legal Journal* 41 (1924): 4–9.

53. Krafft-Ebing, *Psychopathia Sexualis*, 344–46. For background on degeneration theory, see Nathan Hale, Jr., *Freud and the Americans: The Beginnings of Psychoanalysis in the United States, 1876–1917* (New York: 1971), 75–76.

54. C. G. Seligmann, "Sexual Inversion Among Primitive Races," *Alienist and Neurologist* 23 (1902): 580–83; William J. Robinson, " The Bote [abstract of an anthropologist's article]," *Journal of Sexology and Psychoanalysis* 1 (1923): 544–46; Ellis, *Sexual Inversion*, 205–9. One article, however, while making no comment on male homosexuality, described men's violent repression of lesbianism: Douglas McMurtrie, "Legend of Lesbian Love Among the North American Indians," *Urologic and Cutaneous Review* 18 (1914): 192.

55. Edward Carpenter, *Intermediate Types Among Primitive Folk* (London: 1914); John Addington Symonds, *A Problem in Greek Ethics: Being an Inquiry Into the Phenomenon of Sexual Inversion* (privately printed, 1883, 1901); M. H. E. Meier, "Paederastia," in *Allgemeine Encyclopaedie der Wissenschaften und Künste*, ed. J. S. Ersch and J. J. Gruber (Leipzig: 1837), 3.9.149–88. Symonds' privately printed treatise was "Addressed Especially to Medical Psychologists and Jurists" (title page). The work was to have been included as an Appendix to Ellis' *Sexual Inversion*, but Symonds' estate bought out the first English edition in 1897 and withdrew permission for its inclusion in subsequent editions (Weeks, *Coming Out*, 59–60). For examples of the utilization of the Greek evidence introduced by Symonds and others, see I. H. Coriat, "Homosexuality: Its Psychogenesis and Treatment," *New York Medical Journal* 97 (1913): 589–94; Ellis, *Sexual Inversion*, 197–98; Kiernan, "Homosexuality in Early Greek Poetry," *Urologic and Cutaneous Review* 24 (1920): 670; "Sexual Inversion Among Greek Women," *ibid.*, 665–66; McMurtrie, "Principles of Homosexuality and Sexual Inversion in the Female," 145–46; Rivers, "A New Male Homosexual Trait (?)," 22. The wealth of information available did not prevent Freud from misrepresenting Aristophanes' legend of the hermaphrodites (Plato, *Symposium*, 189c–193d) in his *Three Essays*, 2. The original legend explained the creation of what might be described as lesbians and homosexuals (or pedophiles) as well as heterosexuals, but Freud implied that it referred only to the latter.

56. Peter T. Cominos, "Late Victorian Sexual Respectability and the Social System," *International Review of Social History* 8 (1963): 33, 238–40; Smith-Rosenberg, "The Hysterical Woman," 667; Charles Rosenberg, "Sexuality, Class

and Role in Nineteenth Century America," *American Quarterly* 25 (1973): 131–54.

57. Lichtenstein, "The Fairy and the Lady Lover," 374; Krafft-Ebing, "Perversion of the Sexual Instinct: Report of Cases," 565–66.

58. Douglas McMurtrie, "Sexual Inversion Among Women in Spain"; Howard, "Sexual Perversion," 4; Ellis, "Sexual Inversion Among Women," 157.

59. Ellis, *Sexual Inversion*, 209–10.

60. *Ibid.*, 214 (my emphasis; it is extremely uncharacteristic for Ellis to term homosexuality a vice); Douglas McMurtrie, "Record of a French Case of Sexual Inversion," *Maryland Medical Review* 57 (1914): 170–81; "Sexual Inversion Among Women in Spain." Race also plays an important role in sexual ideology, and theories used to stigmatize homosexual relations were used similarly in the case of interracial relations. See, for instance, Charles E. Hughes, "Homo Sexual Complexion Perverts in St. Louis: Note on a Feature of Sexual Psychopathy," *Alienist and Neurologist* 28 (1907): 487–88, which seems to find the interracialism of black and white men found dancing together as disturbing—and pathological—as their homosexuality.

61. Weeks, *Coming Out*, 57–67.

62. Shrady, "Perverted Sexual Instinct," 70; James Kiernan, "Perverted Sexual Instinct," *The Chicago Medical Journal and Examiner* 48 (1884): 264; Kiernan, "Insanity: Sexual Perversion," *Detroit Lancet* 7 (1884): 483.

63. Ellis claimed in 1915 that the frequency of inversion among the near relatives of inverts whose case histories appeared in the literature was "now indisputable" (*Sexual Inversion*, 308).

64. Freud, *Three Essays*, 11–12, note added in 1915.

65. *Ibid.*, esp. pp. 114. Abraham Brill provided the first English translation of this text in 1910, and published an article summarizing the essay on inversion three years later, "The Conception of Homosexuality," *Journal of the American Medical Association* 61 (1913): 335–40. Isadore Coriat's article that year also essentially summarized Freud's essay, "Homosexuality: Its Psychogenesis and Treatment." The American Freudians, and Freud himself, treated male homosexuality almost exclusively in their early writings, as Trigant Burrow pointed out in 1917, "The Genesis and Meaning of 'Homosexuality' and its Relation to the Problem of Introverted Mental States." Freud finally devoted a full essay to the explanation of lesbianism in 1920, "The Psychogenesis of a Case of Homosexuality in a Woman," *The Standard Edition of the Complete Psychological Works of Sigmund Freud,* trans. James Strachey *et al.* (London: 1955), vol. 18, 174–82. An extended analysis of Freudian theories is beyond the scope of this article.

66. Ellis, *Sexual Inversion*, 304–9.

67. C. P. Oberndorf, "Homosexuality," *Medical Record* 46 (1919): 841.

68. Several useful essays on this process appear in Susan Reverby and David Rosner, eds., *Health Care in America: Essays in Social History* (Philadelphia: 1979). See also Michel Foucault, *The History of Sexuality*, I, and the several essays by Carroll Smith-Rosenberg and Charles Rosenberg cited above.

69. Joe L. Dubbert, "Progressivism and the Masculinity Crisis," *Psychoanalytic Review* 61 (1974): 443–55.

70. Harry Braverman, *Labor and Monopoly Capital: The Degradation of Work in the Twentieth Century* (New York: 1974); David Montgomery, *Worker's Control in America* (Cambridge: 1979).

71. Smith-Rosenberg and Rosenberg, "The Female Animal," 332; Aileen Kraditor, *The Ideas of the Woman Suffrage Movement, 1890–1920* (New York: 1971), 12–37.

72. Hamilton, "The Civil Responsibility of Sexual Perverts," 505. "Advanced" was a common codeword for "feminist."

73. Ellis, *Sexual Inversion*, 262.

74. *Ibid.*, 261, n. 3, 262–63. For documents from the German debate, as well as contemporary lesbian literature, see Lillian Faderman and Brigitte Eriksson, eds., *Lesbian-Feminism in Turn-of-the-Century Germany* (Weatherby Lake, Mo.: 1980).

75. Howard, "Effeminate Men and Masculine Women," 687.

76. James Kiernan, "Bisexuality," *Urologic and Cutaneous Review* 18 (1914): 375; Claiborne, "Hypertrichosis in Women," 1183.

77. Howard, "Effeminate Men and Masculine Women," 687.

78. Lydston, "Sexual Perversion, Satyriasis and Nymphomania," 254.

79. Beard, *Sexual Neurasthenia*, 102; Brill, "The Conception of Homosexuality," 335; James Kiernan, "Classification of Homosexuality," *Urologic and Cutaneous Review* 20 (1916): 350.

80. James Kiernan, "Insanity: Sexual Perversion," *Detroit Lancet* 7 (1884): 482; G. Adler Blumer, "A Case of Perverted Sexual Instinct (Conträre Sexualempfindung)," *American Journal of Insanity* 39 (1882): 25. Krafft-Ebing made a similar observation of German "inverts" in "Perversions of the Sexual Instinct: Report of Cases," 570.

81. Michael Gordon, "From an Unfortunate Necessity to a Cult of Mutual Orgasm: Sex in American Marital Literature, 1830–1940," in *The Sociology of Sex*, ed. James Henslin and Edward Sagarin (New York: 1978), 59–84; James McGovern, "The American Woman's Pre–World War I Freedom in Manners and Morals," *Journal of American History* 55 (1968): 315–33. The historical literature on women in this period is thoughtfully reviewed in Estelle B. Freedman, "The New Woman: Changing Views of Women in the 1920s," *Journal of American History* 61 (1974): 372–93.

82. Estelle Freedman, "Separatism as Strategy: Female Institution Building and American Feminism, 1870–1930," *Feminist Studies* 5 (1979): 512–29. The most important works contributing to this argument include Nancy F. Cott, *The Bonds of Womanhood* (New Haven: 1977); Ellen DuBois, "The Radicalism of the Woman Suffrage Movement: Notes Toward the Reconstruction of Nineteenth-Century Feminism," *Feminist Studies* 3 (1975): 63–71; and Blanche Weisen Cook, "Female Support Networks and Political Activism: Lillian Wald, Crystal Eastman, Emma Goldman," in *A Heritage of Her Own*, ed. Nancy F. Cott and Elizabeth H. Pleck (New York: 1979), 412–44.

83. Christina Simmons, "Companionate Marriage and the Lesbian Threat," *Frontiers* 4 (Fall 1979): 54–59. The observers of youth culture were Robert S. Lynd and Helen Merrell Lynd, *Middletown: A Study in American Culture* (New York: 1929), 110. Short autobiographies published in *The Nation* in the 1920s are collected in *These Modern Women*, ed. Elaine Showalter (Old Westbury, N.Y.: 1978). See also J. Stanley Lemons, *The Woman Citizen: Social Feminism in the 1920s* (Urbana: 1975), and Mary Ryan, *Womanhood in America*, 2nd ed. (New York: 1979), 151–82. Discussions in Nancy Cott's seminars at Yale in U.S. women's history also contributed substantially to my thinking on these issues.

84. See, e.g., Henry L. Minton, "Femininity in Men and Masculinity in Women: American Psychiatry and Psychology Portray Homosexuality in the 1930s," *Journal of Homosexuality* 13 (1986): 1–21, which describes the use of masculinity/femininity scales in the psychiatric evaluation of homosexuals by two researchers in the 1930s (although regarding this as a new development rather than a continuation of older patterns of thought).

85. George Chauncey, Jr., "Christian Brotherhood or Sexual Perversion? Homosexual Identities and the Construction of Sexual Boundaries in the World War One Era," *Journal of Social History* 19 (Winter 1985): 189–211.

86. See, e.g., R. W. Shufeldt, who observed that a man he interviewed whom he termed a "loquacious, foul-mouthed and foul-minded 'fairy,'" was "lost to every sense of shame; believing himself designed by nature to play the very part he is playing in life," "Biography of A Passive Pederast," *American Journal of Urology and Sexology* 13 (1917): 457, referring to an interview conducted in 1906.

7

"We Were a Little Band of Willful Women": The Heterodoxy Club of Greenwich Village

Judith Schwarz
Kathy Peiss
Christina Simmons

■ **Historical Introduction**   In the early decades of the twentieth century, Greenwich Village burst upon the national scene as a hotbed of political and cultural ferment. Into this New York City neighborhood poured middle–class women and men fleeing the bourgeois values of their upbringing and seeking radical new ways of thinking and living. In the cafes, bars, and clubs that comprised their social world, Greenwich Villagers developed new modes of political and artistic expression, from *The Masses* magazine to the Paterson pageant of striking silk mill workers. Their commitments ranged from the prosaic to the revolutionary, encompassing feminism, socialism, anarchism and disarmament, as well as demands for women's suffrage, education reform, and an overhaul of municipal politics.

At the same time, the feminists and radicals of Greenwich Village were preoccupied with questions of personal life and social relationships, what would in the 1960s be termed "the politics of the personal." Many Villagers pursued the new psychological and sexual theories of Havelock Ellis, Sigmund Freud, and Edward Carpenter; such figures as Floyd Dell and Margaret Sanger helped to popularize new understandings of female sexuality, heterosexual companionship, and the need for birth control (see Christina Simmons' essay, this volume). Identifying individual self-fulfillment as a legitimate political goal, Villagers experimented with novel social and sexual arrangements that would enhance personal freedom and the meaningfulness of human relationships.

In this world of radical activity, the Heterodoxy Club stands out as among the most innovative and interesting experiments. This "little band of willful women, the most unruly and individualistic you ever fell upon," was founded in 1912 by suffrage leader and minister Marie Jenney Howe. Among its 110 active members during its thirty-year history were such notable feminists and radicals as Charlotte Perkins Gilman, Rose Pastor Stokes, Crystal Eastman, and Elizabeth Gurley Flynn. The roster included leading women doctors, educators, actresses, playwrights, psychologists, writers and radio performers—a cast of the accomplished women of the day.

This "club for unorthodox women" had few formalities: the biweekly luncheons, talks, and debates were occasions for freewheeling, frank yet supportive discussions that were "off the record." Politics, art, and ideas were not the only subjects of conversation, but personal experiences, life histories, and emotions were also revealed in meetings that bear some similarity to the consciousness-raising sessions of the 1960s.

Heterodoxy's members were active in the organized women's movement, particularly the suffrage campaign. Others joined the socialist and labor movements in part as a way to redress the economic inequities that plagued women in the labor force. Most striking, however, are the efforts of Heterodites to rethink the "woman question" and the meaning of feminism in the teens. Marie Jenney Howe and other members of Heterodoxy were among the first to use the term "feminism" in a self-conscious way. To them feminism described a more psychological and cultural idea of women's liberation, one that saw political and economic equality as necessary but not sufficient conditions of women's freedom. Through creative writing and other endeavors, members of Heterodoxy explored women's intellectual and psychological repression, their desire for self-fulfillment, and the historic opening of new experiences and opportunities. And they countered dominant ideas of women's physical and intellectual inferiority and dependency in their work as physicians, lawyers, college teachers, and political activists.

The personal lives of the women of Heterodoxy also embodied their courage and eagerness to challenge the conventional practices of heterosexual marriage and family life that repressed and distorted women's identity. As Judith Schwarz's painstaking research reveals, at least ten and perhaps twenty-four Heterodites were lesbians, some of them living as couples for years. A nascent lesbian subculture seems to have taken form in Greenwich Village in the teens, a subculture experienced in salons, bars, and shared apartments, and articulated in poetry, fiction, and other writing. A strong sense of woman-identification and sisterhood led the heterosexual women in the club to be supportive of its lesbian members in the 1910s, although by the 1920s there are some indications of growing feelings of hostility and fear, spurred by the new Freudian psychoanalytic theory.

The heterosexual members of Heterodoxy also challenged the boundaries of traditional sexual and gender roles. Asserting themselves as sexual beings—and denying the old double standard of sexual morality—some cohabited with men or had a string of affairs. The "new morality" that understood sexual attraction as a vital life force and urged the power of romantic love legitimized behavior that stood outside the conventions of mainstream American society. Other Heterodites married, but fought against the conventional notions of the wife: typically they asserted their economic independence by continuing to pursue their careers; some had "open marriages" or lived in separate residences from their husbands. Divorce rates among married members of Heterodoxy were unusually high for this period.[1]

The following photographs are visual documents of these extraordinary women, who asserted the centrality of feminist principles in their lives, challenged the sexual conventions that uphold male dominance, and experimented with radical new ways of thinking and living. These lives Judith Schwarz has lovingly recovered for us.

—*Kathy Peiss*

■ **Introduction to the Photo Essay**   In 1920 the members of Heterodoxy put together a remarkable photograph album as a Christmas gift to founder Marie Jenney Howe. Each member was apparently asked to contribute a photograph and a short tribute to Marie on the importance of Heterodoxy in their lives. The cover page, entitled "Heterodoxy to Marie" and written in lovely script with a hand-colored purple H, is one of the most moving visual documents of women's friendship and sisterhood I've ever seen. On first viewing the album in 1976, turning page after page of strong women's faces, "the kind men put on cameos or coins," and reading the loving, often very funny, touching, and sometimes cryptic inscriptions, I was inspired to begin the long search for information on the political, social, and personal histories of the women of Heterodoxy. Out of that effort came a book, now in its second printing, and a slide show that has been presented to about 200 colleges and organizations. Each roomful of people who have seen the slide show, whether in groups of twenty or 400, has felt the same response: delight in the evocative images, surprise that such incredibly diverse and powerful women held together in a group for over thirty years, and amazement that Heterodoxy's existence is so little known.

Each member chose a photograph (and in some cases, a cartoon) of herself and wrote a poem or inscription on her page. This makes the book a remarkable act of self-representation. While some simply chose their latest publicity photograph to present an image of their public "self," others selected images that conveyed a sense of the meaning Heterodoxy had given their lives. The clothing in the photographs reflects styles from 1890 to 1920.

This photographic record of the club represents a remarkable relationship among women. "It is the aim of women not to hate, but to love one another," observed the members of Heterodoxy to Marie Jenney Howe in the album's preface. "To realize the spirit of these words is one of the emotional treasures of life which all women desire, many of them fear, some of them seek, and a few of them find. We owe it chiefly to you that we may count ourselves among the fortunate finders."

—*Judith Schwarz*

■ Note

1. For the most complete portrait of Heterodoxy, see Judith Schwarz, *Radical Feminists of Heterodoxy, Greenwich Village, 1912–1940* (Norwich, Vermont: 1986). The history of feminism in the period is recounted in Nancy Cott's *The Grounding of Modern Feminism* (New Haven: 1987).

Marie Jenney and a friend posed together in the 1880s while she was recuperating from a lengthy illness in her youth, long before she studied for the Unitarian ministry, married Progressive lawyer Frederic Howe, and became a suffrage leader. Unless otherwise noted, all photographs in this chapter appear courtesy of The Schlesinger Library, Radcliffe College.

Hello Maria! It's plain to see
That friends have not deserted thee
The joy is writ upon your phiz
So here comes Lou and here comes Liz
With their glad gimmicks
Treat them well — And then
All troubles go to Hell —

Elizabeth Watson
Lou Rogers

Cartoonist Lou Rogers refused to submit a photograph. On her own page, she glued a copy of her hand-drawn newsletter for fans who wrote in about her pioneering radio program on animals. On lawyer Elizabeth Watson's page, Lou drew this cartoon of herself as a small elfin creature with whip and her friend Elizabeth as a giantess with fur muff, walking along in a daze, surrounded by whimsical dogs and a chicken.

Clipping courtesy of the Library of Congress.

"Her Legal Status" cartoon by Lou Rogers, Birth Control Review, May 1919, p. 9. Courtesy of the Library of Congress.

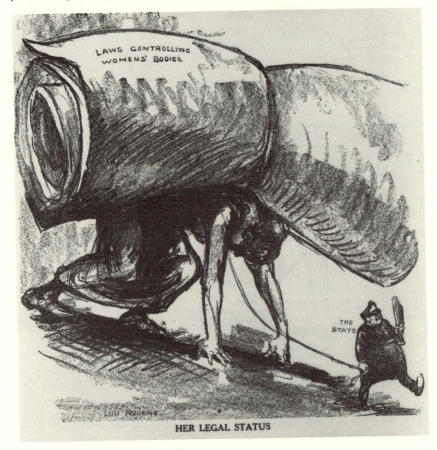

HER LEGAL STATUS

This was the only group photograph in the 1920 Heterodoxy album, probably taken as they waited to march down Fifth Avenue in the 1912 or 1913 suffrage march. Note woman selling Woman Voter *newspaper.*

Elizabeth Gurley Flynn was one of the few working-class members of Heterodoxy. She was a labor organizer, member of the Industrial Workers of the World, and later a leader of the Communist Party. Divorced, with one son, she had a free love relationship with anarchist Carlo Tresca, and a lesbian relationship with Marie Equi, a radical physician.

Rose Pastor Stokes' photograph captures her pensive, almost bitter response to America's growing conservatism. The members of Heterodoxy had suffered greatly under the anti-peace, anti-left, pro-war government actions during the First World War and Red Scare. A writer for the Jewish Daily News and married to James Phelps Stokes, she left socialism to help found the American Communist Party.

Daughter of Progressive Party leader and U.S. Senator Robert La Follette, and considered almost a member of the family by Marie and Fred Howe, Fola La Follette became an actress on Broadway and a noted suffrage speaker. She married playwright George Middleton, but never used his name. Fola found sanctuary among the Heterodoxy members during the height of World War I's anti–La Follette hysteria, when her father was accused of being pro-German.

(above right)
The formidable Henrietta Rodman was a pivotal force in 1910s Greenwich Village. Suffragist, teacher, founder of the Feminist Alliance, she also organized a Village Branch of the Liberal Club after the original Club refused to allow black members. Fashion was of little importance to her; so much so that she practiced nudism at home until she caught too many colds.

Suffragist and birth control advocate Mary Ware Dennett's strong chin and eyeglasses make this an unusually forceful studio photograph. She was arrested and tried on morals charges after writing a pamphlet explaining the facts of life to her two teenage sons.

Caroline Singer is here seated among tribal elders on one of her anthropology field trips. Later in life, she headed the Radcliffe Institute, one of the first women's research centers.

Journalist and later radio show host, Bessie Beatty chose a snapshot taken when she was reporting on the Russian Revolution for the Hearst newspapers.

Life is a series of humps —
But Heterdoxy is delightful.
Mary Knoblauch.

Mary Knoblauch chose a tourist snapshot atop a camel in the Middle East above her simple
but heartfelt inscription.

■ Conventional Female Portraiture and . . .

Journalist, author, and playwright, Zona Gale was a socialist and member of the National Woman's Party. She adopted two daughters and married at age 53.

■ Tensions in the Image

Although this photograph of Grace Nail Johnson is a highly unusual and very tailored view of one of Harlem's most prominent black women, it nevertheless conveys some elements of conventional femininity. Married to poet James Weldon Johnson and herself active in the National Association for the Advancement of Colored People (NAACP), she became Heterodoxy's only black member in 1918.

Feminist author Charlotte Perkins Gilman dropped her membership in Heterodoxy over a disagreement with the more pacifist members during World War I. However, she still contributed her photograph as well as an admiring poem to "Queen Marie."

Katharine Anthony is seated at her desk, possibly writing one of her biographies of famous women like Margaret Fuller or Catherine the Great. She and her lover Elisabeth Irwin called themselves "the gay ladies of Gaylordsville," in reference to their summer home in Connecticut.

■ The Modernist Manner

Crystal Eastman co-edited the radical magazine The Masses *with her brother Max, founded the Women's Peace Party, and was hounded by J. Edgar Hoover's government agents during the first "Red Scare" after World War I.*

■ Bohemian Style

Suffragist Inez Haynes Irwin was unofficial club historian. Her many novels, short stories, and articles were eclipsed by her monumental account of "The Story of the Woman's Party." The 1920 Heterodoxy club album is preserved among her papers at the Schlesinger Library at Radcliffe College.

Attorney Ida Rauh, Max Eastman's first wife and a Provincetown Playhouse actress, chose a theatrically sensuous publicity portrait to represent her in the album.

132

■ Invincible Lesbians

Dr. Sara Josephine Baker, renowned head of the New York Bureau of Child Hygiene, said she was "drawn by psychological suction" into the suffrage movement. She chose her most professional and solemn image.

(below left)
New York Board of Education speaker and socialist Myran Louise Grant had a strong boyish look and a remarkable taste in ties.

Ida Wylie, better known as novelist and screenwriter I. A. R. Wylie, was an Australian who became friends with Radclyffe Hall and Una Troubridge while in her first lesbian relationship in London before World War I. She met Dr. Sara Josephine ("Jo") Baker in 1920. In the 1930s Wylie, Baker, and Dr. Louise Pearce (famed discoverer of the African sleeping sickness virus) began housekeeping together in Princeton, New Jersey. This was before her book Keeper of the Flame became a movie starring Katherine Hepburn and Spencer Tracy.

■ Playing with Gendered Appearance

Paula Jacobi was a prison guard at Framingham Women's Prison in Massachusetts during her own arrest and imprisonment as a suffrage picket at the White House in 1917. One of Marie Howe's closest friends, she was lovers with Anna Van Vechten for fourteen years.

(below left)
Anne Herendeen was a journalist and editor of the 1917 Women's Peace Party's journal Four Lights. *She chose an informal and relaxed image for the club album.*

Stockbroker Kathleen de Vere Taylor chose to include this strikingly handsome informal snapshot of herself wearing a riding habit. Taylor was one of several lesbians who chose photographs taken by friends and lovers.

■ Playfulness

Margaret Wycherly, presumably dressed for one of her many stage and screen roles, was one of the best known actresses among the Heterodites. Among her credits were the movies Sergeant York *(1941) and* Keeper of the Flame *(1943).*

Socialist and writer Frances Maule chose this Peter Pan image for her contribution to the 1920 album. Years later, she made the only addition to the album with a street photographer's snapshot of her striding through downtown Manhattan.

■ Free Spirits

A wonderfully informal snapshot of Elisabeth Irwin, founder of the progressive "Little Red Schoolhouse," which is still active in Greenwich Village. This was probably taken by her lover Katharine Anthony, as they picnicked with their dog. The two women adopted and raised five children.

Sociologist, anthropologist, folklorist, and prolific author, Elsie Clews Parsons chose a snapshot from her last visit to New Mexico.

Salutation

Heterodites, yuletide greetings!
At this season of gifts,
Shall I tell you what gifts you bestow on me,
As we sit at the long tables,
And the years slip along?
Gifts intangible and imponderable,
Yet bright with reality?

For there is no subtler pleasure
Than to know minds capable
Of performing the complete act of thought.
There is no keener joy than to see
Clear-cut human faces, —
Faces like those men choose
For coins, and cameos.

Leta S. Hollingworth

Leta Hollingworth, pioneer educational psychologist, wrote an especially moving tribute to the "Heterodites."

8

The Black Community and the Birth Control Movement

Jessie M. Rodrique

The decline in black fertility rates from the late nineteenth century to World War II has been well documented. In these years the growth rate of the black population was more than cut in half. By 1945 the average number of children per woman was 2.5, and the degree of childlessness, especially among urban blacks, had reached unprecedented proportions. Researchers who explain this phenomenon insist that contraception played a minimal role, believing that blacks had no interest in the control of their own fertility. This belief also affects the interpretation of blacks' involvement in the birth control movement, which has been understood as a movement that was thrust upon an unwilling black population.

This essay seeks to understand these two related issues differently. First, I maintain that black women were, in fact, interested in controlling their fertility and that the low birth rates reflect in part a conscious use of birth control. Second, by exploring the birth control movement among blacks at the grassroots level, I show that despite the racist ideology that operated at the national level, blacks were active and effective participants in the establishment of local clinics and in the birth control debate, as they related birth control to issues of race and gender. Third, I show that despite black cooperation with white birth control groups, blacks maintained a degree of independence that allowed the organization for birth control in their communities to take a qualitatively different form.

Demographers in the post–World War I years accounted for the remarkable decline in black fertility in terms of biological factors. Fears of "dysgenic" population trends coupled with low birth rates among native, white Americans underlay their investigations of black fertility. Population scholars ignored contraception as a factor in the birth decline even as late as 1938. Instead, they focused upon the "health hypothesis," arguing that the fertility drop resulted from general poor health, especially sterility caused by venereal disease. While health conditions seem likely to have had some effect, there is no reason to exclude contraceptive use as an additional cause, especially when evidence of contraceptive knowledge and practice is abundant.[1]

In drawing their conclusions, researchers also made many questionable and unfounded assumptions about the sexuality of blacks. In one large study of family limitation, for example, black women's lower contraceptive use was attributed to the belief that "the negro generally exercises less prudence and foresight than white people do in all sexual matters."[2] Nor is the entire black population represented in many of these studies. Typically their sample consists of women whose economic status is defined as either poor or very poor and who are either illiterate or who have had very little education. Population experts' ideological bias and research design have tended to foreclose the possibility of Afro-American agency, and thus conscious use of contraception.[3]

Historians who have chronicled the birth control movement have focused largely on the activities and evolution of the major birth control organizations and leading birth control figures, usually at the national level. None have interpreted the interests of the movement as particularly beneficial to blacks. Linda Gordon, in her pathbreaking book, *Woman's Body, Woman's Right*, focused on the 1939 "Negro Project," established by the Birth Control Federation of America (BCFA) as a conservative, elitist effort designed "to stabilize existing social relations." Gordon claims that the birth control movement in the south was removed from socially progressive politics and unconnected to any analysis of women's rights, civil rights, or poverty, exemplifying the movement's male domination and professionalization over the course of the twentieth century. Other historians concur, asserting that birth control was "genocidal" and "anathema" to black women's interests, and that the movement degenerated into a campaign to "keep the unfit from reproducing themselves." Those who note its presence within the black community in a slightly more positive light, qualify their statements by adding the disclaimer that support and information for its dissemination came only from the black elite and were not part of a grassroots movement.[4]

There is, however, an ample body of evidence that suggests the importance of birth control use among blacks. Contraceptive methods and customs among Africans as well as nineteenth-century slaves have been well documented. For example, folklorists and others have discovered "alum water" as one of many birth control measures in early twentieth-century southern rural communities. The author of a study of two rural counties of Georgia noted the use of birth control practices there and linked it to a growing race pride. In urban areas a "very common" and distinctive practice among blacks was to place Vaseline and quinine over the mouth of the uterus. It was widely available and purchased very cheaply in drugstores.[5]

The black press was also an abundant source of birth control information. The *Pittsburgh Courier*, for example, carried numerous mail order advertisements for douche powder, suppositories, preventative antiseptics, and vaginal jellies that "destroyed foreign germs."[6] A particularly interesting mail order ad was for a product called "Puf," a medicated douche powder and applicator that claimed to be a "new guaranteed method of administering marriage hygiene." It had a sketch of a calendar with the words "End Calendar Worries Now!" written across it and a similar sketch that read "Tear-Up Your Calendar, Do Not Worry, Use Puf." The instructions for its use indicate euphemistically that Puf should be used "first," meaning before intercourse, and that it was good for hours, leaving little doubt that this product was fully intended to be used as a birth control device.[7]

Advertisements for mail order douches are significant since they appear to reflect a practice that was widespread and well documented among black women. Studies conducted in the mid-thirties overwhelmingly concluded that douching was the preferred method of contraception used by black couples. Yet contemporary researchers neglected to integrate this observation into their understanding of the fertility decline since they insisted that douching was an "ineffective contraceptive." However ineffective the means, the desire for birth control in the black community was readily apparent, as George Schuyler, editor of the *National Negro News*, explained: "If anyone should doubt the desire on the part of Negro women and men to limit their families it is only necessary to note the large sale of preventive devices sold in every drug store in various Black Belts."[8]

Within the black community the practice of abortion was commonly cited by black leaders and professionals as contributing to the low birth rates. Throughout the twenties and thirties the black press reported many cases of abortions that had ended in death or the arrest of doctors who had performed them. Abortion was discussed in the *Pittsburgh Courier* in 1930 in a fictionalized series entitled "Bad Girl," which dealt with a range of attitudes toward childbearing among Harlem blacks. When Dot, the main character, discovers she is pregnant, she goes to a friend who works in a drugstore. The author writes:

> Pat's wonderful remedy didn't help. Religiously Dot took it and each night when Eddie came home she sadly admitted that success had not crowned her efforts. "All that rotten tasting stuff just to keep a little crib out of the bedroom." After a week she was tired of medicine and of baths so hot that they burned her skin.[9]

Next, she sought the advice of a friend who told her that she would have to have "an operation" and knew of a doctor who would do it for fifty dollars.

The *Baltimore Afro-American* observed that pencils, nails, and hat pins were the instruments commonly used for self-induced abortions and the *Birth Control Review* wrote in 1936 that rural black women in Georgia drank turpentine for the same purpose. The use of turpentine as an abortifacient is significant since it is derived from evergreens, a source similar to rue and camphor, both of which were reported by a medical authority in 1860 to have been used with some success by southern slaves. Although statistics for abortions among black women are scarce, a 1938 medical study reported that twenty-eight percent or 211 of 730 black women interviewed said that they had had one or more abortions. A black doctor from Nashville in 1940 asserted in the *Baltimore Afro-American* that abortions among black women were deliberate, not only the result of syphilis and other diseases: "In the majority of cases it is used as a means of getting rid of unwanted children."[10]

These data, while somewhat impressionistic, indicate that a number of contraceptive methods were available to blacks. Many were, and still are, discounted as ineffective "folk methods."[11] There was, however, a discernible consciousness that guided the fertility decline. A discourse on birth control emerged in the years from 1915 to 1945. As blacks migrated within and out of the south to northern cities, they began to articulate the reasons for limiting fertility. It is here that one begins to see how interconnected the issue of birth control was to many facets of black life. For women, it was linked to changes in their status, gender roles within the family, attitudes toward motherhood and sexuality, and, at times, feminism. Birth control was also integral to issues of economics, health, race relations, and racial progress.

In these years blacks contributed to the "official" nationwide debate concerning birth control while also voicing their particular concerns. Frequent coverage was given to birth control in the black press. Newspapers championed the cause of birth control when doctors were arrested for performing abortions. They also carried editorials in favor of birth control, speeches of noted personalities who favored its use, and occasionally sensationalized stories on the desperate need for birth control. Often, the topic of birth control as well as explicit birth control information was transmitted orally, through public lectures and debates. It was also explored in fiction, black periodicals, and several issues of the *Birth Control Review* dedicated to blacks.[12]

Economic themes emerged in the birth control discourse as it related to issues of black family survival. Contraceptive use was one of a few economic strategies available to blacks, providing a degree of control within the context of the family economy. Migrating families who left behind the economy of the rural south used birth control to "preserve their new economic independence," as did poor families who were "compelled" to limit their numbers of children. A 1935 study of Harlem reiterated this same point, adding that the low birth rates of urban blacks reflected a "deliberate limitation of families." Another strategy used by black couples for the same purpose was postponing marriage. Especially in the years of the Depression, birth control was seen as a way to improve general living conditions by allowing more opportunities for economic gain.[13]

Birth control was also linked to the changing status of black women and the role they were expected to play in the survival of the race. On this issue a degree of opposition to birth control surfaced. Some, most notably black nationalist leader Marcus Garvey, believed that the future of the black race was contingent upon increasing numbers and warned that birth control would lead to racial extinction. Both Garveyites and Catholic church officials warned that birth control interfered with the "course of nature" and God's will.[14]

These issues were evident in an exchange between the journalist J. A. Rogers and Dean Kelly Miller of Howard University in 1925. Writing in *The Messenger*, Rogers took Miller to task for his statements concerning the emancipation of black women. Miller is quoted as saying that black women had strayed too far from children, kitchen, clothes, and the church. Miller, very aware that black women had been having fewer children, cautioned against race suicide. Using the "nature" argument of Garvey and the Catholic church, he argued that the biological function of women was to bear and rear children. He stated, "The liberalization of women must always be kept within the boundary fixed by nature." Rogers strongly disagreed with Miller, saying that the move of black women away from domesticity and childbearing was a positive sign. Rogers wrote, "I give the Negro woman credit if she endeavors to be something other than a mere breeding machine. Having children is by no means the sole reason for being."[15]

Other black leaders supported this progressive viewpoint. In his 1919 essay "The Damnation of Women," W. E. B. Du Bois wrote that "the future woman must have a life work and future independence. . . . She must have knowledge . . . and she must have the right of motherhood at her own discretion."[16] In a later essay he described those who would confine women to childbearing as "reactionary barbarians."[17] Doctor Charles Garvin, writing in 1932, believed that it was the "inalienable right of every married woman to use any physiologically sound precaution against reproduction she deems justifiable."[18]

Black women also expressed the need for contraception as they articulated their feelings about motherhood and sexuality. Black women's fiction and poetry in the years from 1916 to the early thirties frequently depicted women who refused to bring children into a racist world and expressed their outrage at laws that prevented access to birth control information. Nella Larsen, for example, in her 1928 novella *Quicksand*, explored the debilitating physical and emotional problems resulting from excessive childbearing in a society that demanded that women's sexual expression be inextricably linked to marriage and procreation.[19]

Others spoke of the right not to have children in terms that were distinctly feminist. For example, a character in the *Courier* serial "Bad Girl" put it this way: "The hospitals are wide open to the woman who wants to have a baby, but to the woman who doesn't want one—that's a different thing. High prices, fresh doctors. It's a man's world, Dot. The woman who wants to keep her body from pain and her mind from worry is an object of contempt."[20] The changing status of women and its relation to childbearing were also addressed in Jessie Fauset's 1931 novel, *The Chinaberry Tree*. Fauset's male characters asserted the need for large families and a "definite place" for women in the home. The female character, however, remained unconvinced by this opinion. She had "the modern girl's own clear ideas on birth control."[21]

Other writers stressed the need for birth control in terms of racial issues and how birth control could be used to alleviate the oppressive circumstances of the black community. For example, Chandler Owen, editor of *The Messenger*, wrote a piece for the 1919 edition of the *Birth Control Review* entitled "Women and Children of the South." He advocated birth control because he believed that general improvements in material conditions would follow from fewer children. Observing that young black women in peonage camps were frequently raped and impregnated by their white overseers, Owen also linked involuntary maternity to racial crimes.[22]

The advocacy of birth control for racial progress occurred most frequently during the Depression, and it helped to mobilize community support for clinics. Newell Sims of Oberlin College, for example, urged that birth control for blacks would be a "step toward independence and greater power" in his 1931 essay "A New Technique in Race Relations." In his opinion a controlled birth rate would free more resources for advancement. The black press hailed the essay as "revolutionary."[23] Other advocates insisted that all blacks, but especially poor blacks, become involved in the legislative process to legalize birth control. It was imperative that the poor be included in the movement since they were the ones most injured by its prohibition. One black newspaper, the *San Francisco Spokesman*, promoted a very direct and activist role for blacks on this issue. "To legalize birth control, you and I should make expressed attitudes on this question a test of every candidate's fitness for legislative office," it argued in 1934. "And those who refuse or express a reactionary opinion should be flatly and uncompromisingly rejected."[24]

For many blacks birth control was not a panacea but one aspect of a larger political agenda. Unlike some members of the white community who myopically looked to birth control as a cure-all for the problems of blacks, most blacks instead described it as a program that would "modify one cause of their unfavorable situation."[25] They stressed that true improvement could come only through the "equalization of economic and social opportunities."[26] Newell L. Sims summed up this position most eloquently in his 1932 essay "Hostages to the White Man." It was a viewpoint stressed well into the forties by numerous and leading members of the black community. He wrote:

> The negro in America is a suppressed class and as such must struggle for existence under every disadvantage and handicap. Although in three generations since slavery he has in many ways greatly improved his condition, his economic, social and political status still remain that of a dominated exploited minority. His problem is, therefore, just what it has been for three quarters of a century, i.e., how to better his position in the social order. Naturally in all his strivings he has found no panacea for his difficulties, for there is none. The remedies must be as numerous and varied as the problem is complex. Obviously he needs to employ every device that will advance his cause. I wish briefly to urge the merits of birth control as one means.[27]

Many also insisted that birth control be integrated into other health care provisions and not be treated as a separate "problem." E. S. Jamison, for example, writing in the *Birth Control Review* in 1938 on the "Future of Negro Health," exhorted blacks to "present an organized front" so that birth control and other needed health services could be made available to them. Yet he too, like Sims, emphasized independence from the white community. He wrote that "the Negro must do for himself. Charity will not better his condition in the long run."[28]

Blacks also took an important stand against sterilization, especially in the thirties. Scholars have not sufficiently recognized this point: that blacks could endorse a program of birth control but reject the extreme views of eugenicists, whose programs for birth control and sterilization often did not distinguish between the two. The *Pittsburgh Courier*, for example, whose editorial policy clearly favored birth control, was also active in the anti-sterilization movement. It asserted in several editorials that blacks should oppose the sterilization programs being advanced by eugenicists and so-called scientists because they were being waged against the weak, the oppressed, and the disfranchised. Candidates for sterilization were likely to be those on relief, the unemployed, and the homeless, all victims of a vicious system of economic exploitation. Du Bois shared this viewpoint. In his column in the *Courier* in 1936 he wrote, "the thing we want to watch is the so-called eugenic sterilization." He added that the burden of such programs would "fall upon colored people and it behooves us to watch the law and the courts and stop the spread of the habit." The *San Francisco Spokesman* in 1934 called upon black clubwomen to become active in the anti-sterilization movement.[29]

Participation in the birth control debate was only one aspect of the black community's involvement; black women and men also were active in the establishment of birth control clinics. From 1925 to 1945 clinics for blacks appeared nationwide, many of which were at least partly directed and sponsored by local black community organizations. Many of the organizations had a prior concern with health matters, creating an established network of social welfare centers, health councils, and agencies. Thus, birth control services were often integrated into a community through familiar channels.[30]

In Harlem the black community showed an early and sustained interest in the debate over birth control, taking a vanguard role in agitation for birth control clinics. In 1918 the Women's Political Association of Harlem, calling upon black women to "assume the reins of leadership in the political, social and economic life of their people," announced that its lecture series would include birth control among the topics for discussion.[31] In March of 1923 the Harlem Community Forum invited Margaret Sanger to speak to them at the Library Building in the Bronx, and in 1925 the Urban League made a request to the American Birth Control League that a clinic be established in the Columbus Hill section of the city.

Although this clinic proved unsuccessful, another clinic, supported by the Urban League and the Birth Control Clinical Research Bureau, opened a Harlem branch in 1929. This particular clinic, affiliated with Margaret Sanger, had an advisory board of approximately fifteen members, including Harlem-based journalists, physicians, social workers, and ministers. There was apparently very little opposition to the work of this clinic, even among the clergy. One minister on the advisory board, William Lloyd Imes of the St. James Presbyterian Church, reported that he had held discussions on birth control at his church; at another meeting he announced that if a birth control pamphlet were printed, he would place it in the church vestibule. Another clergyman, the Reverend Shelton Hale Bishop, wrote to Sanger in 1931 that he believed birth control to be "one of the boons of the age to human welfare."[32] The Reverend Adam Clayton Powell of the Abyssinian Baptist Church both endorsed birth control and spoke at public meetings where he denounced the "false modesty" surrounding questions of sex. Ignorance, he believed, led to unwanted pregnancies among young girls.[33]

Support for birth control clinics by black community organizations was also apparent in other locations throughout the country. Their activism took various forms. In Baltimore, for example, a white birth control clinic had begun to see blacks in 1928. In 1935 the black community began organizing and by 1938 the Northwest Health Center was established, sponsored and staffed by blacks. The Baltimore Urban League played a key role in its initial organization, and the sponsoring committee of the clinic was composed of numerous members of Baltimore's black community, including ministers, physicians, nurses, social workers, teachers, housewives, and labor leaders.[34]

In Richmond, Fredericksburg, and Lynchburg, Virginia, local maternal welfare groups raised funds for expenses and supplies for the birth control clinics at the Virginia Medical College and the Hampton Institute, and publicized birth control services at city health departments. And in West Virginia, the Maternal and Child Health Council, formed in 1938, was the first statewide birth control organization sponsored by blacks.[35]

Local clubs and women's organizations often took part in either sponsoring birth control clinics or bringing the topic to the attention of the local community. In New York these included the Inter-Racial Forum of Brooklyn, the Women's Business and Professional Club of Harlem, the Social Workers Club of Harlem, the Harlem branch of the National Organization of Colored Graduate Nurses, the Harlem YWCA, and the Harlem Economic Forum. In Oklahoma City fourteen black women's clubs sponsored a birth control clinic for black women, directed by two black physicians and one black clubwoman. The Mother's Health Association of the District of Columbia reported to the *Birth Control Review* in 1938 that they were cooperating with black organizations that wanted to start a clinic of their own.[36]

Clinics in other cities were located in black community centers and churches. For example, the Kentucky Birth Control League in 1936 reported that one of the clinics in Louisville was located in the Episcopal Church for Colored People and was operated by a Negro staff. The Cincinnati Committee on Maternal Health reported in 1939 the opening of a second black clinic where a black physician and nurse would work.[37]

Community centers and settlement houses were also part of the referral network directing blacks to birth control services. The Mother's Health Office in Boston received clients from the Urban League, the Robert Gould Shaw House, and the Harriet Tubman House. The Henry Street Settlement sent women to the Harlem clinic, and the Booker T. Washington Community Center in San Francisco directed black women to the birth control clinic in that city. In 1935 the Indiana Birth Control League reported that black clients were directed to them from the Flanner House Settlement for Colored People.[38]

In 1939 the Birth Control Federation of America (BCFA) established a Division of Negro Service and sponsored pilot clinics in Nashville, Tennessee, and Berkeley County, South Carolina. The Division consisted of a national advisory council of thirty-five black leaders, a national sponsoring committee of 500 members who coordinated state and local efforts, and administrative and field personnel. The project in Nashville was integrated into the public health services and located in the Bethlehem center, a black social service settlement, and the Fisk University Settlement House. Both clinics were under the direction of black doctors and nurses. The program was also supplemented by nine black public health nurses who made home visits and performed general health services including birth control. The home visits served the large numbers of women who worked as domestics and could not attend the clinics during the day; 5,000 home visits were made in Nashville in a two-year period. In South Carolina, clinic sessions providing both medical care and birth control services were held eleven times each month at different locations in the county for rural women, seventy percent of whom were black.[39]

Simultaneously with the development of these two projects, the BCFA launched an educational campaign to inform and enlist the services of black health professionals, civic groups, and women's clubs. While professional groups are often credited with being the sole source of birth control agitation, the minutes and newsletters of the Division of Negro Service reveal an enthusiastic desire among a broad cross-section of the black community to lend its support for birth control. In fact, black professional groups often worked closely with community groups and other "non-professionals" to make birth control information widely available. For example, the National Medical Association, an organization of black physicians, held public lectures on birth control in conjunction with local groups beginning in 1929, and when birth control was discussed at annual meetings their otherwise private sessions were opened up to social workers, nurses, and teachers. The National Association of Colored Graduate Nurses, under the direction of Mabel Staupers, was especially active in birth control work. Cooperation was offered by several state and local nursing, hospital, and dental associations. One nurse responded to Staupers' request for help with the distribution of birth control information by writing, "I shall pass the material out, we will discuss it in our meetings and I will distribute exhibits at pre-natal clinics at four health centers and through Negro Home Demonstration Clubs."

The participation of Negro Home Demonstration Clubs in birth control work is significant because it is an entirely overlooked and potentially rich source for the grassroots spread of birth control information in the rural South. Home Demonstration Clubs grew out of the provisions of the Smith-Lever Cooperative Extension Act of 1914 and had, by the early twenties, evolved into clubs whose programs stressed health and sanitation. The newsletter of the Division of Negro Service in 1941 reported that five rural State Negro Agricultural and Home Demonstration Agents offered full cooperation with the division. The newsletter included the response of H. C. Ray of Little Rock, Arkansas. He wrote, "We have more than 13,000 rural women working in home demonstration clubs. . . it is in this connection that I feel our organization might work hand in hand with you in bringing about some very definite and desirable results in your phase of community improvement work. We will be glad to distribute any literature." Also involved with rural birth control education were several tuberculosis associations and the Jeanes Teachers, educators funded by the Anna T. Jeanes foundation for improving rural black schools.[40]

Other groups showed interest in the programs of the Division of Negro Service either by requesting birth control speakers for their conventions or by distributing literature to their members. Similar activities were conducted by the Virginia Federation of Colored Women's Clubs, which represented 400 women's clubs, the Negro Organization Society of Virginia, the National Negro Business League, the National Negro Housewives League, the Pullman Porters, the Elks, the Harlem Citizens City-Wide Committee, and the Social Action Committee of Boston's South End. In 1944, for example, the NAACP and a black boilermakers' union distributed Planned Parenthood clinic cards in their mailings to their California members. Twenty-one Urban Leagues in sixteen states as of 1943 actively cooperated with the BCFA in the display of exhibits, distribution of literature, the promotion of local clinical service, and adult community education programs. These national and local black organizations advocated birth control as one aspect of a general program of health, education, and economic development in the late thirties and early forties.[41]

Even in their cooperation with the BCFA, leading members of the black community stressed their own concerns and disagreements with the overall structure of the birth control movement. Their comments reveal important differences in orientation. At a meeting of the National Advisory Council of the Division of Negro Service in 1942, members of the council made it clear that birth control services and information must be distributed to the community *as* a community. Their goal was one of inclusion; members stated that they were disturbed at the emphasis on doctors, and that teachers, ministers, and other community members must be utilized in birth control work. Even the black physicians on the council stressed the need for keeping midwives, volunteers, and especially women practitioners involved in the movement and suggested that mobile clinics traveling throughout the rural South distribute birth control and other needed health services. This approach to birth control diverged significantly from the conservative strategy of the white BCFA leadership, which insisted that birth control services be dispensed by private, individual physicians. Black physicians, it seems, were more sensitive to the general health needs of their population and more willing to experiment with the delivery of birth control services. They favored the integration of birth control into public health services while many white physicians were opposed.[42]

Others on the council stated that black women could be reached only through community organizations that they trusted, and they stressed again the necessity of not isolating birth control as a special interest to the neglect of other important health needs. Still others pointed to the need for birth control representatives who recognized social differences among urban blacks.

At the level of clinic attendance, clinicians also observed a difference between white and black patrons. Black women, they noted, were much more likely to spread the word about birth control services and bring their relatives and friends to the clinics. Some rural women even thought of "joining" the clinic as they might join a community organization. A white woman, however, was more likely to keep the information to herself and attend the clinic alone. A statistician from the Census Bureau supported this observation when he speculated in 1931 that "grapevine dissemination" of birth control information contributed to low black birth rates. These reports are a testimony to the effectiveness of working-class black women's networks.[43]

Moreover, many local birth control groups were often able to maintain independence from the Planned Parenthood Federation of America (PPFA) even though they accepted and used PPFA's display and educational materials. This situation was evident at the Booker T. Washington community center in San Francisco. A representative from PPFA had sent this center materials and then did not hear from anyone for some time. After almost one year the director of the Washington center wrote back to PPFA, informing the staff that birth control programs were flourishing in the center's area. In fact, the group had used the Federation's materials extensively at community centers and civic clubs, and the local black sorority, Alpha Kappa Alpha, had accepted sponsorship of a mothers' health clinic. The PPFA representative described this situation as typical of many black groups. They would not respond to PPFA communications, but would use PPFA materials and be actively engaged in their own form of community birth control work.[44]

In a speech delivered to PPFA in 1942 Dr. Dorothy Ferebee, a black physician and leader, stated, "It is well for this organization to realize that the Negro at his present advanced stage of development is increasingly interested more in programs that are worked out with and by him than in those worked out for him."[45] This statement reveals a fundamental difference in the goals and strategies of the black and white communities. In the past scholars have interpreted the birth control movement as a racist and elitist set of programs imposed on the black population. While this may describe the intentions of the national white leadership, it is important to recognize that the black community had its own agenda in the creation of programs to include and reach wide segments of the black population.

As this essay demonstrates, black women used their knowledge of "folk methods" and other available methods to limit their childbearing. The dramatic fertility decline from 1880 to 1945 is evidence of their success.

Moreover, the use of birth control was pivotal to many pressing issues within the black community. The right to control one's own fertility emerged simultaneously with changing attitudes toward women in both the black and white communities that recognized their rights as individuals and not only their roles as mothers. And these changing attitudes contributed to the dialogue within the black community about the future of the family and strategies for black survival. Birth control also emerged as part of a growing race consciousness, as blacks saw birth control as one means of freeing themselves from the oppression and exploitation of white society through the improvement of their health and their economic and social status. Birth control was also part of a growing process of politicization. Blacks sought to make it a legislative issue, they opposed the sterilization movement, and they took an active and often independent role in supporting their clinics, educating their communities, and tailoring programs to fit their own needs. In their ideology and practice blacks were indeed a vital and assertive part of the larger birth control movement. What appears to some scholars of the birth control movement as the waning of the movement's original purposes during the 1920s and 1930s was within the black community a period of growing ferment and support for birth control. The history of the birth control movement, and the participation of black Americans in it, must be reexamined in this light.

■ Notes

1. Reynolds Farley, *Growth of the Black Population* (Chicago: 1970), 3, 75; Stanley Engerman, "Changes in Black Fertility, 1880–1940," in *Family and Population in Nineteenth Century America,* ed. Tamara K. Hareven and Maris A. Vinovskis (Princeton: 1978), ch. 3. For an excellent review of the demographic literature, see Joseph McFalls and George Masnick, "Birth Control and the Fertility of the U.S. Black Population, 1880 to 1980," *Journal of Family History* 6 (1981): 89–106; Peter Uhlenberg, "Negro Fertility Patterns in the United States," *Berkeley Journal of Sociology* 11 (1966): 56; James Reed, *From Private Vice to Public Virtue* (New York: 1978), ch. 14.

2. Raymond Pearl, "Contraception and Fertility in 2,000 Women," *Human Biology* 4 (1932): 395.

3. McFalls and Masnick, "Birth Control," 90.

4. Linda Gordon, *Woman's Body, Woman's Right* (New York: 1976), 332–35; Paula Giddings, *When and Where I Enter: The Impact of Black Women on Race and Sex in America* (New York: 1984), 183; Robert G. Weisbord, *Genocide? Birth Control and the Black American* (Westport, Conn.: 1975); William G. Harris, "Family Planning, Socio-Political Ideology and Black Americans: A Comparative Study of Leaders and a General Population Sample" (Ph.D. dissertation, University of Massachusetts, 1980), 69.

A brief chronology of early birth control organizations is as follows: the American Birth Control League was founded in 1921 and operated by Margaret Sanger until 1927. In 1923 Sanger had organized the Clinical Research Bureau and after 1927 controlled only that facility. In 1939 the Clinical Research Bureau and the American Birth Control League merged to form the Birth Control Federation of America. In 1942 the name was changed to the Planned Parenthood Federation of America (hereafter cited as ABCL, BCFA, and PPFA).

5. For contraceptive use among Africans, see Norman E. Himes, *Medical History of Contraception* (New York: 1936). For statements concerning birth control use among black Americans, see W. E. B. Du Bois, "Black Folks and Birth Control," *Birth Control Review* 16 (June 1932): 166–67 (hereafter cited as *BCR*); Herbert Gutman, *The Black Family in Slavery and Freedom 1750–1925* (New York: 1976). Du Bois had first observed the trend toward a steadily decreasing birth rate in *The Philadelphia Negro: A Social Study* (Philadelphia: 1899). For folk methods see Elizabeth Rauh Bethel, *Promiseland: A Century of Life in a Negro Community* (Philadelphia: 1981), 156–57; Newbell Niles Puckett, *Folk Beliefs of the Southern Negro* (New York: 1926); Arthur Raper, *Preface to Peasantry: A Tale of Two Black Belt Counties* (Chapel Hill, N.C.: 1936), 71; "Report of the Special Evening Medical Session of the First American Birth Control Conference" (1921), Box 99, Folder 1017, Margaret Sanger Papers, Sophia Smith Collection, Smith College, Northampton, Mass.

6. *Pittsburgh Courier*, 25 April 1931, n.p. (hereafter cited as *Courier*).

7. *Courier*, 1 December 1934, 7.

8. McFalls and Masnick, "Birth Control," 103; George Schuyler, "Quantity or Quality," *BCR* 16 (June 1932): 165–66.

9. See, for example, *Courier*, 9 March 1935, 2; and *San Francisco Spokesman*, 1 March 1934, 1 (hereafter cited as *Spokesman*); Vina Delmar, "Bad Girl," *Courier*, 3 January 1931, 2.

10. *Baltimore Afro-American*, 3 August 1940, n.p. (hereafter cited as *Afro-American*); "A Clinic for Tobacco Road," *BCR* 3 [New Series] (January 1936): 6; Gutman, *The Black Family*, 80–85; John Gaston, "A Review of 2,422 Cases of Contraception," *Texas State Journal of Medicine* 35 (September 1938): 365–68; *Afro-American*, 3 August 1940, n.p. On abortion see also "Birth Control: The Case for the State," *Reader's Digest* (November 1939).

11. McFalls and Masnick, "Birth Control," 103.

12. "Magazine Publishes Negro Number on Birth Control," *San Francisco Spokesman*, 11 June 1932, 3; "Birth Control Slayer Held Without Bail," *Courier*, 11 January 1936, 4.

13. Alice Dunbar Nelson, "Woman's Most Serious Problem," *The Messenger* (March 1927): 73; Clyde Kiser, "Fertility of Harlem Negroes," *Milbank Memorial Fund Quarterly* 13 (1935): 273–85; Caroline Robinson, *Seventy Birth Control Clinics* (Baltimore, 1930), 246–51.

14. Weisbord, *Genocide?*, 43.

15. J. A. Rogers, "The Critic," *The Messenger* (April 1925).

16. W. E. B. Du Bois, "The Damnation of Women," in *Darkwater: Voices from Within the Veil*, ed. Herbert Aptheker (1921; rpt. Millwood, N.Y.: 1975).

17. W. E. B. Du Bois, "Birth," *The Crisis* 24 (October 1922): 248–50.

18. Charles H. Garvin, "The Negro's Doctor's Task," *BCR* 16 (November 1932): 269–70.

19. For an excellent discussion of the theme of sexuality in black women's fiction, see the introduction to Nella Larsen, *Quicksand and Passing*, ed. Deborah E. McDowell (New Brunswick, N.J.: 1986). See also Mary Burrill, "They That Sit in

Darkness," and Angelina Grimké, "The Closing Door," *BCR* 3 (September 1919); Jessie Fauset, *The Chinaberry Tree* (New York: 1931); Angelina Grimké, *Rachel* (n.p., 1920); Georgia Douglas Johnson, *Bronze: A Book of Verse* (1922; rpt. Freeport, N.Y.: 1971).

20. Delmar, "Bad Girl," *Courier*, 3 January 1931, 2.

21. Fauset, *The Chinaberry Tree*, 131–32, 187.

22. Chandler Owen, "Women and Children of the South," *BCR* 3 (September 1919): 9, 20.

23. Quoted in *Courier*, 28 March 1931, 3, and *Norfolk Journal and Guide*, 28 March 1931, 1.

24. J. A. Ghent, "Urges Legalization of Birth Control: Law Against Contraception Unjust to the Poor," *Spokesman*, 9 July 1932, 3; "The Case of Dr. Devaughn, or Anti-Birth Control on Trial," *Spokesman*, 22 February 1934, 6.

25. W. G. Alexander, "Birth Control for the Negro: Fad or Necessity?" *Journal of the National Medical Association* 24 (August 1932): 39.

26. Charles S. Johnson, "A Question of Negro Health," *BCR* 16 (June 1932): 167–69.

27. Newell L. Sims, "Hostages to the White Man," *BCR* 16 (July–August 1932): 214–15.

28. E. S. Jamison, "The Future of Negro Health," *BCR* 22 (May 1938): 94–95.

29. "Sterilization," *Courier*, 30 March 1935, 10; "The Sterilization Menace," *Courier*, 18 Jan. 1936, 10; W. E. B. Du Bois, "Sterilization," *Courier*, 27 June 1936, 1; "Are Women Interested Only in Meet and Eat Kind of Club?" *Spokesman*, 29 March 1934, 4.

30. For examples of black social welfare organizations see, for example, William L. Pollard, *A Study of Black Self-Help* (San Francisco: 1978); Edyth L. Ross, *Black Heritage in Social Welfare, 1860–1930* (London: 1978); Lenwood G. Davis, "The Politics of Black Self-Help in the United States: A Historical Overview," in *Black Organizations: Issues on Survival Techniques*, ed. Lennox S. Yearwood (Lanham, Md.: 1980). This statement is also based on extensive reading of the *Pittsburgh Courier, Norfolk Journal and Guide, Baltimore Afro-American, San Francisco Spokesman*, and *New York Age* for the 1920s and 1930s.

31. *The Messenger* (July 1918): n.p.

32. "Report of executive secretary" (March 1923), Series I, Box 4, Planned Parenthood Federation of America Papers, American Birth Control League Records, Sophia Smith Collection, Smith College, Northampton, Mass.; Hannah Stone, "Report of the Clinical Research Department of the ABCL" (1925), Series I, Box 4, PPFA Papers; "Urban League Real Asset, Clinic an Example of How it Assists," *Courier*, 2 November 1935, 1; William Lloyd Imes to Margaret Sanger, 16 May 1931 and 23 November 1932, Box 122b, Folders 1333 and 1336, Sanger Papers; Shelton Hale Bishop to Margaret Sanger, 18 May 1931, Box 122b, Folder 1333, Sanger Papers.

33. "Minutes of the first meeting of 1932, Board of Managers, Harlem Branch" (25 March 1932), Box 122b, Folder 1336, Sanger Papers; "Companionate Marriage Discussed at Forum," *New York Age*, 12 May 1928, n.p.

34. E. S. Lewis and N. Louise Young, "Baltimore's Negro Maternal Health Center: How It Was Organized," *BCR* 22 (May 1938): 93–94.

35. "West Virginia," *BCR* 23 (October 1938): 121; "Birth Control for the Negro," Report of Hazel Moore (1937), Box 22, Folder 10, Florence Rose Papers, Sophia

Smith Collection, Smith College; "Negro Demonstration Project Possibilities" (1 December 1939), Box 121, Folder 1309, Sanger Papers.

36. For information on black organizations, see Box 122b, Sanger Papers, especially 25 March 1932; "Minutes of the regular meeting of the Board of Directors of the ABCL," December 1922, Series I, Box 1, PPFA Papers; "Report of the executive secretary" (11 November 1930), Series I, Box 4, PPFA Papers; "ABCL Treasurer's annual reports for the year 1936," Series I, Box 4, PPFA Papers; "Harlem Economic Forum Plans Fine Lecture Series," *Courier*, 14 November 1936, 9; "Birth Control Clinic Set Up for Negroes; Sponsored by Clubs," *Oklahoma City Times*, 28 February and 4 March 1938; "Illinois Birth Control League," *BCR* 22 (March 1938): 64. By 1931 many black organizations in Pittsburgh supported the use of birth control; see "Pittsburgh Joins Nation-Wide League for Birth Control," *Courier*, 21 February 1931, 1.

37. "Annual Reports of the State Member Leagues for 1936, the Kentucky Birth Control League," Series I, Box 4, PPFA Papers; "Annual Report 1938–39, Cincinnati Committee on Maternal Health," Box 119A, Folder 1256, Sanger Papers.

38. "Mother's Health Office Referrals" (5 January 1933), Massachusetts Mother's Health Office, Central Administrative Records, Box 35 and 36, Planned Parenthood League of Massachusetts, Sophia Smith Collection, Smith College; "PPFA field report for California, 1944," Box 119, Folder 1215, Sanger Papers; "Annual Meeting of the BCFA, Indiana Birth Control League, 1935," Series I, Box 4, PPFA Papers.

39. "Chart of the Special Negro Project Demonstration Project," Box 22, Folders 8 and 2, Rose Papers; John Overton and Ivah Uffelman, "A Birth Control Service Among Urban Negroes," *Human Fertility* 7 (August 1942): 97–101; E. Mae McCarroll, "A Condensed Report on the Two Year Negro Demonstration Health Program of PPFA, Inc.," presented at the Annual Convention of the National Medical Association, Cleveland, 17 August 1942, Box 22, Folder 11, Rose Papers; Mabel K. Staupers, "Family Planning and Negro Health," *National News Bulletin of the National Association of Colored Graduate Nurses* 14 (May 1941): 1–10.

40. "Preliminary Annual Report, Division of Negro Service" (7 January 1942), Box 121, Folder 1309, Sanger Papers; "Doctors' Annual Meeting Marked by Fine Program; Local Committee Involved in Planning Meeting," *New York Age*, 7 September 1929, 8; "National Medical Association Meeting Held in Washington," *New York Age*, 27 August 1932, 4. For information on the Smith-Lever Extension Act, see Alfred True, *A History of Agricultural Extension Work in the United States 1785–1923* (Washington, D.C.: 1928). Information on home demonstration clubs also appears in T. J. Woofter, Jr., "Organization of Rural Negroes for Public Health Work," *Proceedings of the National Conference of Social Work* (Chicago: 1923), 72–75; "Activities Report, Birth Control Negro Service," 21 June–21 July 1941, Box 22, Rose Papers; "Progress Outline 1940–42" and "Activities Report, Birth Control Negro Service," 16 June–21 June 1941, Box 22, Rose Papers. For information on Jeanes Teachers see, for example, Ross, *Black Heritage*, 211.

41. Information on organizations is based on numerous reports and newsletters from the years 1940–42, in Box 22, Rose Papers; see also "Newsletter from Division of Negro Service, December, 1941," Box 121, Folder 1309, and "PPFA Field Report for California, 1944," Box 119, Folder 1215, Sanger Papers.

42. "Activities Report, January 1, 1942–February 6, 1942" and "Progress Outline

1940–42," Box 22, Folder 4, Rose Papers; *Family Guardian* (Massachusetts Mother's Health Council) 5 (December 1939): 3, and 10 (July 1940): 3; "Minutes of the National Advisory Council Meeting, Division of Negro Service," 11 December 1942, Box 121, Folder 1310, Sanger Papers; Peter Murray, *BCR* 16 (July–August 1932): 216; M. O. Bousefield, *BCR* 22 (May 1938): 92. James Reed notes the opposition of the American Medical Association to alternative forms of health care systems in *From Private Vice to Public Virtue*, Part IV and 254.

43. "Notes on the Mother's Clinic, Tucson, Arizona," Box 119, Folder 1212, Sanger Papers; "A Clinic for Tobacco Road," *BCR* 3 [New Series] (January 1936): 6–7; Leonore G. Guttmacher, "Securing Patients for a Rural Center," *BCR* 23 (November 1938): 130–31; "Chas E Hall [*sic*] Census Bureau Expert, Gives Figures for Ten States in Which Number of Children Under Five Shows Decrease," *New York Age*, 7 November 1931, 1.

44. "Activities Report, Birth Control Negro Service," 21 November 1942, Box 22, Rose Papers.

45. "Project Reports," *The Aframerican* (Summer and Fall 1942): 9–24.

III

Sexual Conflicts and Cultural Authority, 1920 to 1960

9

Modern Sexuality and the Myth of Victorian Repression

Christina Simmons

For twentieth-century Americans the first sexual revolution popularized the image of the flapper, an ideal of youth, beauty, and freedom of action for women, but also one of sexual vitality. "The emancipated flapper is just plain female under her paint and outside her cocktails," explains a flapper's father in Gertrude Atherton's best-selling novel of 1923, *Black Oxen.* "More so for she's more stimulated. Where girls used to be merely romantic, she's romantic . . . plus sex instinct rampant." But in the shadows stands another figure, the authority against whom the flapper had rebelled—a stern and asexual matron, representative of outmoded Victorianism. "She believed in purity," wrote Sinclair Lewis, describing one such lady, Mrs. Keast, in *Ann Vickers* (1932): "She had, possibly as a result of fifty-five years complete abstinence from tobacco, alcohol, laughter, sexual excitement, and novels, a dark bagginess under her eyes, and twitching fingers." These contrasting images represent two elements in a new discourse on sexuality that appeared in the writings of white liberal commentators on sexual life in the 1920s and 1930s.[1]

This group of thinkers created what I call the myth of Victorian repression to describe and condemn old patterns of sexual behavior and shape new ones. Through this device they interpreted and codified for white middle-class Americans the new morality that had emerged in the 1910s. By proclaiming the existence and legitimacy of female sexual desire, the new morality undermined the basis of the Victorian sexual code and encouraged some women's sexual assertiveness. Other women clung to the influence gained through sexual restraint. The myth of Victorian repression constituted a response to both forms of women's power.

These sexual revisionists proclaimed a modernist liberation from a repressive Victorian past, and subsequent historiography has tended to accept that frame of reference. Michel Foucault has astutely criticized this paradigm, arguing that the supposed repression of the nineteenth century can better be seen as a "deployment of sexuality," the creation of new bourgeois discourses about sexuality, which in fact "incited" a greater intensity of consciousness about and desire for a "truth" of sex than had existed in earlier historical times. Hence, the Victorian prescription of restrained sexual activity and modest sexual speech did not mean the absence or "repression" of sexuality but rather focused psychic attention on it. At the heart of the knowledge produced by such discourses were shifting relations of power between parents and children, women and the male medical establishment, the state and fertile couples, and psychiatry and sexual "deviants." Foucault sees the early twentieth-century sexual revolution, the so-called antirepressive struggle, as "a tactical shift and reversal" in the deployment of sexuality but not a fundamental break with the past.[2]

Analysis of liberal American discourse on sexuality in this period reveals both genuine changes in sexual prescriptions and important continuities with the past. I shall argue here that the myth of Victorian repression represented a cultural adjustment of male power to women's departure from the Victorian order. It constituted a strategic modification rather than a decline of male dominance. Although the new morality was made possible above all by women's greater political and economic activity—suffrage and reform work, college education, labor force participation—the new sexual discourse of the 1920s and 1930s attacked women's increased power. The myth of Victorian repression rehabilitated male sexuality and cast women as villains if they refused to respond to, nurture, or support it. And by identifying women with Victorianism and men with a progressive and realistic understanding of sex, it confirmed men's sexual dominance as normative in modern marriage.

■   Intellectuals, bohemians, and radicals attacked Victorian middle-class sexual mores in the first two decades of the century at the same time that sexual behavior seems to have been changing. Long-standing demands for female-controlled contraception—through voluntary motherhood and the right to say no—shifted toward a new demand for artificial means of birth control to facilitate female sexual pleasure as well as fertility control. Public discussion of these ideas signaled to both critics and proponents that more sexual activity was taking place inside and outside marriage, an increase precipitated by changes in women's sexual attitudes and behavior.[3]

Women had been key figures in the Victorian ideology of sexual control. Nineteenth-century middle-class men and women, whether feminists, free lovers, or conservative moralists, had all feared sexual excess and called for moderation. By the 1850s sexual continence, limiting sexual activity to legal marriage and a reproductive goal, had become the dominant cultural ideal. Allowing women to set the pace in sexual activity was commonly seen as a means to the ideal. Women were thought to be characterized by "passionlessness" and to be guided more by maternal instinct than sexual desire per se. Hence, they were expected to dampen men's unnatural obsession with sex. Although contradicted by women's legal obligation to submit sexually to their husbands, the image of women as upholders of sexual restraint was a powerful element in Victorian culture.[4] Pursuing it, women mounted active campaigns for social purity, including attacks on prostitution and indecency in theater and literature. Victorian men took an equally substantive part in sexual control, however, in their own purity reform work. The YMCA contributed to the enactment in 1873 of the Comstock Act outlawing obscenity, including birth control and abortion devices and information. Federal Agent Anthony Comstock, enforcer of the law named for him, survived into the twentieth century to be mocked by sexual radicals for his efforts to ferret out vice wherever it lurked. While many people's actual behavior or feelings contradicted these prescriptions, the cultural power of this discourse on sexuality was pervasive and long-lasting.[5]

By the early twentieth century, however, Victorian conventions based on these sexual concepts were breaking down. Young women and men in the cities forged a new comradeship in a world of heterosocial leisure sharply different from what Victorian manners had prescribed. In large cities new forms of amusement for unchaperoned couples challenged the sex-segregated or family-controlled recreation of Victorian middle-class life. Mixed-sex restaurants and cabarets, for example, appeared as part of New York night life in the 1890s. Men brought respectable women to establishments where men had previously gone alone or with prostitutes. In movie theaters and dance halls working-class couples set an example of sexually integrated amusement followed quickly by middle-class youth. "Good" and "bad" women now dressed similarly and frequented the same clubs.[6]

For both sexes changing social realities laid the basis for a critique of Victorianism. By the 1910s young middle-class women's foothold in higher education, the labor force, and feminist and reform politics and institutions gave them an increasingly critical perspective on the old sexual order. Wifehood and motherhood no longer formed so exclusively the basis of their social power, and they could press demands for equality beyond suffrage. Many rejected self-restriction and declined to take responsibility for male sexual behavior. They explored female sexuality and espoused a positive romantic outlook on heterosexual relationships. As one feminist noted: "Of late there has been much public discussion of the wantonness of our modern youth; which, being interpreted, means the disposition of our girls to take the same liberty of indulgence in pre-nuptial sexual affairs that has always been countenanced in boys."[7]

Some young middle-class men also evinced alienation from nine-teenth-century mores. Male white-collar workers in large industrial cor-porations faced more specialized and routinized tasks; the self-control and autonomy of the self-made man seemed less relevant or possible. Traditional politics seemed futile and corrupt. Many men turned to women, leisure, art, or radical politics for the fulfillment old masculine roles did not provide. One man, who had quit a demanding office job to spend more time with his wife, wrote in *The Masses* in 1914, "I had begun to feel that the one-sexed world in which I had been living was inade-quate to human needs, that life ought to be lived and shared by men and women together."[8] Both women and men, then, looked for greater equal-ity and companionship, including sexual companionship.

Later sexual studies conducted by Alfred Kinsey and others confirm the impressions of social commentators in the 1910s and 1920s that new patterns of sexual behavior were emerging. Middle-class women born after 1900 were increasingly willing to engage in premarital petting and intercourse and, when married, reached orgasm more often than those born in the nineteenth century. One observer of youth claimed that mid-dle-class high school boys visited prostitutes less often by 1920 because their social class peers were acting as sexual partners.[9] The guardians of purity were descending from their pedestals.

Writers of fiction, religious and moral commentators, physicians, and, increasingly, academic social scientists, published prolific responses to the sexual revolution. Like the nineteenth-century physicians Foucault credits with making sexuality a matter of medical knowledge, these thinkers were generating a new psychological and sociological discourse about sexual behavior and marriage. During the 1910s a conservative movement for sex education attempted to reverse the tide of change in sexual behavior while vociferous sexual radicals exposed Victorian hy-pocrisy. By the 1920s, however, except among fundamentalists and Ca-tholics, the predominant tone was of liberal reform. Realizing the social changes they observed were irreversible, academics, reformers, and a few radicals explained, justified, or criticized prevailing patterns of sexual be-havior and developed a modern sexual ideology to guide behavior. They frequently cited the writings of Sigmund Freud and British sexologist Havelock Ellis, whose ideas were being popularized in the United States in the 1910s, but they reshaped European ideas into a distinctively new American discourse on sexuality and marriage. These writers included, for example, Judge Ben B. Lindsey, author of *Companionate Marriage*, a major text outlining modern marriage; Ira S. Wile, child psychiatrist and sex educator; Lorine Pruette, a psychologist who specialized in women's conflicts between marriage and career; and sociologist Ernest Groves, founder of the field of marriage counseling. Floyd Dell and Margaret Sanger, radical before World War I in their critique of Victorian morality, turned in the 1920s to the pursuit of happiness within a reformed marriage. Sinclair Lewis' and Fannie Hurst's novels offered extended commentaries on sexual relationships. Two radical voices were those of Samuel Schmalhausen and V. F. Calverton, who collaborated in producing the *Modern Quarterly*, a journal of liberal and socialist opinion, between 1925 and 1932. Schmalhausen was a psychoanalyst and Calverton a young radical critic interested in problems of sex.[10]

These thinkers differed in their evaluation of institutional marriage but held in common a revised assessment of the value of sexual activity and a set of male and female stereotypes that they used as positive and negative models of sexual behavior. With these sexual ideas and images, the commentators on sex in the 1920s constructed the myth of the Victorian repression, which demonstrated the errors of the earlier ideology of sexual restraint and attempted to shape an appropriate new dynamic for relations between the sexes.

A clamor against sexual repression marked liberal and radical opinion of the 1920s. Schmalhausen outlined the complaints most dramatically:

> If we survey traditional civilization, we are impressed by one fact as always conspicuously present: the vast array of machinery of intimidation (physical, emotional, intellectual, spiritual) used by the authoritative elders to prevent the free and easy expression of sex desire. The times waited for a Freud to come along and make clear to a blind mankind how tragic the costs of this civilized machinery of intimidation. This exposé of the staggering human cost of sexual frustration I look upon as the ultimate important contribution of Freud. Why were the authoritative elders so concerned with preventing nature from being natural?

Limiting sex expression to reproductive purposes now appeared cruel and arbitrary. Lindsey argued that continence was an idea perpetuated by religious fanatics who saw in sex only "ugliness, original sin, and fig leaves." Dell proclaimed grandly that the destruction of the patriarchal family "has laid the basis for a more biologically normal family life than has existed throughout the whole of the historical period." Thus nineteenth-century American culture appeared as a historical aberration that violated fundamental human nature.[11]

Not only was sex a natural part of life, it was a positive source of energy and creativity rather than a drain on individual powers, as the Victorians had asserted. As Sanger wrote, "To be strongly sexed means that the life force can suffuse and radiate through body and soul. It means radiant energy and force in every field of endeavor." Even rebellion against the code of monogamy, while it was "to be condemned from the higher social point of view," nevertheless "represents biological strength and urge," wrote Wile and Mary Winn. "It is the surplus creative force of the race."[12]

These thinkers felt that the Victorian distance between women and men created an unpleasant tension between husband and wife, especially in sexual interactions. Victorians had seen that tension as a way to limit sexual activity, part of an invigorating moral struggle, but thinkers of the 1920s found sexual conflict exhausting and dangerous. Permitting regular sexual activity was a lesser evil than repression, which seemed to lead to neuroses and weak, unhappy individuals. Groves hoped that asceticism had "passed forever from the category of ideals into that of mental abnormalities." Not only was repression harmful; it did not work. Although many sexual reformers still feared sex outside marriage, they argued that rigid controls exacerbated the danger. Sex could not simply be suppressed, for "futile repression ends in volcanic upheaval and a fresh outbreak of license." Furthermore, denying sexual urges made marriage itself less stable. A great many authors of works on sex and marriage claimed that divorce was caused by sexual maladjustments. Frigidity and impotence were said to result from the ascetic mentality. Hence, Victorian repression undermined the very institution it was supposed to protect.[13]

The hope of many of these critics was to save marriage by "sexualizing it," as Schmalhausen wrote. Companionate marriage represented the new cultural ideal developed during this period. It included birth control to accommodate the new woman's sexuality and to allow men to find sexual satisfaction inside marriage. Sexual and emotional comradeship formed the basis of union. Proponents of companionate marriage stressed early marriage and advocated divorce by mutual consent for the childless.[14] The companionate ideal epitomized twentieth-century liberal criticism of sexual repression.

The new marriage, with its ideal of sexual intimacy, required new behavior from both sexes. In tracts, exposés, and novels that examined heterosexual relations, a series of positive and negative images of men and women dramatized behavior and attitudes both to imitate and to avoid. The images conveyed three important themes of the sexual revisionism of the twenties and thirties: the rehabilitation of male sexuality, an attack on women's power to either control or withdraw from male sexual needs, and the creation of a new female ideal.

As part of the re-evaluation of male sexuality, sexual modernists modified an image of men used by Victorian moral reformers. The "sexual brute" became the "sexual blunderer." Symbolizing men's sexual power over women in the callous infliction of male desire on a passive and innocent wife, the Victorian image of the sexual brute had expressed women's protest against their lack of sexual knowledge and the legal rights husbands possessed over wives' bodies. Accounts of brutal rape on the wedding night demonstrated men's selfish and aggressive sexual impulses and women's victimization. The moral reformers who employed the image defended women's right to refuse intercourse and demanded improved control over male sexuality.[15]

Twentieth-century writers repeated wedding night stories but redefined the nature of the brutality to stress male ignorance of women's sexual needs rather than aggression or cruelty. Women would enjoy sex, it was asserted, if men learned to nurture feminine sexual feelings. Sanger, for example, recounted the story of a bride's disappointment with a husband whose approach on the wedding night "had been in the order of a hurried meal over a lunch counter." In another story a husband met friends in the hotel lobby on his wedding night and stayed up talking with the boys while his bride stewed. "The result was that she became a victim of a neurotic dissociation which completely ruined her marriage by producing a state of long-lasting asexuality."[16] Re-educating men constituted the central recommendation of those who used this image. Women's sexual interest, wrote Ellis, meant that "a new husband is required to meet the new wife." The sexual brute who tyrannized women had been transformed in the new thinking into a less awful personage, merely a blunderer who needed to learn consideration and fairness.[17]

The softening of the Victorian image of men indirectly acknowledged women's increased social power because in the new scenario women appeared less as pathetic victims than in the writings of Victorian reformers. Notions of "masculine supremacy or of female frailty and weakness" were no longer appropriate, wrote Wile and Winn. Yet the assumption in most writings that men had greater knowledge and sexual experience also showed an acceptance of continued male power. Even Sanger, who urged couples to read about and discuss sex and was concerned that women not be sexually coerced, assumed male sexual mastery. In order for the crucial initiation to go exactly right, she argued, the bridegroom must "dominate the whole situation."[18]

The idea that modern men must embrace and not suppress their sexual urges was even clearer in the image of the "poor worm," a repressed and fearful man unable to muster the sexual energy to master women. Far from showing character, a man who failed to pursue and obtain sexual satisfaction appeared unmanly. As one author put it sarcastically,

> Surely there is no sense in . . . ridiculing the activities of a man merely because his intentions chance to be honorable and his motives pure. It is carrying cynicism much too far to regard him as a hypocrite. Perhaps he prefers to manage his affairs in this strange manner. Perhaps he is fooling you.

Inadequate sexual energy was equated with lack of the appropriate aggressiveness: an impotent man might be "kind and gentle," "gentlemanly and refined," but he could not satisfy his wife and was not the man he should be. Created primarily by men, who seemed anxious about what it meant to be male in the modern world, this imagery evoked a sense that young women's sexual liberation required men to jettison Victorian habits in order to retain a dominant role. Acknowledging the existence of female sexuality called for a more vigorous male sexuality in response. Lack of the necessary vigor might hint of homosexuality, increasingly discussed and feared by the professionals producing this commentary.[19]

The sexual revisionists were redefining male sexuality as a less threatening or morally base element of male nature. They offered a positive image of the sexual male as the "healthy animal," responsive to women yet unafraid of his natural drives. Victorians, claimed the writers of the twenties, had taught men to view sexuality as a "weakness," but modern thinkers realized that the sex drive was a man's "most dynamic urge," without which he would be "robbed of his manhood, an enfeebled weakling." The reformers denigrated those who feared aggression toward women as a dangerous part of male sexuality. Lindsey made this clearest when he revealed his admiration for the courage and spontaneity of young boys: "'morality' doesn't play much part in the reactions of the normal lad—not if he is the healthy young animal he should be." As they grew up, the vitality was gradually crushed out of boys, and Lindsey believed women were the primary agents of this tragic maturation. The liberal view of sexuality in the 1920s sought to revise the negative evaluation of aggressive male sexuality and redirect cultural standards that accepted female control over men's energies.[20]

In the sexual revisionists' cautionary tale the blunderer and the poor worm warned men against both ignorant self-assertion in sex and excessive hesitation with women. The healthy animal, when he was sensitive and knowledgeable, made the best husband. He skillfully initiated his bride into sexual intimacy and, though he offered her respect and pleasure, he remained in charge. At the same time several recurrent female images warned readers of both sexes of the threat controlling, neglectful, or exploitive women posed to marriage. The stereotypes of the prudish Victorian matriarch, the demanding and burdensome wife, and the emotionally distant career woman represented caricatures of women who wielded excessive power and were not responsive to men's needs.

The image of the respectable married woman, especially as a mother, had epitomized the sexual purity and domesticity prescribed for bourgeois women in the nineteenth century. As purity became less of a concern, this ideal was rejected as sentimental at best. One reformer called for sociologists to carry on more "scientific" and "objective" discussions of sex, without "the babbling of the term 'mother' with tearstained faces." Sexual reformers expressed both sympathy and impatience toward women raised with traditional modesty about sex. A young wife must "cease to take pride" in "outgrown maidenly reserve," warned Groves. She must abandon herself fully to the sexual embrace and accept the guidance of her husband because "his attitude toward sex is less likely to be warped."[21] Adhering to these outmoded ideas was a bad habit women had to give up to become mature modern adults.

The older woman who upheld Victorian values fared worse. Sexual commentators frequently used the image of the prudish Victorian matriarch, a woman who had the power but not the tenderness of the nineteenth-century mother, yet demanded the customary deference from men for the sacrifices she made as a woman. In the novel *Love Without Money* Dell describes one such mother as "a natural-born policewoman." This woman, a former suffragist, finds even the mention of marriage unpleasant because it raises the topic of sex. She disciplines her children harshly and dominates her husband as well, hindering his career by demanding to stay in her home town, where her family is powerful. Sexual frigidity was central to this image. Lindsey created a vivid account of one such female character who told him, "Sex seems to me a horrible thing. It seemed so to my mother before me. She said the Bible teaches that it is evil, and that its only excuse is for propagating the race." This woman's prudish attitudes had alienated her husband, and he had found a mistress. While Lindsey criticized the husband, too, for his failure to deal more tactfully with his wife, he emphasized the woman's unnatural moral views and rigidity. Women like this were pictured as attempting to control men by withholding sex. They ignored male sexual rights.[22]

The image of the burdensome and demanding wife provided a variation on the theme of the prudish and controlling one: both expressed the fear that women might use men to support them but then not be pliable and attentive to their husbands. The wife who was manipulative behind a front of feminine weakness, expected excessive male attention, and acted as a "noble martyr with unnamed ills" seemed to many modern writers to be taking advantage of men. The image was not of a sexually demanding woman but of a woman who might get her way by playing on men's sexual desires and the traditional conventions of deference to women. For example, in Fannie Hurst's novel *Back Street*, the protagonist's sister, a hypocritical and unattractive young woman, sleeps with her suitor, then uses a pregnancy scare to force him to marry her. Married, she becomes petty and morally conventional. Women's unfair privileges were manifest particularly when they spent money—that is, "men's" money. For an essay on fashion one woman reporter asked men why women spent more on clothes than men. "Because women dominate men in America," answered many of them who are "a shade weary of paying for all the whims of the middle-class woman." The gold-digger, or alimony-hunter, who actually married a man for money, was an extreme case; the more common stereotype was of the woman who expected too much for what she gave.[23]

Interestingly, the image of the burdensome wife was the only one promulgated primarily by female sexual commentators. These writers sensed a shift in the nature of the exchange that constituted marriage and were critical of the dependent and inferior wife. Nineteenth-century homage to the wife and mother had been based on the idea of the tremendous sacrifices women made, especially in the suffering of childbirth, and the general self-abnegation expected of them. But these commentators believed twentieth-century wives and mothers were spoiled and had easy lives. Psychologist Pruette observed, for example, a "tinge of glory" around the "countless greying men who plod to the offices and factories each morning" to feed their families. Women's tasks in the modern world, however, had been diminished in number and significance. Childbearing, for example, no longer required the great courage it once had. Instead, "pregnancy has become a period of neurotic fears and disabilities, ending undramatically in a whiff of anaesthetic." Without the dignity of such noble functions, the magisterial mother became a petty tyrant. These writers, "modern" career women, sensed that motherhood was no longer a source of real dignity and influence as it had been for their mothers and grandmothers. And in their own lives, seeking equality with men in careers and public life, they were no doubt sensitive to the ways dependency could undermine their autonomy. Hence, they sharply rejected Victorian deference and the kinds of women who still wanted it.[24]

A final unappealing character type was the career woman and feminist, often but not always single. Like the matriarch, she was hard, unsympathetic to men's needs, and hostile to sexuality. In the 1922 novel *Broken Barriers*, the male protagonist is married to such a woman. She is a writer and reformer who campaigns for birth control, equal pay for women, and an end to child labor, but who is personally cold and snobbish and who travels so much that she rarely lives with her husband. Her behavior justifies his affair with the young middle-class wage earner who is the heroine of the novel. Those who used this image often implied that single career women were actually disturbed by sex precisely because they suppressed it. Lindsey cited a liberal clergyman who claimed:

> I know women who have never married, and who ought to—who need marriage badly. They have the notion that they have sublimated all the sex they've got in feminist careers. But I've concluded with respect to such people that they either haven't got much, or else that there is an unused surplus of bottled-up sex inside of them that more than accounts for their nerves and their "peculiarities."

Authors pictured women like this as unattractive, unhappy, or personally inadequate.[25]

The career woman threatened men because her independence or her intellectual interests suggested she might refuse to take care of men or do without them altogether. Most of the writers on marriage, male and female, were uncomfortable with such an image of women. This discomfort led them to picture career women as overtly hostile to sexuality but secretly frustrated and desperate for male attention.[26] Other writers suggested that such women might be lesbians. The urgency of the sex instinct as it was now defined meant that when the "normal" channels for its expression were closed, it might emerge in homosexual relationships.[27]

Power and sexual independence from men were the charges leveled against women who resembled these types. The matriarch, the complaining wife, and the career woman gained power from adherence to Victorian conventions of respect for mothers and wives, from feminist activism, or from the economic independence of professional work. All were characterized by resistance to male power and none were marked by a strongly developed female sexuality except for the lesbian career woman. The danger implicit in these stereotypes, then, was not the sexual power of the nineteenth-century whore, potentially overwhelming to men, but the Victorian woman's sexual control. In *Back Street* Fannie Hurst dramatizes this reversal of Victorian images by portraying a kept woman sympathetically. The protagonist, Ray Schmidt, is completely devoted to her lover, Walter Saxel. Far from overpowering him, she has practically no self of her own and epitomizes the adoring, dependent, and subordinate woman. By contrast Saxel's wife is a powerful traditional woman. A respectable Jewish matron, she is spoiled by her husband and dominates his life almost totally by maintaining ties with her own strong family and promoting the interests of the Saxel children. In *Ann Vickers* Sinclair Lewis presents a sexually active single woman as an admirable heroine, not a threatening sexual figure. The only sexuality that appears dangerous and corrupt is lesbian sexuality, which leads to the psychic enslavement and suicide of one of Ann's closest friends. The negative images of women that appear in the writings of sexual revisionists, then, imply a strong fear of women's resistance to male sexuality. The sexual danger was not that women would overcome men but that they would deny male needs. The new, more aggressive male sexuality was required if men were to keep such women in line. As W. J. Robinson wrote in 1930, "militant feminism" would not appear in the woman with a "normal, *i.e.*, properly satisfied, sex life" with a potent man.[28]

The writers of the 1920s captured in the image of the flapper a more positive ideal for modern women. This figure both embodied the popular notion of the free woman and retained a softness that did not threaten men. The flapper participated in the male world, probably working at a job as well as leading an independent, sexually integrated social life. She found men exciting, interesting comrades and did not take a condescending or disapproving attitude toward their ways. Her combination of daring spirit and youthful innocence was precisely what made her attractive to men. As Pruette described her, the flapper "has laid aside many things that would have made life simpler for her: ideals of feminine constancy, of the sacredness of maternity, of her right to a living without working."[29] A vigorous, active companion of men, not a frail and dependent creature, she had given up some of the old claim to special consideration as a woman.

At the same time, the flapper cared more about men and babies than about her paid work or her development as an individual through work. She might be "torn between the desire to be tough-minded, aggressive and self-seeking, and the compulsion to be pleasing" but would probably give way to the latter wish as soon as a man became attentive. These young women saw jobs as necessary to their independence, but they did not want careers that required them to give up love and marriage. As one fictional heroine put it, she was more interested in "experience" than a career and vigorously denied being "cursed with ambitions." Dell particularly stressed the advantages of young women's jobs, which he said were the best way to meet husbands. He criticized "middle-class feminists" for accepting careers on male terms and not helping women adjust work to their inevitable roles as wives and mothers.[30] The flapper scorned the high-minded dedication that characterized the nineteenth-century settlement-house workers and women professionals.

Finally, the ideal flapper was not squeamish about sex. She accepted it as a normal part of human nature and did not condemn men for their desires. She stayed out late, danced close, and necked and petted without feeling imposed upon. One novelist demonstrated this new spirit when he described without condemnation a heroine who actually spends the night with her lover. She chooses freely to do so out of love and is not victimized by a lustful man. Yet the modern young woman was still quite romantic. Lindsey pictures a young woman named Millie, the daughter of the archetypical prude, who exemplified the flapper's virtues. Her father had told her straightforwardly about sex, and she pitied her mother for her antiquated attitudes. Millie had kissed a few boys but was discriminating, postponing further sexual involvement till she met a man she really loved. But, as she told Judge Lindsey, "when I fall in love I'm not going to be stingy."[31]

The flapper's romanticism and youth, however, connoted an innocence that contradicted women's full claim on human sexuality. The ambivalence of many sexual theorists appeared as they struggled to define women's new sexuality. Most asserted that women were not passive and asexual but did have some active interest in sexuality. Like Freud, however, these writers still postulated and, indeed, desired a conventional difference between male and female sexuality. Sanger wrote, for example, that "under stimulation the sexual nature of man asserts itself almost instantaneously ready for action," but that "the sex nature of woman is more deeply hidden in the mysterious recesses of her being. More deeply concealed, it is not so immediately susceptible to stimulation, is far slower in response and thus is not immediately ready for the act of love."[32] Ironically, like the Victorians, some thought women's true interest was in babies rather than sex. Lindsey urged less censure and more sympathy for the red-lipped, "apparently oversexed" flappers on grounds that they were not in fact "fresh bodies offered for the pleasure of men but bodies offered to the agony and bloody sweat of motherhood. That is what it really means with most of them, whether they and we are conscious of it or not."[33] It seemed impossible to deny that young women were exhibiting what by older standards was an immodest interest in sex, but these definitions reassured apprehensive observers that young women were still guided more by traditional nurturing qualities than by an untamed sexuality. The lesbian was threatening precisely because she could enjoy a sexual life of intensity and self-interest unconnected to reproduction, and reproduction represented the payment, the sacrifice that symbolically drained female sexuality of its frightening powers.

A variety of male and female images, then, were used to develop the myth of Victorian repression. The myth criticized the old sexual ideas and roles and suggested alternatives more appropriate to a time when women had supposedly gained equality. The sexual ideologues who created the myth opposed the Victorian ideal of continence and favored more sexual activity. Many were tolerant of some premarital sexual activity; all favored more sexual contact within marriage. Some images reflected the greater social power and sexual demands of women during that time. Criticizing the insensitive blunderer and praising the flapper's adventurous spirit and sexual interest acknowledged women's rights to a fuller life. The ideal of the healthy male animal suggested that coping with women required more vigor, hence indirectly hinted that women were stronger than in the past. At the same time, however, the images served as warnings to men and to women to avoid interactions involving equivalent or greater female power in any form. The image of the poor worm ridiculed timid or overly chivalrous men. The matriarch, complaining wife, and celibate or lesbian career woman served as negative models to warn self-important, willful, or independent women. The flapper figure proclaimed that a youthful and malleable adolescent was more attractive than a sexually experienced adult woman. The sexual revisionists, in short, recognized improvements in women's status and power, yet encouraged women not to go too far, not to abandon men, and not to try to control them.

The sexual commentators of the 1920s and 1930s reworked the sexual code in order to control behavior they feared in three ways: First, they increased the specifically sexual power normatively attributed to men before and within marriage. Men were to set the pace and energetically initiate women into sexual relations. Male deference to female passionlessness was gone. Second, they severely criticized women's capacity to control or withdraw from men sexually. Sexually unresponsive women were caricatured. Victorian women's moral right and duty to limit sexual contact were overthrown. Third, they affirmed a new but still muted female sexuality. Women were supposed to desire and enjoy sexual relations but they were considered less lustful than men and their sexuality was still linked to maternal feeling. To replace the dignified Victorian matron with the youthful flapper as an ideal was to make female power taboo. Young and eager to please, the flapper lacked both the stature of the traditional wife and mother and a developed sexuality that could overpower men. These images attacked women's power and insisted upon men's power to control sexual interactions.

The new sexual discourse created by sexual revisionists had fundamentally altered Victorian ways of thinking. In some ways it was, as claimed, an attack on sexual "repression," if repression means a code of conduct limiting sexual activity. But it was, more specifically, an attack on *women's* control over *men's* sexuality. This control could come either from evasion of marriage (the career woman or lesbian) or from a Victorian sensibility exercised within marriage (the wife and mother figures). Certainly women's increased labor force participation and political activism, the winning of the suffrage, and the growing visibility and public discussion of lesbianism all made it clear that women could be free persons, not as coercively tied to men as in the past.[34]

Moreover, while some women adopted the new fun-loving flapper styles, traditional female expectations of marriage persisted among many women. Women's celebrated "new freedom" was most salient for single women since most white wives did not remain long in the labor force. Financially dependent wives might have been "complainers" because they still looked to men for material rewards they could not get for themselves. Elaine May's study of divorce in the early twentieth century shows that some wives adopted new and higher expectations of what men should provide and were willing to divorce when disappointed. And if young single women's sexual experimentation was based on their new public freedoms and jobs, then dependent wives lost the grounds for sexual assertiveness. Given the strength of persisting messages restricting female sexuality, it would not be surprising if many wives felt more at home looking for domestic influence based on the Victorian model—by attempting to control male sexuality. May found more wives in her sample who were antipathetic to sexual relations than wives claiming unfulfilled desires. Within marriage, then, many women may have retained a Victorian sexual self-definition and may not have been ready for a sexual life that resembled traditional male preferences more than their own.[35] Such resistance might have been even more frustrating to men if public discussion of the new sexuality and women's freedom raised their expectations of sexual responsiveness from women. The myth of Victorian repression both reflected and helped perpetuate anxiety about women dominating men or eluding their control.

On the other hand, a fear of fully developed female sexuality, similar to the Victorian threat of the whore, continued more subtly in the new ideology as well. In this sense "repression" continued, limiting women more than men. The rudimentary revisionist acknowledgment of female sexuality (and its active expression by some young women) was disturbing to many Americans. The subordination and restriction of women had represented sexual control and stability for the whole culture. In this logic, Victorian women's adherence to continence within marriage disciplined men's economic and sexual energies by forcing them to support families. For women to abandon their modesty and follow men's lascivious behavior was to threaten the very basis of civilization. Catholics and fundamentalists argued this most cogently, but liberal reformers were also susceptible to this fear. Even the radicals, much more tolerant of potential disorder, expressed concern about the results of "the increasing subordination . . . of maternity to sexuality, of the mother ethic to the mistress ethic, of love to passion." One could only try to have the faith, wrote Schmalhausen, that through the "peril of the sexual revolution" young people would find a balance between sexual impulse and the need for human harmony and stability.[36] That stability continued to be represented for many by women's domestic and maternal nurturance. Hence, sexual revisionists idealized the flapper, whose explorations of female sexuality remained relatively limited and were driven by romantic love. They condemned lesbians and by omission denied legitimacy to the heterosexually active and independent woman. The legacy of this omission is manifest in the difficulty some female adolescents have today in taking responsibility for their heterosexual activity.[37]

Rebellion against "Victorian repression," then, was much more complex than it appeared on the surface. Bourgeois women's role in sexual control, inherited from the nineteenth century, overlapped in the early twentieth century with the rising economic and social freedom of younger women. Whether sexually active or sexually controlling, women seemed to most liberal sexual theorists to have gained an improper advantage over men in modern life. The myth of Victorian repression conveyed a reaction against women's power in either form but particularly against passionlessness and women's uses of it. The new sexual discourse of the 1920s and 1930s represented not "liberation" but a new form of regulation. The new rules were better adapted to a world where single women of the middle class were asserting a more active sexuality and where men pressed to legitimate theirs. Although some women participated in creating this discourse, it was grounded in a male perspective and reflected primarily fears of female power. The much vaunted new morality gestured in the direction of equality for women but effectively sustained the cultural power of men, focusing that power in the arena of sexuality.[38] Although women's social, political, and economic inequality remain pervasive today, the continuing effects of the myth of Victorian repression may help to account for many women's subjective perception that male sexual power is central to their oppression.

■ Notes

Acknowledgments: I would like to thank Estelle Freedman, Joanne Meyerowitz, Kathy Peiss, and Bruce Tucker for comments on earlier drafts of this article and Kathy Peiss for very helpful editing.

1. Gertrude Atherton, *Black Oxen* (New York: 1923), 126; Sinclair Lewis, *Ann Vickers* (New York: 1932), 395.

2. For earlier historiography see, for example, Sidney Ditzion, *Marriage, Morals, and Sex in America* (1953; rpt. New York: 1969), 374–80, Henry May, *The End of American Innocence* (1959; rpt. Chicago: 1964), 338–47; Steven Marcus, *The Other Victorians* (1966; rpt. London: 1969), 287–88; James R. McGovern, "The American Woman's Pre–World War I Freedom in Manners and Morals," *Journal of American History* 55 (1968): 315–33. Michel Foucault, *The History of Sexuality*, vol. I, *An Introduction* (New York: 1978), trans. Robert Hurley, 69, 92–93, 103–5, 127–31.

3. McGovern, "The American Woman's Pre–World War I Freedom," 316–19; Barbara Epstein, "Family, Sexual Morality, and Popular Movements in Turn-of-the-Century America," 117–19, and Ellen Kay Trimberger, "Feminism, Men, and Modern Love: Greenwich Village, 1900–1925," 132, both in *Powers of Desire: The Politics of Sexuality*, ed. Ann Snitow, Christine Stansell, and Sharon Thompson (New York: 1983); Christina Simmons, "'Marriage in the Modern Manner': Sexual Radicalism and Reform in America, 1914–1941" (Ph.D. dissertation, Brown University, 1982), 64–84.

Interestingly, the radicals of the 1910s, especially birth controllers, tended to attack male power over female sexuality, as is apparent in the cartoons in *The Masses* and the *Birth Control Review*. The mostly liberal group of thinkers discussed here shifted the focus to women's power over male sexuality.

4. See Michelle Zimbalist Rosaldo, "Woman, Culture, and Society: A Theoretical Overview," in *Woman, Culture, and Society*, ed. Michelle Zimbalist Rosaldo and Louise Lamphere (Stanford: 1974), 20–22, 31–34, for an account of women's special role in purity.

On fears of excess and on continence, see Charles E. Rosenberg, "Sexuality, Class and Role in 19th-Century America," *American Quarterly* 25(1973): 134, 137; John S. Haller and Robin M. Haller, *The Physician and Sexuality in Victorian America* (New York: 1974), 200–201, 102–13, 130; G. J. Barker-Benfield, "The Spermatic Economy: A Nineteenth-Century View of Sexuality," in *The American Family in Social-Historical Perspective*, 2nd ed., ed. Michael Gordon (New York: 1978), 377; Ronald G. Walters, *Primers for Prudery: Sexual Advice to Victorian America* (Englewood Cliffs, N.J.: 1974), 2, 17, 32, 49; Linda Gordon, *Woman's Body, Woman's Right: A Social History of Birth Control in America* (New York: 1976), 102–6, 183; Carroll Smith-Rosenberg, "A Richer and a Gentler Sex," *Social Research* 53(1986): 289.

On women's sexuality, see Walters, *Primers*, 67; Nancy F. Cott, "Passionlessness: An Interpretation of Victorian Sexual Ideology, 1790–1850," *Signs* 4(1978): 226–28; Carl N. Degler, "What Ought To Be and What Was: Women's Sexuality in the Nineteenth Century," *American Historical Review* 79(1974): 1469–77. Degler argues that the notion of women's sexual passivity was part of an ideology in the process of being established rather than an account of majority opinion on the question. The fear underlying the ideology was that women did possess sexual drives and might not maintain control. See also Peter Filene, *Him/Her/Self: Sex Roles in Modern America*, 2nd ed. (Baltimore: 1986), 91. Peter Gay, in *Education of the Senses* (New York: 1984), argues like Degler that much behavior violated norms of sexual restraint and that the power of Victorian sexual ideology was thus incomplete.

For the Victorian definition of male sexuality, see Rosenberg, "Sexuality, Class and Role," 140–41; Barbara Welter, "The Cult of True Womanhood: 1820–1860," in *The American Family*, ed. Gordon, 313–16, 318.

5. David J. Pivar, *Purity Crusade: Sexual Morality and Social Control, 1868–1900* (Westport, Conn.: 1973); John Paull Harper, "Be Fruitful and Multiply: Origins of Legal Restrictions on Planned Parenthood in Nineteenth-Century America," in *Women of America: A History*, ed. Carol Berkin and Mary Beth Norton (Boston: 1979), 260–62; Gertrude Marvin, "Anthony and the Devil," *The Masses* (February 1914), reprinted in *Echoes of Revolt: The Masses, 1911–1917*, ed. William L. O'Neill (Chicago: 1966), 39.

6. By 1914 Anglo-Saxon stock was no longer in the majority. Irish, Italian, and Jewish immigrants concentrated in the cities, built political machines that afforded them some control over urban life, and created cultural forms different from both European patterns and those of the native Yankees. Gilman M. Ostrander, *American Civilization in the First Machine Age, 1890–1940* (New York: 1970), 43–45, 277; Epstein, "Family, Sexual Morality," in *Powers of Desire*, ed. Snitow *et al.*, 123. For information on urban culture and leisure, see Lewis A. Erenberg, *Steppin' Out: New York Nightlife and the Transformation of American Culture, 1890–1930* (Westport, Conn.: 1981); Lary May, *Screening Out the Past: The Birth of Mass Culture and the Motion Picture Industry* (New York: 1980); Kathy Peiss, *Cheap Amusements: Working Women and Leisure in Turn-of-the-Century New York* (Philadelphia: 1986); Elizabeth Ewen, "City Lights: Immigrant Women and the Rise of the Movies," *Signs* 5(1980): S45–65.

7. Filene, *Him/Her/Self*, 19–38; Joseph A. Hill, *Women in Gainful Occupations, 1870 to 1920*, Census Monographs IX (Washington, D.C.: 1929), 19, 76; William H. Chafe, *The American Woman: Her Changing Social, Economic, and Political Role, 1920–1970* (New York: 1972), 51, 54; Lorine Pruette, "The Flapper," in *The New Generation: The Intimate Problems of Modern Parents and Children*, ed. V. F. Calverton and S. D. Schmalhausen (New York: 1930), 586–88.

Many sexual commentators made the connection between women's new status and new sexuality. See Horace Coon, *Coquetry for Men* (New York: 1932), 110–11; S. D. Schmalhausen, "The War of the Sexes," in *Woman's Coming of Age: A Symposium*, ed. V. F. Calverton and S. D. Schmalhausen (New York: 1931), 285–86; Dora Russell, "Sex Love," in *The Sex Problem in Modern Society*, ed. John F. McDermott (New York: 1931), 135; Ira S. Wile and Mary Winn, *Marriage in the Modern Manner* (New York: 1929), 28–29, 34; Phyllis Blanchard and Carlyn Manasses, *New Girls for Old* (New York: 1930), 235, 245–46.

The feminist quoted is Suzanne LaFollette, in *Concerning Women* (New York: 1926), 147. See also Gordon, *Woman's Body*, 192; Mari Jo Buhle, *Women and American Socialism, 1870–1920* (Urbana, Ill.: 1981), 260.

8. On men see Gordon, *Woman's Body*, 191–92; Filene, *Him/Her/Self*, 72–78; Joseph F. Kett, *Rites of Passage: Adolescence in America, 1790 to the Present* (New York: 1977), 233–34, 240; Irvin G. Wyllie, *The Self-Made Man in America: The Myth of Rags to Riches* (New York: 1954), 144; Ostrander, *American Civilization*, 256; Erenberg, *Steppin' Out*, 66–67; Lawrence K. Frank, "Social Change and the Family," *Annals of the American Academy of Political and Social Science* 160 (March 1932): 100–101. Quotation from "Confessions of a Feminist Man," *The Masses* (March 1914), 8.

9. Alfred C. Kinsey *et al., Sexual Behavior in the Human Female* (1953; rpt. New York: 1965), 298–300, 380, 362–63, 358–59; Rachelle Yarros, *Modern Woman and Sex: A Feminist Physician Speaks* (New York: 1933), 65; Lewis M. Terman, *Psychological Factors in Marital Happiness* (New York: 1938), 318; Ben B. Lindsey, "The Promise and Peril of the New Freedom," in *Woman's Coming of Age*, ed. Calverton and Schmalhausen, 454–55. Kinsey found similar changes occurring between later generations. Comparing men in their youth between 1910 and 1925 with those growing up between 1930 and 1948, he found the later generation had intercourse with prostitutes only two-thirds to one-half as often as the older group though total sexual contact was of similar frequency. Hence, partners must have been changing from prostitutes to friends. Kinsey, *Sexual Behavior in the Human Male* (Philadelphia: 1948), 396, 411.

The sexual behavior of non–middle-class groups, on the other hand, had begun to diverge from Victorian standards by about 1880. Daniel Scott Smith, "The Dating of the American Sexual Revolution: Evidence and Interpretation," in *The American Family*, ed. Gordon, 431–33, 435.

10. Foucault, *History of Sexuality*, I, 30, 41–46. On Freud's influence, see Nathan Hale, *Freud and the Americans: The Beginnings of Psychoanalysis in the United States, 1987–1917* (New York: 1971), 262, 271, 361, 416, 430; and Fred Matthews, "In Defense of Common Sense: Mental Hygiene as Ideology and Mentality in Twentieth-Century America," *Prospects* 4 (1979): 459–516.

For biographies, see *New York Times*, 27 March 1943, 13; 10 October 1943, 16; Christopher Lasch, *Haven in a Heartless World: The Family Beseiged* (New York: 1977), 16, 23; "Ernest Groves," *Current Biography* 4 (1943): 21–23; Elaine Showalter, "Lorine Pruette," in *These Modern Women: Autobiographical Essays from the Twenties*, ed. Showalter (Old Westbury, N.Y.: 1978), 68; Floyd Dell, *Homecoming: An Autobiography* (New York: 1933), 255, 350, 288, and *Intellectual Vagabondage: An Apology for the Intelligentsia* (New York: 1926), 174, 187–89; Gordon, *Woman's Body*, Chs. 9, 10; Lewis, *Ann Vickers*; Fannie Hurst, *Back Street* (New York: 1930); Haim Gnizi, "V. F. Calverton: Independent Radical" (Ph.D. dissertation, City University of New York, 1968), 25, 31, 52–53, 90–98, 162–63.

11. Samuel D. Schmalhausen, "The Freudian Emphasis on Sex," in *The Sex Problem in Modern Society*, ed. McDermott, 61–62; Floyd Dell, *Love in the Machine Age: A Psychological Study of the Transition from Patriarchal Society* (New York: 1930), 6; Ben B. Lindsey and Wainwright Evans, *Companionate Marriage* (New York: 1927), 227–28.

12. Margaret Sanger, *Happiness in Marriage* (New York: 1926), 21, 48; Wile and

Winn, *Modern Manner*, 213–14; LeMon Clark, *Emotional Adjustment in Marriage* (St. Louis: 1937), 13.

13. Edwin W. Hirsch, *The Power to Love: A Psychic and Physiologic Study of Regeneration* (New York: 1935), 88, 119–20, 126; also Dell, *Machine Age*, 62; Sherwood Eddy, *Sex and Youth* (Garden City, N.J.: 1929), 125, 21; Ernest R. Groves, *The Marriage Crisis* (New York: 1928), 214.

14. Schmalhausen, "Freudian Emphasis," in *The Sex Problem*, ed. McDermott, 69; Lindsey and Evans, *Companionate*, v–vi.

15. Smith-Rosenberg, "Richer and a Gentler Sex," 293–98; Gordon, *Woman's Body*, 103–6.

16. Sanger, *Happiness*, 89; Groves, *Marriage Crisis*, 100; Ernest R. Groves, Gladys Hoagland Groves, and Catherine Groves, *Sex Fulfillment in Marriage* (New York: 1942), 135, 144, 146, 150; Wile and Winn, *Modern Manner*, 54; Ernest R. Groves, *The American Family* (Chicago: 1934), 225. The brute image appeared sometimes, too, in discussion of the relation of Victorian fathers to their modern daughters, describing restrictive, punitive fathers. See Ben B. Lindsey and Wainwright Evans, *The Revolt of Modern Youth* (Garden City, N.J.: 1925), 294.

17. Havelock Ellis, "Woman's Sexual Nature," in *Woman's Coming of Age*, ed. Calverton and Schmalhausen, 238. A few pessimistic female authors despaired of overcoming male aggression and used the same image to argue for a revival of chivalry. See Edith Stern, *Men Are Clumsy Lovers* (New York: 1934), 21.

18. Wile and Winn, *Modern Manner*, xiv, 147; Sanger, *Happiness*, 6.

19. Coon, *Coquetry*, 207, 49–50; Hirsch, *Power to Love*, 182; Lewis, *Ann Vickers*, 277; William J. Robinson, "Sexual Continence and Its Influence on the Physical and Mental Health of Men and Woman," and Victor G. Vecki, "The Dogma of Sexual Abstinence," in *Sexual Continence and Its Influence on the Physical and Mental Health of Men and Women*, ed. Robinson (New York: 1930), 39, 235–36. Several of the authors in this collection were influenced by Freud's 1908 essay "'Civilized' Sexual Morality and Modern Nervousness," first translated into English by Robinson in 1915 (reprinted in *Sexuality and the Psychology of Love*, ed. Philip Rieff [New York: 1963], 20–40). Freud did criticize excessive repression but did not oppose all repression. See also Estelle Freedman, "'Uncontrolled Desires': The Response to the Sexual Psychopath, 1920 to 1960," in this volume.

20. Hirsch, *Power to Love*, 203–4; Eddy, *Sex and Youth*, 134, 316; Wile and Winn, *Modern Manner*, 160; Lindsey and Evans, *Revolt*, 94, 325; Sanger, *Happiness*, 217–18.

21. Harry Elmer Barnes, "Sex in Education," in *Sex in Civilization*, ed. V. F. Calverton and S. D. Schmalhausen (New York: 1929), 303; Groves *et al.*, *Sex Fulfillment*, 183–89; Dell, *Machine Age*, 311.

22. Floyd Dell, *Love Without Money* (New York: 1931), 6, 12, 18, 152–56, 273; Barnes, "Sex in Education," in *Sex in Civilization*, ed. Calverton and Schmalhausen, 302. Barnes emphasizes women's religiosity and role in perpetuating wrong sexual ideas. Lindsey and Evans, *Companionate*, 117–23; Olga Knopf, *Women On Their Own* (Boston: 1935), 245–46; Clark, *Emotional Adjustment*, 97, 109; Lewis, *Ann Vickers*, 476.

23. Wile and Winn, *Modern Manner*, 162–70; Elizabeth M. Gilmer, *Dorothy Dix—Her Book: Every-day Help for Every-day People* (New York: 1926), 63, 157, 283–84; Pruette, "The Flapper," in *The New Generation*, ed. Calverton and Schmalhausen,

589; Hurst, *Back Street*, 54, 92–102; Winifred Rauschenbush, "The Idiot God Fashion," and Alice Beal Parson, "Man-Made Illusions About Woman," in *Woman's Coming of Age*, ed. Calverton and Schmalhausen, 442–43, 23; LaFollette, *Concerning Women*, 14, 83–84, 113; Dell, *Machine Age*, 65–66.

24. LaFollette, *Concerning Women*, 113; Lorine Pruette, "Why Women Fail," in *Woman's Coming of Age*, ed. Calverton and Schmalhausen, 246–47; see also Wile and Winn, *Modern Manner*, 132–33, and Calverton and Schmalhausen, Preface to *New Generation*, 8–10.

These female sexual revisionists were not to my knowledge lesbians, unlike the New Women whom Carroll Smith-Rosenberg describes in "The New Woman as Androgyne: Social Disorder and Gender Crisis, 1870–1936," in her collected essays, *Disorderly Conduct: Visions of Gender in Victorian America* (New York: 1985), 245–96. The situation of the revisionists as heterosexual women participating in the re-creation of heterosexual ideology is complex and needs further examination. For one example, see Mary Trigg, "'The Characterization of Herself': Lorine Pruette on Women, Men, and Marriage in the 1920s," Paper presented at the Seventh Berkshire Conference on the History of Women, Wellesley College, 1987.

25. Meredith Nicholson, *Broken Barriers* (New York: 1922), 79, 241, 320, 313, 315; Gertrude Atherton, *Black Oxen* (New York: 1923), 263; Marjorie Hillis, *Live Alone and Like It: A Guide for the Extra Woman* (Indianapolis: 1936), 90–91; Lindsey and Evans, *Companionate*, 311; Gilmer, *Dorothy Dix*, 56.

26. Knopf, *Women*, 110, 112, 125, 76; Phyllis Blanchard, *The Adolescent Girl* (New York: 1920), 113–14; C. Gasquoine Hartley, *Women's Wild Oats: Essays on the Re-fixing of Moral Standards* (New York: 1920), 21; Groves, *Marriage Crisis*, 3; Lindsey and Evans, *Revolt*, 294, 246; Frances R. Donovan, *The Schoolma'am* (New York: 1938), 39.

27. Gilbert V. Hamilton, "The Emotional Life of Modern Woman," in *Woman's Coming of Age*, ed. Calverton and Schmalhausen, 228–29; Ralph Hay, "Mannish Women or Old Maids?" *Know Yourself* 1 (July 1938), 78; Lindsey and Evans, *Companionate*, 187; David H. Keller, "Abnormal Love Between Women," *Your Body* 3 (March 1938), 426; Knopf, *Women*, 120; Clark, *Emotional Adjustment*, 70. Carroll Smith-Rosenberg discusses the charge of lesbianism extensively in "Androgyne," in her *Disorderly Conduct*.

28. Hurst, *Back Street*, 169, 175, 191, 377, 400–401; Lewis, *Ann Vickers*, 91–92, 189, 207, 320, 420, 460–61; Robinson, "Continence," in *Sexual Continence*, ed. Robinson, 40.

29. Rupert Hughes, *No One Man* (New York: 1930), 58; Gilmer, *Dorothy Dix*, 79, 216–20; Pruette, "The Flapper," in *The New Generation*, ed. Calverton and Schmalhausen, 589.

30. *Ibid.* (Pruette); Gilmer, *Dorothy Dix*, 17; Nicholson, *Broken Barriers*, 76; Dell, *Machine Age*, 139, 353, 358; Blanchard and Manasses, *New Girls*, 237; Robin Wise, *How To Make Love, in Six Easy Lessons* (New York: 1925), 36.

31. Nicholson, *Broken Barriers*, 273; Atherton, *Black Oxen*, 126; Blanchard and Manasses, *New Girls*, 218; Lindsey and Evans, *Companionate*, 124–31.

32. Sanger, *Happiness*, 127; Max J. Exner, *The Sexual Side of Marriage* (1932; rpt. New York: 1937), 20; Hannah M. Stone and Abraham Stone, *A Marriage Manual: A Practical Guide-Book to Sex and Marriage* (New York: 1937), 217–18. In "'A New Generation of Women': Progressive Psychiatrists and the Hypersexual Female,"

Feminist Studies 13 (Fall 1987): 513–43, Elizabeth Lunbeck shows the resistance there was to accepting young women's sexual activity as normal.

33. Lindsey and Evans, *Revolt*, 88; Eddy, *Sex and Youth*, 137; Wile and Winn, *Modern Manner*, 176.

34. John D'Emilio, "Capitalism and Gay Identity," in *Powers of Desire*, ed. Snitow et al., 105.

35. Elaine May, *Great Expectations: Marriage and Divorce in Post-Victorian America* (Chicago: 1980), 137–55, 104–9.

36. Filene, *Him,/Her/Self*, 144–45; Raoul de Guchteneere, *Judgment on Birth Control* (New York: 1931), 177, 191–92; Lindsey and Evans, *Companionate*, 153; Schmalhausen, "War of the Sexes," in *Woman's Coming of Age*, ed. Calverton and Schmalhausen, 173.

37. Rosalind Pollack Petchesky, *Abortion and Woman's Choice: The State, Sexuality, and Reproductive Freedom* (1984; rpt. Boston: 1985), ch. 6, "Abortion and Heterosexual Culture: The Teenage Question."

38. Other writers making similar interpretations of this sexual ideology include Epstein in "Family, Sexual Morality," in *Powers of Desire*, ed. Snitow *et al.*; Smith-Rosenberg in "Androgyne," in her *Disorderly Conduct;* and Margaret Jackson in "Sexual Liberation or Social Control? Some aspects of the relationship between feminism and the social construction of sexual knowledge in the early twentieth century," *Women's Studies International Forum* 6 (1983): 1–17, in which she discusses the ideas of Havelock Ellis.

10

Venereal Disease: The Wages of Sin?

Elizabeth Fee

Ways of perceiving and understanding disease are historically constructed. Our social, political, religious, and moral conceptions influence our perceptions of disease, just as do different scientific and medical theories. Indeed, these different elements often cannot be easily separated, as scientists and physicians bring their own cultural ideas to bear in the construction of scientific theories. Because these cultural ideas may be widely shared, their presence within medical and scientific theory may not be readily apparent. Often, such cultural conceptions are more obvious when reviewing medical and scientific theories of the past than they are in contemporary medical practice.[1]

Just as cultural conceptions of disease may be embodied in the framing of scientific theories, so these theories also influence popular perceptions of disease. At times such scientific theories may reinforce, or contradict, other cultural conceptions, such as religious and moral ideas or racial stereotypes.

In the case of the venereal diseases, it is clear that our attitudes embody a fundamental cultural ambivalence: are venereal diseases to be studied and treated from a purely biomedical point of view—are they infectious diseases like any others—or are they to be treated as social, moral, or spiritual afflictions?[2] As the name implies, venereal diseases are inevitably associated with sexuality—and therefore our perceptions of these diseases tend to be entangled with our ideas about the social meanings and moral evaluation of sexual behaviors. In the case of syph-

Another version of this chapter appears in the *Journal of the History of Medicine and Allied Sciences* 43, no. 2 (1988).

ilis, a major killer in the first half of the twentieth century, health officials could decide that the true "cause" of syphilis was the microorganism *Treponema pallidum*, or they could define the "underlying cause" as "promiscuous sexual behavior." Each claim focuses on a different part of social reality, and each carries different messages of responsibility and blame. Each is part of a different language in which the disease may be described and defined. The first suggests the primacy of the medical clinic for treating disease; the second, the primacy of moral exhortation.

Throughout the twentieth century struggles have been waged over the meaning and definition of the venereal diseases. At times these diseases have been blanketed in silence, as though they belonged to a "private" realm, not open to public discussion. Wars, however, have tended to make venereal diseases visible, to bring them out of the private sphere and into the center of public policy discussions; this has highlighted the struggles over their proper definition and treatment. In World War I, for example, the American Social Hygiene Association consistently equated venereal disease with immorality, vice, and prostitution.[3] Its members thus tried to close down brothels and taverns, to arrest prostitutes, and to advocate continence and sexual abstinence for the soldiers. The Commission on Training Camp Activities tried to suppress vice and liquor and also to organize "good, clean fun": sports events, theatrical entertainments and educational programs.[4] The Army, however, quietly issued prophylactic kits to the soldiers and made early treatment after possible exposure compulsory. Any soldier who failed to get treatment could face trial and imprisonment for neglect of duty. These programs embodied different conceptions of the disease, as the consequence of "vice" or as the result of infection by a microorganism.

When dealing with major disease problems, we often try to find some social group to "blame" for the infection. During the war educational materials clearly presented the fighting men as the innocent victims of disease; prostitutes were the guilty spreaders of infection. Indeed, prostitutes were often presented as implicitly working for the enemy against patriotic American soldiers.[5] In many communities prostitutes would be the focus, and often the victims and scapegoats, of the new attention to venereal infections. Prostitutes—the women responsible for the defilement of the heroic American soldier—would be regularly rounded up, arrested, and jailed in the campaign against vice.

The end of the war, however, brought a waning of interest in venereal disease and a return to "normal life," freed of the restrictions and regulations of military necessity. The energetic public discussion of venereal disease again lapsed into a public silence. Prostitutes and their customers were again permitted to operate without much official harassment; health departments quietly collected statistics on venereal disease but avoided publicity on the subject.[6]

In this essay we will examine the subsequent history of venereal disease, and especially syphilis, by focusing on a major industrial city, Baltimore, to see how the struggle between the moral and biomedical views of disease was played out in the context of city politics in the 1930s and 1940s. Although syphilis is no longer a significant public health problem, this account should be useful in helping us to reflect on the new problem of AIDS (acquired immune deficiency syndrome) today.

■ Treatment for Venereal Disease: The Public Health Clinics   In Baltimore in the 1920s a great social silence surrounded the problem of syphilis. Since venereal diseases carried such negative social stigma, only a small proportion of cases were ever reported. Deaths from syphilis were often attributed to other causes as physicians endeavored to save patients and their families from possible embarrassment. A social conspiracy of silence resulted: patients did not talk about their diseases, physicians did not report them, the health department did not publicize them, and the newspapers never mentioned them. The diseases were thus largely invisible. Most hospitals and some physicians refused to treat patients with venereal diseases; some physicians specialized in these diseases and made a great deal of money from private patients.[7] Many patients, however, could not afford private medical care.

In the aftermath of the war, the city health department began quietly to treat venereal diseases in its public clinics. The first such clinic, opened in 1922, had 13,000 patient visits in its first year of operation. The clinic population grew so fast that the city soon opened a second clinic, and then a third. These patients, brought to the public clinics through poverty, were recorded in health department files as venereal disease cases. Like all the diseases of the poor, these cases attracted little public attention.

The venereal disease problem in Baltimore was, however, made publicly visible by a survey conducted by the United States Public Health Service in 1931.[8] The survey defined syphilis as a major problem in Baltimore, and as a problem of the black population. The reported "colored" rate was 22 per 1000 males and 10 per 1000 women; this contrasted with a reported white rate of 4 per 1000 men and 1.3 per 1000 women. Of course, whites were more likely to be seeing private physicians and thus less likely to have their disease reported to the health department. Syphilis, originally perceived as a disease of vice and prostitution, was now redefined as a black disease.

The treatment of syphilis seemed to have been invented as a punishment for sin. The recommended therapy required sixty or more weekly clinic visits, with painful injections in alternating courses of arsenicals and heavy metals. The minimum effective treatment required forty weekly visits. To the distress of health officials, many patients drifted away as soon as their symptoms had been relieved; only half the white patients and one-third the black patients stayed to receive the minimum necessary treatment.[9] Fewer black patients continued in treatment because most white physicians and nurses were said to have an unsympathetic attitude to black patients. In 1932 the health department employed black physicians and nurses, hoping to increase the rate of successful treatments, and concluded: "The best results are obtained by encouraging the colored race to take care of its own people . . . The success of these clinics is unquestionably due to the fact that colored physicians have a more sympathetic approach and a better understanding of the psychology of the Negro race."[10]

■ The Depression: Restricting Treatment   During the Depression public clinics became more crowded than ever, with over 84,000 visits in 1932 alone. The city health department, already burdened with tight budgets and increasing health problems of every kind, complained that the hospitals in town were dumping poor patients on the city clinics.[11] Ideally, the city health department would have distributed the then current chemotherapy—neoarsphenamine, sulpharsphenamine, and salvarsan—free to physicians and hospitals for treating indigent patients; with cuts in their own budgets, however, they did little beyond helplessly watching while the clinic population continued to grow.

As the Depression deepened, patients who previously would have been able to pay were increasingly forced to depend on free public clinics. In 1933 the problem of overcrowding became so acute that the city health department decided to treat only patients at the infectious stage of syphilis. They discontinued treatment to any patients who had received sufficient drugs to render them noninfectious to others, even though they had not been cured.[12]

The new operating rules effectively changed the character of the health department clinics. Now the clinics no longer pretended to cure, and for the poor, it was now impossible to be properly treated. The unemployed could not afford the expensive series of weekly treatments given by private physicians, but neither could they get a job if they tested positively for infection.

■ Venereal Disease and Racism   In the 1930s as today, health statistics were gathered by race but not by income. The statistics on venereal diseases confirmed the definition of syphilis as predominantly a black or "colored" problem. In fact almost all infectious diseases were far more prevalent among blacks than whites, reflecting the effects of poverty, poor housing, and overcrowding. The distribution of syphilis, for example, was virtually identical with the distribution of tuberculosis, and both were heavily concentrated in the slums and black ghettos. Ferdinand Reinhard, the head of the bureau of venereal diseases, blamed both diseases on economic conditions, noting that the black population "suffered severely under the depression . . . actually existing near the bread line."[13] Reinhard expressed the forlorn hope that "at some future time, when the social conscience of the community becomes more highly developed, something may be done to rectify these conditions."[14]

While Reinhard described the black venereal disease problem as an effect of economics and social conditions, most whites saw venereal disease simply as a question of sexual morality. Blacks were popularly perceived as highly sexual, uninhibited, and promiscuous. James Jones in writing about the "notoriously syphilis-soaked race" has graphically described the sexual perceptions and attitudes underlying syphilis programs in the southern states. Briefly stated, white doctors saw blacks as "diseased, debilitated and debauched," the victims of their own uncontrolled or uncontrollable sexual instincts and impulses.[15] Baltimore, lying on the border between north and south, was little different: if, as nobody doubted, venereal diseases were more prevalent among blacks, this fact was seen as both evidence and consequence of their promiscuity, sexual indulgence, and immorality.

The perception of venereal disease as a black problem tended to be self-reinforcing as physicians and health department officials directed their attention to Baltimore's black population. It is difficult at this point to distinguish the different factors involved in the reported rates of disease—some of the differential must have been a result of the underreporting of white cases, some due to the increased spread of disease and greater susceptibility of the poor to all types of infectious diseases, and some related to different patterns of sexual behavior. Whatever the actual combination of factors involved, health officials were certainly convinced that the main issue was sexual behavior, and they were equally convinced that it was the sexual behavior of the black population that had to be changed.

Since the problem was clearly understood as one of sexual behavior, the city health department began an energetic public education project aimed at changing sexual attitudes—by persuasion or by fear. In 1934 the department directed a new program on sex hygiene at the black population. They gave talks at the Colored Vocational School and the Frederick Douglass High School, and organized exhibits for Negro Health Week and for the National Association of Teachers in Colored Schools. They distributed nearly 14,000 pamphlets on venereal diseases. A "social hygiene motion picture" with the discouraging title *Damaged Lives* played in twenty-three theaters, thus reaching over 65,000 people, one-tenth of Baltimore's adult population.[16]

The main aim of this health propaganda was to stress the dangers of sexual promiscuity, but it also emphasized the need for early detection and treatment of disease. Apparently unaware that the public clinics no longer offered full treatment to their patients, the journalist H. L. Menen thundered in local newspaper columns that "we must either teach and advocate the use of prophylactic measures [condoms] or force patients to take adequate treatment until they are cured."[17] While the first suggestion was perfectly sensible as a method of prevention, it flew in the face of public morality as seeming to encourage "sexual irregularity"— only Mencken seemed to have the courage to publicly advocate such an approach. Pamphlets distributed by the Social Hygiene Association and the city health department continued to urge chastity before marriage and sexual fidelity within marriage as the proper solutions to syphilis.

In 1935 syphilis was by far the most prevalent of the communicable diseases occurring in the city, with 5,754 reported cases; the next most prevalent disease was chickenpox—not a disease considered of much importance—with 3,816 reported cases.[18] The same year, the staff of the bureau of venereal diseases gave twenty-one public talks on syphilis, published five articles in the local press, produced a radio talk for Negro Health Week, and distributed 16,000 pamphlets. The facilities for actually treating syphilis were still completely inadequate.

Syphilis deaths were now running at between 110 and 150 per year. As Reinhard complained, "Any other group of diseases scattered throughout the community to this extent would be considered to have taken on epidemic proportions and would be cause for alarm on the part of health authorities."[19] Perhaps despairing of the efficacy of moral arguments, Reinhard began to stress the economic costs of the refusal to treat syphilis. At least twelve percent of the patients who were refused treatment would end their days in insane asylums; ten percent more would be charges on the public purse because of cardiovascular complications— conservatively estimated at a direct charge to the city of $180,000 annually, without counting the economic costs of lost individual and family earnings, or of medical treatment before complete physical or mental collapse.[20]

Reinhard continued for several years to struggle against the partial treatment plan and to advocate extended clinic facilities, sufficient for all syphilis patients, and staffed with black physicians, nurses, and social workers. It seemed, at the time, to be a one-man campaign. Most physicians approved of the fact that the health department was not offering treatment, the proper domain of fee-for-service medicine. Particularly during the depression years, when many physicians found it difficult to make a living on patient fees, the medical profession was antagonistic to efforts by public health officers to offer free treatments to any patients, whatever their illness.

■ **Syphilis as Everyone's Disease: A National Campaign**   In 1936 Reinhard's "one-man campaign" against syphilis in Baltimore suddenly became part of a major national effort. Thomas Parran, Surgeon-General of the United States Public Health Service, now lent the full weight of his authority to a campaign against venereal diseases. A forceful and dynamic man, Parran decided to break through the wall of silence and make the public confront the magnitude of the problem. To do this, he redefined syphilis as a disease that struck "innocent" victims: the educated, respectable, white population. While his books, *Shadow on the Land* and *Plain Words About Venereal Disease*, are best remembered in public health circles, Parran's short popular article "Why Don't We Stamp Out Syphilis?," published in *Survey Graphic* and the *Reader's Digest* in 1936, reached a much larger popular audience.[21] In this article Parran called syphilis "the great American Disease" and declared: "we might virtually stamp out this disease were we not hampered by the widespread belief that nice people don't talk about syphilis, that nice people don't have syphilis, and that nice people shouldn't do anything about those who *do* have syphilis."[22] Parran's point was that nice people *did* have syphilis; he never tired of pointing out that respectable physicians, innocent children, and heads of industry were among those infected.[23] If people could only free their minds of "the medieval concept that syphilis is the just reward of win" he said, they could "deal with it as we would any other highly communicable disease, dangerous to the individual and burdensome to the public at large."[24] To separate syphilis from its well worn associations with sin, black immorality, vice, and prostitution, Parran peppered his talks and articles with a series of little anecdotes: "Remember that a kiss may carry the germ. In an eastern state recently one of our health officers traced 17 cases of syphilis to a party at which kissing games were played."[25]

Parran declared that half the victims of syphilis were "innocently infected": "Many cases come from such casual contacts as the use of [a] recently soiled drinking cup, a pipe or cigarette; in receiving services from diseased nursemaids, barber or beauty shop operators, etc., and in giving services such as those of a dentist, doctor or nurse to a diseased person."[26] Syphilis was just another contagious disease, although a highly threatening and dangerous one. The point was to find syphilis cases and to treat them; the state should be obliged to provide treatment, said Parran, and the patient should be obliged to endure it. Syphilis would be the next great plague to go—as soon as the public broke with the old-fashioned and pre-scientific notion that syphilis was "the wages of sin." From a financial point of view, the state and the individual could only profit from early identification and treatment before the disease had a chance to produce "human wrecks, the incompetents, the criminals."

In Baltimore, Huntington Williams, the young Commissioner of Health, took up the campaign as articulated by Parran. He termed syphilis "the greatest unmet problem of public health" but declared that "medical science has all the weapons it needs to defeat this tiny but ferocious enemy, once the defenses thrown up by society itself are beaten down."[27]

Beginning in 1936 the new syphilis campaign began to have an impact on the local press. The *Baltimore Health News*, a popular health magazine published by the city, began the process with two issues devoted to syphilis. The American Public Health Association broadcast a radio message on syphilis from its annual meeting in New Orleans; the Baltimore health department reprinted Parran's *Reader's Digest* article; they showed a "talking slide film," *For All Our Sakes*, to large and apparently enthusiastic audiences; the local press and radio stations picked up the campaign.[28]

But while the city health department was consolidating the new bio-medical approach to syphilis, it was suddenly challenged with a resurgent moral crusade against vice and prostitution, led by none other than the redoubtable J. Edgar Hoover.

■ **Medical Treatment or Crusade Against Vice?**   "Captives Taken in Weekend Drive Against City's White Slave Traffic," declared the headlines of the Baltimore *Sun* on May 17, 1937:

> Striking at Baltimore's white slave traffic, thirty-five Federal agents, commanded by J. Edgar Hoover, chief of the Federal Bureau of Investigation, Department of Justice, swept down on ten alleged haunts of vice here late Saturday night and early yesterday morning, taking forty-seven persons into custody . . . Mr. Hoover said the crusade will continue 'until Baltimore is completely cleaned up.'[29]

The raids generated great excitement and controversy, magnified when local prostitutes implicated a number of high level police officers and at least one state senator in Baltimore's "white slave trade."[30] The local newspapers took delight in reporting the activities of this organized racket, playing up Baltimore as a notorious center of vice and iniquity. The series of titillating revelations discredited the Baltimore police force and furthered public admiration of Hoover for his resolute action.

State Senator Raymond E. Kennedy now implied that the city health department, like the police department, was implicitly involved in condoning vice. He demanded that all prostitutes being treated in city clinics be immediately incarcerated. Parran was called to appear as a witness before a Grand Jury investigation. On his arrival in Baltimore, however, Parran managed to turn this into a public relations coup for the health department. He announced a state survey of venereal diseases, suggested that Baltimore follow the successful Swedish model of disease control, including the provision of free drugs, and he declared to enthusiastic mass meetings that Maryland would take the lead in the fight against "social diseases."[31]

Public interest in Parran's speeches was so great that when city budget officials refused a health department request for an extra $21,000 to combat syphilis, their action was publicly denounced as "incredible." Even Senator Raymond Kennedy now joined in the popular demand for adequate medical services and Mayor Jackson was forced to agree to an increased health department budget. As Kennedy declared, "There has been more discussion of syphilis in the last ninety days than in the twenty years before."[32]

By 1938 when the American Society for Social Hygiene complained that prostitution still flourished in Baltimore, the local press had lost interest in exposés of vice, and no local politician emerged to carry a crusade. When "National Social Hygiene Day" was announced for February 2, 1938, Huntington Williams decided to celebrate it in Baltimore under the name "Syphilis Control Day"—perhaps, as he said, to make its purpose more understandable, but perhaps also to dissociate the health department's medical program from the national organization's concern with vice and prostitution.[33] Thanks to citywide publicity and political pressure on Mayor Jackson, Williams was able to expand his budget and open the Druid Hill Health Center for black patients in west Baltimore—the first time that adequate public health facilities had been available in this area of the city.[34]

The city health department now tackled the problem of syphilis in industry. At the time, industrial workers were being fired (or never hired in the first place) if they were found to have positive blood tests for syphilis. Employers fired infected workers on the grounds that they were more likely to be involved in industrial accidents, and thus would increase the costs of workmen's compensation and insurance premiums. The health department started to provide free laboratory blood tests for industrial workers; the test results were kept confidential and those infected were referred for appropriate therapy. The health department followed individual workers to make sure they were receiving treatment but, at least in theory, no worker who accepted treatment could be fired. The fact that no guarantees were offered workers refusing therapy meant, however, that syphilis treatment was essentially made compulsory for industrial workers participating in the plan.[35]

Baltimore's industrial employers were gradually persuaded of the plan's value; by 1940, eight industries with 8,500 workers were participating. Some industries, however, still insisted on their right to fire infected workers, and many of the physicians to whom workers were referred had little idea how to treat syphilis. Despite these problems the "Baltimore Plan" for industry was said to be relatively successful in treating syphilis while protecting workers' jobs.[36]

■ **The Impact of War**   In the late 1930s there were considerable grounds for optimism that the campaign against the venereal diseases was beginning to show results. The more open public health attitude toward syphilis as a problem of disease rather than of morality seemed to be successful. The industrial screening plan was slowly convincing reluctant employers, the city was supporting the health department with larger budget appropriations, and the new Druid Hill Health Center was in operation.[37] The numbers of reported cases of syphilis were decreasing each year, despite increased screening efforts and more effective reporting mechanisms. In 1938, 8,236 new cases were reported; in 1939, 7,509; and in 1940, only 6,213. Spot surveys of selected populations, such as that of the black Dunbar High School in 1939, suggested that syphilis was less prevalent than the more pessimistic reports had suspected. These records of syphilis incidence and prevalence may have been quite unreliable from an epidemiological point of view, but this was the first time that syphilis rates had even seemed to be declining; it was a natural conclusion that health department efforts were finally showing demonstrable results.

In the midst of this optimism, however, came the prospect of war and, with it, the fear that war mobilization and an influx of 60,000 soldiers would upset all previous gains.[38] In 1941, with the institution of selective service examinations, reported venereal disease rates began to climb. In Baltimore that year, 1.7 percent of the white enlistees had positive blood tests for syphilis, as had twenty-four percent of the black recruits.[39] Baltimore City won the dubious distinction of having the second highest syphilis rate in the country, second only to Washington, D.C. Baltimore's rate was 101.3 cases per 1000 men examined, more than twice the national rate.[40] In an effort to justify these statistics, the city health department blamed the situation on the nonwhite population: the relatively high proportion of blacks to whites "explained" why Baltimore had the second highest venereal disease rate among the country's largest cities in the same way that it "explained" Baltimore's soaring tuberculosis rate.[41]

Such justifications were hardly likely to be sufficient for a country at war. With the war mobilization had come renewed national attention to protecting the health and fighting efficiency of the soldiers. As during World War I, the first concern was with the control or suppression of prostitution in the vicinity of army camps and with "social hygiene" rather than treatment programs. The May Act passed by Congress made prostitution a federal offense in the vicinity of military camps.

In Baltimore, as in several other cities, the Federal Bureau of Investigation called a conference of local law enforcement agencies to discuss the problem of prostitution.[42] Almost immediately, wrangling and mutual accusations broke out between the different local authorities involved.[43] The Army accused the police of having failed to control prostitution; the police accused the military officials, the liquor board, and the courts of hampering their fight against prostitution and venereal diseases: the military officials had refused to ban the night clubs and taverns believed to be sources of venereal infections; the liquor board had not revoked their licenses; and the courts had either dismissed charges of prostitution or levied such trivial fines as to be completely ineffective.[44] As if there were not problems enough, Police Captain Joseph Itzel also charged that Baltimore congressmen were protecting some of the establishments his police officers had tried to close.

Perhaps mindful of J. Edgar Hoover's attack on the police department some years previously, the Baltimore police seemed determined to prove their dedication to the attack on prostitution. By early 1943 they claimed to have closed most of Baltimore's brothels and to have driven prostitutes from the streets.[45] Police Commissioner Stanton demanded statewide legislation to allow police officers to arrest prostitutes and force them to submit to medical examination and, if infected, medical treatment.[46]

Dr. Nels A. Nelson, head of the state venereal disease control program, declared that these arrests of prostitutes and compulsory medical examinations were completely ineffective: only a few prostitutes could be arrested at any one time, and as soon as they were treated and released, they would immediately return to the streets to become reinfected and to continue to spread infection until their next arrest. The only real control of venereal disease, concluded Nelson, depended on the complete "repression of sexual promiscuity."[47] Meanwhile, the reported cases of syphilis were rapidly increasing. In 1942 the selective service records showed that almost three percent of the white draftees and over thirty-two percent of the black soldiers had syphilis.[48] Thousands of manhours were being lost in the war industries from hospitalization of workers with venereal diseases. Between 1940 and 1942 new cases of syphilis had almost doubled, from 6,213 to 11,293, and gonorrhea rates were also climbing.

In an attempt to develop some kind of cooperative effort between feuding city agencies, the Baltimore Venereal Disease Council was organized in December 1942. Represented on this Council were the Medical and Chirurgical Faculty of Maryland, the Baltimore Retail Druggists Association, the Venereal Disease Control Office of the Third Service Command, the Baltimore Criminal Justice Commission, the Board of Liquor License Commissioners, the Emergency Medical Services for Maryland, the Johns Hopkins University, the Maryland State Health Department, the Supreme Bench, the Police Commissioner of Baltimore, the Maryland Medical Association, and the City Health Department.[49] They created three committees: on rehabilitation, on legislation, and on medicine, public health, and pharmacy. The committee on rehabilitation concerned itself with prostitution but offered a social, rather than moral, analysis of the problem: "Prostitution exists because of the urge for sexual gratification in numerous males, on the one hand, and the inadequacies of conventional social arrangements to meet these demands." From the women's side, prostitution was bound up with "inadequate income, bad housing, insufficient diet, lack of recreation and other facets of total life," although a small number were thought to enter prostitution because of "an overwhelming craving for sex stimulation."[50] The committee carefully divided all prostitutes into three main types and thirteen subtypes, ranging from "bats or superannuated prostitutes rendered unattractive by drink and drugs and by the least particular of bums and homeless men," to "potential prostitutes who are willing to accept money for sex relations which, however, may also be on a volunteer or free basis."[51] The committee recommended that older "hardened" prostitutes be jailed, that "mental cases" be institutionalized, and that "young and potential" prostitutes be offered rehabilitation services, care, and assistance.

By this time, Nelson of the state health department had, however, abandoned the fight against prostitution. He was busily distributing free drugs for syphilis control to private physicians, while he publicly declared the city venereal disease clinics "little more than drug pumping stations in dirty, unattractive quarters."[52] Nelson told the press he was tired of hearing the VD rate discussed as though it were only a Negro problem: "Negroes are plagued by venereal diseases because of their economic and social position . . . they have had the benefits of only two or three generations of western civilization."[53]

The Army was also under attack for failing to organize an effective VD program.[54] Its programs and policies were plagued by contradictions; publicly, it advocated chastity, while privately, it provided prophylactics for the men. Those in charge of the Army's venereal disease program were caught between advocates of sexual continence and the suppression of prostitution, and many Army officers who felt that "Any man who won't f____, won't fight."[55] The Army finally adopted a pragmatic approach and attempted to reduce the sources of infection as much as possible. The pragmatic approach lacked the fervor of a purity crusade, but tried to steer some middle course between laissez-faire attitudes and moral absolutism.

In Baltimore the new acting directors of the city's venereal disease program, Ralph Sikes and Alexander Novey, shared this pragmatic position. Noting that syphilis cases were continuing their sharp increase during the war, they philosophically began their annual report for 1943 by remarking that "the close association between Mars and Venus has existed since historians first recorded human annals."[56] Under their leadership health officers cooperated with the armed services in distributing prophylactic kits throughout the city: in police stations, fire houses, transportation terminals, hospitals, and clinics.[57] Implicitly, the VD control officers had thus accepted the idea that this was a campaign *against* disease, rather than a campaign *for* sexual morality; they concentrated on a fairly mechanical (if effective) approach to prevention while leaving the struggle around prostitution to social hygiene reformers, the police, and the courts.

■ **Sex Education During the War**   During the war the city health department and a research group at the Johns Hopkins School of Hygiene and Public Health undertook a daring task—to teach "sex hygiene" in the public schools. They gave talks to groups of high school students (separated by sex), showed plaster models of the male and female reproductive systems, and gave simple explanations of "menstruation, conception, pregnancy, nocturnal emissions and masturbation, but omitting intercourse and childbirth."[58] The project organizers found that "the boys frequently asked for further information about masturbation, and often about prophylaxis which had purposely been omitted from the talk."[59]

The talk presented to the students offers an interesting glimpse of sex education in 1944 and of a project regarded with much interest, and some nervousness, in the city health department. Sex was introduced with military metaphors; sex, the students were told, was like "the fast tricky fighter planes of the Army," very difficult to handle:

> Sex is just as difficult a problem to handle as any airplane. . . . It is no wonder then that there are so many crashes in the field of sex. When a plane crashes, a person may not walk away from such an accident, or if he does he may carry injury that will last his lifetime. Similar results occur from crashes in the field of sex.[60]

Having been assured that sex was both exciting and dangerous, students were then given a brief description of male reproductive physiology, ending with a caution against masturbation. Masturbation was not dangerous, students were told, merely unnecessary and possibly habit-forming: "It is true that having formed the habit a person may devote too much time and thought to that sort of thing which will hurt the other things in life, such as studies, athletics, and normal friendships."[61] A brief description of the female reproductive system was followed by a discussion of morals and ethics, warning of the need for judgment, but avoiding specific advice: "Since this problem differs for each one, because of different religions, different stages of financial independence and varied ethical standards, we cannot answer anyone's special problem here."[62] Students were urged to discuss their questions with parents and teachers and to read a social hygiene pamphlet on "Growing Up in the World Today."[63]

The third part of the presentation, on venereal diseases, emphasized the dangers of sex. Intimacy brought the germs of syphilis: sexual intercourse was the most threatening, but even kisses could carry disease. The best strategy was to avoid any possible contact with these sexual germs:

> They can be caught only from an infected person and therefore, we should avoid intimate contact with an infected person. But we cannot tell by *looking* at a person whether he or she is infected or not; the answer is to avoid intimate contact with all persons except in marriage. This is the only sure way of avoiding these diseases.[64]

At least for these high school students, the link between sexual morality and venereal disease was clear: sexual intimacy led to syphilis and was therefore to be avoided except in marriage. Why marital sex should be "safe" was never explained, nor was congenital syphilis ever mentioned.

■ **After the War: The New Penicillin Therapy**   By the end of World War II, the problem of syphilis was beginning to recede, both in public consciousness and in statistical measures. Part of this was the normal relaxation in the immediate aftermath of war, the return to home and family, the desire for stability, and a reluctance to confront social and sexual problems or to dwell on their existence. Even more important, however, was the success of the new drug, penicillin: at last, venereal diseases could, it seemed, be quickly and effectively treated. Many felt it was only a matter of time before the venereal diseases were finally eliminated with the aid of modern medicine's "miracle cures."

By 1940 the new "miracle drug" penicillin had been discovered and purified; in 1943 it was first used against syphilis, but it was not yet generally available; supplies were still strictly rationed.[65] Soon, it would completely transform the old methods of treating venereal diseases. On December 31, 1944, the Baltimore City Hospitals opened the first Rapid Treatment Center for treating syphilis with penicillin. Penicillin doses for syphilis were given over eight days; since supplies of the drug were then very limited, only cases judged to be highly infectious were sent for "an eight-day cure, or what is for the present considered to be a cure."[66] From all initial reports the new experimental treatment was remarkably effective.

On June 20, 1945, Mayor Theodore R. McKeldin approved a new city ordinance making treatment for venereal diseases compulsory for the first time. Those suspected of having syphilis or gonorrhea were required to take penicillin therapy at the Rapid Treatment Center.[67] Those refusing treatment could be quarantined and isolated in the Baltimore City hospitals; members of the Church of Christ Scientist, who could not be forced to take treatment, could still be quarantined. This new ordinance was much stricter than previous health regulations and seems to have been passed with little controversy. The new penicillin therapy was apparently safe and effective, and required at most a few days' treatment. Legislators who might have hesitated to require a prolonged or possibly dangerous therapy—such as the older treatment with arsenic and heavy metals—had few qualms about mandating the new penicillin treatment.

The ordinance was, however, rarely invoked. Most patients were eager to go to the Rapid Treatment Center when diagnosed. In 1946 nearly 2,000 people with infectious syphilis received treatment; most were reported as completely cured. (Before penicillin, only an estimated twenty-five percent of patients completed the lengthy treatments considered necessary for a full cure.)[68] In 1947 the Baltimore *Sun* reviewed the city's experience with the new ordinance:

> On the basis of this experience (over the last 16 months), it is clear that the protection of the public against persons carrying the disease and refusing to be treated more than outweighs the sacrifice of individual rights by so small a number. . . . Under the circumstances, the enactment of a permanent ordinance seems fully justified.[69]

The state health department in 1947 announced that "for the first time in history any resident of Maryland who contracts syphilis can obtain treatment resulting in prompt and almost certain cure."[70]

■ **Conclusion: The End of the Struggle?**   The biomedical approach to venereal diseases had apparently been stunningly successful. Diseases that only ten years before had been described as the most serious of all the infectious diseases had now been tamed by chemotherapy with a simple, safe, and effective cure. Diseases that twenty years previously had been guilty secrets, virtually unmentionable in the public press and quietly ignored by health departments, were now glorious examples of the triumph of modern medicine in overcoming ancient plagues. The ideological struggle between those who had seen the fight against venereal disease as a battle for sexual morality and those who had seen it as simply another form of bacteriological warfare was now over. The social hygiene reformers had to concede defeat to the public health officers, epidemiologists, and laboratory researchers. Or did they?

In 1947 the Maryland State Department of Health, announcing the success of the rapid treatment program, concluded its press bulletin with the warning: "To decrease the number of repeat patients and prevent venereal diseases it will be necessary to reduce sexual promiscuity. If fear of disease is a less powerful restraining factor the problem must be attacked more strongly through moral training and suppression of prostitution."[71] The Baltimore city health department sounded even more pessimistic:

> It may be stated that so far there is little or no evidence that the apparently miraculous one and eight day cures of gonorrhea and infectious syphilis (respectively) with penicillin have accomplished much toward the control of these diseases. . . . Certainly this new therapy has done nothing to correct the promiscuous sexual behavior which is the ultimate cause of the spread of venereal disease.[72]

In 1948 Thomas B. Turner gave a talk to the American Social Hygiene Association entitled "Penicillin: Help or Hindrance?" As the title suggested, he was curiously ambivalent about the new "miracle drug." Turner knew the extraordinary difference the new chemotherapy had made to patients, and he indeed catalogued the successes of penicillin "on the credit side of the ledger." He cautioned, however, against being "dazzled by the apparent potentialities of this fine new drug." On "the debit side of the ledger" was the loss of fear as a deterrent to exposure and the possibility of multiple reinfections; Turner assured his audience that the real concern of venereal disease prevention programs was "the moral, spiritual and economic health of a community," and urged them to "strengthen those forces in the community which help to preserve not only our physical well being, but our spiritual health as well."[73]

Official admiration for the new chemotherapy was thus allied to warnings that the "real" causes of disease were unsolved. Even those most committed to the bacteriological view of disease seemed uneasy about the decoupling of venereal disease from sin and promiscuity: How would sexual morality be controlled if not by the fear of disease? Would "rampant promiscuity" defeat the best efforts of medical treatment?

A brief review of health statistics in the years since the discovery of penicillin suggests that syphilis has, in the main, been effectively controlled. New cases of syphilis are reported each year, and doubtless others go unreported, but the rates are relatively low. In 1986 a total of 373 cases of primary, secondary, and early latent cases were reported in Baltimore; in 1987, a total of 364 cases. Although these cases are of continuing concern to health department officials, at least from the perspective of the 1930s and 1940s, the miracle of control really has occurred.

Gonorrhea, however, is another story. Gonorrhea continues to be the most frequently reported infectious disease in the United States, in Maryland, and in Baltimore City; as press reports like to say, in numbers of cases, it is second only to the common cold.[74] In 1980 there were 18,000 cases in Baltimore, in 1986, 16,000, and in 1987, 13,000 cases. In 1986 the city ranked second in numbers of cases of gonorrhea among cities with populations over 200,000.

Although gonorrhea is of epidemic proportions, it creates little popular concern. A remarkable effort in 1976 to form a coalition in Baltimore against venereal disease—composed of the Boy Scouts, the National Organization for Women, the League of Women Voters, the Benevolent Order of Elks, and the Baltimore Gay Alliance—was unable to fire public interest.[75] Parents were more concerned about drug use than sex; those infected, or potentially infected, knew that the cure was simple, available, and cheap. The vital element of *fear* was missing: Gonorrhea was perceived as an uncomplicated infection, easily treated and readily cured.

As we have since discovered, the fear and underlying ambivalence toward sexuality were only lying dormant. Public concern, horror, and fear about AIDS have recently reignited the older social hygiene movement in a new form. The once prevalent description of the black population as sexually promiscuous, sexually threatening, and a reservoir of disease has now been applied to the gay male population. AIDS is popularly seen as "caused" by gay promiscuity and, even more broadly, as a punishment for unconventional or unapproved sexual behavior, rather than simply as the result of infection by a microorganism. Venereal disease is again perceived as the "wages of sin," or, as the Reverend Jerry Falwell says: "A man reaps what he sows. If he sows seed in the field of his lower nature, he will reap from it a harvest of corruption." Again, the argument is taking place between a new generation of biomedical researchers, eager, in the main, to dissociate a medical problem from a moral crusade, and a new generation of moral reformers, eager to use the new AIDS threat to reform sexual behavior.

The "moral" and "scientific" attitudes toward venereal disease are not, of course, completely separate. As we have seen in the ambivalent responses to the success of penicillin therapy, even the most dedicated scientists tend to share the social and sexual values of their culture—in this case, expressing some regret or misgiving, lest effective and safe chemotherapy act as an encouragement to sexual promiscuity by removing the fear of disease. Moral reformers know that scientific successes, especially in the form of new "miracle drugs," will weaken but not destroy their case. If a new "miracle drug" is discovered to be effective against AIDS, it will weaken, but certainly not destroy their social, moral, and cultural objections to homosexuality.

Both the biomedical and moral perspectives on venereal disease highlight specific aspects of a complex social reality. Venereal diseases, like all other diseases, are experienced and reproduced in a social context. We may separate the biological and social aspects for analysis, but any complete understanding of a disease problem must involve both, as interrelated parts of a single social reality.

Social and cultural ideas offer a variety of ways in which diseases can be perceived and interpreted. The germ theory provides an explanation of disease that largely—but not completely—isolates it from this social context, robbing it of some of its social (and in this case, moral) meaning. But the purely "scientific" interpretation is never wholly victorious, for social and cultural meanings of disease reassert themselves in the interstices of science and prove their power whenever the biomedical sciences fail to completely cure or solve the problem. Only when a disease condition is completely abolished do social and cultural meanings cease to be relevant to the experience and perception of human illness.

■ Notes

1. For a fascinating analysis of the history of cultural and scientific conceptions of syphilis, see Ludwig Fleck, *Genesis and Development of a Scientific Fact* (1935; rpt., Chicago: 1979).

2. For an excellent recent history of the controversies around venereal diseases in the United States, see Allan Brandt, *No Magic Bullet: A Social History of Venereal Diseases in the United States Since 1880* (New York: 1985).

3. National Academy of Sciences, *Scientific and Technical Societies of the United States and Canada*, 8th ed. (Washington, D.C.: 1968), 62.

4. Edward H. Beardsley, "Allied Against Sin: American and British Responses to Venereal Disease in World War 1," *Medical History* 20 (1976): 194.

5. As one widely reprinted article, said to have reached eight million readers, described 'The Enemy at Home': "The name of this invisible enemy is Venereal Disease—and there you have in two words the epitome of all that is unclean, malignant and menacing . . . . Gonorrhoea and syphilis are 'camp followers' where prostitution and alcohol are permitted. They form almost as great an enemy behind the lines as do the Huns in front." "V. D.: The Enemy at Home," as cited by William H. Zinsser, "Social Hygiene and the War: Fighting Venereal Disease a Public Trust," *Social Hygiene* 4 (1918): 519–20.

6. In 1920 William Travis Howard, a member of the city health department, complained: "The Baltimore health department has never inaugurated a single administrative measure directed at the control of the venereal diseases . . . the Baltimore health department has contented itself with receiving such reports as were made and with lending its power, when called upon, to force a few recalcitrant patients to appear at the venereal disease clinic established by the United States Government." Howard, *Public Health Administration and the Natural History of Disease in Baltimore, Maryland: 1797–1920* (Washington, D.C.: 1924): 154–55.

7. Baltimore City Health Department, Annual Report (1930).

8. Taliaferro Clark and Lida Usilton, "Survey of the Venereal Diseases in the City of Baltimore, Baltimore County, and the Four Contiguous Counties," *Venereal Disease Information* 12 (Washington, D.C.: 20 October 1931), 437–56.

9. Ferdinand O. Reinhard, Director, Bureau of Vital Statistics, Baltimore, "Delinquent Patients in Venereal Disease Clinics: Result of a Study in Baltimore City Health Department," *Journal of the American Medical Association* 106 (1936): 1377–90.

10. Baltimore City Health Department, Annual Report (1932), 63.

11. *Ibid.,* 62.

12. Baltimore City Health Department, Annual Report (1933), 93.

13. *Ibid.,* 97.

14. *Ibid.,* 99.

15. James H. Jones, *Bad Blood: The Tuskegee Syphilis Experiment* (New York: 1981), 16–29.

16. Baltimore City Health Department, Annual Report (1934), 107.

17. H. L. Mencken, "Plague," *Evening Sun,* 13 August 1934.

18. Baltimore City Health Department, Annual Report (1935), 115.

19. Ferdinand O. Reinhard, "The Venereal Disease Problem in the Colored Population of Baltimore City," *American Journal of Syphilis and Neurology* 19 (1935): 183–95.

20. Ferdinand O. Reinhard, "Late Latent Syphilis—A Problem and A Challenge," *Journal of Social Hygiene* 22 (1936): 360–63.

21. Thomas Parran, *Shadow on the Land: Syphilis* (New York: 1937); Thomas Parran and R. A. Vonderlehr, *Plain Words About Venereal Disease* (New York: 1941); also see n. 20.

22. Thomas Parran, "Why Don't We Stamp Out Syphilis?" *Reader's Digest* (July 1936), reprinted in *Baltimore Health News* (August 1936): 3.

23. *E.g.* Parran, *Shadow on the Land,* 207, 230.

24. Parran, "Why Don't We Stamp Out Syphilis?" *Baltimore Health News,* 8.

25. *Ibid.,* 3.

26. Parran, "Why Don't We Stamp Out Syphilis?" *Reader's Digest,* 65–73.

27. Avery McBee, "Open Attack on Age-Old Curse," *Baltimore Sun,* 9 August 1936.

28. "War on Venereal Disease Impends," *Baltimore Sun,* 24 December 1936.

29. "G-Men's Haul in Vice Raids Totals 47," *Baltimore Sun,* 17 May 1937.

30. "Vice Witness Names Police Lieutenant," *Baltimore Sun,* 18 May 1937; "Vice Arrests May Total 100; Bierman Named," *Sunday Sun,* 19 May 1937.

31. "Starts to Survey Venereal Disease," *Baltimore Sun,* 29 July 1937; "Venereal Disease Fight is Planned," *Baltimore Sun,* 22 August 1937; "Fight Opens Here on Social Disease," *Baltimore Sun,* 25 August 1937; "Syphilis Control Unit Begins Work," *Baltimore Sun,* 21 October 1937; "Over 2,000 Attend Talks on Syphilis," *Baltimore Sun,* 26 October 1937.

32. "Failure to Assist Syphilis Fight Hit," *Baltimore Sun,* 6 December 1937; "Jackson Pledges Aid in War on Syphilis," *Baltimore Sun,* 7 December 1937.

33. "Attention Called to Syphilis Here," *Baltimore Sun,* 1 February 1938.

34. Baltimore City Health Department, Annual Reports (1938), 159; (1939), 159.

35. Baltimore City Health Department, Annual Report (1938), 16; "21 Employers Asked in Drive on Syphilis," *Baltimore Sun,* 27 March 1938; "Syphilis Control is Under Way Here," *Baltimore Sun,* 22 May 1938; W. M. P., "We Join the Anti-Syphilis Crusade," *The Kalends* (June 1938), reprinted in *Baltimore Health News* 15 (July 1938): 53–54; Baltimore City Health Department, "Syphilis in Industry" (Baltimore: n.d.).

36. Huntington Williams, "Discussion on the Symposium on Syphilis in Industry" (January 15, 1940), Second Annual Conference on Industrial Health Sponsored by the Council on Industrial Health of the American Medical Association, Chicago, 15–16 January 1940; Editorial, "Syphilis and Unemployment," *American*

Journal of Industrial Hygiene and Toxicology (May 1937); *Baltimore Health News* (July 1938).

37. Baltimore City Health Department, Annual Report (1938), 159–63; (1939), 159–63.

38. Baltimore City Health Department, Annual Report (1940), 149–51.

39. Baltimore City Health Department, Annual Report (1941), 139.

40. "City Shown Second in Syphilis Survey," *Baltimore Sun*, 22 October 1941.

41. "High Syphilis Rate Laid to Race Ratio," *Baltimore Sun*, 26 October 1941.

42. "FBI and City Agencies Schedule Parley on Vice," *Evening Sun*, 15 July 1942.

43. "Reckord Tells O'Conor of Vice," *Baltimore Sun*, 17 July 1942.

44. "Itzel Charges War on Vice Hampered," *Baltimore Sun*, 26 January 1943.

45. "Says Vice Control Has Improved Here," *Baltimore Sun*, 27 January 1943.

46. "State Law Held Needed in War on Vice," *Baltimore Sun*, 28 January 1943.

47. "Stanton Idea for Examination of Prostitutes Is Denounced," *Baltimore Sun*, 29 January 1943.

48. "Venereal Picture Dark: Dr. Huntington Williams Says No Improvement Is Expected for Some Time," *Baltimore Sun*, 21 January 1943.

49. "Baltimore Disease Council is Organized," *Baltimore Health News* 20 (February 1943): 109–10.

50. "Three Venereal Disease Council Committee Reports," *Baltimore Health News* 20 (March 1943): 119–20.

51. *Ibid.*, 118–19.

52. "Clinics Here Under Fire," *Baltimore Sun*, 30 March 1943.

53. "Venereal Disease Rate High in State," *Baltimore Sun*, 15 June 1943.

54. Parran and Vonderlehr, *Plain Words About Venereal Disease*, especially 96–120.

55. *Ibid.*, 77.

56. Baltimore City Health Department, Annual Report (1943), 147.

57. *Ibid.*, 148.

58. C. Howe Eller, "A Sex Education Project and Serologic Survey in a Baltimore High School," *Baltimore Health News* 21 (November 1944): 83.

59. *Ibid.*, 84.

60. J. D. Porterfield, Baltimore City Health Department, "A Talk on Sex Hygiene for High School Students," April 1944, Rockefeller Foundation Archives, RG 1.1, Series 200, 1.

61. *Ibid.*, 4.

62. *Ibid.*, 7.

63. Emily V. Clapp, *Growing Up in the World Today* (Boston: n.d.).

64. *Ibid.*, 14.

65. For the development of penicillin therapy, see Harry F. Dowling, *Fighting Infection: Conquests of the Twentieth Century* (Cambridge: 1977):125–57.

66. Baltimore City Health Department, Annual Report (1945), 29.

67. Baltimore City Health Department, Annual Report (1945), 145–46; "Venereal Law Made Specific," *Baltimore Sun*, 26 August 1945.

68. "End of VD—Cure Center Seen as Calamity," *Evening Sun*, 12 June 1946.

69. "A Temporary Power Made Permanent," *Baltimore Sun*, 9 January 1947.

70. "Rapid Treatment," Press Bulletin No. 1043, Maryland State Department of Health, (27 January 1947) Enoch Pratt Library, Maryland Room, Baltimore.

71. *Ibid.*

198 Sexual Conflicts and Cultural Authority

72. Baltimore City Health Department, Annual Report (1946), 28.

73. Thomas B. Turner, "Syphilis: Help or Hindrance?" Talk to American Social Hygiene Association, 2 February 1948, Rockefeller Foundation Archives, RG 1.1, Series 200, 4.

74. Baltimore City STD Fact Sheet, Baltimore City Health Department (November 1981).

75. "City Assembles Coalition to Battle Venereal Disease," *Baltimore Sun*, 10 June 1976.

11

"Uncontrolled Desires": The Response to the Sexual Psychopath, 1920–1960

Estelle B. Freedman

In the 1931 German film *M*, Peter Lorre portrayed a former mental patient who stalked innocent school girls, lured them with candy and balloons, and then, offscreen, murdered them in order to satiate his abnormal erotic desires. Two years later, when the film opened in the United States, the *New York Times* criticized director Fritz Lang for wasting his talents on a crime "too hideous to contemplate." Despite the reviewer's distaste for the public discussion of sexual crimes, the American media soon began to cater to a growing popular interest in stories of violent, sexual murders committed by men like "M." In 1937 the *New York Times* itself created a new index category, "Sex Crimes," to encompass the 143 articles it published on the subject that year. Cleveland, Detroit, and Los Angeles newspapers also ran stories about sexual criminals, while national magazines published articles by legal and psychiatric authorities who debated whether a "sex-crime wave" had hit America.[1]

The sex crime panic soon extended beyond the media and into the realm of politics and law. Between 1935 and 1965, city, state, and federal officials established commissions to investigate sexual crime, passed statutes to transfer authority over sex offenders from courts to psychiatrists, and funded specialized institutions for the treatment of sex offenders. As a result, in most states, a man accused of rape, sodomy, child molestation, indecent exposure, or corrupting the morals of a minor—if diagnosed as a "sexual psychopath"—could receive an indeterminate sen-

This article is reprinted from "'Uncontrolled Desires': The Response to the Sexual Psychopath, 1920–1960," *The Journal of American History* 74 (June 1987): 83–106, and appears courtesy of the *Journal* on behalf of the Organization of American Historians.

tence to a psychiatric, rather than a penal, institution. The laws defined the sexual psychopath as someone whose "utter lack of power to control his sexual impulses" made him "likely to attack . . . the objects of his uncontrolled and uncontrollable desires."[2]

A close look at the sex crime panics that began in the mid-1930s, declined during World War II, and revived in the postwar decade reveals that those episodes were not necessarily related to any increase in the actual incidence of violent, sexually related crimes. Although arrest rates for sexual offenses in general rose throughout the period, the vast majority of arrests were for minor offenses, rather than for the violent acts portrayed in the media. Moreover, when arrest rates accelerated sharply during World War II, the popular discourse on sex crimes quieted, and no new psychopath laws were enacted.[3] The historical evidence also prohibits a conspiratorial interpretation in which power-hungry psychiatrists manipulated the public and politicians to create a sex crime panic and psychiatric solutions to it.[4] Most psychiatrists remained skeptical about psychopath laws. Rather, the media, law enforcement agencies, and private citizens' groups took the lead in demanding state action to prevent sex crimes. In the process, they not only augmented the authority of psychiatrists, but also provoked a redefinition of normal sexual behavior.

This new image of aggressive male sexual deviance that emerged from the psychiatric and political response to sex crimes provided a focus for a complex redefinition of sexual boundaries in modern America. For one thing, public outrage over rare, serious sexual crimes facilitated the establishment of legal and psychiatric mechanisms that were then used to regulate much less serious, but socially disturbing, behaviors. The response to the sexual psychopath, however, was not merely expansion of social control over sexuality by psychiatry and the state. Rather, by stigmatizing extreme acts of violence, the discourse on the psychopath ultimately helped legitimize nonviolent, but nonprocreative, sexual acts, within marriage or outside it. At the same time, psychiatric and political attention to the psychopath heightened public awareness of sexuality in general, and of sexual abnormality in particular, between 1935 and 1960.

Thus the response to the sexual psychopath must be understood in the context of the history of sexuality, for it evidenced a significant departure from the nineteenth-century emphasis on maintaining female purity and a movement toward a modern concern about controlling male violence. In the nineteenth century the ideal of female purity had served symbolically to control male lust and to channel sexual impulses into marital, reproductive relationships. In practice, of course, individuals deviated from the ideal, and periodic sexual reform movements—such as moral reform, social purity, and antiprostitution—attempted to uphold female purity and restore the deviant to the fold. Antebellum sexual reformers typically employed moral suasion and social sanctions, but by the early twentieth century, reformers had increasingly turned to the state to enforce their vision of moral order. During the Progressive Era, for example, city and state governments investigated white slavery, Congress passed the Mann Act to prohibit the interstate transportation of women for immoral purposes, and during World War I the United States Army mobilized against prostitution, incarcerating suspected prostitutes found in the vicinity of military training camps.[5]

By the 1920s the Victorian ideal of innate female purity had disintegrated. Stimulated by Freudian ideas, a critique of "civilized morality" infiltrated American culture. Meanwhile, working-class youth, blacks, immigrants, and white bohemians had created visible urban alternatives to the old sexual order. They engaged in a sexually explicit night life, used birth control, or accepted sexuality outside marriage. Even for the middle classes, a recognition of female sexual desire and of the legitimacy of its satisfaction—preferably in marriage but not necessarily for procreation—came to dominate sexual advice literature by the 1920s. As birth control, companionate marriage, and female sexual desire became more acceptable, female purity lost its symbolic power to regulate sexual behavior. Not surprisingly, by the 1930s calls to wipe out prostitution could no longer mobilize a social movement. Reformers now had to base their arguments more on "social hygiene"—the prevention of venereal disease—rather than on the defense of female virtue.[6]

If the Victorian ideal divided women into the pure and the impure, modern ideas about sexuality blurred boundaries in ways that made all women more vulnerable to the risks once experienced primarily by prostitutes. "If woman in fact should be a sexual creature," Victorian scholar Carol Christ has asked, "what kind of beast should man himself become?" One response to her query was heralded in England during the 1880s by the crimes of Jack the Ripper, whose sexual murders of prostitutes, Judith R. Walkowitz has argued, created a powerful cultural myth associating sex with "violence, male dominance and female passivity."[7] In twentieth-century America the image of the sexual psychopath further specified both the "kind of beast" man might become and the kind of victims he now sought. The sexual psychopath represented man unbounded by the controls of female purity, a violent threat not only to women, but to children as well. But violence against women and children was not the underlying concern of the sex crime panics. Rather, the concept of the sexual psychopath provided a boundary within which Americans renegotiated the definitions of sexual normality. Ultimately, the response to the sexual psychopath helped legitimize less violent, but previously taboo, sexual acts while it stigmatized unmanly, rather than unwomanly, behavior as the most serious threat to sexual order.

To understand how and why this controversial psychiatric diagnosis attracted so much public attention and found its way into American criminal law requires three levels of analysis: of psychiatric ideas, of political mobilization, and of sexual boundaries. Taken together, they reveal a complex relationship between psychiatry, social change, and sexuality. Psychiatrists, journalists, and politicians all helped create the sexual psychopath, but a public concerned with changing gender relationships seized upon the threat of "uncontrolled desires" to help redefine sexual normality and deviance in modern America.

■   When it first appeared in Europe in the late nineteenth century, the diagnosis of psychopathy did not refer exclusively either to sexual abnormality or to men. Akin to the concept of moral insanity, it was applied to habitual criminals who had normal mentality but exhibited abnormal social behavior.[8] The German psychiatrist Emil Kraepelin used the term psychopathic personality in his influential 1904 textbook to refer primarily to criminals with unstable personalities, vagabonds, liars, or beggars, although he also listed prostitutes and homosexuals. In 1905 Adolf Meyer introduced the concept of the psychopath into the United States, where sexual crime remained synonymous with female immorality.[9] William Healy's pathbreaking study, *The Individual Delinquent* (1915), mentioned female hypersexuality and described psychopaths as egocentric, selfish, irritable, antisocial, nervous, and weak willed, but Healy refused to discuss male sexual abnormality and recommended that most readers "should leave the unpleasant subject alone." Until the 1920s American psychiatrists who diagnosed mental patients as psychopaths typically applied the term to either unemployed men or "hypersexual" women.[10]

The transformation of the psychopath into a violent, male, sexual criminal occurred gradually as a result of three convergent trends. First, as courts and prisons became important arenas into which American psychiatry expanded beyond its earlier base in state mental hospitals, the recently established specialization of forensic psychiatry sought new explanations for criminal behavior. Second, the social stresses of the depression drew attention to the problems of male deviance. Third, the social scientific study of sexuality became respectable, and the influence of psychoanalytic theories on American psychiatry during the 1930s provided an intellectual base for a sexual theory of crime.

American criminologists began to use the psychopathic diagnosis during the 1920s partly because of weaknesses in the dominant theory that low mentality ("mental defect" or "feeblemindedness"), if not the cause of crime, was highly correlated with it. During the Progressive Era several states had established separate institutions for the indeterminate commitment of mentally defective prisoners. In practice, however, many of the suspected "defective delinquents" turned out to have normal IQs. With the influx of psychiatrists into courts and prisons after 1915, criminologists increasingly turned to psychiatric diagnoses, such as "constitutional psychopath," to help explain these troublesome prisoners.[11] In 1921 the Massachusetts legislature enacted the Briggs Law, which required psychiatric evaluation of recidivist felons and those convicted of capital offenses. Many of those prisoners who could not be diagnosed as insane or mentally defective were eventually labeled "psychopathic." Such redefinitions expanded the category of insanity and helped create a new deviant population, the psychopaths. In 1918, for example, psychiatrist Bernard Glueck diagnosed almost twenty percent of the inmates at New York's Sing Sing prison as "constitutional inferior, or psychopathic" and recommended a new state institution to house psychopathic and defective delinquents. Between 1919 and 1926 the percentage of inmates classified as psychopaths at one men's reformatory in New York rose from 11.6 to 50.8, while diagnoses of mental defect declined sharply.[12]

Despite increased use of the psychopathic diagnosis, male sexual crimes rarely received the attention of psychiatrists and criminologists during the 1920s. When sexuality and psychopathy were linked at that time, women, not men, remained the likely subjects. Indeed, the first specialized institution for psychopathic criminals, a hospital operated at the Bedford Hills Reformatory for Women between 1916 and 1918, had been established because of John D. Rockefeller, Jr.'s interest in eliminating prostitution. Glueck's Sing Sing study did note an absence of sexual morality among psychopathic male inmates, ten percent of whom had committed sexual crimes. However, his characterization of the psychopath emphasized recidivism, drug and alcohol use, and unstable work patterns, rather than abnormal sexual impulse. Even when sexual crimes against children first became the focus of governmental reports in the 1920s, the psychopath was not associated with such offenses. Nevertheless, the malleable diagnostic category of psychopath had become more widely applied and would soon take on new meanings.[13]

The sexualization of the male psychopath occurred during the 1930s, when American criminologists became increasingly interested in sexual abnormality and male sexual crime. The disruption of traditional family life during the depression, when record numbers of men lost their status as breadwinners, triggered concerns about masculinity. Psychologist Joseph Pleck has argued that during the 1930s psychologists elaborated on sex differences and investigated sexual deviance in order to shore up the psychological basis of masculinity at a time when social and economic support for the traditional male role seemed to be eroding. In the process, the male sexual deviant became the subject of special attention, particularly if he was inadequately masculine (the effeminate homosexual) or hypermasculine (the sexual psychopath). Both categories of deviant males were thought to attack children, thus simultaneously threatening sexual innocence, gender roles, and the social order.[14] The psychopath neatly fit these concerns. From the origin of the concept, the psychopath had been perceived as a drifter, an unemployed man who lived beyond the boundaries of familial and social controls. Unemployed men and vagabonds populated the depression-era landscape, signaling actual family dissolution and symbolizing potential social and political disruption. Like the compulsive child murderer "M," the psychopath could represent the threat of anarchy, of the individual unbound by either social rules or individual conscience. The apparent "sexualization" of the drifter reflected, in part, a merging of economic and psychological identities in modern America.

In this social context, Americans embarked on the serious study of human sexuality, measuring normality and defining deviance. During the twenties and thirties, classic texts by European sexologists, such as Richard von Krafft-Ebing, Havelock Ellis, and Magnus Hirschfeld, became more widely available. A growing number of American researchers, including Katharine Bement Davis and Robert Latou Dickinson, conducted survey and case studies of sexual practices.[15] Within criminology, older biological theories combined with the recent identification of sex hormones to stimulate studies of the mentality of homosexuals, the impact of castration on rapists, and the levels of endocrines in senile sex offenders. New funding sources supported the investigation of sexuality. In 1931 the Rockefeller Foundation helped establish the National Research Council Committee for Research on Problems of Sex, which later supported the work of Alfred Kinsey. The Committee for the Study of Sex Variants, founded in 1935 and chaired by Eugen Kahn (an authority on the psychopath), sponsored a pioneering, two-volume study of homosexuality by psychiatrist George Henry.[16]

A second intellectual current helps account for psychiatric interest in sex criminals, in general, and the sexual component of psychopathic personality, in particular. In the 1920s Freudian concepts of psychosexual development had begun to filter through the fields of psychiatry and criminology, a process that accelerated after the immigration of European analysts to this country. In the early 1930s a few discussions of the psychopath—such as Kahn's important text, translated into English in 1931—referred to infantile sexuality and to arrested sexual development. In the same year psychiatrist Franz Alexander elaborated on the contribution to criminality of the Oedipal complex and of anal and oral eroticism. A 1937 article in the *Psychoanalytic Review* indicated the new direction in psychiatric interpretations when it characterized the psychopath as "the phallic man," fixated at an infantile stage of boundless bisexual energy. By the late 1930s most discussions of the psychopath included at least a section on sexual types, such as "overt homosexuals, exhibitionists, sadists, masochists, and voyeurs." Some authors explicitly linked such deviants to the commission of sexual crimes.[17]

The most prolific advocate of the psychosexual interpretation of psychopathic behavior was Benjamin Karpman, chief psychotherapist at St. Elizabeth's Hospital in Washington, D.C.[18] In voluminous case studies of criminals, Karpman attributed most habitual criminality to arrested sexual development and identified psychopaths by their incapacity to repress or to sublimate their overly active sexual impulses. The typical sexual psychopath was, he believed, "all instinct and impulse." Karpman once claimed, for example, that the psychopath was "always on the go for sexual satisfaction . . . like a cancer patient who is always hungry no matter how much he is fed." Later investigators would attribute sexual psychopathy to underdeveloped, rather than overdeveloped, libido, but Karpman held firmly to his belief that sexual psychopaths always had insatiable and uncontrollable desires.[19] Although his views were extreme among psychiatrists, Karpman's vision of the psychopath as emotionally primitive and sexually ravenous resonated with popular stereotypes that harked back to the theory of the born criminal. Thus, an older, hereditarian tradition merged with new psychiatric concepts to produce a crude model of the psychopath as oversexed, uninhibited, and compulsive. It was this image that found its way into the popular press and ultimately into the law.

■   The incorporation of the sexual psychopath into American criminal law began in the late 1930s in the wake of the first of two waves of popular concern about violent sexual crimes. Three constituencies—the media, citizens' groups, and law enforcement agencies—created the sex crime panic and demanded that politicians offer solutions to the problems of rape and sexual murder of children. Politicians, in turn, seized upon the sexual psychopath as the villain in the sex crime drama and called on psychiatrists as the heroes who might rid society of the danger they posed.

Each of the two major sex crime panics—roughly from 1937 to 1940 and from 1949 to 1955—originated when, after a series of brutal and apparently sexually motivated child murders, major urban newspapers expanded and, in some cases, sensationalized their coverage of child molestation and rape. Between 1937 and 1940, and again during the postwar decade, the *New York Times*, previously silent on the subject, averaged over forty articles per year on sex crimes.[20] In 1937, magazines ranging from *Science* and the *Christian Century* to the *Nation* and the *New Masses* reported on the sex crime panic. After World War II news and family magazines, including *Time*, *Newsweek*, and *Parents' Magazine*, carried articles titled "Queer People," "Sex Psychopaths," and "What Shall We Do About Sex Offenders?" In its 1950 series on "Terror in Our Cities," *Collier's* magazine summarized the newspaper headlines in St. Louis ("The City that *DOES* Something About Sex Crime") in a representative composite.

KINDERGARTEN GIRL ACCOSTED BY MAN—CLERK ACCUSED OF MO-LESTING 2 GIRLS IN MOVIE—MAN ACCUSED BY 8-YEAR-OLD BOY OF MOLESTING HIM IN THEATRE—6-YEAR-OLD GIRL AT ASHLAND SCHOOL MOLESTED—LABORER ARRESTED FOR RAPE OF 10-YEAR-OLD GIRL—FINED FOR MOLESTING 2 BOYS, AGED 8 AND 10—AR-RESTED ON SUSPICION OF MOLESTING 4-YEAR-OLD GIRL—YOUTH WHO MOLESTED BOY 4, IS FINED $500—9 CHARGES AGAINST MO-LESTER OF GIRLS.[21]

Despite the lack of evidence that the incidence of rape, child murder, or minor sex offenses had increased, public awareness of individual acts of sexual brutality led to demands that the state crack down on sex crimes. In 1937, after two child murders had occurred in New York City, residents of Ridgewood, Queens, held a protest meeting and demanded that police be given more power to "take suspicious characters in hand before they commit the crimes."[22] In Chicago, after the rape-murder of two nurses, a police squad was formed to "round up attackers." When a Philadelphia man confessed to attacks on both male and female children, that city's mayor recommended sterilization of sex offenders. In New Jersey when six men were indicted for assaulting girls, the New Jersey Parents and Teachers Congress urged denial of parole to those convicted of sex crimes. In 1937 a mob in Inglewood, California, threatened lynch-ing while the police sought the murderers of three local girls. In 1950 a Connecticut mob attempted to lynch a suspected sex criminal, while the national American Legion called for life sentences without parole for sex offenders.[23]

Federal Bureau of Investigation director J. Edgar Hoover played an important role in fueling the national hysteria and channeling it into sup-port for stronger law enforcement. In 1937 Hoover called for a "War on the Sex Criminal" and charged that "the sex fiend, most loathsome of all the vast army of crime, has become a sinister threat to the safety of Ameri-can childhood and womanhood." In a popular magazine article pub-lished in 1947, Hoover claimed that "the most rapidly increasing type of crime is that perpetrated by degenerate sex offenders." Implying that this threat to social order required total mobilization, Hoover continued: "Should wild beasts break out of circus cages, a whole city would be mobilized instantly. But depraved human beings, more savage than beasts, are permitted to rove America almost at will."[24]

In response to the sex crime panic, police roundups of "perverts" be-came common, especially in the wake of highly publicized assaults on children. The targets of the crackdowns were often minor offenders, such as male homosexuals. A rare glimpse of the reaction of "perverts" to such roundups appeared in a letter written in 1946 by one homosexual male to another after a brutal child murder in Chicago:

"I suppose you read about the kidnapping and killing of the little girl in Chicago—I noticed tonight that they 'thought' (in their damn self right-eous way) that perhaps a pervert had done it and they rounded up all the females [male homosexuals]—they blame us for everything and inci-dentally it is more and more in the limelight everyday—why they don't round us all up and kill us I don't know.

In this case and in others, police justified increased surveillance of all deviant sexual behavior, whether violent or not, by the need to protect women and children from sexual violence.[25]

While some politicians supported the call for law and order, others turned to psychiatrists for solutions to the sex crime problem. In the 1930s the New York State legislature called on institutional psychiatrists to explain how to prevent sex crimes. Mayor Fiorello LaGuardia appoint-ed psychiatrists, lawyers, and criminologists to a Mayor's Committee for the Study of Sex Offenses. In a move that foreshadowed the national po-litical response to sex crimes, LaGuardia also instituted an emergency program that transferred accused and convicted sex criminals from city penitentiaries to Bellevue Hospital for medical observation.[26]

Some psychiatrists expressed discomfort about the sex crime panic. Karl Bowman, then director of the psychiatric division at Bellevue, ob-served that most of the men transferred there were minor offenders who did not belong in a mental hospital. At a 1938 symposium on "The Chal-lenge of Sex Offenders" sponsored by the National Committee on Mental Hygiene, psychiatrists argued that no sudden increase in sex crime had occurred and cautioned against new legislation that would establish ei-ther castration or prolonged imprisonment for sex offenders. Bowman and other panelists called for more frank, rational discussions of sexuality and claimed that sexual repression caused sex offenses. Other psychia-trists, such as Ira Wile, wrote articles opposing prolonged imprisonment or castration for sex offenders. They recommended instead hospital care, psychiatric exams, and research on sex crimes.[27]

Despite psychiatric ambivalence about proposed legislation that would incorporate the psychopathic diagnosis into the law, and despite strong criticism of such statutes within the legal profession, five states—Michi-gan, Illinois, Minnesota, Ohio, and California—passed "sex psychopath" laws between 1935 and 1939. That not simply psychiatric leadership, but the public mobilization to combat the alleged sex crime wave explains their passage is evident in the case of Ohio. In 1934 psychiatrists in that state's mental hospitals had failed to get the legislature to fund separate treatment for psychopathic criminals. In 1938, however, after the *Cleve-land Plain Dealer* ran a series of articles on sex offenders, civic groups created sufficient pressure to achieve quick passage of the Ascherman Act, which permitted the indefinite commitment of psychopaths to the state mental hospital.[28]

Although the psychopath laws were avowedly enacted to protect women and children, they were the product of men's political efforts, not women's. Several women's clubs publicly favored stronger criminal penalties for sex crimes, and male politicians frequently called on representatives of conservative women's organizations to testify in favor of psychopath legislation.[29] However, in contrast to earlier movements for moral reform and social purity, in which organizations such as the Woman's Christian Temperance Union had played a major part, the campaign for sexual psychopath laws had little female, and no feminist, leadership.

The hiatus in the sex crime panic during the early 1940s further suggests that its central concern was men, not women. The legitimization of male aggression during World War II and the shift of national attention toward external enemies combined to reduce the focus on violent sexual crimes. Although arrest rates remained high during the war, both newspaper and magazine coverage of sex crimes tapered off markedly, and only one state—Vermont—enacted a psychopath law. The wartime entry of men into the military and of women into jobs formerly held by men restored the "hypersexual" woman to the foreground. Social workers and government agencies condemned the phenomenon of "victory girls," young women who willingly had sex with soldiers and sailors, and antiprostitution campaigns revived briefly in the name of protecting soldiers from venereal disease.[30]

The postwar years, however, provided a climate conducive to the reemergence of the male sexual psychopath as a target of social concern. The war had greatly increased the authority of psychiatrists, who had been drafted to screen recruits and to diagnose military offenders. Postwar psychiatric and social welfare literature stressed the adjustment problems of returning servicemen, some of whom, it was feared, might "snap" into psychopathic states. In addition, demobilization and reconversion to a peacetime economy stimulated concerted efforts to reestablish traditional family life. Returning male veterans needed jobs that had been held by women, who were now encouraged to marry, bear children, and purchase domestic products. Moreover, the onset of the Cold War, with its emphasis on cultural conformity, intensified efforts to control deviant behavior. Nonconformity—whether political, social, or sexual—became associated with threats to national security. And, amid the pressures for social and sexual stability, Alfred Kinsey published his study of male sexual behavior, igniting unprecedented public debate about normal and abnormal sexuality.[31]

During the postwar decade, the sex crime panic gathered renewed momentum, peaking in the mid-1950s. As if to signal—or to enforce—the return of prewar gender relations, sex crimes once again became a subject of media attention and political action. Although arrests for rape and other sex offenses fell after the war, legislatures revised earlier sexual psychopath laws, and between 1947 and 1955, twenty-one additional states and the District of Columbia enacted new psychopath laws. In the early 1950s arrest rates returned to prewar levels, but only after the second phase of the sex crime panic had begun.[32]

The sexual psychopath laws enacted during the two periods of panic operated alongside older penal codes that punished crimes such as rape and murder with incarceration in state penitentiaries or execution. Most sex offenders continued to be processed under the older codes. During the early 1950s, for example, California superior courts sentenced only thirty-five percent of convicted sex offenders to mental institutions as psychopaths; fifty-four percent went to prisons and eleven percent to the youth authority. Prior to 1953 annual commitments of psychopaths averaged thirty-seven in each state with a special law. Revised laws and new facilities in the 1950s increased commitments in several states; Michigan and Maryland, for example, each averaged one hundred per year. Few of those committed, however, were the homicidal sex maniacs on whom the sex crime panic had originally focused. They tended to be white men, often professionals or skilled workers, who were overrepresented among those convicted of sexual relations with children and minor sexual offenses. Black men, who continued to be overrepresented among those convicted of rape, were more likely to be imprisoned or executed than to be treated in mental institutions. In short, white men who committed sexual crimes had to be mentally ill; black men who committed sexual crimes were believed to be guilty of willful violence.[33]

The sexual psychopath laws did not necessarily name specific criminal acts, nor did they differentiate between violent and nonviolent, or consensual and nonconsensual, behaviors. Rather, they targeted a kind of personality, or an identity, that could be discovered only by trained psychiatrists. Whether convicted of exhibitionism, sodomy, child molestation, or rape, sexual psychopaths could be transferred to state mental hospitals or psychiatric wards of prisons for an indefinite period, until the institutional psychiatrists declared them cured. The laws rested on the premise that even minor offenders (such as exhibitionists), if psychopaths, posed the threat of potential sexual violence. Indefinite institutionalization of sex offenders would protect society from the threat of violent sexual crimes, and psychiatric care would be more humane than castration, life imprisonment, or execution.[34]

In addition to passing laws, elected officials in ten states appointed special commissions to investigate the nature of sexual offenders, the problem of sex crimes, or the legislative means to prevent them. The documents published by such commissions varied in depth and tone from superficial accounts of popular attitudes to serious discussions of the psychiatric, legal, and ethical issues raised by sex-offender legislation. In general, the state reports echoed themes raised by the earlier New York mayor's committee. They found little evidence of increases in local sex crime rates, bemoaned the vagueness of the classification "sexual psychopath," called for scientific study of these mysterious offenders, and recommended new or revised psychopath laws that would, unlike many of the earlier statutes, require conviction of a crime before institutionalization. The preventive measures suggested by state commissions took two forms: specialized psychiatric institutions for men convicted of sex crimes and preventive measures, such as psychiatric screening of potential psychopaths through schools or behavior clinics and sex education to promote healthy family life.[35]

Whatever ambivalence psychiatrists may have had about incorporating the psychopathic diagnosis into law, the postwar response to sexual crimes helped to solidify psychiatric authority within the criminal justice system in two important ways. Following state commission recommendations for more research, a half dozen states provided funding for psychiatric studies of sex offenders. In California, for example, the sex crime panic enabled Karl Bowman, director of the Langley Porter Psychiatric Clinic of the University of California, to obtain funds from the state legislature for programs on sexual deviates, although his previous requests for state funding had been denied. The New Jersey Sex Offender Acts of 1949 and 1950 established a Diagnostic Center for the study of juvenile and adult offenders, and New York State's Sex Delinquency Research Project funded studies of sex offenders at Sing Sing prison.[36]

The second means by which the state expanded both its own and psychiatrists' authority was the establishment of specialized institutions to treat sexual offenders. Under the initial sexual psychopath statutes, men committed for sexual offenses served their indeterminate sentences either on mental wards of prisons or on criminal wards of mental hospitals, such as Howard Hall at St. Elizabeth's Hospital. In 1949 the Ohio legislature appropriated over one million dollars to build a specialized facility for mentally defective and psychopathic criminals at the Lima State Hospital. Maryland legislators authorized the maximum security Patuxent Institution, which opened in 1951, for the psychiatric treatment of habitual offenders, mental defectives, and sexual criminals. In 1954 California transferred the men who had been sentenced as psychopaths from state mental hospitals to the newly completed, ten-million-dollar Atascadero State Hospital. Once institutionalized, the psychopath received treatments according with the therapeutic trends of the era: Metrazol, insulin shock or electro-shock; hormonal injections; sterilization; group therapy; and, in some cases, frontal lobotomy. According to the clinical literature, none of these proved effective in reducing "uncontrolled desires."[37]

The sexual psychopath laws, always controversial among psychiatrists and lawyers, came under renewed criticism in the 1950s and 1960s. In 1949 the Committee on Forensic Psychiatry of the liberal Group for the Advancement of Psychiatry issued a report that argued that the concept of the psychopath was too vague and controversial to be written into law. The following year, in the New Jersey state report on sex offenders, sociologist Paul Tappan attempted to refute the myth of escalation from minor to violent sex crimes, noting that sex offenders had the lowest recidivism rates of all criminals.[38] Legal scholars stepped up their critique of the sexual psychopath laws, and during the 1960s, a "due process revolution" in mental health inspired constitutional challenges to sexual psychopath laws on the grounds that they denied both due process and equal protection to accused sex offenders. By 1968, when Michigan repealed the first of the original state psychopath laws and abolished the legal category of "criminal sexual psychopath," an experiment in psychiatric criminology seemed to have come full circle.[39]

■   As they debated the treatment of the sexual psychopath, psychiatrists and politicians spoke to deeper social concerns about the meaning of sexuality. At a time when the standards of sexual behavior for both women and men were changing rapidly, the psychopath became a malleable symbol for popular fears about the consequences of new sexual values. A close reading of the popular, legal, and psychiatric literature related to the sex crime panics and the psychopath laws reveals at least three ways in which the concept of the sexual psychopath served to create or to clarify boundaries between normal and abnormal behavior. First, the discussion of the sexual psychopath influenced the redefinition of rape as not only a male psychological aberration, but also an act in which both women and children contributed to their own victimization. Second, it drew a strict boundary between heterosexual and homosexual males, labeling the latter as violent child molesters. Finally, the creation of the psychopath as an extreme deviant figure helped Americans adjust to a sexual system in which nonprocreative acts were no longer considered abnormal.

Unlike the Progressive-Era antiprostitution crusade, the sex crime panic of the thirties, forties, and fifties virtually ignored women as perpetrators, while redirecting concern about victims to include not only women, but especially children of both sexes. Child molestation, like rape, clearly predated the sex crime panics, but for the first time the sexual victimization of children became a subject of popular concern. The gradual acceptance of female sexual desire helped focus attention on children, for if women now actively sought sexual fulfillment, they were less accessible as symbolic victims, while childhood innocence remained a powerful image. In the film *M*, for example, a real-life rapist of women was transformed into a child murderer, as if rape alone were not enough to horrify the modern audience. At the same time, Freudian ideas about childhood sexuality and Oedipal desire raised the specter of children's participation in sexual acts. Finally, just as the continued entry of women into the paid labor force evoked fears about unattended children becoming juvenile delinquents, it may have also heightened fears of children's susceptibility to the sexual advances of strangers.

A close investigation of the psychopath literature suggests that women—and to some extent children as well—were paying a high price for the modern recognition of their sexual desire and the removal of female purity as a restraint on male sexuality. Female victims were often portrayed as willing participants in the acts of which men were accused. For example, the New York mayor's committee on sex offenses explained that "In most sex crimes, the fact that a particular girl is a victim of a sex assault is no accident. Generally there is to be found something in the personality, the environmental background, or the family situation of the victim . . . which predisposes her to participation in sex delinquency." The theme that victims were in some way delinquent themselves recurred during the 1950s in the work of relatively liberal critics of the laws, such as Bowman and Bernice Engle, of the influential California Sex Deviate Research Project, and Morris Ploscowe, a lawyer and judge who championed liberalization of laws regulating sexuality. These critics reiterated doubts that a woman could be raped without some predisposition. The legal reforms that they recommended to improve the treatment of the psychopath included corroboration of rape charges by witnesses, investigation of victims' past sexual activity, and proof of "complete sexual penetration"—in short, the very legal mechanisms that feminists would seek to dismantle a decade later. Moreover, in a major study of child sexual abuse and incest, conducted at California's Langley Porter Clinic, the authors described the majority of the victims (eighty percent of whom were female) as "seductive," "flirtatious," and sexually precocious. They labeled those for whom abuse persisted over time as "participating victims." Thus, in a movement allegedly based upon the urgent need to protect women and children, the victims were ultimately as stigmatized as the perpetrators. As in the case of the Southern rape complex, in which black men lived in fear of accusation and white women lived in fear of assault, the threat of the sexual psychopath served to regulate sexual behavior not only for "deviant" men, but also for women.[40]

The image of the rapist in the psychopath literature further attests to the marginal influence of women's interests on the response to the sexual psychopath. The laws rested on the premise that most rapists were "sick" men, suggesting that rape was an isolated act committed by crazed strangers. In fact, recent scholarship has shown that sexual assault is a common experience for women, its perpetrators as likely to be family members or acquaintances as strangers. Even more interesting is a shift in the psychiatric and legal interpretations that occurred by the 1950s. Critics of the psychopath laws increasingly suggested that, in the words of one state report, "aggression is a normal component of the sexual impulse in all males." By this logic, as long as he did not mutilate or murder his victim, the rapist might be considered almost normal and certainly more "natural" than men who committed less violent, and even consensual, sexual acts such as sodomy and pedophilia. Accordingly, men diagnosed as psychopaths were more likely to be accused of pedophilia and homosexuality than of rape or murder.[41]

The response to the sexual psychopath was not, then, a movement to protect female purity; its central concern was male sexuality and the fear that without the guardianship of women, either men's most beastlike, violent sexual desires might run amok, or men might turn their sexual energies away from women entirely. Adult women were now suitable objects for "normal" male sexual desire, even normal male aggression, but the discourse on the psychopath mapped out two new forbidden boundaries for men: sex with children or with other men. The literature frequently played on fears of child molestation, and a significant minority of psychopaths were charged with male homosexual acts, either with children or adults. This fact, and the frequent overlap in use of the terms *sex criminal*, *pervert*, *psychopath*, and *homosexual*, raises the question of whether *psychopath* served in part as a code for *homosexual* at a time of heightened public consciousness of homosexuality.

Social historians have recently identified the 1940s as a critical period in the formation of a public homosexual world in the United States. Although homosexual subcultures had begun to form in American cities as early as the 1890s, it was not until the 1930s that literature and the theatre drew national attention to the existence of homosexuals in this country. The war years provided new opportunities for young men and women to discover homosexuality as they left their families and hometowns to enter the military or defense industries. During the 1940s both homosexual men and lesbians created visible social institutions, including bars, social clubs, and political organizations. By 1950 the early homophile rights movement, the forerunner of gay liberation, was articulating a positive view of homosexuals as a cultural minority group. However, society as a whole remained strongly homophobic. As Barbara Ehrenreich has argued, during the 1950s, "Fear of homosexuality kept heterosexual men in line as husbands and breadwinners."[42] Despite efforts to remove the stigma from homosexuality, the American Psychiatric Association categorized it as a mental disease until 1973. Moreover, in the 1950s the federal government launched a campaign to remove homosexuals from government jobs.[43]

The psychopath literature did reinforce the fear of male homosexuality. At times it appeared that a major motive of the psychopath laws was to prevent the contagion of homosexuality from spreading from adults to youths. Such contagion might corrupt the entire community and might ultimately result in violent death. For example, a 1948 article in the *American Journal of Psychiatry* argued that when adults indulged in homosexual acts with minors, "The minors in turn corrupted other minors until the whole community was involved." As evidence the authors cited "the recent killing of a 7-year-old boy by a 13-year-old because he [the younger child] would not perform the act of fellatio." Furthermore, the beliefs that homosexuals actively recruited among youth and that seduction in youth or childhood was the "commonest single environmental factor" explaining homosexuality were both used to support psychopath legislation. Dr. J. Paul de River, a crude popularizer of theories of sexual psychopathy, stated the case for vigilance in his book *The Sexual Criminal:*

> All too often we lose sight of the fact that the homosexual is an inveterate seducer of the young of both sexes, and that he presents a social problem because he is not content with being degenerate himself; he must have degenerate companions and is ever seeking for younger victims.

Thus, homosexuality was increasingly linked to violence and, especially, to the allegedly coercive recruitment of minors for illicit sexual activity.[44]

The panic over the sexual psychopath, however, did not merely shore up traditional sanctions against male homosexuality by associating it with violence. Rather, even the seemingly repressive aspects of the campaign promoted a new, more open, public discourse on nonmarital, nonprocreative sexuality. The literature on the sexual psychopath helped break down older taboos simply by discussing sexual deviance. At the same time, the literature encouraged a reevaluation of heterosexual behavior during a time of rapid flux in sexual standards. At a basic level, the psychopath literature helped disseminate information about sexual practices that had previously been outside the bounds of proper discourse. Now, in the name of preventing children from either becoming or succumbing to sexual psychopaths, professionals began to argue that sex education should not ignore such practices as oral and anal sex. The state commissions on sex crimes took an especially active part in this education campaign, holding extensive public hearings and conducting attitudinal surveys on sexual abnormality. For example, the Michigan Governor's Study Commission distributed "A Citizens' Handbook of Sexual Abnormalities and the Mental Hygiene Approach to Their Prevention." An Oregon social hygiene council published a fourteen-page "Introduction to the Problem of the Sex Deviate." The city of Long Beach, California, distributed a cartoon-illustrated booklet for children as its "answer to sex fiends." Like the antimasturbation literature of the nineteenth century, the sexual perversion literature of the postwar era was, no doubt, as educative as it was preventive.[45]

In commenting on the widespread concern about psychopaths, many writers pointed to the influence of Kinsey's study of male sexuality, published in 1948, which revealed the extensive practice of nonprocreative sexual acts, within and outside marriage. An editor of the *American Journal of Psychiatry* even argued that Kinsey's evidence of a "gap between cultural mores and private behavior" might have set off a "reaction formation against anxiety and guilt" that led, in turn, to the scapegoating of extreme sexual offenders. Liberal critics of the psychopath laws also referred to Kinsey's study, citing his results to argue that sexual variations were now so common among "normal" couples that they should be excluded from the psychopath laws. For example, Bowman and Engle attempted to differentiate between the dangerous acts of the psychopath and the newly acceptable practices of masturbation, premarital petting, and "unnatural acts" (i.e., oral and anal sex) performed in private between consenting adults. Thus, they assured the public that "serious" perversions did require psychiatric treatment but that healthy sexuality might include nonprocreative heterosexual acts. In this way, the discourse on the psychopath helped redefine the boundaries of normal sexuality and may well have contributed to the sexual liberalism of the 1960s.[46]

■   From the 1930s through the 1950s, the sexual psychopath provided the focus for public discussions of sexual normality and abnormality, while the state played an increasingly important role in defining sexual deviance and in prescribing psychiatric treatment. The debates on the psychopath statutes did more than expand the legal authority of psychiatry. The critics of the laws ultimately helped to legitimize nonprocreative heterosexual acts; the media and national commissions helped educate the public about both "natural" and "perverse" sexual behaviors. At the same time, the psychopath literature tended to stigmatize female and child victims of sexual assault and to draw a firm sexual boundary proscribing all homosexual activity and linking it with extreme violence, especially against youths.

It is difficult to assign any simple meaning to the response to the sexual psychopath. Like "M," or like his later American counterpart in Alfred Hitchcocks's film *Psycho*, the image of the sexual psychopath revealed a deep discomfort with the potential violence of male sexuality unconstrained by female purity—of "uncontrolled desires." The response to the sexual psychopath also confirms that, as in the case of lynching, the fear of sexual violence can provide an extremely powerful tool for mobilizing political support against nonconforming individuals. The ultimate historical legacy of the response to the sexual psychopath, however, was to expand the public discourse on sexuality, to focus attention on male violence, and to heighten the importance of sexuality as a component of modern identity. In so doing, the sexual psychopath helped to redefine the boundaries of acceptable sexual behavior in modern America.

■ Notes

Acknowledgments: The author wishes to thank the following scholars for their helpful comments on earlier versions of this essay: Allan Bérubé, John D'Emilio, Barbara Gelpi, Nathan Hale, Elizabeth Lunbeck, Elaine Tyler May, Peggy Pascoe, Elizabeth Pleck, Leila Rupp, Mary Ryan, and Judith Walkowitz. Research support for this article was provided by an Independent Study Fellowship from the National Endowment for the Humanities.

1. *New York Times,* 3 April 1933, 13; Thea von Harbou, *M,* dir. Fritz Lang, trans. Nicholas Garnham (London: 1968); see also Siegfried Kracauer, *From Caligari to Hitler: A Psychology of the German Film* (London: 1959), 215–22. The film was based on the actual case of the "Dusseldorf Jack the Ripper," reported in *London Times,* 26 May 1930, 13; *London Daily Express,* 26 May 1930, 1; and *New York Times,* 19 July 1931, sec. 8, 2. On sex crimes, see e.g., Sheldon Glueck, "Sex Crimes and the Law," *Nation,* 25 Sept. 1937, 318–20. The *New York Times Index* and the *Readers' Guide to Periodical Literature* (which created a "Sex Crimes" category for its 1937–1939 volume) show parallel fluctuations in newspaper and magazine coverage of sex crimes. The average number of articles per year peaked in 1937–1939, 1949–1951, and 1957–1959.

2. The California, Massachusetts, Nebraska, and Vermont laws used this terminology. Almost every state included the phrase "utter lack of power to control his sexual impulses." For the statutes, see S. J. Brakel and R. S. Rock, *The Mentally Disabled and the Law* (Chicago: 1971), Table 10.1, 362–65. For definitions of the term *psychopath,* see Alan H. Swanson, "Sexual Psychopath Statutes: Summary and Analysis," *Journal of Criminal Law, Criminology and Police Science* 51 (July–Aug. 1960): 228–35.

3. Between 1935 and 1956, arrest rates per 100,000 inhabitants rose from 6.0 to 11.2 for rape and from 24.9 to 48.1 for "other sex offenses," while for prostitution they fell from 108.8 to 35.5. The sharpest increase in arrest rates for rape and other sex offenses occurred in 1936–1937, 1942–1947, and 1953–1956. I calculated all data from a series of annual reports; U.S. Department of Justice, Bureau of Investigation, *Uniform Crime Reports for the United States and Its Possessions* (Washington, D.C.: 1932–1960), III–XXX. The one state for which commitment, rather than arrest, data are available over time is Michigan. There sex offenders committed to state prisons remained a steady 6 to 10 percent of all state prison commitments from 1875 to 1935. After the passage of the Michigan psychopath law in 1936, the rate jumped to 12.4 percent; after 1947, it fell below 10 percent again; Governor's Study Commission, *Report on the Deviated Criminal Sex Offender* ([Lansing] Mich.: 1951), 21, and Table 4, 210–11. On the lack of increase in sex offenses, see also Ira S. Wile, "Society and Sex Offenders," *Survey Graphic* 36 (Nov. 1937): 569–72; Paul Tappan, *The Habitual Sex Offender: Report and Recommendations of the Commission on the Habitual Sex Offender* (Trenton, N.J.: 1950), 19; Edwin Sutherland, "The Sexual Psychopath Laws," *Journal of Criminal Law and Criminology* 40 (Jan.–Feb. 1950): 545–48; California Legislative Assembly, Interim Committee on Judicial System and Judicial Pro-

cess, Subcommittee on Sex Crimes, *Preliminary Report* (Sacramento: 8 March 1950), 20; and Karl M. Bowman, *California Sexual Deviation Research Report to the Assembly* (Sacramento: Jan. 1953), 25.

4. For sociological interpretations of the expansion of psychiatric authority through the psychopath laws, see Edwin H. Sutherland, "The Diffusion of Sexual Psychopath Laws," in *The Collective Definition of Deviance*, ed. F. James Davis and Richard Stivers (New York: 1975), 281–89; and Nicholas N. Kittrie, *The Right to be Different: Deviance and Enforced Therapy* (Baltimore: 1971). For general critiques of the "psychiatric state," see Thomas S. Szasz, *The Manufacture of Madness: A Comparative Study of the Inquisition and the Mental Health Movement* (New York: 1970), 254; Jacques Donzelot, *The Policing of Families* (New York: 1979), esp. 126–50; and Robert Castel, Françoise Castel, and Anne Lovell, *The Psychiatric Society* (New York: 1982), esp. 175–213.

5. On the nineteenth century, see Estelle B. Freedman, "Sexuality in Nine-teenth-Century America: Behavior, Ideology and Politics," *Reviews in American History* 10 (Dec. 1982): 196–215. On moral reform and social purity, see Carroll Smith-Rosenberg, "Beauty, the Beast and the Militant Woman: A Case Study in Sex Roles and Social Status in Jacksonian America," *American Quarterly* 23 (Oct. 1971): 562–84; Mary P. Ryan, "The Power of Women's Networks: A Case Study of Female Moral Reform in Antebellum America," *Feminist Studies* 5 (Spring 1979): 66–86; David J. Pivar, *Purity Crusade: Sexual Morality and Social Control, 1868–1900* (Westport: 1973). On prostitution, see Mark Connelly, *The Response to Prostitution in the Progressive Era* (Baltimore: 1980); and Ruth Rosen, *The Lost Sisterhood: Prostitution in America, 1900–1918* (Baltimore: 1982). On World War I and venereal disease, see Allan M. Brandt, *No Magic Bullet: A Social History of Venereal Disease in the United States since 1880* (New York: 1985), 52–95; and Estelle B. Freedman, *Their Sisters' Keepers: Women's Prison Reform in America, 1830–1930* (Ann Arbor: 1981), 109–42, 146–48.

6. On changing sexual ideas and practices, see Nathan G. Hale, Jr., *Freud and the Americans: The Beginning of Psychoanalysis in the United States, 1876–1917* (New York: 1971), 250–73; John C. Burnham, "The Progressive Era Revolution in American Attitudes toward Sex," *Journal of American History* 59 (March 1973): 885–908; Paul Robinson, *The Modernization of Sex* (New York: 1976); Lewis A. Erenberg, *Steppin' Out: New York Night Life and the Transformation of American Culture, 1890–1930* (Westport: 1981); Christina Simmons, "Marriage in the Modern Manner: Sexual Radicalism and Reform in America, 1914–1941" (Ph.D. dissertation, Brown University, 1982); and Paula S. Fass, *The Damned and the Beautiful: American Youth in the 1920s* (New York: 1977).

7. Carol Christ, "Victorian Masculinity and the Angel in the House," in *A Widening Sphere: Changing Roles of Victorian Women*, ed. Martha Vicinus (Bloomington: 1977), 162; Judith R. Walkowitz, "Jack the Ripper and the Myth of Male Violence," *Feminist Studies* 8 (Fall 1982): 546.

8. On "moral insanity," see Norman Dain, *Concepts of Insanity in the United States, 1789–1865* (New Brunswick: 1964); and Charles E. Rosenberg, *The Trial of the Assassin Guiteau: Psychiatry and Law in the Gilded Age* (Chicago: 1968), esp. 68–70, 247, 254. In this essay I use the terms *psychopathic, the psychopath,* and *psychopathy.* The original term, "constitutional psychopath," reflected the organic explanation of criminal behavior and insanity prevalent in the late nine-

teenth century. During the 1920s and 1930s American usage shifted from "constitutional psychopath" to "psychopathic personality." In 1952 the *Diagnostic and Statistical Manual* of the American Psychiatric Association adopted "sociopathic personality" rather than "psychopathic personality." American Psychiatric Association, *Diagnostic and Statistical Manual* (Washington, D.C.: 1952). But some authors continued to refer to "constitutional psychopaths" and many to "psychopathic personality." Major texts adopting the *psychopathic* category include Eugen Kahn, *Psychopathic Personalities*, trans. H. Flanders Dunbar (New Haven: 1931), and Hervey Milton Cleckley, *The Mask of Sanity: An Attempt to Clarify Some Issues about the So-called Psychopathic Personality* (St. Louis: 1941). For the best overview of terminology, see Henry Werlinder, *Psychopathy: A History of the Concepts: Analysis of the Origin and Development of a Family of Concepts in Psychopathology* (Stockholm: 1978).

9. The European literature is discussed in Werlinder, *Psychopathy*, esp. 21–51, 86–97; Sidney Maughs, "A Concept of Psychopathy and Psychopathic Personality: Its Evolution and Historical Development, Part I," *Journal of Criminal Psychopathology* 2 (Jan. 1941): 330–31; Sidney Maughs, "A Concept of Psychopathy and Psychopathic Personality: Its Evolution and Historical Development, Part II," *ibid.* (April 1941): 466, 470–71; and Pierre Pichot, "Psychopathic Behaviour: A Historical Overview," in *Psychopathic Behaviour: Approaches to Research*, ed. R. D. Hare and D. Schalling (Chicester, Eng.: 1978), 62–65. Early treatments of sexual psychopathy appeared in Richard von Krafft-Ebing. *Psychopathia Sexualis, with Especial Reference to Contrary Sexual Instinct: A Medico-Legal Study*, trans. Charles Gilbert Chaddock (Philadelphia: 1893); and George Frank Lydston, *Diseases of Society and Degeneracy (The Vice and Crime Problem)* (Philadelphia: 1904), 374–91.

10. William Healy, *The Individual Delinquent* (Boston: 1915), 132, 575–89, 411. Similarly, Sheldon Glueck, *Mental Disorder and the Criminal Law: A Study in Medico-Sociological Jurisprudence* (Boston: 1925), does not mention psychopathic sexual behavior. On the association of the psychopath with vagrancy and unemployment in America, see Herman Morris Adler, "Unemployment and Personality: A Study of Psychopathic Cases," *Mental Hygiene* 1 (Jan. 1917): 16–24; and John W. Visher, "A Study in Constitutional Psychopathic Inferiority," *Mental Hygiene* 6 (Oct. 1922): 729–45. On women, see Elizabeth Lunbeck, "'A New Generation of Women': Progressive Psychiatrists and the Hypersexual Female," *Feminist Studies* 13 (Fall 1987): 513–43.

11. On the expansion of psychiatry, see Gerald Grob, *Mental Illness and American Society, 1875–1940* (Princeton: 1983); Ben Karpman, "Milestones in the Advancement of Knowledge of the Psychopathology of Delinquency and Crime," in *Orthopsychiatry, 1923–48: Retrospect and Prospect*, ed. Lawson Gentry Lowry (New York: 1948); Albert Deutsch, *The Mentally Ill in America: A History of Their Care and Treatment from Colonial Times to the Present* (New York: 1949), 405; Walter Bromberg, *Psychiatry between the Wars, 1918–1945: A Recollection* (Westport: 1982), 102–22; and Janet Ann Tighe, "A Question of Responsibility: The Development of American Forensic Psychiatry, 1838–1930" (Ph.D. dissertation, University of Pennsylvania, 1983).

12. Peter L. Tyor, "Segregation or Surgery: The Mentally Retarded in America" (Ph.D. dissertation, Northwestern University, 1972); Aldo Piperno, "A Social-Legal History of the Psychopathic Offender Legislation in the United States" (Ph.D. dis-

sertation, Ohio State University, 1974), esp. 89, 90; Maughs, "Concept of Psychopathy, Part II," 468, 478–79; Deutsch, *Mentally Ill in America*, 369–72. Bernard Glueck, "A Study of 608 Admissions to Sing Sing Prison," *Mental Hygiene* 2 (Jan. 1918): 85, 91–123; Special Committee of the State Commission of Prisons, "The Psychopathic Delinquent," in *31st Annual Report of the State Commissioner of Prisons* (Ossining, N. Y.: 1926), 68–96. See also David J. Rothman, *Conscience and Convenience: The Asylum and Its Alternatives in Progressive America* (Boston: 1980), 200–201.

13. Edith R. Spaulding, *An Experimental Study of Psychopathic Delinquent Women* (New York: 1923), xiii–xvi. On mental defect and female crime, see Freedman, *Their Sisters' Keepers*, 116–21. Glueck, "Admissions to Sing Sing Prison," 93; Reuben Oppenheimer and Lulu L. Eckman, *Laws Relating to Sex Offenses against Children*, U.S. Department of Labor, Children's Bureau Publication No. 145 (Washington, D.C.: 1925). See also Great Britain Home Department, *Committee on Sexual Offenses against Young Persons Report* (London: 1925).

14. Joseph Pleck, "The Theory of Male Sex Role Identity: Its Rise and Fall, 1936 to the Present," in *In the Shadow of the Past: Psychology Portrays the Sexes*, ed. Miriam Lewin (New York: 1983), 205–25.

15. For example, in 1936, Random House published an "unexpurgated edition" of Havelock Ellis, *Studies in the Psychology of Sex*, 4 vols. (New York: 1936). This work, originally published in England in 1897, was widely reviewed. See also Magnus Hirschfeld, *Sexual Pathology: A Study of Arrangements of the Sexual Instincts*, trans. Jerome Gibbs (Newark: 1932); and Richard von Krafft-Ebing, *Psychopathia Sexualis: A Medico-Forensic Study* (New York: 1939). Katharine Bement Davis, *Studies in the Sex Lives of 2200 Women* (New York: 1928); Robert Latou Dickinson and Lura Beam, *The Single Woman: A Medical Study in Sex Education* (Baltimore: 1934).

16. For example, Lowell Selling, "The Endocrine Glands and the Sex Offender," *Medical Record*, 18 May 1938, 441–44; and Clifford A. Wright, "The Sex Offenders' Endocrines," *Medical Record*, 21 June 1939, 399–402. On sex hormone research, see Diana Long Hall, "Biology, Sex Hormones and Sexism in the 1920s," *Philosophical Forum* 5 (Fall–Winter 1973–1974): 81–97. On both the popularity of biological theories of sexual crime and the use of castration in Europe, see Marie E. Kopp, "Surgical Treatment as Sex Crime Prevention Measure." *Journal of Criminal Law and Criminology* 28 (Jan.–Feb. 1938): 692–706. George Henry, *Sex Variants: A Study of Homosexual Patterns* (1941; rpt., New York: 1948), v–viii; John Gagnon, "Sex Research and Social Change," *Archives of Sexual Behavior* 4 (March 1975): 124. See also Aron Krich, "Before Kinsey: Continuity in American Sex Research," *Psychoanalytic Review* 53 (Summer 1966): 69–90; Regina Markell Morantz, "The Scientist as Sex Crusader: Alfred C. Kinsey and American Culture," *American Quarterly* 29 (Winter 1977): 563–89.

17. Kahn, *Psychopathic Personalities*, esp. 102–13; Franz Alexander and Hugo Staub, *The Criminal, The Judge and the Public*, trans. Gregory Zilboorg (New York: 1931), x–xi, 109–18; Fritz Wittels, "The Criminal Psychopath in the Psychoanalytic System," *Psychoanalytic Review* 24 (July 1937): 276–91; Walter Bromberg and Charles B. Thompson, "The Relation of Psychoses, Mental Defect and Personality Types to Crime," *Journal of Criminal Law and Criminology* 28 (May–June 1937): 77–81. For the application of Freud's theories of sexual development to psycho-

pathic behavior, see Werlinder, *Psychopathy*, 154–61; major texts are surveyed there and in Maughs, "Concept of Psychopathy," and Karpman, "Milestones," in *Orthopsychiatry*, ed. Lowry.

18. Benjamin Karpman's work dominates the American listings on the psychopath in the *Index of Psychoanalytic Writings*, ed. Alexander Grinstein, 14 vols. (New York: 1957), II, 1066–68. In 1923 Karpman organized a symposium on the psychopath at St. Elizabeth's Hospital, at which William Alanson White made his often cited comment that the psychopath was the "wastebasket" classification of psychiatry. Nonetheless, Karpman's efforts to define what he called "psychopathology" as a distinct mental disease persisted through the 1950s. In 1940, in the first volume of a journal for the field, he outlined principles; Karpman, "The Principles and Aims of Criminal Psychopathology," *Journal of Criminal Psychopathology* 1 (Jan. 1940): 187–218; and he later called for a national institute to study criminal psychopathology. For colleagues' perception of Karpman in his later years as an "eccentric, slightly pathetic figure as he honed down year after year on the psychopathic individual," see Bromberg, *Psychiatry between the Wars*, 106. Benjamin Karpman, *The Sexual Offender and His Offenses* (New York: 1954), is both a useful bibliographical guide to research to that date and a testament to Karpman's passion for engaging his opponents in debate on the subject of psychopathology. For a bibliography of Karpman's writings, see *ibid.*, 685–86; for his case study approach, see Ben Karpman, *The Individual Criminal: Studies in the Psychogenetics of Crime* (Washington, D.C.: 1935). For his role in symposia, see Benjamin Karpman et al., "Psychopathic Behavior in Infants and Children: A Critical Survey of the Existing Concepts. Round Table, 1950," *American Journal of Orthopsychiatry* 21 (April 1951): 223–72.

19. Karpman, *Sexual Offender*, 501; see also Karpman, "Principles and Aims of Criminal Psychopathology," 204. For the reversal, see, e.g., Cleckley, *Mask of Sanity*, 397.

20. *New York Times Index*, 1936–1960. Many urban newspapers expanded coverage of sex crimes. On Detroit, Cleveland, Omaha, and Lincoln, Nebraska, newspapers, see California Legislative Assembly, Interim Committee on Judicial Systems and Judicial Process, *Final Report of the Subcommittee on Sex Crimes* (Sacramento, 1951), 120; Piperno, "Social-Legal History," 118, 136; Domenico Caporale and Deryl F. Hamann, "Sexual Psychopathy—A Legal Labyrinth of Medicine, Morals and Mythology," *Nebraska Law Review* 36 (1957): 321n.

21. Howard Whitman, "The City That *DOES* Something about Sex Crimes," *Collier's*, 21 Jan. 1950, 21; "Can We End Sex Crimes?" *Christian Century*, 22 Dec. 1937, 154–55; Michael Brush, "Are Sex Crimes Due to Sex?" *New Masses*, 26 Oct. 1937, 15–16; Glueck, "Sex Crimes and the Law," 318–20; "Queer People," *Newsweek*, 10 Oct. 1949, 52. Not until the 1950s and 1960s did the traditional women's magazines begin to feature articles about sex crimes, usually on protecting children. See, for example, Dorothy Diamond and Frances Tenenbaum, "To Protect Your Child from Sex Offenders," *Better Homes and Gardens* 31 (May 1953): 160–62; and Margaret Hickey, "Protecting Children against Sex Offenders, Omaha, Nebraska," *Ladies' Home Journal* 74 (April 1957): 31–33, 37–38.

22. *New York Times*, 21 March 1937, 24; *ibid.*, 23 March 1937, 48; *ibid.*, 27 March 1937, 14; *ibid.*, 11 April 1937, 40; *ibid.*, 6 Aug. 1937, 18; *ibid.*, 12 Aug. 1937, 8; *ibid.*, 13

Aug. 1937, 19; *ibid.,* 15 Aug. 1937, 20; *ibid.,* 24 Aug. 1937, 27; *ibid.,* 25 Aug. 1937, 3; *ibid.,* 31 Aug. 1937, 11. For the call for action against "suspicious characters," see *ibid.,* 15 Aug. 1937, 20.

23. *Ibid.* 24 Sept. 1937, 46; *ibid.,* 8 Sept. 1937, 16; *ibid.,* 6 Nov. 1937, 18; Wile, "Society and Sex Offenders," 571; *New York Times,* 24 Jan. 1950, 22; *ibid.,* 4 Feb. 1950, 6. For a criminologist's response to public vengefulness, see *ibid.,* 24 Oct. 1951, 26.

24. *New York Herald Tribune,* 26 Sept. 1937, quoted in Jack Frosch and Walter Bromberg, "The Sex Offender—A Psychiatric Study," *American Journal of Orthopsychiatry* 9 (Oct. 1939): 761–67; J. Edgar Hoover, "How Safe Is Your Daughter?" *American Magazine* 144 (July 1947): 32. J. Edgar Hoover's views were quoted to a subcommittee of the U.S. House Judiciary Committee considering a bill making it a federal offense to flee across state borders to escape prosecution for degenerate acts with a minor. Sheldon S. Levy, "Interactions of Institution and Policy Groups: The Origins of Sex Crime Legislation," *Lawyer and Law Notes* 5 (Spring 1951): 32.

25. "Marty" to "Howard," pseudonyms, 8 Jan. 1946 (in the possession of Allan Bérubé, San Francisco). I am grateful to Allan Bérubé for sharing this and other sources. A burglar confessed to the killing; there was no mention of "degeneracy" in the coverage of his conviction, and the murderer was eventually committed to the penitentiary for the criminally insane. *Chicago Tribune,* 8 Jan. 1946, 1–2; *ibid.,* 9 Jan. 1946, 1–2; *ibid.,* 10 Jan. 1946, 1–3; *ibid.,* 11 Jan. 1946, 1–2; *ibid.,* 12 Jan. 1946, 4; *ibid.,* 13 Jan. 1946, 1, 6; *ibid.,* 14 Jan. 1946, 1–2.

26. *New York Times,* 1 Oct. 1937, 46; *ibid.,* 14 Oct. 1937, 52; *ibid.,* 15 Oct. 1937, 17; Mayor's Committee for the Study of Sex Offenses in the City of New York, *Report* (New York: 1943), 1–5. The Bellevue program is also discussed in Joseph Wortis, "Sex Taboos, Sex Offenders and the Law," *American Journal of Orthopsychiatry* 9 (July 1939): 554; and Donald Shaskan, "One Hundred Sex Offenders," *ibid.,* 565–66. In 1937 the Commonwealth of Massachusetts established a Committee of Four to recommend changes in laws relating to sexual delinquency. *New York Times,* 5 Sept. 1937, 7.

27. Mayor's Committee of New York, *Report,* 5, 11–14; "The Challenge of Sex Offenders," *Mental Hygiene* 22 (Jan. 1938): 10–24. See also Wile, "Society and Sex Offenders," 571–72. For other criticisms of the expansion of psychiatric authority and of sexual psychopath laws, see Frederick Wertham, "Psychiatry and the Prevention of Sex Crimes," *Journal of Criminal Law and Criminology* 28 (March–April 1938): 848–50; William Scott Stewart, "Concerning Proposed Legislation for the Commitment of Sex Offenders," *John Marshall Law Quarterly* 3 (March 1938), 407–21; Gregory Zilboorg, "The Overestimation of Psychopathology," *American Journal of Orthopsychiatry* 9 (Jan. 1939): 90–91; James E. Hughes, "The Minnesota 'Sexual Irresponsibles' Law," *Mental Hygiene* 25 (Jan. 1941): 76–86; and George H. Dession, "Psychiatry and the Conditioning of Criminal Justice," *Yale Law Journal* 47 (Jan. 1938): 319–40.

28. Piperno, "Social-Legal History," 117–18, 72. Similarly, in 1935 the Michigan state legislature passed the "Goodrich Act" in response to publicity surrounding the mutilation-murder of a young girl by a former mental institution inmate, named Goodrich, who had a record of sex offenses. Although the original Michi-

gan Law of 1935 (rev. 1937) was declared unconstitutional, a 1939 revision remained in force. *Ibid.*, 91–96.

29. For example, members of women's clubs testified in favor of the Ohio law. *Ibid.*, 118, 134–35.

30. The number of magazine articles about sex crimes dropped from eleven between 1937 and 1939 to three between 1940 and 1947. The number rose to thirty for the decade 1947–1957. *Readers' Guide to Periodical Literature*, 1937–1957. For the renewal of antiprostitution campaigns, spearheaded by the American Social Hygiene Association, see its publication, the *Journal of Social Hygiene* 29 (1943); see also, for example, Paul Kinsie, "To Combat the Return of Commercialized Prostitution," *American City* 64 (Aug. 1949): 102–3. On World War II, see Francis E. Merrill, *Social Problems on the Homefront* (New York: 1948), 122–44; and Karen Anderson, *Wartime Women: Sex Roles, Family Relations and the Status of Women during World War II* (Westport: 1981), 103–11.

31. Rebecca Greene, "The Role of the Psychiatrist in World War II" (Ph.D. dissertation, Columbia University, 1977); Allan Bérubé, "Coming Out Under Fire," ch. 7 (in Bérubé's possession); William Chafe, *The American Woman: Her Changing Social, Economic and Political Roles, 1920–1970* (New York: 1972), 174–225; Elaine Tyler May, "Explosive Issues: Sex, Women and the Bomb in Postwar America," paper presented at the annual meeting of the American Historical Association, Washington, D.C., Dec. 1982 (in May's possession). On the relation of the postwar political reaction to strictures against sexual nonconformity, see John D'Emilio, *Sexual Politics, Sexual Communities: The Making of a Homosexual Minority in the United States, 1940–1970* (Chicago: 1983), 40–53. On Kinsey, see Morantz, "The Scientist as Sex Crusader."

32. Karl Bowman, "Review of Sex Legislation and Control of Sex Offenders in the United States of America," *International Review of Criminal Policy* 4 (July 1953): 20–39; Swanson, "Sexual Psychopath Statutes," 228–35; and Brakel and Rock, *Mentally Disabled and the Law*, 341–75. The postwar laws, most of which passed between 1949 and 1953, and revisions of older ones remedied some of the most blatant abuses of due process rights by requiring criminal conviction before psychiatric observation and indeterminate sentencing. However, in some states, notably California, released sexual psychopaths were required to register with local police whenever they moved, even if their convictions had been set aside or expunged. Piperno, "Social-Legal History," 94–107, gives an excellent summary of the legal cases concerning the psychopath laws.

33. Bowman, *California Report*, 13; California Assembly, *Final Report*, 43–45; Brakel and Rock, *Mentally Disabled and the Law*, 348–59; Kittrie, *Right to Be Different*, 192; Piperno, "Social-Legal History," 181, and Table 3, 176. On the types of offenses and characteristics of offenders, see Bowman, "Review of Sex Legislation," 22–23, and Appendix, 33–39; Paul Gebhard et al., *Sex Offenders: An Analysis of Types* (New York: 1965), 865–66; Governor's Study Commission, *Report on the Deviated Criminal Sex Offender*, 35–36; California Assembly, *Preliminary Report*, 30–40. On the race of sex offenders, see A. R. Mangus, "Study of Sex Crimes in California," in Bowman, *California Report*, esp. 28; Leonard D. Savitz and Harold I. Lief, "Negro and White Sex Crime Rates," in *Sexual Behavior and the Law*, ed. Ralph Slovenko (Springfield, Ill.: 1965), 210–30; Karl M. Bowman and Bernice Engle, "Review of Scientific Literature on Sexual Deviation: A Review of Recent Medi-

colegal Opinion regarding Sex Laws," in California Department of Mental Hygiene, *Sexual Deviation Research* ([Sacramento]: 1953), 115; Piperno, "Social-Legal History," 182; Irwin August Berg, "Mental Deterioration among Sex Offenders," *Journal of Criminal Law* 34 (Sept. 1943): 184; and Frosch and Bromberg, "Sex Offender," 761–76.

34. The concept of sexual identity, as opposed to sexual act, has been influenced by Mary McIntosh, "The Homosexual Role," *Social Problems* 16 (Fall 1968): 184; see also Jeffrey Weeks, *Coming Out: Homosexual Politics in Britain, from the Nineteenth Century to the Present* (London: 1977), 9–44. In 1931 a Maryland judge explained that he was sentencing a sex offender to death because there was no suitable institution in which this type of criminal could be treated; see Piperno, "Social-Legal History," 72.

35. Commonwealth of Massachusetts, House Doc. 2169, *Final Report of the Special Commission Investigating the Prevalence of Sex Crimes* (Boston: 1948); New Hampshire Interim Commission to Study the Cause and Prevention of Serious Sex Crimes, *Report* (Concord: 1949); Tappan, *Habitual Sex Offender;* California Assembly, *Preliminary Report;* Governor's Study Commission, *Report on the Deviated Criminal Sex Offender;* Pennsylvania General Assembly, Joint State Government Commission, *Sex Offenders: A Report to the General Assembly* (Harrisburg: 1951); Virginia Commission to Study Sex Offenses, *The Sex Offender and the Criminal Law: Report to the Governor and the General Assembly* (Richmond: 1951); Illinois Commission on Sex Offenders, *Report to the 68th General Assembly of the State of Illinois* (Springfield: 1953); Oregon Legislative Assembly, Interim Committee to Study Sex Crime Prevention, *Report Submitted to the 49th Legislative Assembly, 1955* (Portland: 1956); Minnesota Legislature, Interim Commission on Public Welfare Laws, *Sex Psychopath Laws Report* (St. Paul: 1959).

36. State-funded research projects on sex offenders were conducted in New York, California, New Jersey, Nevada, Pennsylvania, and Oregon. Between 1951 and 1954, Bowman's Sexual Deviation Study received almost $200,000 to conduct biochemical research on sexual psychopaths in the state mental hospitals, analyze police statistics on sex crimes, and study the child victims of sexual assault. See California Assembly, *Final Report*, 107–8; and Marian Robinson, *The Coming of Age of the Langley Porter Clinic: The Reorganization of a Mental Health Institute* (University of Alabama, 1962), 7; David Abrahamson, "Study of 102 Sex Offenders at Sing Sing," *Federal Probation* 14 (Sept. 1950), 26–32. Albert Ellis and Ralph Brancale, with Ruth R. Doorbar, *The Psychology of Sex Offenders* (Springfield, Ill.: 1956), is based on psychiatric evaluation of 300 men at the New Jersey Diagnostic Center, conducted under the Sex Offender Acts of 1949 and 1950.

37. Bowman, "Review of Sex Legislation," Appendix; California Assembly, *Preliminary Report*, 50–55; George N. Thompson, "Electroshock and Other Therapeutic Considerations in Sexual Psychopathy," *Journal of Nervous and Mental Diseases* 109 (June 1949): 531–39. For a critical summary of treatment methods, see Group for the Advancement of Psychiatry, *Psychiatry and Sex Psychopath Legislation: The 30s to the 80s* (New York: 1977).

38. Committee on Forensic Psychiatry, Group for the Advancement of Psychiatry, *Psychiatrically Deviated Sex Offenders* (Topeka, Kans.: 1949); Tappan, *Habitual Sex Offender*, 14, 22; Bowman and Engle, "Review of Scientific Literature," 115, 120. See also an influential 1950 essay, Sutherland, "Diffusion of Sexual Psycho-

path Laws," *Collective Definition of Deviance*, ed. Davis and Stivers, 281–89; and Karl M. Bowman and Milton Rose, "A Criticism of Current Usage of the Term 'Sexual Psychopath,'" *American Journal of Psychiatry* 109 (Sept. 1952): 177–82; Manfred S. Guttmacher and Henry Wiehofen, *Psychiatry and the Law* (New York: 1952), 111–16.

39. Legal critics include Morris Ploscowe, *Sex and the Law* (New York: 1951); Caporale and Hamann, "Sexual Psychopathy"; Ferd Paul Mihm, "A Re-Examination of the Validity of Our Sex Psychopath Statutes in the Light of Recent Appeal Cases and Experience," *Journal of Criminal Law and Criminology* 44 (March–April 1954): 716–36; and Stanton Wheeler, "Sex Offenses: A Sociological Critique," *Law and Contemporary Problems* 25 (Spring 1960): 258–78. For a summary, see Kittrie, *Right to Be Different*, 194–201. On the "due process revolution" and constitutional challenges to sex offender laws, see Piperno, "Social-Legal History," 223–25, and the following cases: *U.S. ex rel Gerchman v. Maroney*, 355 F2d 302 (1966); *Specht v. Patterson*, 386 U.S. 605 (1967), 87 S. Ct 1209 (1967); *Millard v. Cameron*, 125 U.S. App. D.C. 383 (1966), 373 F2d 468 (1966); *Tippett v. St of Md*, 436 F2d 1153 (1971); *Davis v. Sullivan*, 354 F. Supp 1320 (1973).

40. Mayor's Committee of New York, *Report*, cited in California Assembly, *Preliminary Report*, 34; Karl Bowman, *Sexual Deviation Research*, March 1952 Report to the California Assembly ([Sacramento], 1952), 45–68; A. R. Mangus, "Child Victims of Adult Sex Offenders," in Bowman, *California Report*, 31–34; Estelle Rogers and Joseph Weiss, "Study of Sex Crimes against Children," *ibid.*, 47–84; and Joseph Weiss, Estelle Rogers, Charles E. Dutton, and Miriam E. Darwin, "Summary of the Study of Child Victims of Adult Sex Offenders," in California Legislative Assembly, *Final Report on California Sexual Deviation Research* (Sacramento: 1954), 59–62. For the feminist critique of the treatment of rape, see Susan Brownmiller, *Against Our Will: Men, Women and Rape* (New York: 1975), esp. 283–404.

41. See Wini Breines and Linda Gordon, "The New Scholarship on Family Violence," *Signs* 8 (Spring 1983): 490–531. Quoted report is Commonwealth of Massachusetts, *Final Report*, 7; see also California Assembly, *Preliminary Report*; Louise V. Frisbie and Ernest H. Dondis, *Recidivism among Treated Sex Offenders*, Research Monograph No. 5, California Department of Mental Hygiene ([Sacramento], 1965), 14, Cf. Stanton Wheeler on the use of sexual psychopath laws to institutionalize "passive" rather than aggressive offenders: "In a society stressing active mastery of the environment over passive acquiescence, perhaps it is not surprising that the aggressive sex offender who overresponds is judged less disturbed than the passive exhibitionist." Wheeler, "Sex Offenses," 277. For example, of felons convicted of sex crimes and diagnosed as sexual psychopaths in New York City between 1932 and 1938, a majority had been accused of pedophilia or homosexuality. Frosch and Bromberg, "Sex Offender," 762–63. See also Tappan, *Habitual Sex Offender*, 20, 29; Ploscowe, *Sex and the Law*, 216–41; and Mayor's Committee of New York, *Report*, 39, 54–55. Of the men committed to the Nebraska state hospital under the sexual psychopath law between 1949 and 1956, half had been charged with sexual relations with children (under age thirteen) or sex with force; the other half had engaged in consensual homosexuality (7.3 percent), exhibitionism (19.5 percent), or statutory rape (22 percent). Caporale and Hamann, "Sexual Psychopathy," 325.

42. D'Emilio, *Sexual Politics*, 23–33; Allan Bérubé, "Coming Out under Fire," *Mother Jones* 8 (Feb.–March 1983): 23–29, 45. See also Weeks, *Coming Out*, 1–7. Barbara Ehrenreich, *The Hearts of Men: American Dreams and the Flight from Commitment* (Garden City: 1983), 26.

43. Ronald Bayer, *Homosexuality and American Psychiatry: The Politics of Diagnosis* (New York: 1981), 28–40; D'Emilio, *Sexual Politics*, 40–53. In 1955, when members of the American Law Institute suggested decriminalizing homosexuality in the institute's model penal code, the Council rejected the proposal because homosexuality "is a cause or symptom of moral decay in a society and should be repressed by law." American Law Institute, *Model Penal Code: Tentative Draft No. 4* (Philadelphia: 1955), 276.

44. William Jaines, H. R. Hoffman, and H. A. Esser, "Commitments under the Criminal Sexual Psychopath Law in the Criminal Court of Cook County, Illinois," *American Journal of Psychiatry* 105 (Dec. 1948): 425. The fear of community-wide sexual corruption—and the exploitation of that fear for political ends—is explored in John Gerassi, *The Boys of Boise* (New York: 1966), a journalist's investigation of the homosexual scandals in Boise, Idaho, in 1955–1956. J. Paul de River, *The Sexual Criminal: A Psychoanalytic Study* (Springfield, Ill.: 1949), xii. On the fear of homosexual recruitment, see also Norwood W. East, "Sexual Offenders," *Journal of Nervous and Mental Diseases* 103 (June 1946): 648–49; and Bowman and Engle, "Review of Scientific Literature," 117–19. For the attribution of most perversion to unconscious homosexuality, see Sandor Lorand, "Perverse Tendencies: Their Influence on Personality," *Psychoanalytic Review* 26 (April 1939): 178.

45. The call for greater public discussion of sexuality appeared early and consistently in the psychopath literature, e.g., Karl M. Bowman, "The Challenge of Sex Offenders: Psychiatric Aspects of the Problem," *Mental Hygiene* 22 (Jan. 1938): 10–20; Guttmacher and Wiehofen, *Psychiatry and the Law*, 136; Ellis and Brancale with Doorbar, *Psychology of Sex Offenders*, esp. 91–92. Public hearings and attitudinal surveys are described in California Assembly, *Preliminary Report*, 9, 81–223; and Tappan, *Habitual Sex Offender*, 11, 57–67. On the Oregon booklet, see William J. Petrus, "Can We Prevent, Control and Treat Deviated Sex Offenders?" typescript, 1954 or later, file L3:10, Papers of the American Social Hygiene Association, Social Welfare History Archives (University of Minnesota, Minneapolis). On Long Beach, see Jeree Crowther, "Answer to Sex Fiends," *American City* 119 (April 1950): 65.

46. "Comment: The Spectral Evidence of Sex Offenses," *American Journal of Psychiatry* 108 (Feb. 1952): 629–30; on scapegoating, see also Paul Tappan, "Sentences for Sex Criminals," *Journal of Criminal Law and Criminology* 42 (Sept.–Oct. 1951): 335–36. For the importance of Kinsey's work in reassessing "normal" sexuality, see Group for the Advancement of Psychiatry, *Psychiatrically Deviated Sex Offenders*, 2; Bowman, "Review of Sex Legislation," 26–28; and Bernard C. Glueck, Jr., "An Evaluation of the Homosexual Offender," *Minnesota Law Review* 41 (Jan. 1957): 192. Bowman and Engle, "Review of Scientific Literature," and Bernice Engle, "Sex Offenders and the Law," *Nation*, 4 Nov. 1954, 198. See also Wortis, "Sex Taboos," 563; Guttmacher and Wiehofen, *Psychiatry and the Law*, 136–37; and Ellis and Brancale with Doorbar, *Psychology of Sex Offenders*, 93–94, 97, 127–32.

12

The Homosexual Menace: The Politics of Sexuality in Cold War America

John D'Emilio

Over the last two decades, new social historians, feminist historians, and historical demographers together have shifted the focus of the discipline away from its traditional concern with politics, war, and diplomacy toward an examination of what might broadly be called the private realm. Gradually, this reorientation has expanded to include the sexual. Community studies, the reconstruction of family life, examination of marriage patterns and fertility rates, the investigation of the domestic sphere in which many women moved, the exploration of popular culture, and other topics often intersect at the point of sexuality. Historians have pursued these connections and are now directing more attention than ever before to the study of erotic life.

Meanwhile, events since the 1960s have alerted us to the importance of sexuality as an area of political contention. Eroticism in contemporary America is clearly more than a private matter. During the 1970s both women's liberation and gay liberation became major social forces in part by their assertion that the personal is political. They succeeded in mobilizing millions of women and men around sexual concerns. In local, state, and national politics, issues of abortion and reproductive rights, rape, sexual harassment, and homosexuality stimulated intense debate and, in many cases, substantive changes in policy and public attitudes took place. By the late 1970s, moreover, the victories of the feminist and gay movements had provoked a backlash. A well-organized, well-financed movement, often referred to as the New Right and strongly grounded in Christian fundamentalism, attempted to erase the changes of the previous few years. With sexual issues as its motivating force, the New Right provided much of the energy behind Ronald Reagan's successful campaign for the presidency. During the 1980s sexuality moved even closer to center stage in American politics, as the issues of abortion, gay rights, pornography, and, most recently, AIDS (acquired immune deficiency syndrome), have polarized Americans.

The contemporary scene certainly suggests that it is worth investigating the intersection of sexuality and politics in the American past—how sexuality has worked its way into politics and, conversely, how politics has impinged upon sexual expression. In this essay I would like to turn attention to the 1950s, the decade when Cold War tensions were at their height, and explore a moment when the American political system seized upon one particular aspect of sexual life. Throughout these years the state mobilized considerable resources against homosexuals and lesbians. The image of the homosexual as a menace to society sharpened in the 1950s and the sanctions faced by gay men and women intensified. In the first part of the essay I will examine the anti-homosexual campaigns of the Cold War era and then move on to suggest what lay behind them.

■ I   Homosexuality made its unexpected debut as an issue of Cold War domestic politics in February 1950. During hearings before the Senate Appropriations Committee, Undersecretary of State John Peurifoy mentioned that most of the ninety-one employees who had been dismissed for reasons of "moral turpitude" were homosexuals.[1] The revelation could hardly have come at a less fortunate time for the Truman administration or for gay Americans. The previous few months had witnessed a series of events that encouraged the exploitation of fears about national security—the Communist victory in China, the detonation of an atom bomb by the Soviet Union, the conviction of Alger Hiss on charges of perjury, and the trial in New York of Judith Coplon for espionage. A few days before Peurifoy testified, Senator Joseph McCarthy had delivered his famous Wheeling, West Virginia speech in which he claimed that the State Department was riddled with Communists. Eager to discredit President Truman and the Democrats, Republicans saw in Peurifoy's remarks another opportunity to cast doubt upon the administration's competence to safeguard the nation's security.[2]

In the succeeding months the danger posed by "sexual perverts" became a staple of partisan rhetoric. Several Republican senators charged that homosexuals had infiltrated the executive branch of the government and that the Truman administration had failed to take corrective action. Governor Thomas Dewey of New York, the Republican presidential candidate in 1948, accused Truman of condoning the presence of sex offenders on the federal payroll. When the officer in charge of the District of Columbia vice squad testified at a Congressional hearing that thousands of "sexual deviates" worked for the government, pressure for an investigation built. Finally, in June 1950 the Senate authorized a formal inquiry into the employment of "homosexuals and other moral perverts" in government.[3]

The report that the Senate released in December 1950 painted a threatening picture of homosexual civil servants. Significantly, the Senators never questioned the assumption that government employment of gay men and women was undesirable; instead, they treated it as a self-evident problem. The investigating committee offered two closely connected arguments to buttress its conclusion that homosexuals should be excluded from government service. The first pertained to the "character" of the homosexual who allegedly lacked "emotional stability" and whose "moral fiber" had been weakened by sexual indulgence. Homosexuality took on the form of a contagious disease that threatened the health of anyone who came near it. Even one "sex pervert in a Government agency," the committee warned,

> tends to have a corrosive influence upon his fellow employees. These perverts will frequently attempt to entice normal individuals to engage in perverted practices. This is particularly true in the case of young and impressionable people who might come under the influence of a pervert. . . . One homosexual can pollute a Government office.

The second rationale for exclusion concerned the danger of blackmail. "The social stigma attached to sex perversion is so great," the committee noted, that blackmailers made "a regular practice of preying upon the homosexual." Already morally enfeebled by sexual indulgence, homosexuals would succumb to the blandishments of the spy and betray their country rather than risk the exposure of their sexual identity. The only evidence the committee provided to support its contention was the case of an Austrian intelligence officer early in the twentieth century.[4]

The homosexual menace remained a theme of American political culture throughout the McCarthy era. In committee hearings legislators persistently interrogated federal officials about the employment of "sex perverts." Right-wing organizations combined charges of Communist infiltration with accusations about sex offenders on the government payroll.[5] Lee Mortimer, a columnist for the Hearst-owned *New York Daily Mirror*, published a series of sensationalistic "Confidential" books that capitalized on the homosexual issue. Lesbians, according to Mortimer, formed cells in schools and colleges that preyed upon the innocent. They infiltrated the armed services where they seduced, and sometimes "raped," their peers. Mortimer warned that "10,000 faggots" had escaped detection and that the government remained "honeycombed in high places with people you wouldn't let in your garbage wagons." The pens of right-wing ideologues transformed homosexuality into an epidemic infecting the nation, actively spread by Communists to sap the strength of the next generation.[6]

The Senate report, as well as the rhetoric and articles on homosexuality, served as prelude to the imposition of heavier penalties against gay men and women. During the 1950s the web of oppression tightened around homosexuals and lesbians. An executive order barred them from all federal jobs, and dismissals from government service rose sharply. The military intensified its purges of gay men and lesbians. The Post Office tampered with their mail, the FBI initiated widespread surveillance of homosexual meeting places and activities, and urban police forces stepped up their harassment.

Dismissals from civilian posts in the federal government increased as soon as the sexual pervert issue arose. From 1947 through March 1950, they had averaged only five per month, but in the next six months the figure increased twelvefold. Within weeks after Eisenhower's inauguration, the Republican president issued an executive order that made homosexuality sufficient and necessary grounds for disbarment from federal employment. In addition, all applicants for government jobs faced security investigations, and the number of homosexuals and lesbians who never made it past the screening process far exceeded those whose employment was terminated. States and municipalities, meanwhile, followed the lead of the federal government in demanding moral probity from their personnel. The states also enforced rigorous standards in the licensing of many professions. Corporations under government contract applied to their workers the security provisions of the Eisenhower administration. The Coast Guard enforced a similar system of regulations for merchant sailors, longshore workers, and other maritime laborers. One study in the mid-1950s estimated that over 12,600,000 workers—more than twenty percent of the labor force—faced loyalty-security investigations.[7]

The military, too, intensified its search for homosexuals and lesbians in its ranks. During the late 1940s discharges for homosexuality averaged slightly over 1,000 per year. But in the atmosphere of heightened concern for national security that the Cold War provoked, even the military worked overtime to purge homosexuals. Separations averaged 2,000 per year in the early 1950s and rose to over 3,000 by the beginning of the next decade. Exploiting the sense of terror and helplessness that an investigation provoked, military authorities often trampled upon the rights of gay and nongay personnel alike.[8] Late in 1950, for example, the military began a "housecleaning" of lesbians at its bases in the South. As one corporal under investigation reported:

> Eleven girls were called in and questioned as to their alleged homosexuality . . . The girls being sick of the worry and strain of being under suspicion and being promised by a very likable chap Capt. Dickey of the OSI (Office of Special Investigation) that they would receive General Discharges if they confessed, all proceeded to do so and after confessing

were informed that it wasn't enough to incriminate only themselves—
they must write down also someone else with whom they had homosexual relations—this done they waited and at the end of January they
were all out with Undesirables.

Altogether, at least three dozen women received separations at Lackland,
Keesler, and Wright-Patterson Air Force Bases. The cost in human suffering hidden behind these numbers, and the thousands of other dis-
charged women and men, defies calculation. Two of the women caught
in the investigation mentioned earlier committed suicide; the others carried a burden that one study called "a life stigma."[9]
    Since most homosexuals and lesbians could mask their identity, the
presumption that they imperiled national security led the government to
adopt extraordinary measures to break their cover. In 1950 the FBI, responsible for supplying the Civil Service Commission with information
on government employees and applicants, established liaisons with police departments throughout the country. Not content merely to screen
particular individuals, it adopted a preventive strategy that justified widespread surveillance. Cooperative vice squad officers supplied the bureau
with records of morals arrests, regardless of the disposition of a case.
Regional FBI offices clipped press articles about the gay subculture,
gathered data on gay bars, compiled lists of other places frequented by
homosexuals, and infiltrated gay rights organizations such as the Mattachine Society and the Daughters of Bilitis. Agents sometimes exhibited
considerable zeal in using the information they collected.[10] In an affidavit
submitted to the American Civil Liberties Union, one former employee of
the federal government described how the FBI hounded him for over a
decade after he left his civil service job. Agents informed his employers
and coworkers about the man's sexual identity, and he experienced mer-
ciless ridicule at work. When an arm injury left him disabled, he was
denied vocational retraining by the state of Illinois because of his homosexuality. As late as the early 1960s, FBI agents visited him at home in an
effort to extract the names of homosexual acquaintances.[11]
    The Post Office, too, participated in extralegal harassment. Using ob-
scenity statutes as a rationale, the department established a watch on the
recipients of physique magazines and other gay male erotica. Postal in-
spectors joined pen pal clubs that were often used by male homosexuals
as a way of meeting one another, began writing to men they believed
might be gay, and if their suspicions proved correct, placed tracers on the
victim's mail to locate other homosexuals. A professor in Maryland and
an employee of the department of highways in Pennsylvania lost their
jobs after the Post Office revealed to their employers that the men received mail implicating them in homosexual activity.[12]
    The highly publicized labeling of lesbians and homosexuals as moral
perverts and national security risks, and the anti-gay policy of the federal

government, gave local police forces across the country a free rein in harassing them. Throughout the 1950s lesbians and gay men suffered from unpredictable, brutal crackdowns. Women generally encountered the police in and around lesbian bars while men also faced arrest in public cruising areas, but even the homes of gay men and women lacked immunity from vice squads. Newspaper headlines would strike fear into the heart of the gay population by announcing that the police were combing the city for nests of deviates. Editors often printed names, addresses, and places of employment of men and women arrested in bar raids.[13] Arrests were substantial in many cities. In the District of Columbia they topped 1,000 per year during the early 1950s; in Philadelphia misdemeanor charges against lesbians and homosexuals averaged 100 per month. Arrests fluctuated enormously as unexpected sweeps of gay bars could lead to scores of victims in a single night. New York, New Orleans, Dallas, San Francisco, and Baltimore were among the cities that witnessed sudden upsurges in police action against homosexuals and lesbians in the 1950s. A survey of male homosexuals conducted by the Institute for Sex Research revealed how far police action extended into the gay world: twenty percent of the respondents had encountered trouble with law enforcement officers.[14]

In some localities the concern about homosexuality became an obsession. In Boise, Idaho, the arrest of three men in November 1955 on charges of sexual activity with teenagers precipitated a fifteen-month investigation into the city's male homosexual subculture. A curfew was imposed on Boise's youth, and the city brought in an outside investigator with experience in ferreting out homosexuals. Over 150 news stories appeared in the local press, and newspapers in neighboring states gave prominent coverage to the witch hunt. Gay men fled Boise by the score as the police called in 1,400 residents for questioning and pressured homosexuals into naming friends.[15]

The issue of homosexuality also surfaced repeatedly in Florida throughout the 1950s and early 1960s. In Miami in 1954, the murder of two homosexuals by "queerbashers" who had picked up their victims in a gay bar led the mayor to reverse a long-standing policy of closing his eyes to the existence of the establishments. In a strange twist, the individuals most in need of protection became the targets of the police, who made sweeps of the bars and beefed up their patrols of local parks and beaches. The Miami City Council passed a law mandating special attendants in movie theaters to protect youth and another that prohibited establishments selling liquor from employing or serving homosexuals. In testimony before a Senate committee investigating juvenile delinquency, the mayor of Miami called for an amendment to the so-called white slavery act so that homosexuals could be prosecuted under it. A special file containing the names of those arrested on homosexual-related charges was circulated to police departments throughout southern Florida.[16] In 1958 concern spread to the state legislature as a special committee spearheaded a sensationalistic investigation in Gainesville. The committee collected several thousand pages of testimony, grilled hundreds of witnesses, and exhibited few compunctions about releasing information based on hearsay and unsubstantiated accusations. Sixteen staff and faculty members of the University of Florida eventually lost their positions on charges of homosexuality; significantly, all of them had been active in the civil rights movement in Florida.[17]

■ **II**   Although the preoccupation with "sexual perversion" appears, in retrospect, bizarre and irrational, the incorporation of gay women and men into the demonology of the McCarthy era required little effort. According to right-wing ideologues, leftist teachers poisoned the minds of their students; lesbians and homosexuals corrupted the bodies of the young. Since Communists bore no identifying physical characteristics, they were able to infiltrate the government and commit treason against their country. Bereft of integrity, they exhibited loyalty only to an alien ideology that inspired fanatical passion. Homosexuals, too, could escape detection and thus insinuate themselves in every branch of the government. The slaves of their sexual passions, they would stop at nothing to gratify their desires until the satisfaction of animal needs finally destroyed their moral sense. Communists taught children to betray their parents; "mannish" women mocked the ideals of marriage and motherhood. Lacking toughness, the effete men of the eastern establishment lost China and Eastern Europe to the enemy, while weak-willed, pleasure-obsessed homosexuals—"half-men"—feminized everything they touched and sapped the masculine vigor that had tamed a continent. The congruence between the stereotype of Communists and homosexuals made the scapegoating of gay men and women a simple matter.

Still, the special targeting of homosexuals and lesbians during the Cold War marked a significant departure from the past. Although it grew out of a centuries-long cultural tradition that was clearly hostile to homoerotic activities, there was no model for it in America's history. In 1920, for instance, the Senate investigated "immoral conditions" of a homosexual nature at the naval training station in Newport, Rhode Island. In important ways the political context resembled that of the McCarthy era—a world war had recently ended, a major Communist revolution had taken place, the nation was in the midst of a red scare, and Republicans were trying to discredit a Democratic administration. Yet, although the Senate report expressed intense loathing for homosexuals, it reserved its strongest condemnation for the methods used to entrap them and made no effort to arouse an anti-homosexual campaign.[18]

The need to explain the scapegoating of gay men and lesbians becomes even more apparent when one recalls that the initial attacks grew out of the belief that they endangered national security, that the vulnerability of homosexuals to blackmail made them likely candidates for treason. The threat to security informed the Senate investigation into their employment by the government, pushed the government to exclude them from its service, and rationalized the widespread surveillance by the FBI. Yet at no time during this period did the government present evidence to sustain its contention about blackmail. How then does one explain the massive mobilization of resources at every level of government to unmask the homosexual menace? Why did the 1950s witness so great an intensification of the penalties directed at lesbians and gay men? The answer, I think, may be found by looking at the changes in sexual expression, gender roles, and family stability that occurred in the previous two decades.

Taken together, the Great Depression and World War II seriously disrupted family life, traditional gender arrangements, and patterns of sexual behavior. The prolonged economic dislocations of the 1930s led to a significant drop in both marriage and birth rates. The inability of young adults to find stable employment and achieve financial independence from parents forced a postponement of marriage. The discrimination that married women in particular faced in the labor market encouraged young single women to remain unwed. Although birth rates had been declining steadily for over a century, the depression years witnessed an acceleration of this trend. Extreme economic hardship may have drawn some families together, but it also certainly meant that many young women and men never realized their expectation of a family of their own.[19]

Wartime brought the return of prosperity and full employment and, for a short time in the early 1940s, a rush toward marriage and childbearing. But far more significant were the disruptions caused by war. Families endured prolonged separations, divorce and desertion occurred more frequently, and the trend toward sexual permissiveness accelerated. Juvenile delinquency emerged as a perplexing social problem, and the rate of premarital pregnancy and illegitimacy rose. Women, especially those who were married and had children, entered the workforce in unprecedented numbers. They not only took the low-paying jobs traditionally available to them, but also filled positions that were normally occupied by men and that promised them financial security. At the same time the widespread use of psychiatrists by the government during the war enormously increased the prestige and influence of the profession. The emphasis of mental health professionals on family dynamics as a source of individual maladjustment focused concern on the instability of family life.[20]

World War II also marked a critical turning point in the social expression of homosexuality. It created a substantially new "erotic situation" that led to a sudden coalescence of an urban gay subculture in the 1940s. The war plucked millions of young men and women, whose sexual identities were just forming, out of their homes, out of towns and small cities, and away from the heterosexual environment of the family, and dropped them into essentially sex-segregated situations—as GIs, as WACs and WAVEs, in same-sex roominghouses for women workers who had relocated to find employment. Wartime society freed millions of the young from the settings where heterosexuality was normally encouraged. For men and women who were already gay, the war provided the opportunity to meet persons like themselves, while others were able to act on erotic desires they might otherwise have denied. World War II was something of a nationwide "coming out" experience for homosexuals and lesbians.[21]

The evidence to support this contention is accumulating as the exploration of the social history of the gay subculture progresses. Lisa Ben, for instance, came out during the war. Leaving the small California farming community where she was born and raised, she came to Los Angeles to find work and lived in a women's boardinghouse. There, she met for the first time lesbians who took her to gay bars and introduced her to other gay women. Donald Vining, a young man with lots of homosexual desire but few gay experiences, moved to New York during the war and worked at a large YMCA. His diary reveals numerous erotic adventures with soldiers, sailors, marines, and civilians who were also away from home. Even oppression could have positive side effects. When Pat Bond, a lesbian from Davenport, Iowa, was caught up in a purge of lesbians from the WACs in the Pacific, she did not return to Iowa. She stayed in San Francisco and became part of a community of lesbians.[22]

These changes added up to more than the sum of the individual biographies. Lesbians and gay men in association with one another created institutions to bolster their identity. Places as diverse as San Jose, Denver, Kansas City, Buffalo, and Worcester, Massachusetts had their first gay bars in the 1940s. The immediate postwar period also witnessed a minor efflorescence of gay male and lesbian literature. The social expression of homosexual behavior took on a substantially new form during these years as a stable urban gay subculture appeared in many American cities.[23]

Finally, the publication in 1948 of the Kinsey study of male sexual behavior put in bold relief concerns about American sexual morality. The release of the huge scientific tome was the publishing event of the year. The book remained high on the best-seller list for several months, sold a quarter of a million copies, and received widespread attention in the press, popular magazines, and specialized journals. Most men, the study found, were sexually active by age fifteen. Premarital and extramarital sex was typical rather than exceptional, and virtually all men had violated the law at least once in pursuit of an orgasm. Worst of all, perhaps, were

Kinsey's conclusions about the incidence of homosexuality. Over a third of his sample had had at least one adult homosexual experience, homoerotic activity predominated for at least a three-year period in one of eight cases, and four percent of American men were exclusively homosexual. The sexual portrait of the American male that the Kinsey study sketched could only have horrified moral conservatives.[24]

The disruptions created by depression and war, as well as the evolution of a stable gay subculture, did not occur in isolation. From the 1920s to the 1950s, the place of sexuality in American life was also changing in profound ways. Influenced by the spread of Freudianism, marital advice literature highlighted the importance of erotic pleasure in achieving a successful marriage. Youth were enjoying greater autonomy in sexual matters. A school-based peer culture, the availability of the automobile, and innovations in mass culture allowed them to date and go steady without the chaperonage of adults. The success of the birth control movement in making contraceptives more widely available helped sustain the shift to a sexuality that was nonprocreative and, increasingly, nonmarital. And, after World War II, the spread of pornography beyond its traditional place in a marginal, illicit underground accentuated the flux in sexual values.[25]

■ **III**   Government policymakers and business leaders approached the end of World War II with two overriding and interlocking concerns. With memories of the Great Depression still vivid, they set their minds on achieving a stable international order and a prosperous domestic economy. Postwar conditions, however, did not augur well for either goal. The Soviet Union retained hegemony in Eastern Europe, civil wars raged in China and Greece, the economy of Western Europe was in ruins, and Communists were making a serious bid for power in Italy and France. At home, the first year of peace brought a wave of strikes in basic industries, and labor militancy threatened to escalate. Inflation immediately after the war was followed later in the decade by recession.

The policies that political leaders pursued in the international arena helped to condition their response to domestic instability. The rhetoric about Communist aggression abroad inevitably fed concerns about subversion at home and justified extraordinary measures. As American Communists were pushed beyond the pale of political legitimacy, the fragile popular front of the 1930s in which New Deal liberals, progressives, and Communists worked together collapsed. The Attorney General's list of subversive organizations destroyed the effectiveness of many reform efforts, and labor militancy declined as Communists were expelled from positions of union leadership. The House Un-American Activities Committee's highly publicized hearings inhibited the expression of dissent in the field of education and in cultural activity. The political spectrum both shifted to the right and narrowed considerably in the postwar years.[26]

Accompanying these efforts were a series of initiatives that one can reasonably describe as a politics of personal life tailored to restore a different form of domestic tranquility. Some of these measures were decidedly benevolent. A generous GI Bill of Rights and federal home mortgages, for instance, subsidized millions of young men so that they could more easily and quickly assume the role of husband and father. Other measures fell on the side of coercion, psychological or otherwise. Even before the war ended, women faced a barrage of propaganda informing them that their jobs really belonged to men and extolling the virtues of marriage and childrearing. In the media, pictures of sparkling, well-equipped kitchens occupied by young mothers with babies dangling from their arms replaced images of women in hardhats surrounded by heavy machinery. Popular psychology books and women's magazines equated femininity with marriage and motherhood. Where these methods failed, employers could simply fire women, since female workers lacked the support of either organized labor or federal antidiscrimination statutes. From 1944 to 1946 the number of women workers fell by four million.[27]

Most extreme, however, were those currents that induced fear and promised punishment. For example, an extensive popular literature in the late 1940s described the grave threat that a surge in sex crimes posed to the women and children of America. Just as hidden enemies imperiled the security of the nation, dangerous criminals lurking in the shadows menaced the postwar family. J. Edgar Hoover himself sounded the alarm, and a dozen states convened special commissions to find ways of containing the sexual psychopath. Eventually, more than half the states passed sexual psychopath laws. Those enacted at the height of the Cold War tended to wreak havoc on constitutional rights.[28]

When placed in this context, the Cold War era's preoccupation with the homosexual menace appears less like a bizarre, irrational expression of McCarthyism and emerges, instead, as an integral component of postwar American society and politics. The anti-homosexual campaigns of the 1950s represented but one front in a widespread effort to reconstruct patterns of sexuality and gender relations shaken by depression and war. The targeting of homosexuals and lesbians itself testified to the depth of the changes that had occurred in the 1940s since, without the growth of a gay subculture, it is difficult to imagine the homosexual issue carrying much weight. The labeling of sexual deviants helped to define the norm for men and women. It raised the costs of remaining outside the traditional family even as other, nonpunitive approaches encouraged a resurgence of traditional male and female roles. There was a congruence between anti-Communism in the sphere of politics and social concern over homosexuality. The attempt to suppress sexual deviance paralleled and reinforced the efforts to quash political dissent.

Finally, one should note the unintended consequence of the McCarthy era campaigns. In marshaling the resources of the state and the media against the more extensive gay subcultures of midcentury, political and moral conservatives unwittingly helped weld that subculture together. The penalties directed at gay men and lesbians grew so intense that they fostered a collective consciousness of oppression. Thus, in the 1950s a gay emancipation movement first took shape, spreading slowly until the political radicalism of the 1960s infiltrated the gay world. By the end of the 1960s, a resurgent feminism and a militant gay liberation movement would usher in a new era of sexual politics, assaulting the policies and practices of Cold War America.

■ Notes

1. *New York Times*, 1 March 1950, 1. A more detailed discussion of these events may be found in John D'Emilio, *Sexual Politics, Sexual Communities: The Making of a Homosexual Minority in the United States, 1940–1970* (Chicago: 1983), ch. 3.

2. See Athan Theoharis, *Seed of Repression: Harry S. Truman and the Origins of McCarthyism* (Chicago: 1971); Alan Harper, *The Politics of Loyalty: The White House and the Communist Issue, 1946–52* (Westport, Conn.: 1969); Robert Griffith and Athan Theoharis, eds., *The Specter: Original Essays on the Cold War and the Origins of McCarthyism* (New York: 1974); Allen Weinstein, *Perjury: The Hiss-Chambers Case* (New York: 1978); and David M. Oshinsky, *A Conspiracy So Immense: The World of Joe McCarthy* (New York: 1983).

3. For discussions of the "sexual pervert" issue see *New York Times*, 9 March 1950, 1; 15 March 1950, 1; 19 April 1950, 25; 25 April 1950, 5; 26 April 1950, 3; 5 May 1950, 15; 20 May 1950, 8; 15 June 1950, 6. See also the series of articles by Max Lerner in the *New York Post*, 10–23 July 1950.

4. U.S. Senate, 81st Cong., 2nd Sess., Committee on Expenditures in Executive Departments, *Employment of Homosexuals and Other Sex Perverts in Government* (Washington, D.C.: 1950). The quotations may be found on pages 3–5.

5. *New York Times*, 28 March 1951, 1; 5 October 1951, 2; 26 June 1953, 4; 13 April 1953, 20; *Senator McCarthy's Methods*, a pamphlet published by the Committee for McCarthyism of the Constitutional Educational League, New York City, 1954, copy in Herbert Lehman papers, Columbia University.

6. Lee Mortimer, *Washington Confidential Today* (New York: 1952; Paperback Library ed., 1962), 110–19; Jack Lait and Lee Mortimer, *U.S.A. Confidential* (New York: 1952), 43–45.

7. *Employment of Homosexuals*, 7–9, 12–13; Executive Order 10450, reprinted in the *Bulletin of the Atomic Scientists* (April 1955): 156–58; *New York Times*, 4 January 1955, 14; Eleanor Bontecou, *The Federal Loyalty-Security Program* (Ithaca: 1953), 272–99, 323–35; Ralph S. Brown, Jr., *Loyalty and Security: Employment Tests in the United States* (New Haven: 1958), 256–60; Karl M. Bowman and Bernice Engle, "A Psychiatric Evaluation of the Laws of Homosexuality," *Temple Law Quarterly Review* 29 (1956): 299–300. The twenty percent figure comes from Ralph S. Brown, Jr., "Loyalty-Security Measures and Employment Opportunities," *Bulletin of the Atomic Scientists* (April 1955): 113–17.

8. *Employment of Homosexuals*, 8; Colin Williams and Martin Weinberg, *Homosexuals and the Military: A Study of Less Than Honorable Discharge* (New York: 1971), 31–36, 45–47, 53; Clifford A. Dougherty and Norman B. Lynch, "The Administrative Discharge: Military Justice?" *George Washington Law Review* 33 (1964): 498–528; Jerome A. Susskind, "Military Administrative Discharge Boards: The Right to Confrontation and Cross-Examination," *Michigan State Bar Journal* 46 (1965): 25–32.

9. Barbara J. Scammell to ACLU, 15 February 1951, and June Fusca to ACLU, 16 March and 23 April 1951, all in General Correspondence, Vol. 16, 1951, ACLU papers, Princeton University. The phrase "life stigma" comes from Williams and Weinberg, *Homosexuals and the Military*, 36. See also Allan Bérubé and John D'Emilio, "The Military and Lesbians during the McCarthy Years," *Signs* 9 (1984): 759–75.

10. See J. Edgar Hoover, "Role of the FBI in the Federal Employee Security Program," *Northwestern University Law Review* 49 (1954): 333–47. The information on the FBI surveillance program comes from several hundred pages of documents obtained from the FBI under the Freedom of Information Act, File Classification Nos. 94-843, 94-1001, 94-283, 100-37394, and 100-45888.

11. B. D. H., "Personal and Confidential History," in General Correspondence, Vol. 43, 1964, ACLU papers.

12. The postal surveillance did not come to light until the mid-1960s. See Alan Reitman to Affiliates, Memo, 1 September 1965; Ernest Mazey to Reitman, 10 September 1965; and Spencer Coxe to Reitman, 5 August 1965, all in General Correspondence, Vol. 1, 1965, ACLU papers. See also *New Republic*, 21 August 1965, 6–7; *Newsweek*, 13 June 1966, 24.

13. With the exception of the Boise scandal, discussed below, local police activities against gay men and women did not receive coverage beyond the pages of local papers. It is, accordingly, a laborious process to uncover incidents of harassment. The most accessible sources are the publications of gay organizations which, beginning in the mid-1950s, covered police practices extensively. *One* magazine is by far the best source, with news items from around the country, but the *Ladder* and the *Mattachine Review* are also valuable sources. James Kepner, who wrote articles on police practices for *One*, has saved the clippings from local newspapers that readers of *One* sent to him. The clippings may be found in the National Gay Archives in Los Angeles.

14. On the District of Columbia see *Employment of Homosexuals*, 15–19; *Kelly v. U.S.*, 194 F .2d 150 (D.C. Circuit, 1952); 90 A .2d 233 (D.C. Munic. Ct. App., 1952); *McDermott v. U.S.*, 98 A .2d 287 (D.C. Munic. Ct. App., 1953). On Philadelphia, see Council on Religion and the Homosexual, *The Challenge and Progress of Homosexual Law Reform* (San Francisco: 1968), 18. On New York, see *One* (November 1953): 19, and Lee Mortimer's columns in the *Daily Mirror*, 12 August 1959, 3 November 1959, and 26 January 1960. On New Orleans, see Elly Bulkin, "An Old Dyke's Tale: An Interview with Doris Lunden," *Conditions: Six* (1980): 18. On San Francisco, see the *Ladder* (November 1956): 5. On Baltimore, see *One* (April 1955): 14, and (December 1955): 10, and *Baltimore Evening Sun*, 3 and 5 October 1955, clippings in National Gay Archives. On other cities, see *One* (November 1955): 8; (November 1958): 17; (December 1958): 15; and (June 1959): 13. For the ISR survey, see John H. Gagnon and William Simon, *Sexual Conduct* (Chicago: 1973), 138–39.

15. On Boise, see *Time*, 12 December 1955, 12; John Gerassi, *The Boys of Boise* (New York: 1966); Jonathan Katz, *Gay American History* (New York: 1976), 109–19; Washington Mattachine *Newsletter* (January 1957) 1–3.

16. On Miami, see "Miami Junks the Constitution," *One* (January 1954): 16–21, and "Miami Hurricane," (November 1954): 4–8; John Orr to Herbert Levy, 13 September 1954, in General Correspondence, Vol. 19, 1954, ACLU papers. See also the extensive collections of clippings from the *Miami Herald* and the *Miami Daily News*, August and September 1954, National Gay Archives.

17. Weekly Bulletin 2015, 26 October 1958; Stuart Simon to Charlie Johns, 5 February 1959; clippings; and other material on the Johns Committee in General Correspondence, Vol. 55, 1959, ACLU papers. For the final report of the investigation, which continued for several years, see *Homosexuality and Citizenship in Florida: A Report of the Florida Legislative Investigating Committee* (Tallahassee: 1964).

18. U.S. Senate, 67th Cong., 1st Sess., Committee on Naval Affairs, *Alleged Immoral Conditions at Newport (R.I.) Naval Training Station* (Washington, D.C.: 1921).

19. For demographic information on the 1930s, see Conrad and Irene Taeuber, *The Changing Population of the United States* (New York: 1958), and Joseph Spengler, *Facing Zero Population Growth* (Durham, N.C.: 1978). On the economic status of women, see William Chafe, *The American Woman* (New York: 1972), 58–65, 81–88, 107–11.

20. On domestic society during the war years, see Richard Polenberg, *War and Society* (Philadelphia: 1972); Francis Merrill, *Social Problems on the Home Front* (New York: 1948); Ruth Milkman, "Women's Work and the Economic Crisis: Some Lessons from the Great Depression," in *A Heritage of Her Own*, ed. Nancy F. Cott and Elizabeth H. Pleck (New York: 1979); William Chafe, *The American Woman*, chs. 6–8; Geoffrey Perrett, *Days of Sadness, Years of Triumph* (New York: 1973); Roy Hoopes, *Americans Remember the Home Front* (New York: 1977); and Richard R. Lingeman, *Don't You Know There's a War On?* (New York: 1970). On psychiatry, see Rebecca Schwartz Greene, "The Role of the Psychiatrist in World War II" (Ph.D. dissertation, Columbia University, 1977), and William C. Menninger, *Psychiatry in a Troubled World* (New York: 1948).

21. On the impact of World War II on homosexual expression, see John D'Emilio, *Sexual Politics, Sexual Communities*, ch. 2. The description of wartime and military life as a new "erotic situation" comes from Williams and Weinberg, *Homosexuals and the Military*, 57. See also Allan Bérubé, "Marching to a Different Drummer," *The Advocate*, 15 October 1981, 20–24, and "Coming Out Under Fire," *Mother Jones* (February–March 1983): 23–29.

22. Leland Moss, "An Interview with Lisa Ben," *Gaysweek*, 23 January 1978, 14–16, and Lisa Ben, interview with the author, 9 January 1977, Los Angeles; Donald Vining, *A Gay Diary, 1933–1946* (New York: 1979); "Pat Bond," in Nancy and Casey Adair, *Word is Out: Stories of Some of Our Lives* (New York: 1978), 55–65.

23. On the spread of gay bars, see Gene Tod, "Gay Scene in Kansas City," *Phoenix* (Newsletter of the Phoenix Society of Kansas City) (August 1966): 5–6; Karla Jay and Allen Young, eds., *Lavender Culture* (New York: 1978), 146–54. On literature, see Roger Austen, *Playing the Game: The Homosexual Novel in America* (Indianapolis: 1977), 93–142, and Jeannette Foster, *Sex Variant Women in Literature*, 2nd ed. (Baltimore: 1975), 324–41.

24. Alfred Kinsey et al., *Sexual Behavior in the Human Male* (Philadelphia: 1948), 301, 392, 499, 585, 610–66. For discussions of Kinsey and his work, see Wardell Pomeroy, *Dr. Kinsey and the Institute for Sex Research* (New York: 1972); Paul Robinson, *The Modernization of Sex* (New York: 1976), 42–119; and Regina Markell Morantz, "The Scientist as Sex Crusader: Alfred C. Kinsey and American Culture," *American Quarterly* 29 (1977); 563–89. For the opinion of one moral conservative, see Henry P. Van Dusen, "The Moratorium on Moral Revulsion," *Christianity and Crisis*, 21 June 1948, 81.

25. See John D'Emilio and Estelle Freedman, *Intimate Matters: A History of Sexuality in America* (New York: 1988), chs. 11 and 12.

26. On anti-Communist measures and the isolation of the Communist party in the postwar period, see David Caute, *The Great Fear: The Anti-Communist Purge under Truman and Eisenhower* (New York: 1978); Griffith and Theoharis, eds., *The Specter;* Norman Markowitz, *The Rise and Fall of the People's Century* (New York: 1973); Lawrence S. Wittner, *Cold War America* (New York: 1974); and Joseph Starobin, *American Communism in Crisis, 1943–1957* (Berkeley: 1972).

27. On women's and men's roles in the postwar decade, see Mary P. Ryan, *Womanhood in America* (New York: 1975), 298–303, 316–20, 335–38; Chafe, *The American Woman*, 174–95; Sara Evans, *Personal Politics* (New York: 1979), 3–14; Betty Friedan, *The Feminine Mystique* (New York: 1963); Peter Filene, *Him/ Her/ Self* (New York: 1975), 169–202; Joe L. Dubbert, *A Man's Place: Masculinity in Transition* (Englewood Cliffs, N.J.: 1979), 230–55.

28. See Estelle B. Freedman, "'Uncontrolled Desires': The Response to the Sexual Psychopath, 1920–1960," in this volume. For a sampling of the popular literature, see J. Edgar Hoover, "How Safe is Your Daughter," *American Magazine* (July 1947): 32–33; "Biggest Taboo: Crimes Committed by Sexually Maladjusted," *Collier's*, 15 February 1947, 24; "What Can We Do About Sex Crimes," *Saturday Evening Post*, 11 December 1948, 30–31; "Terror in the Cities," *Collier's*, 11 November 1949, 13–15; and "Murder as a Sex Practice," *American Mercury* (February 1948): 144–50. Among the state commission reports are Commission to Study Sex Offenses, *The Sex Offender and the Criminal Law: Report to the Governor and the General Assembly of Virginia* (Richmond: 1951); Interim Commission of the State of New Hampshire to Study the Cause and Prevention of Serious Sex Crimes, *Report* (Concord: 1949); Joint State Government Commission of Pennsylvania, *Sex Offenders: A Report to the General Assembly* (Harrisburg: 1951); and Michigan Governor's Study Commission on the Deviated Criminal Sex Offender, *Report* (Lansing: 1950). For critiques of the laws, see Edwin H. Sutherland, "The Sexual Psychopath Laws," *Journal of Criminal Law and Criminology* 40 (1950): 543–54; Bowman and Engle, "A Psychiatric Evaluation"; Bowman and Engle, "Sexual Psychopath Laws," in *Sexual Behavior and the Law*, ed. Ralph Slovenko (Springfield, Ill.: 1965); Alan Swanson, "Sexual Psychopath Statutes: Summary and Analysis," *Journal of Criminal Law, Criminology and Police Science* 51 (1960): 215–35.

13

The Reproduction of Butch-Fem Roles: A Social Constructionist Approach

Elizabeth Lapovsky Kennedy
Madeline Davis

All commentators on twentieth-century lesbian life have noted the prominence of butch-fem roles.[1] Their presence was unmistakable in prefeminist communities where the butch projected the male image of her particular time period—at least in dress and mannerism—and the fem, the female image; and all members were usually one or the other. The tenacity of butch-fem roles underlines the appeal of an essentialist theory, which assumes that sexuality and gender transcend time and culture and reflect biological or psychological givens. However, our study of the Buffalo lesbian community's culture, social organization, and consciousness reveals significant changes within this seeming continuity. Our approach views sexuality as socially constructed, that is, created by human actors in culturally and historically conditioned ways. In this essay we argue that social constructionism provides a necessary dimension for understanding how butch-fem roles have operated in the community and in the development of individual identity.[2]

Essentialist approaches to butch-fem roles, as well as to homosexuality in general, have a long tradition.[3] The nineteenth-century medical literature considered the "invert," the man or woman whose character and mannerisms appeared to imitate those of the "opposite sex," as congenitally flawed. These researchers had little commentary on cases of more "normal" appearing behavior—passivity in women, aggressiveness in men—in which the desired object was nevertheless of the same sex. By the early 1900s psychologists and sexologists, led by Sigmund Freud, began to explore homosexuality in terms of childhood trauma and parental insufficiency.[4] This approach never fully supplanted theories of congenital causation but nevertheless was extremely powerful as a new kind of essentialism, which viewed homosexuality as a psychological disorder caused by abnormal personality development.[5] Over the years essentialism has at times been adopted by the lesbian and gay community and used as a basis from which to argue for tolerance and acceptance. Radclyffe Hall's *The Well of Loneliness* is an apt example; the novel pleads for the acceptance of Stephen, an unmistakably masculine lesbian, who cannot help being who she is.[6] The essentialist tradition still has a powerful influence on contemporary thinking about sexuality. For instance, the dominant ideology of our society considers the distinction between men and women as fixed and ultimately based in biology. Similarly, it categorizes lesbians and gay men as distinct kinds of people.[7] Such ideas unquestionably lurk in the background of popular thinking about butch-fem roles as well.

The relatively new social constructionist approach aims to reveal the temporal and cultural dimensions of the continuities that essentialists take for granted. Jonathan Katz explains this eloquently in his pioneering *Gay American History:*

> I will be pleased if this book helps to revolutionize the traditional concept of homosexuality. This concept is so profoundly ahistorical that the very existence of Gay history may be met with disbelief. The common image of the homosexual has been a figure divorced from any temporal-social context. The concept of homosexuality must be historicized. Ancient Greek pederasty, contemporary homosexual "marriages" and lesbian-feminist partnerships all differ radically. Beyond the most obvious fact that homosexual relations involve persons of the same gender, and include feelings as well as acts, there is no such thing as homosexuality in general, only particular historical forms of homosexuality. There is no evidence for the assumption that certain traits have universally characterized homosexual (or heterosexual) relations throughout history. The problem of the historical researcher is thus to study and establish the character and meaning of each varied manifestation of same-sex relations within a specific time and society.[8]

In this essay we want to further the scope of social constructionist research by addressing ourselves to the subject of butch-fem roles: are they indeed constant in community culture and individual identity, and therefore subject to a fixed biological or psychological interpretation, or do they need to be seen in the total social context of a developing lesbian community? After providing some background information for our research, we will document the meaning of roles for this community and show how the specific content of roles has changed over time. We will then look at how our narrators came to their role identities and consider their understanding of lesbianism as inborn or a product of social forces.

Lesbian communities began to develop in the large industrial centers of Europe and America at the turn of the century; Buffalo was no exception.[9] Our research has positively identified an upper-class community in Buffalo during the 1920s and black and white working-class communities during the 1930s, and it suggests that these communities existed even earlier. (This difference in dates is more a reflection of the sources available for learning about each community than of age. Our data on the upper-class women come from articles about them in local newspapers, while our information on the working-class women comes primarily from their own testimonies, and therefore can go only as far back as their ages and memories permit.)[10] Our research has focused on working-class lesbians from 1930 to 1965, because we wanted to check our hunch that their consciousness, culture, and social life were formative in the emergence of the gay liberation movement of the 1960s.[11] In this article we will treat the working-class lesbian community as a unified whole, even though it consisted of separate black and white communities that overlapped only to a limited degree, and we will use material from both black and white women. Over nine years we have collected oral histories from forty-five narrators, including nine women of color, all of whom were participants in this community at some time, and some of whom were leaders. Our narrators' stories were much richer than we had ever imagined and confirmed our suspicions about their role in shaping lesbian history and politics.

Our primary concern has been to document the political and social evolution of this working-class lesbian community, looking at both its internal dynamics and its response to the changing nature of oppression. During this period the community existed predominantly in bars, since these were the only places where people could gather publicly, break the isolation of lesbian life, and develop both friendships and lover relationships. The oppressive tenor of the times is captured in a narrator's memory of what her older sister, who was already a lesbian, said to her upon learning that she was going to join the life in the early 1950s. They had gone to an after-hours club together in New York City, and a friend of her sister asked our narrator to dance. After two or three dances our narrator returned to the table and noticed that her sister was crying. When she asked why, her sister said:

> "I don't like the way you're looking around here. This isn't the life for you." I said, "If it's good enough for you why isn't it good enough for me?" My sister replied, "Look around at all these people that are laughing, joking, they're having a ball—you think they are. Inside they're being ripped apart. Do you know what it's like to live this kind of life?

Every day when you get out of bed, before your feet hit the floor, you've gotta say to yourself, come on, get up, you may get smacked right in the face again today, some way, somehow. . . . If you can get up everyday not knowing what this day's gonna bring, whether your heart's gonna be ripped out, whether you're gonna be ridiculed, or whether people are gonna be nice to you or spit in your face, if you can face living that way, day in and day out, then you belong here; if you can't . . . get the hell out."[12]

Although the risks involved in coming together were great, lesbians persevered and began to forge a community with a rich culture and a strong sense of solidarity and pride.[13]

Despite the fact that butch-fem roles were prominent in our narrators' memories, we at first viewed them as peripheral to the growth and development of the community. Only after several years of study did we come to understand that we could not even conceive of the transformation of the community without analyzing them. They were a complex phenomenon that pervaded all aspects of community life.[14] These roles had two dimensions: First, they constituted a code of personal behavior, particularly in the areas of image and sexuality. Butches affected a masculine style, while fems appeared characteristically female. Butch and fem also complemented one another in an erotic system in which the butch was expected to be both the doer and the giver; the fem's passion was the butch's fulfillment.[15] Second, butch-fem roles were what we call a social imperative. They were the organizing principle for this community's relation to the outside world and for its members' relationships with one another. The presence of the butch with her distinctive dress and mannerism, or the butch-fem couple, announced lesbianism to the public. The butch, in her willingness to affirm who she was and take the consequences, was the primary indicator of lesbianism to the heterosexual world. Her aggressive style set the tone of resistance to lesbian oppression. In addition, butch-fem roles established the guidelines for forming love relationships and friendships. Two butches could be friends but never lovers; the same was true for two fems. Given this social dimension of butch-fem roles, whether her identity felt like a natural expression of self or something falsely imposed, a lesbian needed to adopt a role to participate comfortably in the community and receive its benefits.

This social dimension of roles helps to explain their tenacity. But why should the opposition of masculine and feminine be woven into lesbian culture and become a fundamental organizing principle? Modern lesbian culture developed in the context of the late nineteenth and early twentieth century when elaborate hierarchical distinctions were made between the sexes, and gender was a fundamental organizing principle of cultural life. Given the nineteenth-century polarization of masculinity and femininity, Jonathan Katz argues, one of the few ways for women to achieve independence in work and travel and to escape passivity was to "pass" as men.[16] In a similar vein, Jeffrey Weeks holds that the adoption of male images by lesbians at the turn of the century broke through women's and lesbians' invisibility, a necessity if lesbians were to become part of public life.[17] Expanding this approach, Esther Newton situates the adoption of male imagery in the context of the New Woman's search for an independent life, and delineates how male imagery helped to break through nineteenth-century assumptions about the sexless nature of women and to introduce overt sexuality into women's relationships with one another.[18]

We agree with these interpretations and modify them for the conditions of the 1930s, 1940s, and 1950s. During this period an effective way for the lesbian community to express the challenge presented by its affirmation of women's sexual love of women was to manipulate the basic ingredient of patriarchy—the hierarchical distinction between male and female. Butch-fem couples flew in the face of convention and outraged society by usurping male privilege in appearance and sexuality. At a time when the community was developing solidarity and consciousness, but had not yet formed lesbian political groups, butch-fem roles were the only structure for organizing against heterosexual dominance.[19] In a sense they were a prepolitical form of resistance.[20]

The social imperative of butch-fem roles is most apparent in the evolution of lesbian bar culture even in the short period from 1930 to 1965. During the forties lesbian bar life began to flourish in Buffalo, developing a rich culture and consciousness of kind. World War II established an atmosphere where women could easily go out alone, thereby creating more space for the lesbian community. This growth in community culture and social life, in conjunction with the repression of the McCarthy era, some of which was directed specifically against homosexuals and lesbians, created a new element of defiance. Bar lesbians in the fifties went even further in asserting their identities than those in the forties and aggressively fought for the right to be themselves. Their bold rebelliousness generated the kind of consciousness that made gay liberation possible.

Butch-fem roles were the key element in this transformation of the community's stance toward the straight world. In the forties butches and butch-fem couples endured the harassment they received from being obvious lesbians with a strategy of passive resistance similar to that of "turning the other cheek." But in the fifties one segment of the community, the street dykes, aggressively fought back when provoked, defending their relationships and community standards.

> Even right now it's very easy for the kids coming out now, but back then it wasn't, and I've been beaten up, I've been hit by guys. And I've fought back; sometimes I won; sometimes I lost. But I wasn't fighting to prove

that I was big and bad and tough and wanted to be a man. I was fighting to survive. And I just can't see it. Things back then were horrible and I think that because I fought like a man to survive I made it somehow easier for the kids coming out today. I did all their fighting for them. I'm not a rich person. I don't even have a lot of money; I don't even have a little money. I would have nothing to leave anybody in this world, but I have that that I can leave to the kids who are coming out now, who will come out into the future. That I left them a better place to come out into. And that's all I have to offer, to leave them. But I wouldn't deny it. Even though I was getting my brains beaten up I would never stand up and say, "'No don't hit me. I'm not gay; I'm not gay." I wouldn't do that. I was maybe stupid and proud, but they'd come up and say, "Are you gay?" And I'd say, "Yes I am." Pow, they'd hit you. For no reason at all. It was silly and it was ridiculous, and I took my beatings and I survived it.

(By acknowledging the different responses to maltreatment in the 1940s and 1950s, we do not mean to imply that the fifties butch was braver or more courageous than her predecessors. Rather we argue that each kind of butch behavior was appropriate for the general situation in the society at large, and for internal developments in the community itself. All stages of lesbian history required courage, initiative, and persistence.)

Our narrators' memories of their first impression of the bars capture vividly the differences between the butch roles in the 1940s and the 1950s. One narrator who went to Ralph Martin's, a popular lesbian and gay bar of the forties, remembers the butches she met there with affection:

And the butches were very butchie, but they were gentle, they were a gentle group. I was only fifteen when I met a lot of these real real machos, but they were gentle. Of course I had hair down to my rear end when I really went to my first club, and they accepted me, there was nothing where they . . . Hey, you got long hair, you don't belong in our group, something like that you know. They just had respect for me and I did for them.

In the fifties this mode of behavior was completely replaced by a tough image. One narrator remembers an influential conversation with two new friends shortly after entering the bars:

They were two of the, I guess, the star dykes around town, and I remember one time the three of us were together, we must have been standing at the bar, because I remember when (one) pounded her fist on the bar or table, we were talking about being gay, and she said, "If you want to be butch you gotta be rough, tough, and ready," boom! She pounded her fist on the bar. And well, it scared me, I didn't know if I could measure up to all of that but I figured I would have to try 'cause I knew I was a butch, I knew that's what I was.

Other changes occurred in butch-fem roles that correlated with the move toward public defiance. As suggested by the quotations, the forties community adamantly refused to instruct newcomers, while the fifties community reached out to them and helped them learn their butch role. One narrator remembers a younger butch who in the early forties kept asking her questions. She always told her, "I will not tell you anything. Anything you find out will be on your own. Do what you have to do." In contrast all of our narrators who entered the bars in the fifties remember either reaching out to someone or someone reaching out to them: "With new butches you [tried] to befriend them. It ain't easy bein' alone. . . . Today it's a little more difficult. Someone walks into a bar and they're totally ignored. Before . . . you wanted to take them in for their own protection."

At the same time that the fifties community accepted the responsibility of instructing newcomers, it became less tolerant of deviance in butch-fem roles, another change from the 1940s. In the forties lesbians belonged to a role-identified community that tolerated the small number who didn't conform to roles and allowed much latitude in the way people expressed their role identity. One of our narrators said of the forties, "At that time almost everyone was in roles. For at least ninety-five percent there was no mistaking." Then she wondered out loud, "Did we do it to them, push people into roles?" She answered herself, "No they preferred it that way, we didn't do it." By the fifties those who did not conform could not be in the community. As one narrator, a well respected butch of the late fifties, remembers:

> Well, you had to be [into roles]. If you weren't, people wouldn't associate with you . . . You had to be one or the other or you just couldn't hang around. There was no being versatile or saying, "Well, I'm either one. I'm just homosexual or lesbian." You know, they didn't even talk about that. It was basically a man-woman relationship. . . . You had to play your role.

Although this rigidification paralleled what was happening in the larger society, it cannot be interpreted simply as imitative. The increasingly defiant stand of the community in relation to the heterosexual world increased the pressure and strain associated with butch-fem roles and hence produced a greater concern with rules and appropriate behavior. Butches had to know how to be tough and how to handle themselves in a fight. If they didn't, they could be in great danger.

Our analysis that the powerful continuity of butch-fem roles derives from their contribution to lesbian social organization, not the inherent biological or psychological makeup of every lesbian, is also supported by our narrators' varied experiences in developing their role identities. Although some narrators knew their identity from an early age, many had to develop an identity as part of the community. Two of our butch narrators who found the bars in the thirties remember being sure of their roles as butches before finding a gay community. One remembers that she was always more masculine. She looked that way and had that air about her. The other gives many examples of her tendencies toward being butch in early life. She remembers reveling in the boyish shoes her father made her wear because she was so hard on her shoes and related a humorous tale of getting her first short hair cut in the thirties:

> Then the boy's bob came out. My father took me to a barber he knew, and he got carried away and was telling the guy how to cut it up around the ears. My mother screamed, "What happened to your hair?" [Then] I used to take a scissors into the bathroom and cut my hair, and my mother would say, "How come your hair doesn't grow?" I would say, "Gee, I don't know!"

This same narrator couldn't remember a time when she wasn't "after the girls. . . . A father caught me rubbing against his daughter, standing on the running board of the car. I was sent home and forbidden to play with the girl again." When we asked if she was consciously initiating sexual contact, even though she was young at the time, she responded, "Definitely." These two women did not have to learn a role identity when they entered the bars but simply learned appropriate ways to develop and express their already established identity.

Our third narrator who came out in the thirties, however, does not emphasize her early butch identity, but rather the quest involved in finding a role. "If you're in gay life, you're in gay life, whichever—if you want to play the fem or be the butch, you certainly have to go out and find it, one way or the other, what part you are going to play." This captures the experience of those who came to the lesbian community without knowing their role identity. Since butch-fem was built on the opposition of masculine and feminine characteristics, it was harder for a fem to realize a distinctive identity while growing up in the context of customary expectations of feminine behavior. In addition, a significant portion of butch narrators also were not conscious of a role identity before entering the community. One narrator recalls that she went to her first bar with her boyfriend in the 1940s, not knowing what to expect and certainly with no preconceived idea of a butch identity. She learned from the community itself that she was butch, as is evident in her description of her first dance:

> I never danced, never, not even at proms. I danced, let's face it, but I didn't follow good; so I got out and it was just a natural thing. I grabbed her and I led. She was tiny and cute, and she says, "You're gay." I says, "Oh yeh, I'm happy," and I meant it. It was sincere. She thought I was pulling her leg.

And of course you're always going to try to act older because of where you are. And she said, "No," she said, "I knew you were a butch when you walked in the door. I don't care if you've got long hair or what." And I said, "Oh, I'm engaged to be married." She said, "I don't care if you're engaged, got long hair, I know you're a gay butch." I says, "Oh, no. I'm going, Oh God." Well, we finished our dance and I joined her group.

We have much more information on the complex process of creating role identity for women who entered the bars in the fifties, because we have been able to interview many more. Like their predecessors, some of our narrators knew they were butch from an early age and simply had to learn appropriate butch behavior upon entering the community:

Nine years old, I knew [I was a stud]. I used to beat up boys; girls—I would just treat them like little doll babies. But I never cared for a doll. . . . I had two brothers and a sister and my younger brother used to get cap pistols, trucks and things, I got dolls. . . . I used to beat him up and take his trucks and cap pistols and give him my dolls.

Another common memory of butch narrators who spent their child-hoods in the forties is feeling comfortable in boys' clothes at an early age. One narrator remembers, "I was under ten when I was wearing [my brother's] clothes when nobody was around. I always felt that I was in drag in women's clothing even as a child." This same narrator had powerful fantasies of being a cowboy:

I was a little chubby . . . so when I was in fifth grade . . . I used to have this fantasy that I was a cowboy. This excess weight I had was just sort of like props that I had on my body, and when I would leave the classroom I'd take off this excess weight and put on my cowboy suit and get on my horse and ride away.

Cowboy fantasies were common for young lesbians of this period. Another narrator who was called "Tom" for Tomboy, from about age six or seven, always envisioned herself as the heroic Roy Rogers. After school she would race home, take off her girl's clothes, and don her cowboy outfit. "I was Roy Rogers."

The clarity and forcefulness of these women's perceptions of their butch identities from an early age are striking, but their experiences were not those of all butch lesbians. Other narrators did not know their identities until they entered the community, and still others had difficulty finding the appropriate role for themselves. In some cases people came out one way and then changed their identification. One narrator remembers with humor that her mother had more insight into her developing role identity than she herself did:

She [my second relationship] was on the masculine side but I was very attracted to her, and so I naturally took the feminine approach. We started to see each other and then we started to go together and we really loved each other but we weren't making it, we were constantly hassling and fighting and arguing. And I talked to my mother and said, "Gee I don't know what it is. I really like her" . . . And my mother said, "Maybe you're not happy in the way you're living your life with her." I said, "What do you mean?" She said—my mother would get embarrassed when she tried to explain things in daylight—and she said, "Before you met [Joan] you used to dress a little different, you wore slacks and that. Now you're in dresses all the time and you put makeup on. You don't seem like you're happy. Maybe you should go back to what you were and let her be a little more feminine." I kind of thought about that and I talked it over with this girl, and do you know that that relationship lasted for six years?

Although lesbians only rarely switched roles during a relationship, it was common for people to change their roles after their first relationships. Such a change was associated with coming out and finding your place in the community and your sexual preferences. Coming out fem and then becoming butch was the most usual direction of this early change. There was a common saying among butches in the lesbian community, "Today's love affair is tomorrow's competition." One butch narrator remembers the pain that fems could cause by switching roles, "especially when they come back and take the girl you are with away. The only way she can get at you is that way, and it works; and then you're alone." Another narrator explains this switching as due not only to inexperience, but to the kind of vulnerability required of fems:

> Some would start out real fem and the minute they got hurt by a butch . . . the next time you'd see them they'd be real butchie . . . They'd be dressed up really butchie . . . Usually the butches broke up with them. They'd start getting really butchie too. I don't know if they think butch is better.

Changing of roles even occurred after a person had been out a long time:

> I've seen a lot of girls come out and be fem and wind up butch. I've seen a lot of girls that were butch turn fem . . . a lot, a whole lot. Sometimes it shocks me. Me, I could never do that. To say, well I'm gonna turn a fem, and go out with a man, or I'm gonna turn a fem and just be that. No, I couldn't do that. I've been livin' the way I am too long. But I've seen a lot do it. I've seen a lot of girls who I wouldn't even believe they could switch, turn from one side to the other.

This phenomenon of switching indicates both the power and social nature of roles. A lesbian who was not sure of her role could not simply explore. She had to take a role, and if she was not comfortable in one, then she could take the other. For many lesbians, roles had to be learned and involved an element of conscious choice. One fem who was—and still is—very famous for her beauty and attractiveness, emphasizes this element of conscious choice when explaining what she feels determines a person's role: "I don't know how they get their role because, I think it's a matter of choice, what they feel like they want to do, I suppose. It's hard to say. Because sometime, I feel like I might want to turn stud. Really!"

In addition to those who switched roles, this community also had members who were never completely comfortable in roles, even though they appeared to adapt.

> I think on the surface I identified . . . when I was involved in the gay community, on the surface, you know, you either had to be butch or fem. And I was always the, I guess you'd say, the butch appearing one—back to the days when DA haircuts were popular.[21]

But this woman did a lot of joking about roles even at a time when rules were strict and serious:

> Thinking back I can remember one of the things I used to say, people would say, "Are you butch or are you fem?" And I used to say, "Well, the only difference to me between the butch or a fem is when you get up on the dance floor so you don't have to argue who's going to lead." And I have another saying since then: "My biggest decision when I get up every morning is whether to be an aggressive fem or a nelly butch."

Although the women we interviewed who were uncomfortable in roles were not the majority of this community, a surprising number expressed some degree of discomfort. The fact that they adapted just enough to get by, is yet another confirmation that roles are not an intrinsic part of lesbians' biological or psychological makeup, but are a fundamental organizing principle of participation in the community.

In keeping with our narrators' varied experiences in finding their role identities, the community has not had, nor does it now have, a hegemonic view about what constitutes a true lesbian. Many narrators see the butch lesbian as the true lesbian. Other narrators consider anyone who stays with women, and is part of the community, a lesbian. Two of our butch narrators who came out in the thirties disagree with one another on the subject, and their argument, which they said was quite common among members of the community in the past, eloquently explores the central issues.

During the interview Leslie took the position that only butches are lesbians. She is a lesbian [butch] and is never attracted to another like herself. Rather, she is always attracted to a more feminine type of person. Arden, on the other hand, thought that all women who stay with women are lesbians, butch or fem, as long as they don't flip back and forth between women and men. Each tried to convince the other of the rightness of her position but neither was successful. Leslie asked Arden about two women who had been Arden's instructors in sex. These women had been married; didn't Arden consider them bisexual? Arden: "No, they didn't go back and forth. Once they were in the crowd they stayed. It was good fun and they liked it." The friends then discussed the women who had started seeing lesbians during the war while their husbands were away. Some of these women went back and forth, while others did not. Leslie again did not agree with Arden that those who stayed with women were lesbians. A final argument revolved around the identity of Ramona, a past lover of Leslie's, who was very feminine and had never been with a man. Arden saw her as a lesbian while Leslie did not. Leslie believed that her own involvement with sixteen-year-old Ramona had indelibly influenced the impressionable young woman, who might not otherwise have pursued relationships with women. It was impossible for the two friends to come to an agreement.

At another interview Leslie and Arden continued their disagreement on a different level. Leslie emphasized how the pressures of heterosexual life might influence a non-lesbian: "Women of all kinds get involved in the fun of gay life. They like the fun and freedom of gay life, and it has nothing to do with sexual preference." Arden countered, underlining the forces that encouraged lesbians to pursue heterosexual marriage: "But also there is another side. I think that there were many women who liked being with women, who preferred women, but who get the Mrs. because they wanted that status."

The similarity of Leslie's position to that of the Kinsey reports, which were published after she came of age, is quite striking.[22] Leslie is using a continuum model in which there are "true lesbians" who only have sex with women, and fems whom she considers bisexuals, who can have sex with either men or women. In fact she believes that the majority of the world is bisexual. In addition her idea that only butches are true lesbians bears a striking similarity to early medical theories.[23] Arden, on the other hand, has the incipient analysis of a social constructionist. In her view, if women spend time in the lesbian community and consider themselves lesbians, they are lesbians, whether they are butch or fem. Furthermore, even though they hold these differing views about the nature of lesbianism, both women are cognizant of the social forces that influence a woman to participate in either the lesbian or heterosexual world.

In the fifties community similar disagreements existed. "There was always that . . . jealousy. If you'd see [a fem] looking at a man, you'd think, 'What are you looking at him for?' You couldn't think of them as a lesbian—a lesbian wouldn't do that." When pressed further this narrator said, "They're not as true as we are. I bet mostly all of the old [butches] feel that way." And to our surprise, some fems of that period concurred with this opinion. In their view, because they weren't the initiators, or because they didn't frequently make love to another woman, they weren't true lesbians. However, some fems disagreed. One fem who came out in the fifties, and left the life for sixteen years of marriage beginning in the early sixties, felt that she was a lesbian during the fifties when she moved with the crowd and is a lesbian again today.

Disagreements about what created a true lesbian went beyond this one issue of whether butches and fems were both lesbians. Women in the community also disagreed about the role of biology. Those who came to their butch identity at an early age tend to attribute it to physiological causes. Others claim that they don't know what ultimately caused their lesbianism. One respected butch humorously relates her opinion of how she became a lesbian:

> I don't know. You know people ask me . . . when I tell them I've been gay all my life . . . "How did you get to be gay all your life?" And I tell them the story. I say, "Well you see, the way it was with me is when I was born the doctor was so busy with my mother, it was a hard birth for her, . . . that it was the nurse that slapped my ass to bring that first breath of life into me. And I liked the touch of that feminine hand so much that I've been gay ever since."

In conclusion, our research suggests that the reproduction of butch-fem roles involves complex issues of psychosocial identity as well as community instruction and pressure, and that the power and continuity of roles derive in part from their centrality in organizing lesbian relations with the straight world. We argue that an analysis of butch-fem roles that is located in the context of the growth and development of a specific community has more explanatory power than essentialism. In Buffalo, as lesbians moved from a situation of relative isolation toward the political stance of the homophile and gay liberation movements, the content and meaning of butch-fem roles changed from that of building culture and community to confronting heterosexual society and fighting for dignity and respect. Some lesbians knew their role identity before entering the community, while others had to learn it, and all had to learn the content of butch-fem roles for the Buffalo community at the particular time they entered. Many members of the community adhered to essentialist explanations of their situation. This echoed essentialism in the dominant culture and provided for many a supportive sense of inescapable identity. However, others did not find essentialism a good description of their own experiences or of the variety of ways women participated in the community. They generated, from the social relations of their lives, alternative explanations that approached those of present day social constructionists.

■ Notes

Acknowledgments: The original version of this paper was written for the International Scientific Conference on Gay and Lesbian Studies, "Homosexuality, Which Homosexuality?" at the Free University of Amsterdam. We want to thank the conference organizing committee for granting permission to publish the paper in this volume, especially since the conference is publishing its own proceedings. We thank Christina Simmons and Kathy Peiss for their careful reading of this chapter, and helpful suggestions for revisions. We also thank Lisa Duggan, Joan Nestle, Bobbi Prebis, and David Schneider for their general support of our work and the reading of a draft of this essay.

1. See, for instance, Del Martin and Phyllis Lyon, *Lesbian/Woman* (New York: 1972); Audre Lorde, "Tar Beach," *Conditions* no. 5 (1979): 34–47; Joan Nestle, "Butch-Fem Relationships, Sexual Courage in the 1950s," *Heresies* 12 (1981): 21–24; John D'Emilio, *Sexual Politics, Sexual Communities; The Making of a Homosexual Minority in the United States, 1940–1970* (Chicago: 1983); Esther Newton, "The Mythic Mannish Lesbian: Radclyffe Hall and the New Woman," *Signs* 9 (Summer 1984): 557–75. Butch-fem roles are also apparent in twentieth-century novels and pulp fiction. For an example of the former, see, for instance, Gale Wilhelm, *We Too Are Drifting* (New York: 1935); and of the latter, Ann Bannon, *Beebo Brinker* (Greenwich, Conn.: 1962).

2. Our research is part of the work of the Buffalo Women's Oral History Project, founded in 1978 with three goals: (1) to produce a comprehensive, written history of the lesbian community in Buffalo, New York, using as its major source oral histories of lesbians who came out before 1970; (2) to create and index an archive of oral history tapes, written interviews, and supplementary materials; and (3) to give this history back to the community from which it derives. Madeline Davis and Elizabeth Lapovsky Kennedy are the directors of the project. Avra Michelson was an active member from 1978 to 1981. Wanda Edwards has been an intermittent member of the project since 1981, particularly in regard to research on the black lesbian community and on racism in the white lesbian community.

3. For a helpful overview of essentialist positions, see Diane Richardson, "The Dilemma of Essentiality in Homosexual Theory," *Journal of Homosexuality* 9 (Winter 1983): 79–90.

4. For a helpful discussion of this nineteenth- and early twentieth-century literature, see George Chauncey, Jr., "From Sexual Inversion to Homosexuality: The Changing Medical Conceptualization of Female 'Deviance,'" in this volume; and Newton, "The Mythic Mannish Lesbian," 565–68.

5. It is with hesitation that we call these psychological theories essentialist. Can there be an essentialist approach other than one that attributes homosexuality to genetic factors? Freudian theory certainly has the potential to explain the construction of homosexual identity in the context of social and cultural forces. But until recently it has only rarely been used in this way. Rather, most psychiatrists have worked with a model that dichotomized heterosexual and homosexual behavior and considered the former as normal and the latter as pathological. Carroll Smith-Rosenberg makes this point in her article, "The Female World of Love and Ritual: Relations Between Women in Nineteenth-Century America," *Signs* 1 (Autumn 1973): 2–28. For an article that delineates some of the

complex factors distinguishing an essentialist approach from a social construc-tionist approach and suggests some confusion in our current thinking about these distinctions, see Steven Epstein, "Gay Politics, Ethnic Identity: The Limits of Social Constructionism," *Socialist Review* 93/94 (May–August 1987): 9–56.

6. Radclyffe Hall, *The Well of Loneliness* (1928; rpt. London: 1974). For useful discussions of the novel's contribution to homosexual resistance, see Jonathan Katz, *Gay American History: Lesbians and Gay Men in the U.S.A.* (New York: 1976), 397–405; and Jeffrey Weeks, *Coming Out: Homosexual Politics in Britain, From the Nineteenth Century to the Present* (London: 1977) 107–11.

7. The dominant ideas about homosexuality are not monolithic; contradictory ideas exist alongside one another. The idea that homosexuality is a sickness, or a moral flaw, and can spread among people is also prevalent. The different ideas about homosexuality can be more or less homophobic depending on the con-text—the time period or the social group.

8. Katz, *Gay American History*, 6–7.

9. For a discussion of the conditions that might give rise to lesbian commu-nities at this time, see Ann Ferguson, "Patriarchy, Sexual Identity, and the Sexual Revolution," *Signs* 7 (Autumn 1981): 158–72. The earliest references to lesbian bar communities appear in French fiction, Emile Zola's *Nana* (1880), and Guy du Maupassant's "Paul's Mistress" (1881). For a discussion of these sources, albeit a negative one, see Lillian Faderman, *Surpassing the Love of Men: Romantic Friend-ship and Love Between Women from the Renaissance to the Present,* (New York: 1981), 282–84. For commentary on early twentieth-century lesbian communities, see Gayle Rubin's introduction to *A Woman Appeared to Me*, by Renée Vivien (Nevada: 1976), iii–xxvii; Vern Bullough and Bonnie Bullough, "Lesbianism in the 1920s and 1930s: A Newfound Study," *Signs* 2 (Summer 1977): 895–904; and Eric Garber, "Tain't Nobody's Business: Homosexuality in Harlem in the 1920s," *The Advocate* no. 342 (May 1982): 39–43.

10. One of our narrators gave us an upper-class woman's obituary she had saved, which said that this woman was survived by a lifelong companion. From this lead we found other obituaries and learned of a group of women who had been active in business and the arts in the 1920s and 1930s. A copy of these articles is on file at the Lesbian Herstory Archives, P.O. Box 1258, New York, N.Y. 10016.

11. This hypothesis was shaped by our personal contact with Buffalo lesbians who came out in the 1940s and 1950s, and by discussion with grassroots gay and lesbian history projects around the country, in particular, the San Francisco Les-bian and Gay History Project, the Boston Area Gay and Lesbian History Project, and the Lesbian Herstory Archives. In addition we were influenced by the early social constructionist work in lesbian and gay history. See, in particular, Katz, *Gay American History;* Rubin, "Introduction" to *A Woman Appeared to Me,* Vivien; and Weeks, *Coming Out.* We want to thank all these people who have been inspira-tional to our work.

12. All quotations are taken from the oral histories collected for this project between 1978 and 1986.

13. For further discussion of Buffalo bar life and the development of the lesbian community, see Madeline Davis, Elizabeth Lapovsky Kennedy, and Avra Michel-son, "Buffalo Lesbian Bars in the Fifties," paper presented at the National Wom-

en's Studies Association, Bloomington, Ind., May 1980, and "Buffalo Lesbian Bars: 1930–1960," paper presented at the Fifth Berkshire Conference on the History of Women, Vassar College, Poughkeepsie, N.Y., June 1981. Both papers are on file at the Lesbian Herstory Archives. We are currently rewriting them for our monograph *Boots of Leather, Slippers of Gold: The History of a Lesbian Community*.

14. For a detailed discussion of our research on butch-fem roles, see Madeline Davis and Elizabeth (Liz) Lapovsky Kennedy, "Butch/fem Roles in the Buffalo Lesbian Community: 1940–1960," paper presented at the Gay Academic Union Conference, Chicago, October 1982. This paper is on file at the Lesbian Herstory Archives.

15. For additional information on butch-fem roles and sexuality in the Buffalo lesbian community, see Madeline Davis and Elizabeth Lapovsky Kennedy, "Oral History and the Study of Sexuality in the Lesbian Community: Buffalo, New York, 1940–1960," *Feminist Studies* 12 (Spring 1986): 7–26.

16. Katz, *Gay American History*, 209–11.

17. Weeks, *Coming Out*, 89, and *Sex, Politics and Society: The Regulation of Sexuality Since 1800* (London: 1981), 115–17.

18. Newton, "The Mythic Mannish Lesbian."

19. We do not mean to relegate butch-fem roles to history. They are unquestionably meaningful for a number of lesbians today. This analytical framework explains why they continue today, as well as alerts us to expect that their current meaning is somewhat different from twenty years ago.

20. The concept of prepolitical comes from Eric Hobsbawm, *Primitive Rebels: Studies in Archaic Forms of Social Movement in the Nineteenth and Twentieth Centuries* (New York: 1959), 2.

21. The DA—the letters stand for duck's ass—was a popular hairdo for working-class men and butches during the 1950s. All side hair was combed back and joined the back hair in a manner resembling the layered feathers of a duck's tail, hence the name. Pomade was used to hold the hair in place and give a sleek appearance.

22. Alfred Kinsey, Wardell B. Pomeroy, Clyde E. Martin, Paul H. Gebhard, *Sexual Behavior in the Human Female* (1953; rpt. New York: 1965), 468–76.

23. She could have been exposed to these ideas through Hall's the *Well of Loneliness*, which she had read.

IV

Private Passions and Public Debates, 1960 to the Present

14

Mass Market Romance:
Pornography for Women Is Different

Ann Barr Snitow

■ **I**   In 1978, 109 million romantic novels were sold under an imprint you will not see in the *New York Times* best-seller lists or advertised in its *Book Review*. The publisher is Harlequin Enterprises, Ltd., a Canadian company, and its success, a growth of 400 percent since 1976, is typical of the boom in romantic fiction marketed for women.[1]

Harlequin romances can be purchased cheaply in bookstores and drugstores, but the company does a large percentage of its business through the mail, sending eight titles a month to twelve million subscribers in North America. Since a Harlequin is almost always 188 pages long (55,000–58,000 words), subscribers could be reading about 375 pages a week. Reading is more private and more absorbing than television. A book requires stopping the housework, waiting for that lunch or coffee break at the office. "Your passport to a dream," say the television ads for Harlequins, which picture a weary secretary sinking gratefully into solitary reading on her lunch hour.

If one includes the large number of novels published by other companies but essentially keeping to the Harlequin formula— "clean, easy-to-read love stories about contemporary people, set in exciting foreign places"[2]—the number of books of this specific genre being sold has risen to several hundred million a year. This is a figure in another statistical universe from the sales of books we usually call "best sellers." This article offers a series of hypotheses about the appeal Harlequin romances have for the women reading them.

Reprinted from *Radical History Review* 20 (Spring/Summer 1979): 141–61.

■ **II**   To analyze Harlequin romances is not to make any literary claims for them. Nevertheless, it would be at best grossly incurious, and at worst sadly limited, for literary critics to ignore a genre that millions and millions of women read voraciously. Though I propose to do a literary analysis of Harlequin romances as a way to get at the nature and power of their appeal, they are not art but rather what Lillian Robinson has called "leisure activities that *take the place* of art."[3] This is to say that they fill a place left empty for most people. How do they fill it, and with what?

After a recent talk I gave about Harlequin romances, a member of the audience asked, "Would a reader of Harlequin romances be insulted by your lecture?" This is a disturbing question because the terms I use here to describe the Harlequin formula and its appeal *are* insulting, but to whom? In describing the sensibility of the Harlequin type of romance, I am not presuming to describe the sensibility of its readers. In matters of popular culture, we are not what we eat.

The old line about commercial popular culture, that it is soma for the masses produced by a cynical elite, has been replaced, and properly so, by a more complex idea of the relation between the consumers and sellers of mass culture: in this newer view, popularity is by definition considered as a species of vitality. In other words, consumers are not seen merely as passive repositories, empty vessels into which debilitating ideologies are poured. This recognition of the force of popular forms, of their appeal to the depth structures in all our minds, is an important development in our critical thinking.[4]

Certainly the romantic novels for women I will discuss here reflect a complex relationship between readers and publishers. Who is manipulating whom? Each publisher is the prisoner of past successes, trying to find again the somewhat mysterious combination of elements that made a particular book hit the taste of the street. The way in which people experience mass cultural products in a heterogeneous society is erratic, subject to many forces. Harlequins, for example, are only one strain in the mass paperback market aimed primarily at women readers. There are also gothics (now rather passé), spectaculars, historical romances, family sagas, fotonovelas, and true confessions.[5] Each one of these has its own species of appeal. Does each also have its own specific audience? The mass audience may be manipulated in some ways and may be controlling the market in others but it is also and always omnivorous, capable of digesting contradictory cultural impulses and at the same time resisting suggestion altogether.

In this article I try to steer a careful course between critical extremes, neither assuming that romance novels are dope for catatonic secretaries, nor claiming for them a rebellious core of psychological vitality. I observe in these books neither an effective top down propaganda effort against women's liberation, nor a covert flowering of female sexuality. Instead, I see them as accurate descriptions of certain *selected* elements of female consciousness. These novels are too pallid to shape consciousness but they feed certain regressive elements in the female experience. To observe that they express primal structures in our social relations is not to claim either a cathartic usefulness for them or a dangerous power to keep women in their place.

The books are interesting because they define a set of relations, feelings, and assumptions that do indeed permeate our minds. They are *mass* paperbacks not only because they are easy to read pablum but also because they reflect—sometimes more, sometimes less consciously, sometimes amazingly naively—commonly experienced psychological and social elements in the daily lives of women. That the books are unrealistic, distorted, and flat are all facts beside the point. (I am not concerned here with developing an admiration for their buried poetics.) Their particular sort of unreality points to what elements in social life women are encouraged to ignore; their distortions point to larger distortions culture wide; their lack of richness merely bares what is hidden in more inclusive, more personally controlled works of art, the particular nature of the satisfactions we are all led to seek by the conditions of our culture.

■ **III**   What is the Harlequin romance formula? The novels have no plot in the usual sense. All tension and problems arise from the fact that the Harlequin world is inhabited by two species incapable of communicating with each other, male and female. In this sense these Pollyana books have their own dream-like truth: our culture produces a pathological experience of sex difference. The sexes have different needs and interests, certainly different experiences. They find each other utterly mystifying.

Since all action in the novels is described from the female point of view, the reader identifies with the heroine's efforts to decode the erratic gestures of "dark, tall and gravely handsome"[6] men, all mysterious strangers or powerful bosses. In a sense the usual relationship is reversed: woman is subject, man, object. There are more descriptions of his body than of hers ("Dark trousers fitted closely to lean hips and long muscular legs"[7]) though her clothes are always minutely observed. He is the unknowable other, a sexual icon whose magic is maleness. The books are permeated by phallic worship. Male is good, male is exciting, without further points of reference. Cruelty, callousness, coldness, menace, etc., are all equated with maleness and treated as a necessary part of the package: "It was an arrogant remark, but Sara had long since admitted his arrogance as part of his attraction."[7] She, on the other hand, is the subject, the one whose thoughts the reader knows, whose constant re-evaluation of male moods and actions makes up the story line.

The heroine is not involved in any overt adventure beyond trying to respond appropriately to male energy without losing her virginity. Virginity is a given here; sex means marriage and marriage, promised at the end, means, finally, there can be sex.

While the heroine waits for the hero's next move, her time is filled by tourism and by descriptions of consumer items: furniture, clothes, and gourmet foods. In *Writers Market* (1977) Harlequin Enterprises stipulate: "Emphasis on travel." (The exception is the occasional hospital novel. Like foreign places, hospitals offer removal from the household, heightened emotional states, and a supply of strangers.) Several of the books have passages that probably come straight out of guide books, but the *particular* setting is not the point, only that it is exotic, a place elsewhere.[8]

More space is filled by the question of what to wear.

> She rummaged in her cases, discarding item after item, and eventually brought out a pair of purple cotton jeans and a matching shift. They were not new. She had bought them a couple of years ago. But fortunately her figure had changed little, and apart from a slight shrinkage in the pants which made them rather tighter than she would have liked, they looked serviceable.[9]

Several things are going on here: the effort to find the right clothes for the occasion, the problem of staying thin, the problem of piecing together outfits from things that are not new. Finally, there is that shrinkage, a signal to the experienced Harlequin reader that the heroine, innocent as her intent may be in putting on jeans that are a little too tight, is wearing something revealing and will certainly be seen and noted by the hero in this vulnerable, passive act of self exposure. (More about the pornographic aspects later. In any other titillating novel one would suspect a pun when tight pants are "serviceable" but in the context of the absolutely flat Harlequin style one might well be wrong. More, too, about this style later on.)

Though clothes are the number one filler in Harlequins, food and furniture are also important and usually described in the language of women's magazines:[10] croissants are served hot and crispy and are "crusty brown,"[11] while snapper is "filleted, crumbed and fried in butter" and tomato soup is "topped with grated cheese and parsley"[12] (this last a useful, practical suggestion anyone could try).

Harlequins revitalize daily routines by insisting that a woman combing her hair, a woman reaching up to put a plate on a high shelf (so that her knees show beneath the hem, if only there were a viewer), a woman doing what women do all day, is in a constant state of potential sexuality. You never can tell when you may be seen and being seen is a precious opportunity. Harlequin romances alternate between scenes of the hero and heroine together in which she does a lot of social lying to save face, pretending to be unaffected by the hero's presence while her body melts or shivers, and scenes in which the heroine is essentially alone, living in a cloud of absorption, preparing mentally and physically for the next contact.

The heroine is alone. Sometimes there is another woman, a competitor who is often more overtly aware of her sexuality than the heroine, but she is a shadow on the horizon. Sometimes there are potentially friendly females living in the next bungalow or working with the patient in the next bed, but they, too, are shadowy, not important to the real story which consists entirely of an emotionally isolated woman trying to keep her virginity and her head when the only person she ever really talks to is the hero, whose motives and feelings are unclear: "She saw his words as a warning and would have liked to know whether he meant [them] to be."[13]

The heroine gets her man at the end, first, because she is an old-fashioned girl (this is a code for no premarital sex) and, second, because the hero gets ample opportunity to see her perform well in a number of female helping roles. In the course of a Harlequin romance, most heroines demonstrate passionate motherliness, good cooking, patience in adversity, efficient planning, and a good clothes sense, though these are skills and emotional capacities produced in emergencies, and are not, as in real life, a part of an invisible, glamorless work routine.

Though the heroines are pliable (they are rarely given particularized character traits; they are all Everywoman and can fit in comfortably with the life style of the strong willed heroes be they doctors, lawyers, or marine biologists doing experiments on tropical islands), it is still amazing that these novels end in marriage. After 150 pages of mystification, unreadable looks, "hints of cruelty"[14] and wordless coldness, the thirty page denouement is powerless to dispel the earlier impression of menace. Why should this heroine marry this man? And, one can ask with equal reason, why should this hero marry this woman? These endings do not ring true, but no doubt that is precisely their strength. A taste for psychological or social realism is unlikely to provide a Harlequin reader with a sustaining fantasy of rescue, of glamor, or of change. The Harlequin ending offers the impossible. It is pleasing to think that appearances are deceptive, that male coldness, absence, boredom, etc., are not what they seem. The hero *seems* to be a horrible roúe; he *seems* to be a hopeless, moody cripple; he *seems* to be cruel and unkind; or he *seems* to be indifferent to the heroine and interested only in his work; but always, at the end a rational explanation of all this appears. In spite of his coldness or preoccupation, the hero really loves the heroine and wants to marry her.

In fact, the Harlequin formula glorifies the distance between the sexes. Distance becomes titillating. The heroine's sexual inexperience adds to this excitement. What is this thing that awaits her on the other side of distance and mystery? Not knowing may be more sexy than finding out. Or perhaps the heroes are really fathers—obscure, forbidden objects of desire. Whatever they are, it is more exciting to wonder about them than to know them. In romanticized sexuality the pleasure lies in the distance itself. Waiting, anticipation, anxiety—these represent the high point of sexual experience.

Perhaps there is pleasure, too, in returning again and again to that breathless, ambivalent, nervous state *before* certainty or satiety. Insofar as women's great adventure, the one they are socially sanctioned to seek, is romance, adventurousness takes women always back to the first phase in love. Unlike work, which holds out the possible pleasures of development, of the exercise of faculties, sometimes even of advancement, the Harlequin form of romance depends on the heroine's being in a state of passivity, of not knowing. Once the heroine knows the hero loves her, the story is over. Nothing interesting remains. Harlequin statements in *Writers Market* stress "upbeat ending essential here" (1977). Here at least is a reliable product that reproduces for women the most interesting phase in the love/marriage cycle and knows just when to stop.

■ **IV**   What is the world view implied by the Harlequin romance formula? What are its implicit values? The novels present no overt moral superstructure. Female virginity is certainly an ideal, but an ideal without a history, without parental figures to support it or religious convictions to give it a context. Nor can one say money is a value; rather it is a given, rarely mentioned. Travel and work, though glamorous, are not really goals for the heroine either. They are holding patterns while she awaits love.

Of course, the highest good is the couple. All outside events are subordinated to the psychodrama of its formation. But the heroine must struggle to form the couple without appearing to do so. Her most marketable virtue is her blandness. And she is always proud when she manages to keep a calm facade. She lies constantly to hide her desires, to protect her reputation. She tries to cover up all signs of sexual feeling, upset, any extreme of emotion. She values being an ordinary woman and acting like one. (Indeed, for women, being ordinary and being attractive are equated in these novels. Heroes are of course expected to have a little more dash and sometimes sport scars.) Finally, the heroine's value system includes the given that men are all right, that they will turn into husbands, despite appearance to the contrary.

The world of Harlequin novels has no past. (At most, occasionally the plot requires a flashback.) Old people hardly appear except as benevolent peripheral presences. Young women have no visible parents, no ties to a before. Everyone is young though the hero is always quite a bit older than the heroine. Is this why there are no parents, because the lover is really *in loco parentis?*

Harlequins make no reference to a specific ethnic group or religion. (In this they differ from a new popular mass form, the family saga, which is dense with ethnic detail, national identity, *roots.*) Harlequins are aggressively secular: Christmas is always the tinsel not the religious Christmas. One might expect to find romance linked, if only sentimentally, to nature, to universal categories, to first and last things. Harlequins assiduously avoid this particular short cut to emotion (while of course exploiting others). They reduce awe of the unknown to a speculation on the intentions of the cold, mean stranger and generally strip romance of its spiritual, transcendent aspect.

At the other extreme from the transcendent, Harlequins also avoid all mention of local peculiarities beyond the merely scenic. They reduce the allure of difference, of travel, to a mere travelogue. The couple is alone. There is no society, no context, only surroundings. Is this what the nuclear family feels like to many women? Or is this, once again, a fantasy of safety and seclusion, while in actuality the family is being invaded continually and is under pressures it cannot control?

The denatured quality of Harlequins is convenient for building an audience: anyone can identify. Or, rather, anyone can identify with the fantasy which places all the characters in an upper-class, polite environment familiar not in experience but in the ladies' magazines and on TV. The realities of class—workers in dull jobs, poverty, real productive relations, social divisions of labor—are all, of course, entirely foreign to the world of the Harlequin. There are servants in the novels lest the heroine, like the reader, be left to do all the housework, but they are always loyal and glad to help. Heroines have familiar service jobs—they are teachers, nurses, nursery-maids—but the formula finds a way around depicting the limitations of these jobs. The heroine can do the work which ordinary women do while still seeming glamorous to the reader either because of *where* the heroine does her work or how she is rescued from doing it.

All fiction is a closed system in many respects, its language mainlining into areas of our conscious and subconscious selves by routes that bypass many of the things we know or believe about the real world of our daily experience. This bypassing is a form of pleasure, one of art's pleasing tricks. As Fred Kerner, Harlequin's director of publishing, said when describing the formula to prospective authors in *The Writer:* "The fantasy must have the same appeal that all of us discovered when we were first exposed to fairy tales as children."[15] I do not wish to imply that I would like to remove a Harlequin romance from the hands of its readers to replace it with an improving novel which includes a realistically written catalog of woman's griefs under capitalism and in the family. My purpose here is diagnostic. A description of the pared-down Harlequin formula raises the question: What is it about this *particular* formula that makes it so suggestive, so popular, with such a large female readership, all living under capitalism, most living—or yearning to live—in some form of the family?

Harlequins fill a vacuum created by social conditions. When women try to picture excitement, the society offers them one vision, romance. When women try to imagine companionship, the society offers them one vision, male, sexual companionship. When women try to fantasize about success, mastery, the society offers them one vision, the power to attract a man. When women try to fantasize about sex, the society offers them taboos on most of its imaginable expressions except those that deal directly with arousing and satisfying men. When women try to project a unique self, the society offers them very few attractive images. True completion for women is nearly always presented as social, domestic, sexual.

One of our culture's most intense myths, the ideal of an individual who is brave and complete in isolation, is for men only. Women are grounded, enmeshed in civilization, in social connection, in family, and in love (a condition a feminist culture might well define as desirable) while all our culture's rich myths of individualism are essentially closed to them. Their one socially acceptable moment of transcendence is romance. This involves a constant return in imagination to those short moments in the female life cycle, courtship. With the exception of the occasional gourmet meal which the heroine is often too nervous to eat, all other potential sources of pleasure are rigidly excluded from Harlequin romances. They reinforce the prevailing cultural code: pleasure for women is men. The ideal of romance presented in these books is a hungry monster that has gobbled up and digested all sorts of human pleasures.

There is another way in which Harlequin romances gloss over and obscure complex social relations: they are a static representation of a quickly changing situation—women's role in late capitalism. They offer a comfortably fixed image of the exchange between men and women at the very moment when the social actuality is confusing, shifting, frightening. The average American marriage now lasts about five years. A rape takes place every twelve minutes. While the social ferment of the sixties gave rise to the gothic form in cheap fiction—family dramas that were claustrophic and anti-erotic compensations for an explosion of mobility and sexuality—in the seventies we have the blander Harlequins, novels that are picaresque and titillating, written for people who have so entirely suffered and absorbed the disappearance of the ideal of home that they don't want to hear about it any more. They want instead to read about premarital hopefulness.

Harlequin romances make bridges between contradictions; they soothe ambivalence. A brutal male sexuality is magically converted to romance;

the war between men and women who cannot communicate ends in truce. Stereotyped female roles are charged with an unlikely glamor, and women's daily routines are revitalized by the pretense that they hide an ongoing sexual drama.

In a fine piece about modern gothic romances, Joanna Russ points out that in these novels, "'Occupation: Housewife' is simultaneously avoided, glamorized, and vindicated."[16] Female skills are exalted: it is good to nurture, good to observe every change in expression of the people around you, important to worry about how you look. As Russ says, the feminine mystique is defended and women are promised all sorts of psychological rewards for remaining loyal to it. Though in other respects, gothics are very different from Harlequins, they are the same in this: both pretend that nothing has happened to unsettle the old, conventional bargain between the sexes. Small surface concessions are made to a new female independence (several researchers, misreading I believe, claim that the new heroines are brave and more interested in jobs than families[17]) but the novels only mention the new female feistiness to finally reassure readers that "plus ça change, plus c'est la même chose." Independence is always presented as a mere counter in the sexual game, like a hairdo or any other flirtatious gesture; sexual feeling utterly defeats its early stirrings.

In fact, in Harlequin romances, sexual feeling is probably the main point. Like sex itself, the novels are set in an eternal present in which the actual present, a time of disturbing disruptions between the sexes, is dissolved and only a comfortably timeless, universal battle remains. The hero wants sex; the heroine wants it, too, but can only enjoy it after the love promise has finally been made and the ring is on her finger.

■ **V**   Are Harlequin romances pornography?

> She had never felt so helpless or so completely at the mercy of another human being . . . a being who could snap the slender column of her body with one squeeze of a steel-clad arm.
>   No trace of tenderness softened the harsh pressure of his mouth on hers . . . there was only a savagely punishing intentness of purpose that cut off her breath until her senses reeled and her body sagged against the granite hardness of his. He released her wrists, seeming to know that they would hang helplessly at her sides, and his hand moved to the small of her back to exert a pressure that crushed her soft outlines to the unyielding dominance of his and left her in no doubt as to the force of his masculinity.[18]

In an unpublished talk,[19] critic Peter Parisi has hypothesized that Harlequin romances are essentially pornography for people ashamed to read pornography. In his view, sex is these novels' real *raison d'être*, while the romance and the promised marriage are primarily salves to the conscience of readers brought up to believe that sex without love and marriage is wrong. Like me, Parisi sees the books as having some active allure. They are not just escape; they also offer release, as he sees it, specifically sexual release.

This is part of the reason why Harlequins, so utterly denatured in most respects, can powerfully command such a large audience. I want to elaborate here on Parisi's definition of *how* the books are pornography and, finally, to modify his definition of what women are looking for in a sex book.

Parisi sees Harlequins as a sort of poor woman's D. H. Lawrence. The body of the heroine is alive and singing in every fiber; she is overrun by a sexuality that wells up inside her and that she cannot control. ("The warmth of his body close to hers was like a charge of electricity, a stunning masculine assault on her senses that she was powerless to do anything about."[20]) The issue of control arises because, in Parisi's view, the reader's qualms are allayed when the novels invoke morals, then affirm a force, sexual feeling, strong enough to override those morals. He argues further that morals in a Harlequin are secular; what the heroine risks is a loss of social face, of reputation. The books uphold the values of their readers who share this fear of breaking social codes, but behind these reassuringly familiar restraints they celebrate a wild, eager sexuality which flourishes and is finally affirmed in "marriage" which Parisi sees as mainly a code word for "fuck."

Parisi is right: *every* contact in a Harlequin romance is sexualized:

> Sara feared he was going to refuse the invitation and simply walk off. It seemed like an eternity before he inclined his head in a brief, abrupt acknowledgement of acceptance, then drew out her chair for her, his hard fingers brushing her arm for a second, and bringing an urgent flutter of reaction from her pulse.[21]

Those "hard fingers" are the penis; a glance is penetration; a voice can slide along the heroine's spine "like a sliver of ice." The heroine keeps struggling for control but is constantly swept away on a tide of feeling. Always, though, some intruder or some "nagging reminder" of the need to maintain appearances stops her. "His mouth parted her lips with bruising urgency and for a few delirious moments she yielded to her own wanton instincts." But the heroine insists on seeing these moments as out of character: She "had never thought herself capable of wantonness, but in Carlo's arms she seemed to have no inhibitions."[22] Parisi argues that the books' sexual formula allows both heroine and reader to feel wanton again and again while maintaining their sense of themselves as not that sort of women.

I agree with Parisi that the sexually charged atmosphere that bathes the Harlequin heroine is essentially pornographic (I use the word pornographic as neutrally as possible here, not as an automatic pejorative). But do Harlequins actually contain an affirmation of female sexuality? The heroine's condition of passive receptivity to male ego and male sexuality is exciting to readers, but this is not necessarily a free or deep expression of the female potential for sexual feeling. Parisi says the heroine is always trying to humanize the contact between herself and the apparently undersocialized hero, "trying to convert rape into love making." If this is so, then she is engaged on a social as well as a sexual odyssey. Indeed, in women, these two are often joined. Is the project of humanizing and domesticating male sexual feeling an erotic one? What is it about this situation that arouses the excitement of the anxiously vigilant heroine and of the readers who identify with her?

In the misogynistic culture in which we live, where violence toward women is a common motif, it is hard to say a neutral word about pornography either as a legitimate literary form or as a legitimate source of pleasure. Women are naturally overwhelmed by the woman-hating theme, which obscures what might be women's own stake in arousing reading.

In recent debates, sex books that emphasize both male and female sexual feeling as a sensuality that can exist without violence are being called "erotica" to distinguish them from "pornography."[23] This distinction blurs more than it clarifies the complex mixture of elements that make up sexuality. "Erotica" is soft core, soft focus; it is gentler and tenderer sex than that depicted in pornography. Does this mean true sexuality is diffuse while only perverse sexuality is driven, power hungry, intense, and selfish? I cannot accept this particular dichotomy. It leaves out too much of what is infantile in sex—the reenactment of early feelings, the boundlessness and omnipotence of infant desire and its furious gusto. In pornography all things tend in one direction, a total immersion in one's own sense experience, for which one paradigm must certainly be infancy. For adults this totality, the total sexualization of everything, can only be a fantasy. But does the fact that it cannot be actually lived mean this fantasy must be discarded? It is a memory, a legitimate element in the human lexicon of feelings.

In pornography, the joys of passivity, of helpless abandonment, of response without responsibility are all endlessly repeated, savored, minutely described. Again this is a fantasy often dismissed with the pejorative "masochistic" as if passivity were in no way a pleasant or a natural condition.

Yet another criticism of pornography is that it presents no recognizable, delineated characters. In a culture where women are routinely objectified it is natural and progressive to see as threatening any literary form that calls dehumanization sexual. Once again, however, there is another way to analyze this aspect of pornography. Like a lot of far more respectable twentieth century art, pornography is not about personality but about the explosion of the boundaries of the self. It is a fantasy of an extreme state in which all social constaints are overwhelmed by a flood of sexual energy. Think, for example, of all the pornography about servants fucking mistresses, old men fucking young girls, guardians fucking wards. Class, age, custom—all are deliciously sacrificed, dissolved by sex.

Though pornography's critics are right—pornography *is* exploitation—it is exploitation of *everything*. Promiscuity by definition is a breakdown of barriers. Pornography is not only a reflector of social power imbalances, sexual pathologies, etc., but it is also all those imbalances run riot, run to excess, sometimes explored *ad absurdum*, exploded. Misogyny is one content of pornography; another content is an infant desire for complete, immediate gratification, to rule the world out of the very core of passive helplessness.

In a less sexist society, there might be a pornography that is exciting, expressive, interesting, even, perhaps, significant as a form of social rebellion, all traits which, in a sexist society, are obscured by pornography's present role as escape valve for hostility toward women, or as metaphor for fiercely guarded power hierarchies, etc. Instead, in a sexist society, we have two pornographies, one for men, one for women. They both have, hiding within them, those basic human expressions of abandonment I have described. The pornography for men enacts this abandonment on women as objects. How different is the pornography for women, in which sex is bathed in romance, diffused, always implied rather than enacted at all. This pornography is the Harlequin romance.

I described above the oddly narrowed down, denatured world presented in Harlequins. Looking at them as pornography obviously offers a number of alternative explanations for these same traits: the heroine's passivity becomes sexual receptivity and, though I complained earlier about her vapidity, in pornography no one need have a personality. Joanna Russ observed about the heroines of gothic romances something true of Harlequin heroines as well: they are loved as babies are loved, simply because they exist.[24] They have no particular qualities, but pornography bypasses this limitation and reaches straight down to the infant layer where we all imagine ourselves the center of everything by birthright and are sexual beings without shame or need for excuse.

Seeing Harlequins as pornography modifies one's criticism of their selectivity, their know-nothing narrowness. Insofar as they are essentially pornographic in intent, their characters have no past, no context; they live only in the eternal present of sexual feeling, the absorbing interest in the erotic sex object. Insofar as the books are written to elicit sexual excitation, they can be completely closed, repetitive circuits always returning to the moment of arousal when the hero's voice sends "a velvet finger"[25] along the spine of the heroine. In pornography, sex is the whole content; there need be no serious other.

Read this way, Harlequins are benign if banal sex books, but sex books for women have several special characteristics not included in the usual definitions of the genre pornography. In fact, a suggestive, sexual atmosphere is not so easy to establish for women as it is for men. A number of conditions must be right.

In *The Mermaid and the Minotaur,* an extraordinary study of the asymmetry of male and female relationships in all societies where children are primarily raised by women, Dorothy Dinnerstein discusses the reasons why women are so much more dependent than men on deep personal feeling as an ingredient, sometimes a precondition, for sex. Beyond the obvious reasons, the seriousness of sex for the partner who can get pregnant, the seriousness of sex for the partner who is economically and socially dependent on her lover, Dinnerstein adds another, psychological reason for women's tendency to emotionalize sex. She argues that the double standard (male sexual freedom, female loyalty to one sexual tie) comes from the asymmetry in the way the sexes are raised in infancy. Her argument is too complex to be entirely recapitulated here but her conclusion seems crucial to our understanding of the mixture of sexual excitement and anti-erotic restraint that characterizes sexual feeling in Harlequin romances:

> Anatomically, coitus offers a far less reliable guarantee of orgasm—or indeed of any intense direct local genital pleasure—to woman than to man. The first-hand coital pleasure of which she is capable more often requires conditions that must be purposefully sought out. Yet it is woman who has less liberty to conduct this kind of search: . . . societal and psychological constraints . . . leave her less free than man to explore the erotic resources of a variety of partners, or even to affirm erotic impulse with any one partner. These constraints also make her less able to give way to simple physical delight without a sense of total self-surrender—a disability that further narrows her choice of partners, and makes her still more afraid of disrupting her rapport with any one partner by acting to intensify the delight, that is, by asserting her own sexual wishes. . . .
>
> What the double standard hurts in women (to the extent that they genuinely, inwardly, bow to it) is the animal center of self-respect: the brute sense of bodily prerogative, of having a right to one's bodily feelings. . . . Fromm made this point very clearly when he argued, in *Man for Himself,* that socially imposed shame about the body serves the function of keeping people submissive to societal authority by weakening in them some inner core of individual authority. . . . On the whole . . . the female burden of genital deprivation is carried meekly, invisibly. Sometimes it cripples real interest in sexual interaction, but often it does not: indeed, it can deepen a woman's need for the emotional rewards of carnal contact. What it most reliably cripples is human pride.[26]

This passage gives us the theoretical skeleton on which the titillations of the Harlequin formula are built. In fact, the Harlequin heroine cannot afford to be only a mass of responsive nerve endings. In order for her sexuality, and the sexuality of the novels' readers, to be released, a number of things must happen that have little to do directly with sex at all. Since she cannot seek out or instruct the man she wants, she must be in a state of constant passive readiness. Since only one man will do, she has the anxiety of deciding, "Is this *the* one?" Since an enormous amount of psychic energy is going to be mobilized in the direction of the man she loves, the man she sleeps with, she must feel sure of him. A one night stand won't work; she's only just beginning to get her emotional generators going when he's already gone. And orgasm? It probably hasn't happened. She couldn't tell him she wanted it and couldn't tell him *how* she wanted it. If he's already gone, there is no way for her erotic feeling for him to take form, no way for her training of him as a satisfying lover to take place.

Hence the Harlequin heroine has a lot of things to worry about if she wants sexual satisfaction. Parisi has said that these worries are restraints there merely to be deliciously overridden, but they are so constant an accompaniment to the heroine's erotic feelings as to be, under present conditions, inseparable from them. She feels an urge toward deep emotion; she feels anxiety about the serious intentions of the hero; she role plays constantly, presenting herself as a nurturant, passive, receptive figure; and all of this is part of sex to her. Certain social configurations feel safe and right and are real sexual cues for women. The romantic intensity of Harlequins—the waiting, fearing, speculating—are as much a part of their functioning as pornography for women as are the more overtly sexual scenes.

Nor is this just a neutral difference between men and women. In fact, as Dinnerstein suggests, the muting of spontaneous sexual feeling, the necessity which is socially forced on women of channeling their sexual desire, is in fact a great deprivation. In *The Mermaid and the Minotaur* Dinnerstein argues that men have a number of reasons, social and psychological, for discomfort when confronted by the romantic feeling and the demand for security that so often accompany female sexuality. For them growing up and being male both mean cutting off the passionate attachment and dependence on woman, on mother. Women, potential mother figures themselves, have less need to make this absolute break. Men also need to pull away from that inferior category, Woman. Women are stuck in it and naturally romanticize the powerful creatures they can only come close to through emotional and physical ties.

The Harlequin formula perfectly reproduces these differences, these tensions, between the sexes. It depicts a heroine struggling, against the hero's resistance, to get the right combination of elements together so that, for her, orgasmic sex can at last take place. The shape of the Harlequin sexual fantasy is designed to deal women the winning hand they cannot hold in life: a man who is romantically interesting—hence, distant, even frightening—while at the same time he is willing to capitulate to her needs just enough so that she can sleep with him not once but often. His intractability is exciting to her, a proof of his membership in a superior class of beings but, finally, he must relent to some extent if her breathless anticipation, the foreplay of romance, is to lead to orgasm.

Clearly, getting romantic tension, domestic security, and sexual excitement together in the same fantasy in the right proportions is a delicate balancing act. Harlequins lack excellence by any other measure, but they are masterly in this one respect. In fact, the Harlequin heroine is in a constant fever of anti-erotic anxiety, trying to control the flow of sexual passion between herself and the hero until her surrender can be on her own terms. If the heroine's task is "converting rape into love-making" she must somehow teach the hero to take time, to pay attention, to feel, while herself remaining passive, undemanding, unthreatening. This is yet another delicate miracle of balance which Harlequin romances manage quite well. How do they do it?

The underlying structure of the sexual story goes something like this:

1. The man is hard (a walking phallus).

2. The woman likes this hardness.

3. But, at the outset, this hardness is *too hard.* The man has an ideology that is anti-romantic, anti-marriage. In other words, he will not stay around long enough for her to come, too.

4. Her final release of sexual feeling depends on his changing his mind, but *not too much.* He must become softer (safer, less likely to leave altogether) but not too soft. For good sex, he must be hard, but this hardness must be *at the service of the woman.*

The following passage from Anne Mather's *Born Out of Love* is an example:

His skin was smooth, more roughly textured than hers, but sleek and flexible beneath her palms, his warmth and maleness enveloping her and making her overwhelmingly aware that only the thin material of the culotte suit separated them. He held her face between his hands, and his hardening mouth was echoed throughout the length and breadth of his body. She felt herself yielding weakly beneath him, and his hand slid from her shoulder, across her throat to find the zipper at the front of her suit, impelling it steadily downward.

"No, Logan," she breathed, but he pulled the hands with which she might have resisted him around him, arching her body so that he could observe her reaction to the thrusting aggression of his with sensual satisfaction.

"No?" he probed with gentle mockery, his mouth seeking the pointed fullness of her breasts now exposed to his gaze. "Why not? It's what we both want, don't deny it." . . .

Somehow Charlotte struggled up from the depth of a sexually-induced lethargy. It wasn't easy, when her whole body threatened to betray her, but his words were too similar to the words he had used to her once before, and she remembered only too well what had happened next. . . .

> She sat up quickly, her fingers fumbling with the zipper, conscious all the while of Logan lying beside her, and the potent attraction of his lean body. God, she thought unsteadily, what am I doing here? And then, more wildly: Why am I leaving him? *I want him!* But not on his terms, the still small voice of sanity reminded her, and she struggled to her feet.[27]

In these romantic love stories, sex on a woman's terms is romanticized sex. Romantic sexual fantasies are contradictory. They include both the desire to be blindly ravished, to melt, and the desire to be spiritually adored, saved from the humiliation of dependence and sexual passivity through the agency of a protective male who will somehow make reparation to the woman he loves for her powerlessness.

Harlequins reveal and pander to this impossible fantasy life. Female sexuality, a rare subject in all but the most recent writing, is not doomed to be what the Harlequins describe. Nevertheless, some of the barriers that hold back female sexual feeling are acknowledged and finally circumvented quite sympathetically in these novels. They are sex books for people who have plenty of good reasons for worrying about sex.

While there is something wonderful in the heroine's insistence that sex is more exciting and more momentous when it includes deep feeling, she is fighting a losing battle as long as she can only define deep feeling as a mystified romantic longing on the one hand, and as marriage on the other. In Harlequins the price for needing emotional intimacy is that she must passively wait, must anxiously calculate. Without spontaneity and aggression, a whole set of sexual possibilities is lost to her just as, without emotional depth, a whole set of sexual possibilities is lost to men.

Though one may dislike the circuitous form of sexual expression in Harlequin heroines, a strength of the books is that they insist that good sex for women requires an emotional and social context that can free them from constraint. If one dislikes the kind of social norms the heroine seeks as her sexual preconditions, it is still interesting to see sex treated not primarily as a physical event at all but as a social drama, as a carefully modulated set of psychological possibilities between people. This is a mirror image of much writing more commonly labeled pornography. In fact one can't resist speculating that equality between the sexes as child rearers and workers might well bring personal feeling and abandoned physicality together in wonderful combinations undreamed of in either male or female pornography as we know it.

The ubiquity of the books indicates a central truth: romance is a primary category of the female imagination. The women's movement has left this fact of female consciousness largely untouched. While most serious women *novelists* treat romance with irony and cynicism, most women do not. Harlequins may well be closer to describing women's hopes for love than the work of fine women novelists. Harlequins eschew irony; they take love straight. Harlequins eschew realism; they are serious about fantasy and escape. In spite of all the audience manipulations inherent in the Harlequin formula, the connection between writer and reader is tonally seamless; Harlequins are respectful, tactful, friendly toward their audience. The letters that pour in to their publishers speak above all of involvement, warmth, human values. The world that can make Harlequin romances warm is indeed a cold, cold place.

■ **Postscript (1988)**   In the decade since this article was published a wide discussion of women's romance fiction has developed, including studies by Tania Modleski, Janice Radway, and Leslie Rabine. In addition, Harlequins themselves and other, related genres have changed rapidly and repeatedly, confirming the hypothesis that romance is a very malleable material, lending itself to extensive reworkings. Therefore, what is written here marks a specific historical point in the feminist work on popular fiction and in the evolving life of that fiction itself.

■ **Notes**

1. Harlequin is fifty percent owned by the conglomerate controlling the *Toronto Star*. If you add to the Harlequin sales figures (variously reported from 60 million to 109 million for 1978) the figures for similar novels by Barbara Cartland and those contemporary romances published by Popular Library, Fawcett, Ballantine, Avon, Pinnacle, Dell, Jove, Bantam, Pocket Books, and Warner, it is clear that hundreds of thousands of women are reading books of the Harlequin type.

2. Blurb in Harlequin Romance. Elizabeth Graham, *Mason's Ridge* (Toronto: 1978), and others (Quotation cited from *Best Sellers*, N.Y.)

3. Lillian S. Robinson, *Sex, Class, and Culture* (Bloomington, Ind.: 1978), 77.

4. In her article "Integrating Marxist and Psychoanalytic Approaches to Feminist Film Criticism," *Jump Cut* (Fall 1979), Ann Kaplan gives a useful survey of this shift in Left critical thinking about mass culture. See also Lillian Robinson, *Sex, Class, and Culture*, and Stuart Ewen *Captains of Consciousness* (New York: 1976).

5. Kate Ellis has explored the nature and history of gothic romances: "Paradise Lost: The Limits of Domesticity in the Nineteenth-Century Novel," *Feminist Studies* 2, no. 2/3 (1975): 55–63; "Charlotte Smith's Subversive Gothic," *Feminist Studies* 3 (Spring–Summer 1976): 51–55; and "Feminism, Fantasy, and Women's Popular Fiction" (unpublished essay). In "Women Read Romances that Fit Changing Times," *In These Times*, 7–13 Feb. 1979, she gives a more general survey of the different kinds of mass market paperbacks available to women, each with its own particular appeal.

6. Rachel Lindsay, *Prescription for Love* (Toronto: 1977), 10.

7. Rebecca Stratton, *The Sign of the Ram* (Toronto: 1977) 56, 147.

8. Here is an example of this sort of travelogue prose: "There was something to appeal to all age groups in the thousand-acre park in the heart of the city—golf for the energetic, lawn bowling for the more sedate, a zoo for the children's plea-

sure, and even secluded walks through giant cedars for lovers—but Cori thought of none of these things as Greg drove to a parking place bordering the Inlet." Graham, *Mason's Ridge*, 25.

9. Anne Mather, *Born Out of Love* (Toronto: 1977), 42.

10. See Joanna Russ, "Somebody's Trying to Kill Me and I Think It's My Husband: The Modern Gothic," *Journal of Popular Culture*, 6 (Spring 1973): 666–91.

11. Mather, *Born Out of Love*, 42.

12. Daphne Clair, *A Streak of Gold* (Toronto: 1978), 118.

13. Lindsay, *Prescription for Love*, 13.

14. Stratton, *The Sign of the Ram*, 66. The adjectives "cruel" and "satanic" are commonly used for heroes.

15. May 1977, 18.

16. Russ, "Somebody's Trying to Kill Me," 675.

17. See, for example, Josephine A. Ruggiero and Louise C. Weston, "Sex Role Characterizations of Women in 'Modern Gothic' Novels," *Pacific Sociological Review* 20 (April 1977): 279–300.

18. Graham, *Mason's Ridge*, 63.

19. Delivered 6 April 1978, Livingston College, Rutgers University.

20. Stratton, *The Sign of the Ram*, 132.

21. *Ibid.*, 112.

22. Ibid., 99, 102, and 139.

23. Gloria Steinem, "Erotica and Pornography: A clear and present difference," *Ms.* (November 1978), and other articles in this issue. An unpublished piece by Brigitte Frase, "From Pornography to Mind-Blowing," MLA talk, 1978, strongly presents my own view that this debate is specious. See also Susan Sontag's "The Pornographic Imagination," in *Styles of Radical Will* (New York: 1969), and Jean Paulhan, "Happiness in Slavery," preface to Pauline Reage, *Story of O* (New York: 1965).

24. Russ, "Somebody's Trying to Kill Me," 679.

25. Stratton, *The Sign of the Ram*, 115.

26. Dorothy Dinnerstein, *The Mermaid and The Minotaur: Sexual Arrangements and Human Malaise* (New York: 1976), 73–75.

27. Mather, *Born Out of Love*, 70–72.

15

(De)Constructing Pornography: Feminisms in Conflict

Daphne Read

Pornography has dominated the political imagination of the United States and Canada for nearly a decade, but the moment of "closure" is approaching.[1] As energies have been funneled into formulating legislation to control pornography, AIDS (acquired immune deficiency syndrome) has displaced pornography from the center of the emotional/ political landscape. The three single most powerful issues in the past twenty years—abortion, pornography, and now AIDS—have rudely transgressed the thin boundary between the private and the public, arousing public passions and exposing the crude violence of fear. What these three issues have in common is that they tap and intensify fears, anxieties, and phobias about the relationship between individual freedom, sexuality, and death.

On the surface pornography belongs to a different order of experience than abortion or AIDS—it does not appear to be a matter of life and death[2]—but the radical feminist discourse of pornography that has emerged in the last decade links pornography directly to male violence against women, to women's oppression in general, and more globally to all oppression. This discourse has redefined pornography, expanded its field, invested it with multiple social meanings, and threatened to subsume all social evil under its name. But no discourse is seamless; there have been multiple disruptions and resistances to the negative totalizing tendencies of the feminist pornography discourse: from activists and theorists resisting any authoritarian closure of the exploration of sexuality and sexualities, from civil libertarians wary of the repressive implications of legislative control in a conservative moral and political climate,

277

and from sex trade workers who challenge the tragic monological voices of the anti-pornography movement.

The debates within the feminist community have been fierce and acrimonious (particularly in the United States), but these hostilities have pushed feminist activism and theory in productive directions. An analysis of the construction of pornography within radical feminist discourse *and* its deconstruction points to the success of feminist organizing against violence against women, the risks in attempting to re-vision (or to appropriate) patriarchal concepts for feminist purposes (putting new wine in old skins, so to speak), and the ongoing, creative instabilities of feminist theory and practice.

■ (Re)Constructing Pornography

> Pornography is the ideology of a culture which promotes and condones rape, woman-battering, and other crimes of violence against women.
>
> —*Take Back the Night*[3]

The ways in which pornography has been theorized have varied with shifts in contemporary ideological discourse. In the late 1960s and early 1970s, the sexual revolution formed the context of discussion of pornography and sexuality. In "The Pornographic Imagination," for example, Susan Sontag argued radically that some pornography constitutes a literary genre and as art offers a particular knowledge, a truth, about human experience. She wrote:

> This truth—about sensibility, about sex, about individual personality, about despair, about limits—can be shared when it projects itself into art. . . . That discourse one might call the poetry of transgression is also knowledge. He [sic] who transgresses not only breaks a rule. He goes somewhere that the others are not; and he knows something the others don't know.[4]

She argued that pornography satisfies some human craving for transcendence. Its seductive power lies in its vision of a total universe focused exclusively on "the erotic imperative" or sexual exchange.

> All action is conceived of as a set of sexual *exchanges*. Thus, the reason why pornography refuses to make fixed distinctions between the sexes or allow any kind of sexual preference or sexual taboo to endure can be explained "structurally." The bisexuality, the disregard for the incest taboo, and other similar features common to pornographic narratives function to multiply the possibilities of exchange. Ideally, it should be possible for everyone to have a sexual connection with everyone else.[5]

In this view gender and the different experiences of men and women portrayed in pornography are not at issue; the field of pornography is sexuality, sexual exchanges, and self-transcendence.

In the early 1970s two critical shifts occurred in the way feminists read and interpreted cultural texts and events. We began to assert ourselves as reading subjects, and we began to question the relationship between representations of women and the lives women led, that is, the relationship between ideology and lived experience for women. Feminists read pornography differently from Sontag: through the lens of gender and as a reflection of everyday life. This change was fueled by two grassroots issues: the critique of sexist images of women and organizing against violence against women.

While Sontag was discussing pornography in terms of consciousness and human knowledge, a more urgent task for feminists was that of differentiating between power and dominance in heterosexual relationships on the one hand, and female sexual pleasure on the other. Kate Millett, one of the great iconoclasts of the 1970s, began to hold literary works accountable to women's lives. Forging a radically new critical terrain, she introduced the concept of sexual politics into cultural criticism and insisted on reading as a woman. *Sexual Politics* was a breathtakingly daring critique of the literary men who had had such an impact on the rebellious sexual libertarians of the 1960s: D. H. Lawrence, Henry Miller, Norman Mailer.[6] Literary sexual activity was turned inside out and upside down and exposed as an expression of male power and domination. It became impossible for women to read these male authors without the discomfort of a double consciousness—without an awareness of male violence and misogyny. The mirror Millett held to these literary men reduced them from the Voice of Humanity to merely male members of the human species. But disturbingly, her mirror also brought to the foreground the violence in sexual relations between men and women.

The magnitude of this violence became depressingly clear to feminists working on rape, wife battering, incest, and sexual harassment in the 1970s, but it was extremely difficult to put "private" violence against women on the "public" agenda. At the same time the public sex industry was growing exponentially and becoming more diversified and more accessible—moving out of its shadowy ghetto into the middle-class home—through the multiplication of porn magazines and the emergence of the video market among other developments. Analysts noted the increasing violence in pornography as well as new trends in the degradation, humiliation, and infantilization of women. For feminists the contrast between the appalling "normalcy" of everyday violence against women, which went unchecked and unpunished because "invisible," and the apparent legitimation of violence against women both in and by the pornography industry, ignited a prolonged protest against pornography. The ideological critique of sexist images of women and political activism against violence against women were fused brilliantly in the slogan: "Pornography is the theory, and rape the practice."[7] This slogan signals the maturing of a radical feminist discourse of pornography, which has generated enormous creative political energy; it also marks the codification of that discourse into an ideology with its own blindnesses, gaps, and unacknowledged margins.

The powerful appeal of the radical feminist analysis of pornography builds on the tenets of radical feminist theory. Three points can be made in this regard. First, the anti-pornography analysis puts women at the center, both as subject/agent and as subject/victim. Pornography is defined from the standpoint of "woman" and in terms of the harm it does to women. Second, in attempting to define pornography for legal purposes, feminists have focused specifically on sexual violence, linking representations of violence to real violence against women. Following the radical feminist first principle that women are oppressed through their sexuality, pornography is variously defined as a form of sexual coercion and violence against women, as a form of sexual discrimination, as hate literature, as the ideology of patriarchal societies. As patriarchal ideology it is perceived to disseminate and condone misogyny—woman-hating—and to promote, even cause, violence against women. Thus, radical feminists argue, there is a direct causal relationship between pornography and violence against women. Finally, feminists have extended the field of pornography so that it has become more than a metaphor for oppression; radical feminists have developed a (problematic) cultural critique of western society in which pornography stands as a totalizing self-destructive system that includes all oppressions within its boundaries (racism, homophobia, anti-semitism, imperialism).[8]

As the radical feminist anti-pornography movement grew in strength and was beginning to make some headway in its crusade for legislative reform, other feminists began to sound alarm bells about the direction of the movement and the broader implications of the single-issue focus. Critics questioned the politics of alliances between the anti-pornography movement and conservative forces that are explicitly anti-feminist—forces that favor the traditional family and sex roles and are anti-abortion, homophobic, anti-sexual, and moralistic.[9] They argued that the feminist anti-pornography movement had participated in the shift to the right in the United States.

Willingly or not, feminist expressions of outrage about violence against women and pornography have been appropriated by the state in the United States and Canada. In the early to mid-1980s, when public passions were at their peak, the concern with violence against women and children was subsumed within a more generalized moral panic about violence in society and the deterioration of family life. Stan Cohen has described periods of moral panic thus:

> A condition, episode, person or group of persons emerges to become defined as a threat to societal values and interests; its nature is present-ed in a stylized and stereotypical fashion by the mass media; the moral barricades are manned by editors, bishops and politicians and other right-thinking people; socially accredited experts pronounce their diag-noses and solutions; ways of coping are evolved, or (more often) resorted to; the condition then disappears, submerges or deteriorates. . . . Some-times the panic is passed over and forgotten, but at other times it has more serious and long term repercussions and it might produce changes in legal and social policy or even in the way in which societies conceive themselves.[10]

Though pornography was first targeted by feminists as a threat to the values and interests of women, it has subsequently become a generalized target for activists from the entire political spectrum, politicians, social scientists, and "right thinking people." It seems reasonable to fear that new legislation aimed at censoring or regulating pornography might be used more broadly to repress gays and lesbians, artists, and others since in spite of a feminist presence in the political process, daily reality in-cludes continued attacks on gays and lesbians, on progressive artists, and on sex education in schools.

Feminists interested in legal reform have worked hard on definitions of pornography that are both comprehensive and specific in an effort to forestall the possibility of government intervention outside the bound-aries of pornography. The most influential—and controversial—work in this regard has been the legislation developed by Catharine MacKinnon and Andrea Dworkin, which has been proposed or enacted in Min-neapolis, Indianapolis, Long Island, and Cambridge, Massachusetts, and declared unconstitutional by the Supreme Court in 1986. Rejecting the traditional concept of obscenity as the legal basis for restricting pornog-raphy, MacKinnon and Dworkin argued that pornography harms women by infringing on their civil rights, as it causes men to treat women as second-class citizens. A trafficking provision that would have allowed a woman to secure an injunction against the production, distribution, sale, or exhibition of pornographic material was widely condemned for violat-ing First Amendment protection of free speech.[11] In addition, however, the Feminist Anti-Censorship Task Force and other feminist critics at-tacked the definition of pornography, arguing that in its inclusiveness, the categories of sexual explicitness, sexism, and violence were con-flated.[12] On their own, none of these categories constitutes an adequate definition of pornography. The primary target, some feminists argue, ought to be only those images that are simultaneously sexually explicit, sexist, and violent. However, a conceptual slide that occurs in both feminist anti-pornography polemic and conservative rhetoric underlies the proposed legislation: that is, sexually explicit images that are neither violent nor sexist are seen to be as dangerous as images that are all three. The ease with which this conceptual conflation is achieved rhetorically—and accepted—attests to the emotional strength of more traditional attitudes toward sexuality, especially fear and ambivalence, which persist in spite of the sexual "enlightenment" of the past twenty years.

A question that emerges in thinking about pornography as the focus of feminist energies concerns the complicity of the anti-pornography movement in the larger moral panic. The sense of a social and moral crisis that pornography aroused has since shifted to AIDS, but for a moment in the early 1980s it can be argued that there was a moral panic focused on pornography. Jeffrey Weeks has pointed out that moral panic "crystallises widespread fears and anxieties, and often deals with them not by seeking the real causes of the problems and conditions which they demonstrate but by displacing them on to 'Folk Devils' in an identified social group (often the 'immoral' or 'degenerate')."[13] Did the single-minded focus on pornography as the *ideology* of violence against women serve to displace attention from a deeper analysis of the causes of that violence and the development of a complex strategy for dealing with it? Single-issue organizing provides a sense of emotional satisfaction and achievement in that individuals are doing something concrete toward creating social change. The satisfaction is all the greater if the issues can be seen as representative of all oppression.[14] But clearly, what the anti-pornography movement has mobilized in many women is not a sense of power, but the *fear* of violence. Paraphrasing Weeks, it might be argued that the anti-pornography movement has provided a focus for some women's fears and anxieties and deals with them by displacing them on to the "immoral" and "degenerate" pornography and sex trade industries.[15]

Sexuality, sexual practices, and sexual politics constitute the contested terrain that a single-minded focus on pornography narrows and obscures. At the core of the debates in the United States is the question of sexual freedom. Ellen Willis writes:

> The arguments have crystallized around specific issues: pornography; the causes of sexual violence and how best to oppose it; the definition of sexual consent; the relation of sexual fantasy to action and sexual behavior to political practice (is there such a thing as "politically correct" sex?); the nature of women's sexuality and whether it is intrinsically different from men's; the meaning of heterosexuality for women; the political significance of "fringe" sexualities like sadomasochism.[16]

These issues "raise the question of whether sexual freedom, as such, is a feminist value, or whether feminism ought rather to aim at replacing male-defined social controls over sexuality with female-defined controls."[17] Willis places the emergence of the bitter conflict over sexuality and the hardening of positions within the women's movement in the context of the rise of the New Right and the collapse of liberalism.

> Confronted with a right-wing backlash bent on suppressing all non-marital, non-procreative sex, feminists who saw sexual liberalism as deeply flawed by sexism but nonetheless a source of crucial gains for women found themselves at odds with feminists who dismissed the sexual revolution as monolithically sexist and shared many of the attitudes of conservative moralists.[18]

What appears to be at stake in the American feminist debates on sexuality is the issue of civil rights for women. Is the freedom of the individual, when that individual is a woman, to be interpreted as simply freedom *from* or as freedom *to:* freedom from danger (male violence) or freedom to act (sexual choice)? If women are viewed primarily as victims, then we narrow the range of our vision and limit ourselves to defensive and protective strategies rooted in sexual fear. But if we are open to the possibilities created by the very changes we have fought for, then we are able to push our knowledge and our visions of the possible even further (without, however, giving up the reality of the need for self-protection).[19]

■ **Not A Love Story**   The radical feminist anti-pornography discourse raises complex questions about the relationship between feminist analysis and the object of the analysis. Radical feminist discourse constructs pornography as an ideology, but the discourse is itself ideological. Ideologies work through narrative and a compelling emotional logic that dominates the cognitive dimension.[20] As an ideology, from the radical feminist perspective, pornography tells an anti-woman story that reinforces patriarchal attitudes to women. To counter the power of this patriarchal ideology, radical feminists have constructed a compelling pro-woman vision of intimate, loving relationships rooted in eros, mutuality, connection, and communication. However, ideologies can be simultaneously liberating and repressive. Where Sontag saw (some) pornography as offering a deep knowledge about human sexuality and consciousness, feminists have seen violence against women. Where radical feminists emphasize an ethos of love and connectedness, other feminists point out the dangers of a new essentialism that turns women into the naturally superior sex and denies both the differences and inequality among women (due to race, class, and other factors) and the place of conflict and difference within relationships.

The double ideological construction of pornography that radical feminism undertakes—that is, the critique of pornography as a patriarchal ideology and the creation of an alternate vision of eros—depends on two dialectical processes: reading and telling. We "read" pornography in order to retell its story. In the Anglo-American education system, we have been trained to read and interpret linearly: we read from the beginning to the end and we expect to be satisfied with "answers" at the end. We have also been trained to read—to recognize, interpret, and evaluate—realist narratives that are, not surprisingly, the narratives of bourgeois culture. Conventional realist novels, for example, are expected to develop progressively (linearly) themes of a high moral nature and to reveal the truth about life through the thoughts and behavior of characters with whom we identify emotionally.[21] We evaluate novels, films, and other narratives on the basis of how well they meet our criteria: we measure them against our own lived experience and our analysis of that experience.

Radical feminism reads pornography as a debased form of realism and constructs a high realist narrative as antidote.[22] This double movement is at play in *Not A Love Story*, a feature-length film from Studio D, the women's studio of the National Film Board in Canada. Released in 1981 this film complements *Take Back the Night*, the classic radical feminist anthology on pornography. The film exposes viewers to various aspects of the sex trade industry and offers testimony about the effects of pornography from noted radical feminists (Susan Griffin, Kate Millett, Robin Morgan, Kathleen Barry), a social scientist (Edward Donnerstein), members of a men's group, and entrepreneurs and workers in the trade. Ironically, in spite of its obvious intention to educate and raise public awareness of the dangers of pornography, the film was initially banned from public screening in Ontario by the Ontario Censorship Board. As a major text of the anti-pornography movement, *Not A Love Story* continues to have a powerful effect in educating new viewers about pornography. But as a text it also illustrates the ideological construction of the anti-pornography analysis.[23]

Not A Love Story may be seen as a sort of "pilgrim's progress," which involves the descent of two women into the bowels of the sex trade industry and a kind of purification ritual that reestablishes the values of wholeness, eros, and autonomy. The originator of the quest is the filmmaker, Bonnie Sherr Klein, and the woman who legitimizes that quest is a stripper, Linda Lee Tracey, who, we are informed, is "questioning." Tracey is shown at the beginning of the film as a woman who takes creative pleasure in her work and doesn't feel humiliated and degraded—the concluding lines for her strip act resound with confidence, humor, and pride: "God bless the working woman!" However, the filmmaker "knows" the "truth": pornography is anti-woman and causes violence against women. Her message is validated by Tracey's experience in different subject-positions within the sex trade industry. As a working woman, whom Klein admires because she is at home with her body and sexuality, Tracey takes delight in the comedy and parody she incorporates into her strip act. But her pleasure in her work, its eroticism, and her autonomy are undermined as she becomes Klein's collaborator as a sex trade investigator, where the emotional script has already been determined.

In mediating between the filmmaker and the sex trade, Tracey's consciousness is raised through experiences in which she is both observer and participant, subject-as-agent and subject-as-victim. As investigator she observes sex films and shows which are presented (by the filmmaker) as an extension of Tracey's own work. At one point Klein asks Tracey how she feels about herself, her work. Tracey answers that she is confused: "It's getting to me on an emotional level, a humanity level. But I do believe in what I'm doing." "But," Klein rejoins, "you're a part of it." Tracey has embarked on the path leading from "false" consciousness to feminist consciousness. She is, for a moment, a soapbox activist outside sex businesses; she experiences the feminist rage of Robin Morgan and shares vicariously the pain and tears of Morgan's family about the damage pornography does to human relationships and the (heterosexual, nuclear) family; finally, she experiences herself as object under the phallic lens of Suze Randall, photographer for porn magazines. This is both the nadir and the culmination of Tracey's experiences in the sex trade: she is recuperated as a "feminist" subject, mourning the tragedy of pornography and affirming her own wholeness and autonomy—and thus affirming the filmmaker's version of "truth."

The meanings of the film are condensed in the opening images of valentine hearts-and-women in commercialized (read: pornographic) contexts. Susan Griffin's voice-over informs us that these images represent "the heart imprisoned . . . the heart on its knees, and if necessary, rendered silent." The message slides from humanism to essentialist feminism: pornography is "the heart imprisoned," but *woman* is the "heart." *Not A Love Story* presents a narrative of women's pain, of "the heart imprisoned." The film's title inscribes both the feminist critique of pornography and its alternative. If pornography is not about love and it is not a "love story," traditionally a women's genre, then it is both a perversion of the genre—to a men's genre—and an inversion, from heterosexual romance and love to sexual objectification, degradation, abuse, and violence against women. The alternative, which women want and which represents wholeness and life, is love, eros, and intimacy. The quest for Tracey is the discovery of "the heart imprisoned" and its/her release—a vision of freedom from sexual bondage.

A number of issues arise, however, if we read the radical feminist story of pornography in *Not A Love Story* deconstructively from the perspective of socialist feminism, the sexuality debates, and in a historical context. To read from a contemporary postmodernist sensibility rather than from the nineteenth-century realist tradition is to search for the plurality and heterogeneity of meanings that disrupt and undermine the production of a single, linear, ideological "truth." Deconstructing a text produces many meanings and opens up possibilities of conflicting meanings by bringing into the foreground what is marginalized, minimized, or silenced in the text. In *Not A Love Story* and in the radical feminist (re)construction of pornography, it is possible to discern emotional slides, where sharper analysis is required, and to raise unasked questions about class, race, and sexuality that shake the solidity of the discourse.

■ **(De)Constructing Pornography**   In the 1970s feminists challenged pornography on the basis of certain crucial assumptions. The most contentious today is the assumption that there is a homogeneous unified class of women and that we can speak of "woman" as an inclusive, fixed category. Thus, the perspective on pornography in *Take Back the Night*, for example, is that all women are victimized by pornography: pornography is a crime against women. But the subtitle, *Women on Pornography*, reveals the classic slide in feminist analysis—the apparently fluid substitution of "women" for "feminist." In feminist writing, the feminist standpoint and "woman's" standpoint are often assumed to be synonymous and universal, but political debates and experiences have eloquently and consistently refused this consensus. Differences between women are the raw nerve of the women's movement. Throughout the history of the contemporary movement in North America, there has been angry resistance to homogenizing views of feminists and of women. This resistance has come from the women who have been excluded from or marginalized within the women's movement and feminist theory: lesbians, black women, women of color, Native women, working-class women, sex trade workers, disabled women, and others. The emphasis on difference, which has entered into feminist discourse both through political struggle and through the theories of poststructuralism and psychoanalysis, undermines the unity of the anti-pornography position.

The issue of difference is not addressed directly in *Not A Love Story*. The film's point of view reflects a white middle-class ideology. Within this perspective the issue of class difference is subsumed within an assumption of a shared sex/gender consciousness. The film appears to illustrate the feminist credo that "sisterhood is powerful" both in the narrative plot and in the relationship between the filmmaker and the stripper. However, class structures their relationship. The filmmaker controls the learning experience and the analysis of it: her moral authority resides in her position as a white middle-class woman who is the mother of a young daughter whom she wishes to protect; her interpretive authority resides in the fact that she controls the script and the camera. The stripper is a willing convert: she is white, working-class, and shown only in relation to her work and the filmmaker's investigation; that is, she is not situated in her own social context. What is the message here? That her worth as a human being is embodied in her work, or worse, reduced to her work—reinforcing the stereotypic association of the working class with the body and sexuality and the middle class with intellect? Implicitly, a class-based "good girl"/"bad girl" dichotomy is established between the "good mother," who is concerned about the world of values her daughter encounters, and the "bad sister," who participates in the world of debased sexuality and tarnished feminine identity.

The line between the "good girl" and the "bad girl" continues throughout the film; the filmmaker maintains her position as the distanced—and protected—observer/outsider while her subject explores the sex trade from the inside. The most disturbing aspect of the relationship between the two women is the complicity of the filmmaker with the voyeurism of the camera. This complicity is revealed in the ambiguity of the presentation of Tracey's strip act at the beginning of the film. The context in which it is shown skews our response: we cannot view it without a double consciousness—our capacity to appreciate Tracey's art/work is shadowed by the critical perspective of the film. However, this moment in the film is also the moment that perversely undermines the coherence of the radical feminist critique of the sex trade; Tracey clearly delights in her power and in the pleasures of eroticism. But a later moment in the film is much bleaker: when Tracey very reluctantly consents to become the sexual object of Randall's camera lens, the filmmaker is complicit in the objectification that occurs. It is Tracey who takes the risks, not Klein. What difference might it have made had the filmmaker stepped out of the safety of her position to become the camera's sexual object, or had she examined more self-reflectively her own relationship to Tracey and the sex trade industry?

Not A Love Story does not challenge the fundamentally conservative, even oppressive, dualistic thinking that persists in some feminist discourse. The subject-object split between the filmmaker and the stripper is one such instance of a dualism that creates a hierarchy of perception and value (or worth). This subject-object split characterized relations between nineteenth-century feminist reformers and prostitutes. The "good girl"/"bad girl" dualism is another example of a conservative hierarchy in contemporary feminism with roots in nineteenth-century feminism.

The emotional resonance of these dualisms is very powerful and infuses radical feminist attempts to analyze the sexual oppression of women and to create alternative visions. The "good girl"/"bad girl" dualism, for example, persists in the distinction some feminists have made between pornography and erotica. Gloria Steinem's discussion of the difference between them is based on the etymology of the two words, but her interpretation is problematic:

> "Erotica" is rooted in "eros" or passionate love, and thus in the idea of positive choice, free will, the yearning for a particular person. (Interestingly, the definition of erotica leaves open the question of gender.)

"Pornography" begins with a root "porno," meaning "prostitution" or "female captives," thus letting us know that the subject is not mutual love, or love at all, but domination and violence against women. (Though, of course, homosexual pornography may imitate this violence by putting a man in the "feminine" role of victim.) It ends with a root "graphos," meaning "writing about" or "description of," which puts still more distance between subject and object, and replaces a spontaneous yearning for closeness with objectification and voyeurism. The difference is clear in the words.[24]

Steinem's discussion of pornography depends on a view of prostitutes solely as sexual victims, and her description of eros assumes a link between "good" sexuality and "good" love. These assumptions mirror those of nineteenth-century reformers. Ellen DuBois and Linda Gordon have pointed out that in the nineteenth century the "inability to see anything in prostitution but male tyranny and/or economic oppression affected not only 'bad' women, but the 'good' ones as well. Feminists' refusal to engage in a concrete examination of the actuality of prostitution was of a piece with their inability to look without panic at any form of sexual nonconformity."[25] These double-edged observations are also appropriate in relation to the radical feminist analysis of pornography in the twentieth century.

Steinem's attempt to distinguish erotica from pornography is a response to the desire for intimacy in sexual relationships, but the feminist vision of sexuality *solely* in a context of mutual love and equality has been translated into a code of "proper" sexuality and sexual behavior, wittily satirized by Mariana Valverde:

> Some people think that eroticism in a feminist utopia would be androgynous, non-violent, soft and fuzzy, and perfectly symmetrical, with both partners doing exactly the same thing for the same amount of time at precisely the same time. You know the myth: two happy significant others of no particular gender meet, like each other, talk, quietly kiss, and disappear between the sheets as the light fades. No lust; no sweat; no power struggle.[26]

This "myth," however, has had disturbing implications for feminist theorizing and politics. Feminist critics of the anti-pornography movement argue that the radical themes of feminism in the 1970s have codified into rigid and prescriptive positions. The radical edges of the critique of compulsory heterosexuality and the politics of lesbianism and woman-bonding have been blunted in a conservative feminist discourse of sexuality. In its most extreme version, this discourse is marked by essentialist and moralizing views of male and female sexuality that are rooted in a male/female dichotomy. Male sexuality is perceived, and thus defined, as naturally dominating, aggressive, violent, and bad. In contrast, female sexuality is both perceived and defined as naturally egalitarian, mutual, warm, and good. This is the homogenized view of female sexuality. Lesbian sexuality is appropriated to what is ideologically a white middle-class view of female sexuality. Furthermore, in the effort to create an unproblematic sisterhood of woman-bonding women, lesbianism is effectively desexualized. This codification of human sexuality—dichotomizing male and female sexuality and homogenizing female sexuality—entrenches a very negative and static view of society as a place where women and men will always be enemies.[27]

There have always been sexual rebels, however. In addition to charting sexual dangers, women also have a history of exploring the terrain of sexual pleasure, pushing beyond the bounds of social prescription. Sexual libertarians pose a threat to anti-pornography feminists because they transgress the limits of the new "true womanhood," refusing to conform to the vision of female psychology and sexuality prescribed in radical feminist ideology. Sexual "outlaws," like lesbian sadomasochists and sex trade workers, challenge feminists to come to terms with the tabooed in their analysis of the social construction of both gender and sexuality. On the one hand, lesbian sadomasochism is threatening because it explores the dynamics of dominance and submission in sexual relationships between women. It forces the issue of power in relationships into the open, directly challenging the view that all women desire "vanilla sex" and claiming the dominance/submission pattern as a positive feminist possibility and not just a form of male oppression. On the other hand, sex trade workers, empowered through organizing, articulate a class consciousness that challenges the complicity of feminists with mainstream views of both the sex trade and the women who work in it.[28] Sex trade workers defend their right to work and demand recognition and respect from feminists.

■   Feminist critiques of the radical feminist construction of pornography reveal that pornography is fundamentally unstable as a feminist category. In fact, the persistence of difference and conflict between women and among feminists opens a space for moving beyond the patriarchal construct of pornography. Without question, the feminist attempt to interpret and expose pornography as woman-hating has had a tremendously powerful appeal. Pornography has served as an important and energizing heuristic device for feminists as a symbolic condensation of misogyny, male violence against women, and the sexualization of female subordination. However, it is extremely difficult, if not impossible, to transform a concept entirely unless it is re-visioned and renamed, which, paradoxically, shifts the terrain of the debates and struggles. The limits of the feminist transformation of pornography are reflected in some of the political consequences. The attempt to redefine pornography in feminist terms has been co-opted by conservative governments, which are all too willing to reaffirm conservative, patriarchal views of sexuality and morality; yet worse, the radical feminist discourse of pornography has itself perpetuated the patriarchal division between "good girls" and "bad girls" that lingers on in cultural stereotypes and analysis and in internalized ideologies of gender. Deconstructing the radical feminist reconstruction of pornography points to the theoretical and practical/experiential spaces that disrupt both the patriarchal and the feminist normative paradigms of pornography. Critics of the feminist anti-pornography movement have raised questions of female desire and have challenged feminism to articulate the relations between gender, race, and class. In so doing they have shifted the terrain of the debates and have moved us out of the problematic of pornography in directions that will, in their turn, generate new contradictions and blind spots.

■ Notes

Acknowledgments: I would like to thank Margie Wolfe and Connie Guberman for initiating and supporting the research and writing of an early version of this article. My most heartfelt thanks go to Christina Simmons, whose support as friend and editor has been invaluable.

1. The 1980s might be regarded as the "political moment" of pornography. Jeffrey Weeks defines a political moment as "that period when moral attitudes are transformed into formally political action" *Sex, Politics and Society: The Regulation of Sexuality Since 1800* [London: 1981], 15). Regardless of whether the issues raised by pornography can ever be "resolved," one can argue that "closure" occurs with the passing of new legislation.

In the United States the Indianapolis Ordinance and its ultimate legal defeat in February 1986 (when the Supreme Court affirmed a lower court ruling of unconstitutionality) represented the culmination of feminist efforts to use the legal system to define and control pornography and to empower its victims. The Meese Commission (which presented its report in July 1986) was arguably more concerned with child pornography and threats to male children, male family power, and traditional morality than with harm to women, but it did support some of the radical feminist analysis. It more clearly represented the conservative perspective of the state, however, in recommending stricter enforcement of traditional obscenity laws. See Chiquita Rollins, "When Conservatives Investigate Porn," *Off Our Backs* (December 1985): 1, 12–13; Carol Anne Douglas, "Supreme Court Strikes Down Indianapolis Pornography Law," *Off Our Backs* (April 1986): 6; and "Pornography: The Meese Report," *Off Our Backs* (August–September 1986): 4–5.

In Canada in 1983 the federal government established a special committee on pornography and prostitution, the Fraser Committee, to which feminist groups submitted carefully articulated briefs arguing a feminist definition of pornography and presenting an analysis of the harmful effects of pornography. In spite of this input, the proposed new legislation before the House of Commons in 1987 was widely seen as extremely conservative, with disturbing implications for the imposition of censorship on *all* sexually explicit materials. However, the bill was shelved when abortion and free trade took precedence in public debates in 1988.

2. Pornography is seen to be a matter of death in relation to snuff films. Feminists have also argued that pornography is anti-life and an expression of thanatos, the death drive. See Susan Griffin, *Pornography and Silence: Culture's Revenge Against Nature* (New York: 1981).

3. Laura Lederer, "Introduction," *Take Back the Night: Women on Pornography*, ed. Lederer (New York: 1982), 6.

4. Susan Sontag, "The Pornographic Imagination," in *A Susan Sontag Reader* (New York: 1982), 232.

5. *Ibid.*, 229.

6. Kate Millett, *Sexual Politics* (Garden City, N.Y.: 1970).

7. Robin Morgan, "Theory and Practice: Pornography and Rape," in *Take Back the Night*, ed. Lederer, 131.

8. These ideas are articulated by the contributors to *Take Back the Night*. Susan Griffin develops the cultural critique of western society through the prism of pornography in *Pornography and Silence*.

9. See, for example, Lisa Duggan, Nan Hunter, and Carole Vance, "False Promises: Feminist Antipornography Legislation in the U.S.," in *Women Against Censorship*, ed. Varda Burstyn (Vancouver: 1985), 130–51; Alice Echols, "The New Feminism of Yin and Yang," in *Powers of Desire: The Politics of Sexuality*, ed. Ann Snitow, Christine Stansell, and Sharon Thompson (New York: 1983), 439–59; Ann Snitow, "Retrenchment versus Transformation: The Politics of the Antipornography Movement," in *Women Against Censorship*, 107–20.

10. Stan Cohen, *Folk Devils and Moral Panics* (London: 1972), 9; cited in Weeks, *Sex, Politics and Society*, 14.

11. Rosemarie Tong, "Women, Pornography, and the Law, *Academe* (September–October 1987), 14–22.

12. This critique is developed in Duggan, Hunter, and Vance, "False Promises," in *Women Against Censorship*, ed. Burstyn. See also Tong, "Women, Pornography, and the Law."

13. Weeks, *Sex, Politics and Society*, 14.

14. Carole S. Vance and Ann Barr Snitow, "Toward a Conversation about Sex in Feminism: A Modest Proposal," *Signs* 10 (1984): 132.

15. In a scathing attack on the feminist anti-pornography movement, B. Ruby Rich writes: "Women today are terrified at the levels of violence being directed at us in society—and, to take it further, at powerless people everywhere. . . . Terror is not an effective emotion, though. It paralyzes. The fear of escalating violence, accompanied by the larger social backlash, has resulted not in massive political action by feminists but rather in a reaction of denial, a will *not to see* the dangers . . . a desperate desire to see, instead, their disguises. Turning away from a phalanx of assaults too overwhelming to confront, the Women Against Pornography groups turn instead to its entertainment division, pornography. But whether symptom or cause, pornography presents an incomplete target for feminist attack. The campaign against pornography is a massive displacement of outrage that ought to be directed at a far wider sphere of oppression." ("Anti-Porn: Soft Issue, Hard World," *Village Voice*, 20 July 1982, 18; rpt. in *Feminist Review* 13

[1983], 61.) Gayle Rubin writes, in a more moderate tone, "It is precisely at times such as these, when we live with the possibility of unthinkable destruction, that people are likely to become dangerously crazy about sexuality. . . . Disputes over sexual behavior often become the vehicles for displacing social anxieties, and discharging their attendant emotional intensity." ("Thinking Sex: Notes for a Radical Theory of the Politics of Sexuality," in *Pleasure and Danger: Exploring Female Sexuality*, ed. Carole S. Vance [Boston: 1984], 267.)

16. Ellen Willis, "Toward a Feminist Sexual Revolution," *Social Text: Theory/Culture/Ideology* 6 (1982): 3.

17. *Ibid.*

18. *Ibid.*

19. See Ellen Carol DuBois and Linda Gordon, "Seeking Ecstasy on the Battlefield: Danger and Pleasure in Nineteenth-Century Feminist Sexual Thought," *Feminist Studies* 9 (1983): 7–25; rpt. in *Pleasure and Danger*, ed. Vance, 31–49.

20. Terry Eagleton, "Ideology, Fiction, Narrative," *Social Text: Theory/Culture/Ideology* 2 (1979): 64.

21. See Catherine Belsey, *Critical Practice* (London: 1980), esp. 67–84, for a discussion of realism. See also Roland Barthes, *S/Z*, trans. Richard Miller (New York: 1974).

22. Although I have chosen to focus on reading strategies rooted in realism, one could also work with the genres, ideologies, and reading strategies of romance and melodrama in relation to *Not A Love Story*. For a different theory of reading rooted in radical feminism, see Patrocinio P. Schweickart, "Reading Ourselves: Toward a Feminist Theory of Reading," in *Gender and Reading: Essays on Readers, Texts, and Contexts*, ed. Elizabeth A. Flynn and Schweickart (Baltimore: 1986), 31–62.

23. See B. Ruby Rich's review of *Not A Love Story* in "Anti-Porn." The value of focusing on a film as text is that the problems raised in interpreting the film illustrate the problems of developing a monolithic interpretation of pornographic films. That is, if an anti-pornography film contains its own contradictions and ambiguities, aren't other films also likely to contain contradictions and to resist a single totalizing interpretation?

24. Gloria Steinem, "Erotica and Pornography: A Clear and Present Difference," in *Take Back the Night*, ed. Lederer, 23.

25. DuBois and Gordon, in *Pleasure and Danger*, ed. Vance, 39.

26. Mariana Valverde, "Pornography, Power and Passion," *International Women's Day Committee Newsletter* (Toronto: May 1984); rpt. as "Lesbiantics: The True Joy of Sex," *Rites for Lesbian and Gay Liberation* 1 (June 1984): 17. See also her book *Sex, Power and Pleasure* (Toronto: 1985).

27. Ann Ferguson, Ilene Philipson, Irene Diamond, Lee Quinby, Carole S. Vance, and Ann Barr Snitow, "Forum: The Feminist Sexuality Debates," *Signs* 10 (1984): 106–35: B. Ruby Rich, "Feminism and Sexuality in the 1980s," *Feminist Studies* 12 (1986): 525–61; Gayle Rubin, "Thinking Sex," in *Pleasure and Danger*, ed. Vance, 267–319; Ann Snitow, Christine Stansell, and Sharon Thompson, "Introduction," *Powers of Desire*, 9–47; Carole S. Vance, "Pleasure and Danger: Toward A Politics of Sexuality," in *Pleasure and Danger*, 1–27.

28. For example, see Laurie Bell, ed., *Good Girls/Bad Girls: Sex Trade Workers and Feminists Face to Face* (Toronto: 1987).

16

Gay Villain, Gay Hero: Homosexuality and the Social Construction of AIDS

Robert A. Padgug

■ **I** Patterns of disease are as much the product of social, political, and historical processes as of "natural history." From a historian's perspective, the current AIDS epidemic in the United States is "socially constructed"—the product of multiple historical determinations involving the complex social interaction of human beings over time. It is not, as the National Academy of Sciences would have it, "the story of a virus."[1] The emphasis here is on *historical* determination because AIDS, an event of the present, is imagined and dealt with on the basis of ideologies and institutions developed over time. As Marx wrote, "Human beings do make their own history, but they do not make it just as they please; they do not make it under circumstances chosen by themselves, but under circumstances directly encountered, given and transmitted from the past."[2]

The circumstances of AIDS certainly involve an epidemiologic pattern as well as associated illnesses and their effects on individual human lives; viewed more broadly these circumstances also involve beliefs, struggles, and institutions that have developed over time. That is, social, political, ideological, economic, religious, and public health realities define the meaning and treatment of AIDS both for its victims and the entire society.

AIDS, like other life-threatening diseases whose causes, means of spreading, and ultimate trajectory are not adequately known, has become, in Susan Sontag's now-classic formulation, a "metaphor," or a set of sometimes conflicting metaphors.[3] That is, most of us can comprehend and confront AIDS only if its social meaning is extended well beyond the relatively narrow spheres of medicine and epidemiology. The metaphors that have been constructed around the AIDS epidemic appear to have an unusual power for good or for evil. This power derives from the unanticipated emergence of a deadly new contagion of uncertain course and extent in an era when fatal infectious diseases were believed to have been eliminated. It is also linked to the nature of the groups first affected by AIDS, groups already included in powerful social metaphors.

As metaphor, social struggle, or disease management, AIDS is a contemporary crisis that impels us to draw upon a wide variety of historical material in the struggle to comprehend and deal with it. At the same time, however, we should recognize that such material can be interpreted differently and can be combined to form contradictory ideological and institutional responses to AIDS.

This essay develops these themes by exploring a central feature of the social construction of AIDS—sexuality, particularly, male homosexuality in the United States. Equally important aspects of the crisis, involving medical, epidemiological, economic, class, gender, and racial issues, are slighted here, although they clearly are essential elements in a full comprehension of the epidemic.

■ **II**   Sexuality is central in the social construction of AIDS in the United States because sexuality in general and male homosexuality in particular appear to play a paramount role in its etiology and spread. This distinguishes AIDS from most other diseases. As Michel Foucault and others have argued, sexuality is immensely important in the construction of personality as well as of ethics and morality in the modern world. A vast array of competing sexual ideologies, forming the basis for complicated ethical and political positions and struggles, demonstrates this in everyday American practice. In a word, sexuality is itself a set of metaphors and the product of a complicated social history.

Closely connected to sexuality, AIDS has become "moralized" to a much greater degree than, for example, tobacco- or alcohol-related diseases despite the fact they can also be seen as "self-inflicted" and devastatingly costly when measured in lives, health, and social resources. This heightened moralism is possible because AIDS in the United States has been constructed largely in the image of male homosexuality, as that image itself has been constructed in the scientific and popular mind from the mid-nineteenth century to the present.

During the first stages of the epidemic, essentially 1981 and 1982, few aside from gay men—certainly not the popular press and only to a limited degree the government and medical community—paid much attention to AIDS. The disease was happening to "them"—outsiders.[4] This silence—this absence from public discourse—is essentially the way homosexuality has been treated in our society except in periods of moral panic. The moral panic that brought AIDS to the attention of the so-called general public in periodic waves of hysteria, was the possibility that the disease might be spreading to "us," might be crossing that invisible, but ever-present ideological line that divides the normal from the abnormal, the moral from the immoral, the deserving from the undeserving. The definition of AIDS as a disease of homosexual men became entrenched in popular and medical attitudes in spite of growing evidence to the contrary and was used to describe both the disease and the majority of its sufferers. A complex history has shaped the beliefs about homosexuality that were marshalled for the AIDS crisis. The English historian Jeffrey Weeks summarizes those most often chosen:

> Certain forms of sexuality, socially deviant forms—homosexuality especially—have long been promiscuously classified as "sins" *and* "diseases," so that you can be born with them, seduced into them and catch them, all at the same time. . . . In the fear and loathing that AIDS evokes there is a resulting conflation between two plausible, if unproven theories—that there is an elective affinity between disease and certain sexual practices, and that certain practices cause disease—and a third, that certain types of sex *are* diseases.[5]

Implicit in Weeks' description is the nineteenth-century "medicalization" of homosexuality at the hands of physicians and psychiatrists, a conception that has become widely accepted in the twentieth century. Men and women who were categorized as sodomites, practitioners of a sinful sexuality, became "inverts" and, later, homosexuals, that is, they were seen as individuals with physically or mentally diseased personalities who had, in effect, *become* their sexuality.[6] Their sexuality, and therefore their personality, bore the features of its own corruption: it was confused as to gender, it was uncontrollable, it was irresponsible, it sought ever-new pleasures[7] and it was, above all, "promiscuous" or, in more contemporary terms, "addictive."[8]

These features were used to draw the character of the person with AIDS and the person who was thought to infect others. Diseased in mind and body, the man was also "contagious" with respect to both his sexuality and his disease. AIDS was the very mark of his inner disorder, revelatory of his homosexuality as well as the "self-inflicted" result of it. As the conservative journalist Patrick Buchanan put it, "The poor homosexuals—they have declared war upon Nature, and now Nature is exacting an awful retribution."[9] Right-wing polemicists like Buchanan, followed by many ordinary citizens, used these medicalized and moralistic views of homosexuality in their most extreme and hostile forms, proclaiming AIDS a natural or divine judgment upon all homosexuals, regardless of whether they actually had AIDS. And this punishment could spread more widely if the rest of "us" were not morally careful.

The American right wing has shown an "elective affinity" for attacking homosexuality, most notably during the McCarthy period and, in response to the 1970s gay liberation movements, even before the appearance of AIDS. Aversion to homosexuality, which can be connected with a fear of social change and modernism, has its own long and complicated history.[10] But even more temperate and sympathetic observers, including some gays, have adopted two key elements of the historical indictment of homosexuality: "willful irresponsibility" and "promiscuity." Irresponsibility was linked to disregard for the effects of immoral acts, a lack of interest in dealing with the crisis that resulted from them, and, indeed, a certain *desire* to see the crisis unresolved. Thus envisioned, those who wished to "spread" their sexuality in the manner of a contagion desired to spread their contagion in the manner of their sexuality. Elizabeth Fee captures this attitude well:

> It has proved an easy cultural move from the idea of populations at risk to that of populations guilty of harboring disease: from a gay plague to a plague of gays. A member of a population at risk is thus not only a potential victim but a potential villain of the epidemic: to be a member of a risk group is to be a dangerous person.[11]

Just as significantly, promiscuity—shorthand for that set of irresponsible sexual practices gay men stand accused of—is central to the entire construction of AIDS metaphors around homosexuality. In both popular and scientific fantasy over the last century, the characteristic feature of homosexuality was precisely its narrowing to pure sexuality—a sexuality lacking in order, in discrimination, in rules—a sexuality in some sense outside social institutions, and, therefore, dangerous. It is precisely this reduction that underlies the definition of homosexuality as quintessentially the "other," the utterly different, that which lies outside society. Well-entrenched in European and American culture during the nineteenth century, this definition had begun to dissipate by the 1970s, but it has been partly revived by the AIDS crisis. The "swishy queen" has been replaced in the popular and medical imagination by the dying AIDs victim as the exemplar of male homosexuality. What has not changed is the reduction of all homosexuals to the image of the supposedly most "visible" minority among them.

Many measures commonly suggested to deal with AIDS victims are patterned on those traditionally used to deal with homosexuals. Various forms of expulsion—real and symbolic—from society as a whole and, especially, from the realm of politics and public discourse have been proposed: quarantine and other forms of isolation for AIDS sufferers, public surveillance of HIV-positive individuals, HIV antibody testing without sufficient provision for confidentiality or anonymity, the general refusal to discuss homosexual sex acts publicly, as well as the strong desire of much of the population to remove AIDS patients from schools, jobs, and housing. These measures are not only entirely congruent with the definition of homosexuals as outsiders, but threaten to reinforce it significantly. As two commentators unusually sensitive to the practical effects of the metaphors of AIDS have noted: "With AIDS now regarded as man-ifest 'proof' of the profoundly 'diseased' and 'decadent' nature of 'queers' and 'junkies,' reactionary calls to remove gays and IVDUs [intravenous drug users] from the midst of so-called 'civil society' have truly reached new depths."[12]

The effects of such thinking have gone beyond rhetoric to produce massive discrimination against those who have contracted AIDS, inade-quate funding for AIDS research and for social welfare programs for AIDS sufferers, great resistance to public health education—including an over-whelming Congressional vote on October 14, 1987, to ban federal funding for education efforts that "promote homosexuality"—and a politics of not-so-benign neglect of the epidemic by the federal government.

Ultimately, the construction of a disease from this complex, historically elaborated imagery leaves us with a view of homosexual persons with or likely to contract AIDS as either individual victims or immoral agents; they become the bearers of a disease just as they are the bearers of a psychological, social, or biologically determined (homo)sexuality. Even as an epidemiological "risk group," they tend to be considered a "group" only insofar as they share individually determined and very narrowly de-fined behavioral patterns (sexual acts) that bring them into contact with a specific viral agent. Such a view is insufficient on both epidemiological and historical grounds. Disease patterns are epidemiologically mean-ingful only when applied to groups, not to individuals. In any case, the point is not that homosexuals form a "risk group" but that certain sexual acts are "risky."[13] And whatever the biological or psychological roots of homosexuality and heterosexuality, they are historically meaningful only when viewed as socially constructed within specific societies; as such, they cannot simply be posed as opposites nor reduced to purely physical sexuality. The obsession with homosexuality, especially as a descriptor of individual personality, is seriously misleading and leaves both homosex-uals and AIDS outside history.

In reality, no group has ever been outside history altogether, without rules, without internal order of some sort, except in the minds of its en-emies. (This is surely as true of drug users and other groups at "higher risk" for AIDS as it is of homosexuals.) The attitudes and fantasies dis-cussed above stem from defining homosexuals negatively by their failure to conform rather than by their actual history. This other and more com-plicated history involves changing social definitions of homosexuality, the emergence of homosexuals as a special class of person, and their exclusion from the rest of society. Largely in response, homosexuals have created their own communities or subcultures with specific self-defini-tions, institutions, and ideologies.[14]

In *this* history, the role of gay men in the AIDS crisis can be explored only insofar as we view them as a historically defined and developed group and not as predefined and ahistorical individuals. In the intersection between this history and the history of attitudes toward homosexuality it makes sense to study the AIDS epidemic as social history. Even the concept of gay men as a "risk group" ultimately is meaningful only on this wider, nonepidemiological level.

■ **III**   For gay men, the AIDS crisis has exacerbated serious problems of discrimination and homophobia. In a society that does not provide adequate funds, care, and sympathy for dealing with AIDS, the crisis means the continuation of gay men's medical and social isolation. Above all, the crisis means living with the threat and the reality of disease, death, and bereavement.

As a whole, the gay community has shown a rational fear of the disease, but it also has demonstrated a remarkably capacity to avoid panic. This relative calm undoubtedly derives from a familiarity with AIDS that is significantly greater than that of the general public, as well as the self-knowledge as a community that rejects ordinary metaphors of AIDS built on fear and loathing of homosexuality. Unlike the heterosexual world, the gay world cannot construct AIDS as a disease of "the other," but is forced to "normalize" it and to construct its own series of metaphors for so doing.

The AIDS crisis is remarkable due to the degree to which the group that appeared most affected by the disease became extensively involved in its management. Gays have been in the forefront of groups providing social aid and health care to persons with AIDS (whether homosexual or not), conducting research, lobbying for funds and other governmental intervention, creating education programs, negotiating with legislators and health insurers, and the like.[15] A recent report in the *New York Times* assesses the effort in New York City:

> City officials say they shudder to think of what would have happened in New York if the homosexual community had not formed the Gay Men's Health Crisis and other spinoff organizations to care for the sick, educate the healthy and lobby for attention and funds. . . . "When the story of New York's AIDS epidemic is written, that self-help effort will be the bright part of it," said Dr. [Stephen] Joseph, the City Health Commissioner.[16]

The same could be written of other cities as well, in San Francisco, for instance, where the most successful gay "self-help" efforts to date have been carried out.

The gay community has demonstrated a remarkable willingness and ability to work within and outside the established governmental and private institutions that normally handle health emergencies. When gays have not succeeded in persuading or forcing established institutions to provide money, care, and compassion to deal with AIDS, they have provided the needed resources through their own institutions. This insistence on taking an active role in disease management serves as notice that gays will not be forced to remain outsiders, as the victims or villains of popular metaphor.

Ironically, despite the obvious danger of doing so, the gay community has in a sense embraced the identification of AIDS with homosexuality that is central to popular and medical metaphors of the disease, but has redefined this concept significantly to make effective self-management of the disease central to it. Comprehension of this effort requires a close look at the actual history of the community.

■ **IV**   The gay community—as a community of interacting and self-defining persons rather than as a pool of victims—has been noticeably and continually absent from the media and public discourse (except for the gay press). Silence about gay people and the realities of their lives is at the very center of homosexual oppression. Almost from its inception in the nineteenth century, the gay community has struggled for the right to control its own fate, to free itself from the interference of the state, the church, and the medical and psychiatric professions. The struggle has, therefore, always been about *power:* the power to define, to victimize, to deny entry into the public realm as a legitimate group.

This struggle is evident in the long history of the gay communities[17] that grew mainly within large urban centers, particularly in New York, San Francisco, and Los Angeles, precisely the communities where AIDS made its first and most deadly appearance. And the power struggle is equally apparent in the closely connected struggle for political identity and power, beginning before World War II and growing to national significance in the period of "gay liberation" in the 1970s and 1980s.[18]

This continued struggle for political and social power molded the struggle over AIDS; that is, gay men have fought, most often against the same groups that denied their rights, to retain some degree of control over the definition of the disease and the way it was combated. Refusing to see themselves as victims or to be expelled from society again, while political, medical, and moral "professionals" determine their fate, gay men are building on many decades of political and social organizing and using that experience to create new forms of resistance. The speed with which gay self-help and political organizations sprang up to meet the AIDS crisis, and the efficiency with which they achieved their aims, was a measure of the community's organizational and institutional sophistication. The gay community, and the so-called gay ghettos, had long since developed a wide variety of social, cultural, political and legal institutions—including a large number of newspapers and magazines—that could be enlisted in the fight against AIDS. As Michael Bronski puts it, the huge effort of AIDS organizing "is in the tradition of the gay movement—a direct response to an oppressive situation."[19] It is also a very American response to crisis as well; this society characteristically creates a wide range of voluntary organizations to meet social, welfare, and health needs of portions of the population.

The gay community, of course, has never been monolithic. Like all communities that have emerged in a context of struggle against oppression, it is highly complex and continually developing. Not all who are homosexual in "orientation" or practice belong to it; one must embrace one's homosexuality more or less publicly for that. People move in and out of the community as need and circumstance require. The character and strength of gay communities differ considerably depending upon location, with the greatest strength and development evident mainly in large urban centers. And each has its idiosyncratic features, differences largely correlated with the cities where they formed. Moreover, the gay community is subject to the same differentiation across class, political, income, gender, age, ethnic, and racial lines as the rest of American society. Insofar as it has spawned a number of political and social movements, however, the community has tended to be white and middle class, a characteristic that has led to significant tensions.

Most notable, perhaps, has been the tendency for contradictions to develop between gay men and lesbians. Many lesbians find an alternative political and social practice in the women's movement and do not share gay men's way of life and attitudes toward sexuality. What has, in fact, largely brought the varied strands of the gay community together is an abstract "sexual orientation," originally defined by hostile outsiders, and, above all, a common history of struggle against oppression.

Despite these internal tensions and continued hostility from outsiders, the AIDS crisis neither destroyed nor weakened the community. In fact, its maturity enabled the community to meet the challenge of AIDS with a noticeably strengthened sense of identity, inner cohesion, and ability to work for common aims. Gay men and lesbians, for example, have worked together more closely than ever in the political struggle surrounding AIDS as well as in the care of the ill and dying, mainly gay men. Lesbians have indeed performed heroically in a struggle that on many grounds need not have been theirs at all. This new cohesion is best symbolized by the march in Washington, D.C. on October 11, 1987, in which an estimated 500,000 gay men and lesbians challenged continuing homophobia and inadequate attention to AIDS in one of the most massive political outpourings in the United States in many years. These and other accomplishments resulted from fundamental changes in lesbian and gay politics, organizations, and social institutions.

On the simplest level, lesbian and gay political organizations, fundamentally oriented toward a familiar kind of pressure-group activity, have been joined or replaced by many new groups that combine health care and organizing with gay politics and legal action. Society's failure to address the health and social needs of the gay community, as well as the limitations of existing institutions, forced gays and lesbians to create their own institutions to confront the crisis. Once these community-based organizations were in place (approximately 250–300 now exist), their members realized that they had to broaden their scope by adding political goals and activities, that is, they would have to combat both homophobia and discrimination as well as AIDS. As Eric Rofes, an activist in AIDS health care issues, has noted:

> If we have learned anything from AIDS, it's that you cannot separate politics from health care. They are one and the same. Women have understood that for a long time. People of color have understood that for a long time. A lot of gay white men have. But too many haven't.[20]

The new politics of AIDS has succeeded in procuring additional funding and health resources for the struggle against AIDS, as well as in combating homophobia in the government, the health sector, and the insurance industry. It is beginning to build bridges to other groups who see health care as a central issue. However, stretching itself to the limit in the struggle against AIDS, the gay community has reduced the degree to which the remainder of society is responsible for providing the money, care, and volunteers it supplies for most other epidemics.[21] Peter Arno and Karyn Feiden observe:

> The fact that the SSA [Social Security Administration] has ruled that AIDS patients are eligible for presumptive disability illustrates the gay community's ability to influence public health policy. In cities with large gay populations, such as New York and San Francisco, the supportive care received by many AIDS patients is actually superior to that received by the victims of other severe chronic illnesses. The Federal Government, however, cannot take credit for this. The development and growth of community-based AIDS service organizations, largely through massive gay-organized volunteer efforts, is helping to create a high-quality integrated care delivery system. Whether the current level of voluntarism can continue to match the pace of the epidemic or serve the growing segment of IV [intravenous] drug users; whether volunteer care is viable outside major metropolitan areas and can serve victims of other diseases; and whether voluntarism allows the government to abdicate its obligations to its people, remains to be seen.[22]

Thus, the success of the gay community's crisis intervention might have the paradoxical effect of leaving most of the responsibility for care with the community and perpetuating the segregation of gay men and lesbians. One task for gay organizations is to devise ways to share the responsibility for combatting AIDS with the rest of society.

AIDS has profoundly affected the style and nature of gay politics in other ways as well. Gay political organizations originated in the context of a distinctive American political structure that has incorporated minority-group activity into political life;[23] in some circumstances, as in the AIDS crisis, a minority group largely despised by the wider society can exercise considerable political power for certain purposes. Because of this, the American gay community, unlike its counterparts in other nations, has always had a strong impetus toward seeing itself as a more-or-less typical minority demanding recognition and jockeying for position vis-à-vis other minorities in the political arena rather than as a part of a wider political, usually leftist, movement.

The nascent gay self-identity as a minority group that emerged in the 1950s was, however, challenged strongly after the Stonewall riots in New York in 1969. At this time a number of more radical, left-leaning groups, emerging in part from the ferment of the anti–Vietnam War movements, gained temporary domination with a political agenda aimed at broad human liberation and overcoming the homosexual/heterosexual distinction rather than at minority rights and group privileges. Cutting across the distinction between minority-group and liberatory politics was a substantial difference in political styles that pitted pressure-group activities by representational organizations working within established American institutions against a style of protest that was street-oriented, anti-"establishment," and directly involved as many ordinary gay men and women as possible.[24]

In the late 1970s the political pendulum, influenced by the partial institutionalization of the gay "revolution" of the post-Stonewall period and by the desire to protect earlier accomplishments, swung once again toward the minority-group outlook. This shift involved a strong emphasis on membership organizations (such as the National Gay Task Force, now the National Lesbian and Gay Task Force) whose major role was to deal with federal and state legislative and judicial bodies. The notion that gay struggle aimed at *human* liberation was largely abandoned, street politics was denigrated as a sign of community immaturity, and the distinction between homosexual and heterosexual was paradoxically strengthened as a precondition for political success within, not against, the American political system.

The AIDS crisis forced another major shift in political style. The community quickly discovered that working purely within a system either unable or unwilling to meet the needs of AIDS patients and the gay community was no longer feasible. The need for direct action to procure funds, health care, and social welfare, as well as the necessity to confront a government and public that remained unacceptably homophobic, led to the revival of a more confrontational, direct-action style of politics.

The renewed politics of direct action supplemented rather than replaced a more conservative politics of membership organizations and lobbying legislatures and politicians. Both types of organization have grown in numbers and importance, and their supporters and organizers have learned to work together relatively well. They have discovered that popular demonstrations against the most blatant examples of homophobia and street actions aimed at increasing funding for AIDS work and research complement more traditional styles of politics as often as they clash. In addition, many gay organizations, most notably the increasing number that deal with the broad spectrum of legal, social, and civil rights of gay persons and persons with AIDS, have managed to combine an aggressive, confrontational style with a more traditional membership-organization structure.

This new combination of styles, although imperfect, has enabled the gay community to protect past gains while making new gains both within and opposed to established institutions. Correspondingly, the struggle between a gay minority identity and one that sees the gay community at the forefront of a radical restructuring of humanity itself has become less important and interesting in the face of the AIDS epidemic. The minority group perspective remains dominant but the outcome is still uncertain. Nevertheless, the new style of gay politics appears to be a creative response to an unusual crisis and has given the gay community a political presence and weight lacking in earlier years.

■ V   Like politics, gay male sexuality has substantially changed as a result of AIDS. Those gay institutions largely devoted to sexual activity—bars, baths, backrooms, public spaces—were of great importance, although they hardly exhausted the content of gay community life. The fundamental link among gay persons was, after all, sexual, but these institutions have represented far more than sites of sexual activity. Such places have developed a far greater symbolic and social significance to the gay community than is readily understood by non-gays.[25] For decades they represented the only public spaces that could in any sense be termed homosexual and where homosexuals could discover each other as well as a wider homosexual world, in spite of frequent police raids and moral crusades against them. Outsiders probably cannot imagine the significance of these spaces in the complicated double process of "coming out"—that is, entering the homosexual world as well as publicly committing oneself to one's homosexuality.

Not surprisingly, when gay people asserted their right to exist in the gay liberation period that began in the 1960s, sexual institutions expanded astronomically. The room for sexual experimentation and creativity also expanded immensely, as an expression of gay identity, as a protest against the earlier suppression of homosexuality, and as a genuine, although sometimes utopian, attempt to fashion a society under new conditions of freedom. And the public nature of much of this sexuality became another expression of the fact that gay sex was a product of a community, not merely of a group of pre-existing homosexual individuals.

Gay men, like feminists, have been quite aware for some time that sexuality has a deeply political aspect. Because of its role in their identity, this sexuality was central to their political struggles against the oppressive institutions of society. The rightists who chose the gay community as one of their primary targets appear to have comprehended this as well.

Gay identity itself may be said to have been built largely on sexual identity and sexual institutions. But in the context of the gay liberation movements of the late 1960s and 1970s, the existence of sexual institutions and identity encouraged the expansion of nonsexual institutions, including political and protest groups, self-help groups, and cultural institutions. In the 1970s both sexual and nonsexual institutions grew in importance as a real gay community emerged in the wake of gay liberation. It was, however, precisely the sexual institutions and the role of sexuality within the gay community that were most definitively shaken by AIDS, a disease spread, at least in part, through some forms of sexual intercourse. The gay community is still struggling to cope with the challenge of AIDS to its sexual beliefs and practices. But the strong emphasis on sexuality in its multiple forms is too deeply rooted in gay history simply to be abandoned. The forces—church, state, or medical—that seek to use the AIDS crisis to restore their authority will not easily banish all homosexual acts. Certainly the gay community's efforts to repeal all sodomy laws, especially on the federal level, have been impeded by AIDS (see the Supreme Court's decision in *Bowers v. Hardwick* in June 1986, declaring that sodomy laws are constitutional and that the private practice of gay sexuality is not protected by the United States Constitution[26]). But the struggle for control of sexuality is only in part a legislative or judicial struggle; it also encompasses the community's struggle to control its own sexuality and the ability to control, through sexuality, such disparate aspects of human life as health care, the body, and the family. The gay community well recognizes the nature of this struggle and its implications for the community's ability to survive the challenge of AIDS.

Under the impetus of AIDS, sexual institutions themselves have declined in importance within the gay community. They are increasingly being replaced by nonsexual social, cultural, and political institutions, including the community-based health, social welfare, and related organizations mentioned earlier. The nature of the gay community, the institutions that provide its cohesion, and the way gay people deal with one another have all changed considerably. At the same time, gay sexuality has increasingly been reconstructed under the impetus of AIDS along the lines of sexuality found in the majority heterosexual world. This has, for example, meant a new emphasis on "dating" and on longer-term, more monogamous relationships among gay men. The new sexuality is perhaps symbolized by the "wedding" ceremony that brought together thousands of gay and lesbian couples to reaffirm their commitment to each other on October 10, 1987, as part of the activities that led up to the massive march in Washington, D.C. But change has also meant a decline in the various forms of sexual experimentation, spontaneity, unorthodox relationships, community "flamboyance," willingness to cross social boundaries, and sense of "celebration"—the "Dionysian" aspects of life—that made the gay community so interesting and creative in the 1970s.

Gay men will need many years to come to terms with the current realities of sexuality and its place within their community and self-identity. In the meantime they need to undertake the serious theoretical work— lesbians and the women's movement in general have done far better in this sphere—of understanding sexuality in an age of crisis and reconstructing its role within gay identity. Broadly theoretical concerns have attached themselves to narrowly defined issues such as the debates, both within and outside the gay community in San Francisco and New York in 1984 and 1985, over whether gay baths should be allowed to operate in a time of epidemic. But the largely symbolic nature of these concerns ultimately makes them poor arenas for elaborating a new gay sexuality. The debates fed on the rhetoric of "promiscuity" among non-gays as well as old and not particularly well-conceived arguments over the role of monogamy and multiple sexual partners among gay men. In fact, only a minority of gay men regularly used the baths, and there was never substantial evidence to suggest that closing the baths would decrease the spread of HIV infection. Closing baths and similar institutions in many cities represents less a restructuring of gay sexuality than a partial defeat for the gay community's control over its own sexuality.

To date, the major changes in gay male sexual practice are mainly the product of a practical need to meet the AIDS crisis directly. A significant "safe-sex" movement, largely staffed, operated, and funded by the gay community, has been created to carry out the necessary work of educating gay men (and others) regarding sexual practices in a crisis, using pamphlets, discussion groups, safe-sex pornography, and the like. Substantial evidence suggests that this movement has helped change the behavior of the majority of gay men.[27] While some gay men are evidently abandoning sex altogether—a few even appear to have accepted the assertion that all gay sex equals death—most are adapting to the crisis by building new sexual identities around safe-sex activities.

This restructuring of gay institutions and deeply rooted sexual practices may reflect a certain malleability that enables the gay community to respond rapidly to external changes. This malleability appears to be conditioned by a long history of oppression and by the fact that gay traditions are not passed on through the family. A history that at first sight seems to demonstrate significant weaknesses may turn out in retrospect to offer important advantages as well.

And, in fact, gay men were never as "obsessed" with sex as their enemies and even many in their own community believed. A significant proportion of gay men never made sex central to their lives, and the main gay tradition, which did privilege sexual relations especially in the 1970s and early 1980s, did not sexualize the entire world or foster an obsession with sex. Ironically, sex became tame, an ordinary part of everyday life, and necessary changes became easier.

■ **VI**   In contrast to its surprising development of strength in other areas, the gay community has been less successful and shown more ambivalence in relation to medicine. Ronald Bayer perceptively suggests that gay men find themselves "between the specter and the promise of medicine."[28] Medicine offers both the promise of solutions to AIDS and the danger that physicians and medical researchers will reassume control over the gay community or work with the state to do so. After all, physicians and psychiatrists "medicalized" homosexuality in the first place, and only in 1973, after a long struggle, was the American Psychiatric Association "persuaded"—some would say forced—to remove homosexuality from its list of mental disorders.[29]

The AIDS crisis has rekindled much of that long history of hostility between the homosexual community and the medical world. Physicians and other health workers have not been notably sympathetic to gay men or persons with AIDS. Homophobia has risen dramatically as AIDS threatens to link gay men permanently with a specific, deadly disease, thought to be of their own making.[30] The association of gay men with other "medicalized" risk groups, such as illicit drug users and prostitutes, has similar effects. In addition, gay male health—like that of other oppressed or poor groups in our society—has been neglected by the medical community. When gay men receive excellent medical treatment, they do so as middle-class men, rarely as gays. Not until the mid-to-late 1970s did anyone recognize that the gay male community might suffer from specific diseases that would best be treated in the context of the community. This recognition, which grew out of the liberation movement and the sense of community that accompanied it, was largely confined to gays.[31]

Before the 1970s most physicians and psychologists refused to recognize the existence of a gay community, insisting that gay people were merely individuals with certain medical or psychological characteristics. For the medical establishment gay men were mentally or physically sick and their other diseases were the expected byproduct of their homosexuality. With a heavy dose of moralism, the medical profession acted as if—and often stated that—it preferred to see people suffer from venereal disease than commit acts it did not approve.[32] Moreover, many gays feared that seeking treatment for particular sexually transmitted diseases would, in effect, be an admission of their homosexuality before a hostile world— precisely what happens when gay men are diagnosed as suffering from AIDS or AIDS-related complex (ARC). And, finally, the neglect of gay men's health derived also from gay men's willingness to accept the typical twentieth-century emphasis, especially in the age of antibiotics, on curative medicine rather than preventive measures, particularly condoms and other devices that might have prevented the spread of infectious disease through sexual contact. This multi-sided mismanagement of the gay community's health left it peculiarly vulnerable to new diseases, among which AIDS is only the most devastating example. As Cindy Patton notes:

> The opportunistic infections (other than KS [Kaposi's sarcoma] and PCP [*Pneumocystis carinii* pneumonia]) that accompany AIDS in gay men are precisely those minor infections that have, at least for the last few decades been a part of the gay male health picture. . . . Yet the historical relationship between lesbians and gay men and their physicians has been hostile and fraught with deception and fear.[33]

The new emphasis on self-management of health and illness among feminists, poverty advocate groups, and, in somewhat different ways, middle-class people in general, has contributed to the determination of the gay community and particularly people with AIDS to play a significant role in the medical management of AIDS.

Gay persons with AIDS have undertaken to educate themselves in technical matters relating to their disease and its possible cures and treatments. They have actively demanded services from the medical and epidemiological establishments and have even occasionally provided them directly. Especially in San Francisco and New York, these services are, arguably, superior to those available for most other types of patients in the United States. As Richard Dunne, executive director of the New York–based Gay Men's Health Crisis, recently put it:

> What's happening today is something that has not happened before in modern medicine—maybe never before. The patient walks in to see the doctor and says, "I'm on AZT and I'm having some side effects. What do you think of my taking cyclovir?" Physicians are overwhelmed that the P.W.A. [person with AIDS] is the expert. A P.W.A. said to me recently that his physician is someone he consults but that he makes the decisions.[34]

In a closely related development, the gay community has been forced to pay particular attention to the private health insurance industry. In America, unlike almost every other industrial nation, private health insurance represents health care access to all but the elderly or very poor. Gay men, never in favor with the insurance industry,[35] are in danger of being denied adequate insurance against illness. The gay community, largely through its legal organizations, has actively combated discrimination that would deny them health insurance or employee benefits. While not uniformly successful, its efforts have helped ensure that gay men and others thought to be at risk for AIDS will not automatically be denied access to insurance and, therefore, to health care itself. For example, the National Association of Insurance Commissioners, whose regulations are usually accepted by the various state insurance departments, was persuaded to adopt guidelines banning inquiries into applicants' sexual orientation and any use of information regarding sexual orientation in insurance underwriting.[36] That the gay community, whose legitimacy is barely recognized, should be able to "negotiate" with the powerful insurance industry is impressive evidence of its ability to intervene in all aspects of the AIDS epidemic and alter the terms in which they are discussed and managed.

The gay community, however, has tended to remain aloof from other groups (many of the poor, the aged, and a substantial number of health care workers) who are pressing for a national health care system. This is a surprising development in that it is precisely minority-group members who are, in addition to gay men, those most at risk for AIDS and AIDS-related conditions.

Many middle-class, white gay men have been surprised to discover the substantial inadequacies of the private health insurance system in meeting the AIDS crisis and in meeting their personal needs for access to health care. However, their organizations have neither joined the struggle to reform it in more than essentially minor ways, nor demanded in a forthright manner a system of nationally provided health care or insurance. Perhaps the reason the gay movement has been unable to work fully with minority and other protest groups for common aims is the continuing racism among white, middle-class gays and homophobia among other minorities as well as belief on each side that they compete for limited resources. A significant exception was the boycott of Coors Beer that began in San Francisco and brought together gays, women, unions, blacks, and other minorities, was spearheaded partly by the gay community, and at the beginning was led by Harvey Milk.[37] And recent developments, including the courting of the gay movement by Jesse Jackson's Rainbow Coalition, may yet bring major changes.

In health-related activities the gay community has begun to move closer to the heterosexual world in general. Many gay health organizations, caring agencies, and related institutions have become large and successful bureaucracies, dispensing hundreds of thousands of dollars and becoming attentive to public fund-raising and government grants. In addition, they are becoming integrated into the wider health-care world. Some radical gay political groups, however, see such mainstreaming as political timidity, an overemphasis on the purely clinical aspects of the epidemic, and too great a willingness to cooperate with governmental bodies, which are thereby allowed to escape justified charges of having done too little to meet the crisis.[38] Such tensions are probably inevitable as the gay community's position on the complicated problems of medicine and health care involved with AIDS continues to evolve.

■ **VII**   The detailed responses to AIDS coalesce into two complex and parallel sets of metaphors—two types of discourse, two varieties of practice—built on the relationship between AIDS and homosexuality. Both sets of metaphors accept the reality of that relationship, resting upon the complicated ideological and institutional history of American homosexuality. But they draw on different aspects of that heritage, reconfigurating them in response to the AIDS crisis and creating significantly different amalgams of past and present. In fact, they form the materials for two sides of a massive political and ideological struggle that extends far beyond the reality of AIDS as a disease.

The two discourses do not speak directly to one another, but they "echo" each other strongly. Both regard AIDS as a moral crisis, but where the first defines AIDS as the breakdown of the dominant "traditional" morality of sexual behavior and social organization, the second considers it the breakdown of a new "social contract" that includes all people as full members of the body politic. Where the first seeks to exclude homosexuality from public view and shroud it in silence, the second argues that "silence is death" with respect to both AIDS and homosexuality.[39] Where the first finds sexual irresponsibility and lack of self-control at the heart of homosexuality, the second demonstrates an unusual capacity on the part of gay people to alter their own sexual behavior. Where the first sees victims and villains, the second sees actors and heroes.

The gay community, in an ironic reversal of popular views of AIDS, constructed the AIDS crisis and its metaphors in the image of its own history. But the metaphors we find here, unlike those of homophobic approaches, are socially, institutionally, and ideologically rich, because they build on the history of a real community coming to terms with its past and its need to take control of its present and future. They are also useful metaphors, in that they allow for a rational intervention in the management of the disease while they let us remove at least some of the hysteria that has prevented us from treating AIDS like any other disease.

The gay community has largely succeeded in removing AIDS from the category of the new, the terrifying, and the special and made it more ordinary, normal, and therefore, manageable. In the same manner, people with AIDS have shown that it is possible—indeed necessary—to live with AIDS and not merely die from it.

The best summation of this story can perhaps be found in the moving remarks of Paul Monette in the preface to a cycle of poems on the death of his lover from AIDS:

> The story that endlessly eludes the decorum of the press is the death of a generation of gay men. What is written here is only one man's passing and one man's cry, a warrior burying a warrior. May it fuel the fire of those on the front lines who mean to prevail, and of their friends who stand in the fire with them. We will not be bowed down or erased by this. I learned too well what it means to be a people, learned in the joy of my best friend what all the meaningless pain and horror cannot take away—that all there is is love. Pity us not.[40]

■ Notes

Acknowledgments: This essay is a considerably revised version of papers presented at the annual meeting of the American Historical Association in December 1986; at the Marxist School in New York City in April 1987; at the Socialist Scholars Conference in New York City in April 1987; and at a panel organized by the Association of Social Scientists in Health Care at the October 1987 annual meeting of the American Public Health Association in New Orleans. It has been much improved by the generous comments of Gerald Oppenheimer (Brooklyn College), in dialogue with whom many of my views on AIDS have been developed.

1. Institute of Medicine, National Academy of Sciences, *Mobilizing Against AIDS: The Unfinished Story of a Virus* (Cambridge, Mass.: 1986).

2. Karl Marx, *The 18th Brumaire of Louis Bonaparte* (New York: 1963), 15. I have altered the customary translation from "men" to "human beings," a change I feel is warranted by the German "menschen."

3. Susan Sontag, *Illness As Metaphor* (New York: 1978).

4. Cf. Ronald Bayer, "AIDS and the Gay Community: Between the Specter and the Promise of Medicine," *Social Research* 52 (Autumn 1985): 581–606 at 587ff.

5. Jeffrey Weeks, *Sexuality and Its Discontents* (London: 1985), 45–46.

6. On the process in general, see Jeffrey Weeks, *Coming Out* (London: 1977); Jonathan Katz, *Gay American History* (New York: 1976) 129–207; and *Gay/Lesbian Almanac* (New York: 1983), 1–19. For further details: Vernon L. Bullough, "Homosexuality and the Medical Model," *Journal of Homosexuality* 1 (1974): 99ff; George Chauncey, Jr., "From Sexual Inversion to Homosexuality: The Changing Medical Conceptualization of Female 'Deviance,'" in this volume; Georges Lanteri-Laura, *Lecture des perversions: histoire de leur appropriation médicale* (Paris: 1979); Peter Conrad and Joseph W. Schneider, *Deviants and Medicalization: From Badness to Sickness* (St. Louis: 1980), ch. 7. Cf. Michel Foucault, *The History of Sexuality*, vol. I, *An Introduction* (New York: 1978), 44.

7. Cf. Philippe Ariès, "Thoughts on the History of Homosexuality," in *Western Sexuality: Practice and Precept in Past and Present Times*, ed. Philippe Ariès and André Béjin (Oxford: 1985), 62–75.

8. Cf. Patrick Carnes, *The Sexual Addiction* (Minneapolis: 1983); Craig Rowland, "Reinventing the Sex Maniac," *The Advocate*, 21 Jan. 1986, 43–49; Daniel Goleman,

"Some Sexual Behavior Viewed as an Addiction," *New York Times*, 16 October 1984, C1. Not surprisingly in light of the historical associations of this concept, it turns out that women and gay men are the groups most at risk for this supposed "addiction."

9. *New York Post*, 24 May 1983.

10. Cf. the material collected in Jonathan Katz, *Gay American History* and *Gay/Lesbian Almanac*.

11. Elizabeth Fee, commentary on the session "AIDS in Historical Perspective," annual meeting of the American Historical Association, Chicago, Ill., December 1986.

12. Nancy Krieger and Rose Appleman, *The Politics of AIDS* (Oakland, Cal.: 1986), 18. See most recently Randy Shilts, *And the Band Played On: Politics, People, and the AIDS Epidemic* (New York: 1987); and Daniel M. Fox, "AIDS and the American Health Polity: The History and Prospects of a Crisis of Authority," *Milbank Quarterly* 64 (1986), Supplement I, "AIDS: The Public Context of an Epidemic," ed. Ronald Bayer, Daniel M. Fox, and David P. Willis, 7–33.

13. See William H. McNeill, *Plagues and Peoples* (New York: 1976), for a good historical overview.

14. See the works cited in note 6 and Dennis Altman, *The Homosexualization of America and the Americanization of the Homosexual* (New York: 1982); John D'Emilio, *Sexual Politics, Sexual Communities: The Making of a Homosexual Minority in the United States, 1940–1970* (Chicago: 1983), and "Gay Politics, Gay Community: San Francisco's Experience," *Socialist Review* 55 (Jan.–Feb. 1981): 77–104; and Toby Marotta, *The Politics of Homosexuality: How Lesbians and Gay Men Have Made Themselves a Political and Social Force in Modern America* (New York: 1981).

15. On all these aspects and the reaction of the gay community in general to the AIDS epidemic, see Shilts, *And the Band Played On;* Dennis Altman, *AIDS in the Mind of America* (Garden City, N.Y.: 1986); "AIDS: The Politicization of an Epidemic," *Socialist Review* 78 (Nov./Dec. 1984): 93–109; "The Politics of AIDS," in *AIDS: Public Policy Dimensions*, ed. John Griggs (New York: 1987), 23–33; and, in some ways most perceptively, Cindy Patton, *Sex and Germs: The Politics of AIDS* (Boston: 1985). In addition, it is important to look at coverage of AIDS in the gay press from 1981 on in some detail, particularly the *New York Native*, the (national) *Advocate*, and the San Francisco *Bay Area Reporter*.

16. *New York Times*, 16 March 1987, 17. On the Gay Men's Health Crisis and its role in the crisis in New York, cf. Richard Dunne, "New York City: Gay Men's Health Crisis," *AIDS: Public Policy Dimensions*, ed. Griggs, 155–69.

17. On the gay ghettoes in general, see: Martin P. Levine, "Gay Ghetto," *Journal of Homosexuality* 4 (1979): 363–78; Martin P. Levine, ed., *Gay Men: The Sociology of Male Homosexuality* (New York: 1979); Manuel Castels, *The City and the Grassroots: a Cross-Cultural Theory of Urban Social Movements* (Berkeley: 1983).

18. An overview of the various gay liberation movements can be found in Barry Adam, *The Rise of a Gay and Lesbian Movement* (Boston: 1987).

19. Michael Bronski, "Death and the Erotic Imagination," *Gay Community News* (Boston), 7–13 Sept. 1986, 8–9 at 8.

20. Quoted by Mark Vandervelden, "Gay Health Conference," *The Advocate*, 28 April 1987, 12. The occasion for Rofes' statement was the eighth annual "National

Lesbian and Gay Health Conference," held in Los Angeles on 26–29 March 1987, and attended by representatives of more than 250 organizations.

21. On the limits of voluntarism, cf. Peter S. Arno and Karyn Feiden, "Ignoring the Epidemic: How the Reagan Administration Failed on AIDS," *Health-PAC Bulletin* 17 (December 1986): 7–11, and Peter S. Arno, "The Contributions and Limitations of Voluntarism," in *AIDS: Public Policy Dimensions*, 188–92.

22. Arno and Feiden, "Ignoring the Epidemic," 11.

23. Cf. Altman, *AIDS in the Mind of America*, who strongly argues for the unique nature of the AIDS crisis in the United States, due in part to this peculiarly American type of political system.

24. On the general development of gay politics and gay self-identity, see the works cited in notes 14 and 18 and, in particular, the works listed by John D'Emilio and Barry Adam.

25. Cf. Dennis Altman, "Sex: The New Frontline for Gay Politics," *Socialist Review* (Sept./Oct. 1982).

26. 106 S.Ct. 2841, 2842–56 (1986).

27. The increasingly large literature on changes in gay sexual behavior due to AIDS is summarized and discussed in Marshall H. Becker and Jill G. Joseph, "AIDS and Behavioral Change to Reduce Risk: A Review," *American Journal of Public Health* 78 (April 1988): 394–410.

28. Bayer, "AIDS and the Gay Community: Between the Specter and the Promise of Medicine."

29. See Ronald Bayer, *Homosexuality and American Psychiatry: The Politics of Diagnosis*, 2nd ed. (New York: 1988).

30. See, in general, Dan DeNoon, "AIDS Takes its Psychological Toll on the Health-Care Community," *In These Times*, 14–20 October 1987, 6–7.

31. The first relatively thorough and scientific survey and analysis of diseases specific to the gay community that I am aware of appeared in 1981: William W. Darrow, Donald Barrett, Karla Jay, and Allen Young, "The Gay Report on Sexually Transmitted Diseases," *American Journal of Public Health* 71 (Sept. 1981): 1004–11; cf. the accompanying editorial of H. Hunter Handsfield, 989–90, who cites other, less complete studies.

32. Cf. Allan M. Brandt, *No Magic Bullet*, 2nd ed. (Cambridge, Mass.: 1987).

33. Patton, *Sex and Germs*, 8.

34. Quoted in Anne-Christine D'Adesky, "Breaking the F.D.A. Drugjam," *The Nation*, 17 October 1987, 405. See also the various PWA (persons with AIDS) newsletters, magazines such as "AIDS Treatment News," and the pages of the gay press, in particular the *New York Native*, all of which provide substantial coverage on AIDS treatments (in addition to AIDS politics and organizing). For work by PWAs themselves, see Michael Callen, ed., *Surviving and Thriving with AIDS* (Boston: 1978) and Peter Tatchell, *AIDS: a Guide to Survival* (Boston: 1987).

35. Cf. the 1906 remarks of Dr. William Lee Howard, "The Sexual Pervert in Life Insurance," quoted in Katz, *Gay/Lesbian Almanac*, 319f.

36. See *New York Native*, 5 Jan. 1987, 7; *National Underwriter*, 29 Dec. 1986.

37. Cf. Randy Shilts, *The Mayor of Castro Street: The Life and Times of Harvey Milk* (New York: 1982).

38. The most notable example of such an attack was by Larry Kramer, "An Open Letter to Richard Dunne and Gay Men's Health Crisis, Inc.," *New York*

Native, 26 January 1987, 1ff., which in part led to a slightly more activist stand by the GMHC as well as to the formation of several direct action groups in New York City, most notably the civil disobedience–oriented group ACT-UP.

39. "Silence = Death" is the organizing slogan of the New York–based ACT-UP, an AIDS activist group that uses street demonstrations to demand more funding for AIDS-related treatment.

40. Paul Monette, *Love Alone: Eighteen Elegies for Rog* (New York: 1988), xii–xiii.

Notes About the Contributors

Marybeth Hamilton Arnold is a doctoral candidate in history at Princeton University. She is currently completing her dissertation, a study of actress Mae West.

George Chauncey, Jr., has written on the history of sexuality in the *Journal of Social History, Salmagundi,* and other journals and is coeditor, with Martin Duberman and Martha Vicinus, of a forthcoming collection of essays, *The New Social History of Homosexuality* (New American Library). A doctoral candidate in history at Yale University, he currently lives in New York, where he is finishing his dissertation, "Gay New York: A Social and Cultural History of Male Homosexuality in New York City, 1890–1970."

Madeline Davis is the chief conservator for the Buffalo and Erie County Public Library System and a cofounder of the Buffalo Women's Oral History Project. She has been active in the gay liberation and lesbian feminist movements since 1970. A singer/songwriter, she has produced a tape of lesbian-feminist music, "Daughter of All Women" (1982). She is currently working on a book, *Boots of Leather, Slippers of Gold: The History of a Lesbian Community,* with Elizabeth Kennedy.

John D'Emilio is assistant professor of history at the University of North Carolina in Greensboro. He is the author of *Sexual Politics, Sexual Communities: The Making of a Homosexual Minority in the United States, 1940–1970* (University of Chicago Press, 1983) and, with Estelle Freedman, of *Intimate Matters: A History of Sexuality in America* (Harper & Row, 1988).

Elizabeth Fee is associate professor of health policy at the Johns Hopkins School of Hygiene and Public Health. She is author of *Disease and Discovery* (Johns Hopkins University Press, 1987) and editor of *Women and Health* (Baywood, 1983).

Estelle B. Freedman teaches social, women's, and sexual history at Stanford University. She is the author of *Their Sisters' Keepers: Women's Prison Reform in America, 1830–1930* (University of Michigan Press, 1981) and coauthor with John D'Emilio of *Intimate Matters*.

Elizabeth (Liz) Lapovsky Kennedy is associate professor of American studies and women's studies at the State University of New York at Buffalo and a cofounder of the Buffalo Women's Oral History Project. Since 1970, she has actively worked to build a women's studies B.A., M.A., and Ph.D. program at SUNY/Buffalo and to further the field of women's studies. She is coauthor of *Feminist Scholarship: Kindling in the Groves of Academe* with Ellen DuBois *et al.* (University of Illinois Press, 1985) and is currently working on a book on the lesbian community of Buffalo with Madeline Davis.

Robert A. Padgug received his doctorate in classical history. He has been researching the history of sexuality, in particular in Greek antiquity, for a number of years. Currently employed in the health insurance industry, his recent interests have focused on social and economic aspects of the AIDS crisis.

Kathy Peiss teaches history and women's studies at the University of Massachusetts at Amherst. Her book, *Cheap Amusements: Working Women and Leisure in Turn-of-the-Century New York* (Temple University Press, 1986) examines working women's culture and the social construction of gender and sexuality. She is currently working on a social history of the cosmetics industry, gender, and consumption.

Daphne Read completed her Ph.D. in English at York University, Toronto, Canada, where she has also taught women's studies. Her dissertation, "Rereading *Burger's Daughter*: A Feminist Deconstruction," is a study of Nadine Gordimer's writing in relation to feminist and critical theory and attempts to develop a socialist-feminist deconstructive criticism.

Jessie M. Rodrique is a Ph.D. candidate in American history at the University of Massachusetts at Amherst and a predoctoral Fellow at the Smithsonian Institution. Her dissertation is on black women and the birth control movement from 1915 to 1945.

Judith Schwarz is a coordinator of the Lesbian Herstory Archives/Lesbian Herstory Educational Foundation. She was special consulting editor of *Frontiers: A Journal of Women Studies*, Lesbian History Issue (1978), and author of *Radical Feminists of Heterodoxy, Greenwich Village 1912–1940* (New Victoria Publishers, 1986). She lives and works in New York City.

Christina Simmons teaches American history and women's studies at the University of Cincinnati–Raymond Walters College. She is completing a monograph entitled *The Modern American Woman: Redefining Sexuality, 1914–1941.*

Ann Barr Snitow was a founding member of New York Radical Feminists in 1970. She writes about feminism and literature and teaches at the Eugene Lang College of the New School for Social Research in New York. She coedited *Powers of Desire: The Politics of Sexuality* (Monthly Review Press, 1983) with Christine Stansell and Sharon Thompson.

Jeffrey Weeks is the author of *Coming Out: Homosexual Politics in Britain from the Nineteenth Century to the Present: Sex, Politics and Society* and *Sexuality and Its Discontents.* He has taught at the Universities of Essex, Kent, and Southampton. He currently lives and works in London.